—THE—

ANOINTED
Life

Other Titles by Charles Spurgeon

THE
ANOINTED
Life

C. H. SPURGEON

WHITAKER
HOUSE

Publisher's Note:
The author's selection of Bible versions has been retained whenever possible, including the Revised Version when it was originally cited. The text of this book, however, has been edited for the modern reader. Words, expressions, and sentence structure have been updated for clarity and readability.

Unless otherwise indicated, all Scripture quotations are from the King James Version (KJV) of the Holy Bible. Quotations marked (RV) are from the Revised Version.

THE ANOINTED LIFE
a 5-in-1 anthology

Titles included in this anthology:
All of Grace
ISBN: 978-0-88368-857-1   © 1981, 1983 by Whitaker House
Faith (previously titled *Strong Faith*)
ISBN: 978-0-88368-637-9   © 1995 by Whitaker House
Spurgeon on the Holy Spirit
ISBN: 978-0-88368-622-5   © 2000 by Whitaker House
How to Have Real Joy (previously titled *The Joy of the Lord*)
ISBN: 978-0-88368-662-1   © 1998 by Whitaker House
The Power in Praising God
ISBN: 978-0-88368-526-6   © 1998 by Whitaker House

ISBN-13: 978-0-88368-473-3 • ISBN-10: 0-88368-473-X
Printed in the United States of America
© 2002 by Whitaker House

Whitaker House
1030 Hunt Valley Circle
New Kensington, PA 15068
www.whitakerhouse.com

Library of Congress Cataloging-in-Publication Data

Spurgeon, C. H. (Charles Haddon), 1834–1892.
  The anointed life / by Charles Spurgeon.
    p. cm.
  ISBN 0-88368-473-X
  1. Christian life—Baptist authors. I. Title.
  BV4501.3 .S668 2002
  248.4—dc21
                2002012162

2 3 4 5 6 7 8 9 10 11 12 **LIJ** 16 15 14 13 12 11 10 09

Contents

All of Grace

Contents

Chapter 1

To You

Whosoever will, let him take the water of life freely.
—Revelation 22:17

My intention in writing this message is that many will be led to the Lord Jesus. It is sent forth in childlike dependence on the power of God the Holy Spirit to be used in the conversion of millions, if He so pleases. No doubt many men and women will read this volume, and the Lord will bless them with grace. For this reason, the clearest language has been chosen, and many simple expressions have been used. However, if scholars should happen to glance at this book, the Holy Spirit can impress them, also. Oh, that some might read this who will become great winners of souls!

Who knows how many will find their way to peace by what they read here? A more important question for you is this: Will you be one of them?

A certain man placed a fountain along a busy road. Then he hung a cup near to it by a little chain. He was told some time afterward that a great art critic had found much fault with its design. "But," he asked, "do many thirsty people drink at it?" Then they told him that thousands of poor people, men, women, and children, quenched their thirst at this fountain. He smiled and said that he was not troubled by the critic's observation. He only hoped that on some hot summer's day the critic himself might fill the cup, be refreshed, and praise the name of the Lord.

Here is my fountain, and here is my cup. Find fault if you wish, but do drink of the water of life. I care only for this. I would rather bless the soul of the poorest street cleaner or rag-gatherer than please a prince and fail to convert him to God.

Are you serious about reading these pages? If so, we are agreed at the outset. However, my goal is nothing short of your finding Christ and heaven. Oh, that we may seek this together! I do so by dedicating this book with prayer. Will you not join me by looking up to God and asking Him to bless you while you read? Providence has put these pages before you. You have a little spare time in which to read them, and you feel willing to give them your attention. These are good signs. Who knows, maybe the time of blessing has come for you. At any rate, *"the Holy Ghost saith, To day if ye will hear his voice, harden not your hearts"* (Hebrews 3:7–8).

Chapter 2

Open the Door

Behold, I stand at the door, and knock: if any man hear my voice, and open the door, I will come in to him.
—Revelation 3:20

I heard a story; I think it came from the north country. A minister called on a poor woman intending to help her, for he knew that she was very poor. With his money in hand, he knocked at the door, but she did not answer. He concluded she was not at home and went his way. A little later he met her at the church and told her that he had remembered her need. "I called at your house and knocked several times. I suppose you were not at home because there was no answer." "At what hour did you call, sir?" "It was about noon." "Oh, dear," she said, "I heard you, sir, and I am so sorry I did not answer. I thought it was the man calling for the rent." Many poor people know what this means. Now, it is my desire to be heard, and therefore I want to say that I am not calling for the rent. Indeed, it is not the purpose of this book to ask anything of you. I want to tell you that salvation is *all of grace*, which means free, gratis, for nothing.

Often when we are anxious to win attention, our listener thinks, "Oh! Now I am going to be told what to do. It is the man calling for what is due God, and I have nothing to pay it with. I will not be at home." No, this book does not come to make a demand on you, but to bring you something. We are not going to talk about law and duty and punishment, but about love and goodness and forgiveness and mercy and eternal life. Therefore, do not act as if you were not at home. Do not turn a deaf ear or a careless heart. I am asking nothing of you in the name of God or man. It is not my intent to make any requirement at your hands. I come in God's name to bring you a free gift that will be your present and eternal joy to receive.

Open the door and let my pleadings enter. *"Come now, and let us reason together"* (Isaiah 1:18). The Lord Himself invites you to a conference concerning your immediate and endless happiness. He would not have done this if He did not mean well toward you. Do not refuse the Lord Jesus who knocks at your door, for He knocks with a hand that was nailed to the tree for such as you are. Since His only and sole objective is your good, incline your ear and come to Him. Listen diligently, and let the good Word sink into your soul. It may be that the hour has come for you to enter that new life that is the beginning of heaven. *"Faith cometh by hearing"* (Romans 10:17), and reading is a type of hearing. Faith may come to you while you are reading this book. Why not? O blessed Spirit of all grace, make it so!

Chapter 3

God Justifies the Ungodly

To him that worketh not, but believeth
on him that justifieth the ungodly,
his faith is counted for righteousness.
—Romans 4:5

This message is for you: *"To him that worketh not, but believeth on him that justifieth the ungodly, his faith is counted for righteousness."*

I call your attention to the words, *"Him that justifieth the ungodly."* They seem to me to be very wonderful words.

Are you surprised that there is such an expression as that in the Bible, *"That justifieth the ungodly"*? I have heard that men who hate the doctrines of the Cross bring the charge against God that He saves wicked men and receives to Himself the vilest of the vile. See how this Scripture accepts the charge and plainly states it! By the mouth of His servant, Paul; by the inspiration of the Holy Spirit, He takes to Himself the title of *"Him that justifieth the ungodly."* He makes those just who are unjust. He forgives those who deserve no favor. Did you think that salvation was for the good and that God's grace was for the pure and holy who are free from sin? Perhaps you think that

14

if you were excellent, then God would reward you. Maybe you have thought that, because you are not worthy, there could be no way for you to enjoy His favor. You must be somewhat surprised to read a text like this: *"Him that justifieth the ungodly."* I do not wonder at your surprise. For, with all my familiarity with the great grace of God, I never cease to wonder at it, either.

No One Is Righteous before God

It does sound surprising, does it not, that it should be possible for a holy God to justify an unholy man? We, according to our natural reliance on good works for our salvation, are always talking about our own goodness and our own worthiness. We stubbornly believe that there must be something in us in order to win the notice of God. Now, God, who sees through all deceptions, knows that there is no goodness whatsoever in us. He says that *"there is none righteous, no, not one"* (Romans 3:10). He knows that *"all our righteousnesses are as filthy rags"* (Isaiah 64:6). Therefore, the Lord Jesus did not come into the world expecting to find goodness and righteousness, but to bestow them upon those who do not have them. He comes, not because we *are* just, but to make us so; He *"justifieth the ungodly."*

When a lawyer comes into court, if he is an honest man, he desires to plead the case of an innocent person and justify him before the court from the things of which he has been falsely accused. It should be the lawyer's objective to justify the innocent person, and he should not attempt to protect the guilty party. It is not man's right nor in his power to truly justify the guilty. This is a miracle reserved for the Lord alone. God, the infinitely just Sovereign, knows that there is not a just man on earth who does good and does not sin. Therefore, in the infinite sovereignty of His divine nature and in the splendor of His ineffable love, He undertakes the task not so much of justifying the just as of justifying the ungodly. God has devised ways and means of making the ungodly man stand justly accepted before Him. He has set up a system by which, with perfect justice, He can treat the guilty as if he had been free from offense. Yes, He can treat him as if he were wholly free from sin. He justifies the ungodly.

*"Christ Jesus came into the world to save **sinners**"* (1 Timothy 1:15, emphasis added). This truth is a very surprising thing—a thing to be marveled at most of all by those who enjoy it. I know that it is to me, even to this day, the greatest wonder that I have ever heard of—that God would ever justify *me*. I feel myself to be a lump of unworthiness, a mass of corruption, and a heap of sin apart from His almighty love. I know and am fully assured that I am justified by *"faith which is in Christ Jesus"* (2 Timothy 3:15). I am treated as if I had been perfectly just and made an heir of God and a joint-heir with Christ. And yet by nature, I must take my place among the most sinful. Though altogether undeserving, I am treated as if I had been deserving. I am loved with as much love as if I had always been godly, whereas before I was ungodly. Who can help being astonished at this demonstration of grace? Gratitude for such favor stands dressed in robes of wonder.

Now, while this is very surprising, I want you to notice how available it makes the Gospel to you and to me. If God justifies the ungodly, then He can justify you. Is that not the very kind of person that you are? If you are unconverted at this moment, it is a very proper description of you. You have lived without God; you have been the reverse of godly. In one word, you have been and are *ungodly*. Perhaps you have not even attended a place of worship on Sundays, but have lived in disregard of God's day and house and Word. This proves that you have been ungodly. Sadder still, it may be that you have even tried to doubt God's existence and have gone to the point of saying that you did so. You have lived on this fair earth, full of the blessings of God's presence, and all the while you have shut your eyes to the clear evidences of His power and Godhead. You have lived as if there were no God. Indeed, you would have been very pleased if you could have positively demonstrated to yourself that there is no God. Possibly you have lived a great many years this way so that you are now pretty well settled in your ways. Yet God is not in any of them. If you were to be labeled ungodly, it would describe you as well as if the sea were to be labeled salt water, would it not?

Possibly you are a person of another sort. You have regularly attended to all the outward forms of religion. Yet you have had no heart in them at all but have been truly ungodly. Though meeting with the people of God, you have never met with God yourself. You have sung in the choir and yet have not praised the Lord with your heart. You have lived without any love for God in your heart or regard for His commands in your life. Well, you are just the kind of person to whom this Gospel is sent, this Gospel that says that God justifies the ungodly. It is very wonderful and is happily available for you. It just suits you, does it not? How I wish that you would accept it! If you are a sensible person, you will see the remarkable grace of God in providing for someone such as you are. You will say to yourself, "Justify the ungodly! Why, then, should I not be justified, and justified at once?"

Self-Righteousness Is a Delusion

Now, observe further that it must be so. The salvation of God is for those who do not deserve it and have no preparation for it. It is reasonable that this statement is in the Bible, for no others need justifying but those who have no justification of their own. If any of you are perfectly righteous, you desire no justifying. You feel that you are doing your duty well and almost putting heaven under an obligation to you. What do you want with a Savior or with mercy? What do you want with justification? You will be tired of this book by this time, for it will have no interest to you.

If any of you are giving yourselves such proud airs, listen to me for a little while. You will be lost as surely as you are alive. You righteous men, whose righteousness is all of your own working, are either deceivers or deceived. Scripture cannot lie, and it says plainly, *"There is none righteous, no, not one"* (Romans 3:10).

In any case, I have no Gospel to preach to the self-righteous, no, not a word. Jesus Christ Himself did *"not come to call the righteous"* (Matthew 9:13), and I am not going to do what He did not do. If I called you, you would not come. Therefore, I will not call you. Rather, I ask you to look at that righteousness of yours until you see what a delusion it is. It is not half as substantial as a cobweb. Be finished with it! Flee from it! Believe that the only people who need justification are those who are not just in themselves. They need something to be done for them to make them just before the judgment seat of God. You can depend on this: The Lord does only what is needful. Infinite wisdom never attempts what is unnecessary. Jesus never undertakes what is superfluous. To make him just who is just is no work for God. That is a labor for a fool. However, to make him just who is unjust, that is work for infinite love and mercy. To justify the ungodly is a miracle worthy of God, and it is.

Pardon Is for the Guilty

Now, look. If there is a physician anywhere in the world who has discovered sure and precious remedies, to whom is that physician sent? To those who are perfectly healthy? I think not. Send him down to a place where there are no sick people, and he feels that he is out of place. There is nothing for him to do. *"They that are whole have no need of the physician, but they that are sick"* (Mark 2:17). Is it not equally clear that the great remedies of grace and redemption are for the sick in soul? They cannot be for the whole, for they cannot be of use to such. If you feel that you are spiritually sick, the Physician has come into the world for you. If you are altogether undone by reason of your sin, you are the very person aimed at in the plan of salvation.

I say that the Lord of love had just such as you in His eye when He arranged the system of grace. Suppose a man of generous spirit were to resolve to forgive all those who were indebted to him. It is clear that this could apply only to those really in his debt. One person owes him a thousand dollars, and another owes him fifty dollars; each one has but to have his bill receipted, and the liability is wiped out. However, the most generous person cannot forgive the debts of those who do not owe him anything. It is out of the power of Omnipotence to forgive where there is no sin. Pardon, therefore, cannot be for you who have no sin. Pardon must be for the guilty. Forgiveness must be for the sinful. It would be absurd to talk of forgiving those who do not need forgiveness or pardoning those who have never offended.

Do you think that you must be lost because you are a sinner? This is the reason you can be saved. Because you realize that you are a sinner, I would encourage you to believe that grace is ordained for such as you. The hymn-writer Joseph Hart even dared to say,

> A sinner is a sacred thing;
> The Holy Ghost hath made him so.

It is true that Jesus seeks and saves those who are lost (Luke 19:10). He died and made a real atonement for real sinners. When men are not playing with words or calling themselves "miserable sinners" in false humility, I feel overjoyed to meet with them. I would be glad to talk all night to bona fide sinners. The inn of mercy never closes its doors on such, neither on weekdays nor on Sunday. Our Lord Jesus did not die for imaginary sins. His heart's blood was spilled to wash out deep crimson stains that nothing else can remove.

He who is a dirty sinner is the kind of man that Jesus Christ came to make clean. A gospel preacher on one occasion preached a sermon from the verse, *"Now also the ax is laid unto the root of the trees"* (Luke 3:9). He delivered such a sermon that one of his hearers said to him, "One would have thought that you had been preaching to criminals. Your sermon ought to have been delivered in the county jail." "Oh, no," said the good man, "if I were preaching in the county jail, I would not preach from that text. There I would preach, *'This is a faithful saying, and worthy of all acceptation, that Christ Jesus came into the world to save sinners'* (1 Timothy 1:15). This is true." The law is for the self-righteous, to humble their pride. The Gospel is for the lost, to remove their despair.

If you are not lost, what do you want with a Savior? Should the shepherd go after those sheep that never went astray? Why should the woman sweep her house for the pieces of money that were never out of her purse? (See Luke 15:8–9.) No, the medicine is for the diseased; the quickening is for the dead. The pardon is for the guilty; liberation is for those who are bound. The opening of eyes is for those who are blind. How can the Savior, His death on the cross, and the Gospel of pardon be accounted for unless it is true that men are guilty and worthy of condemnation? The sinner is the Gospel's reason for existence. If you are undeserving, ill-deserving, hell-deserving, you are the sort of person for whom the Gospel is ordained and arranged and proclaimed. God justifies the ungodly.

Come Just as You Are

I want to make this very plain. I hope that I have done so already. Yet, still, plain as it is, it is only the Lord who can make a man see it. At first it does seem most amazing to man that salvation would really be for him when he is lost and guilty. He thinks that it must be for him when he is penitent, forgetting that his penitence is a part of his salvation. "Oh," he says, "but I must be this and that," all of which is true, for he will be this and that as the result of salvation. However, salvation comes to him before he has any of the results of salvation. In fact, it comes to him while he deserves only this bare, beggarly, base, abominable description: *ungodly.* That is all he is when God's Gospel comes to justify him.

Therefore, may I urge any who have no good thing about them—who fear that they do not have even a good feeling or anything at all that can recommend them to God—to firmly believe that our gracious God is able and willing to take them without anything to recommend them. He is willing to forgive them spontaneously, not because *they* are good, but because *He* is good. Does He not make His sun to shine on the evil as well as on the good? Does He not give fruitful seasons and send the rain and the sunshine in their time even on the most ungodly nations? (See Matthew 5:45.) Yes, even Sodom had its sun and Gomorrah had its dew. The great grace of God surpasses my conception and your conception. I would like you to think worthily of it. As high as the heavens are above the earth, so high are God's thoughts above our thoughts (Isaiah 55:9). He can *"abundantly pardon"* (v. 7). *"Christ Jesus came into the world to save sinners"* (1 Timothy 1:15); forgiveness is for the guilty.

Do not attempt to touch yourself up and make yourself something other than what you really are. Come as you are to Him who justifies the ungodly. Some time ago, a great artist had painted a picture of a part of the city

21

in which he lived. He wanted, for historic purposes, to include in his picture certain characters well known in the town. A street sweeper, who was unkempt, ragged, and filthy, was known to everybody, and there was a suitable place for him in the picture. The artist said to this ragged and rugged individual, "I will pay you well if you will come down to my studio and let me paint you." He came around in the morning but was soon sent away for he had washed his face, combed his hair, and donned a respectable suit of clothes. He was needed as a beggar and was not invited in any other capacity. In the same way, the Gospel will receive you into its halls if you come as a sinner, not otherwise. Do not wait for reformation, but come at once for salvation. God justifies the *ungodly,* and that takes you up where you are now. It meets you in your worst state.

Come in your disorder. I mean, come to your heavenly Father in all your sin and sinfulness. Come to Jesus just as you are: leprous, filthy, naked, neither fit to live nor fit to die. Come, you who are the very sweepings of creation. Come, though you hardly dare to hope for anything but death. Come, though despair is brooding over you, pressing on your heart like a horrible nightmare. Come and ask the Lord to justify another ungodly one. Why should He not? Come, for this great mercy of God is meant for such as you. I put it in the language of the text, and I cannot put it more strongly: The Lord God Himself takes to Himself this gracious title, *"Him that justifieth the ungodly."* He makes just, and causes to be treated as just, those who by nature are ungodly. Is that not a wonderful word for you? Do not delay in considering this matter well.

Chapter 4

"It Is God That Justifieth"

It is God that justifieth.
—Romans 8:33

I t is a wonderful thing to be justified, or made just. If we had never broken the laws of God, we would not have needed justification, for we would have been just in ourselves. He who has always done the things that he should have done, and has never done anything that he should not have done, is justified by the law. However, I am quite sure that you are not one of that sort. You are too honest to pretend to be without sin, and therefore you need to be justified.

Now, if you justify yourself, you will simply be a self-deceiver. Therefore, do not attempt it. It is never worthwhile. If you ask your fellowmen to justify you, what can they do? You can make some of them speak well of you, for small favors; and others will backbite you for less. Their judgment is not worth much.

Our text says, *"It is God that justifieth."* This is much more to the point. It is an astonishing fact, and one that we should consider with care. Come and see.

A Plan Only God Could Think Of

In the first place, nobody else but God ever would have thought of justifying those who are guilty. They have lived in open rebellion. They have done evil with both hands and have gone from bad to worse. They have turned back to sin even after they have smarted for it and have, therefore, been forced to leave it for a while. They have broken the law of God and trampled on the Gospel. They have refused proclamations of mercy and have persisted in ungodliness. How can they be forgiven and justified? Their fellowmen, despairing of them, say, "They are hopeless cases." Even Christians look on them with sorrow rather than with hope. But not so their God. He, in the splendor of His electing grace, having chosen them *"before the foundation of the world"* (Ephesians 1:4), will not rest until He has justified them and made them to be *"accepted in the beloved"* (v. 6). Is it not written, *"Whom he did predestinate, them he also called: and whom he called, them he also justified: and whom he justified, them he also glorified"* (Romans 8:30)? Thus you see there are some whom the Lord resolves to justify. Why should you and I not be among them?

No one but God ever would have thought of justifying me. I am a wonder to myself. I do not doubt that grace is equally viewed as such by others. Look at Saul of Tarsus, who foamed at the mouth against God's servants. Like a hungry wolf, he worried the lambs and the sheep right and left. And yet God struck him down on the road to Damascus and changed his heart. (See Acts 8:3; 9:1–22.) God so fully justified him that, before long, this man became the greatest preacher of justification by faith who ever lived. He often must have marveled that he was justified by faith in Christ Jesus, for he was once a determined stickler for salvation by the works of the law. None but God ever would have thought of justifying such a man as Saul the persecutor. Yet the Lord God is glorious in grace.

A Plan Only God Could Fulfill

Even if anybody *had* thought of justifying the ungodly, no one but God could have done it. It is quite impossible for any person to forgive offenses that have not been committed against himself. A person has greatly injured you. You can forgive him, and I hope you will, but no third person can forgive him apart from you. If the wrong is done to you, the pardon must come from you. If we have sinned against God, it is in God's power to forgive, for the sin is against Himself. That is why David said in Psalm 51:4, *"Against thee, thee only, have I sinned, and done this evil in thy sight,"* for then God, against whom the offense was committed, could put the offense away.

What we owe to God, our great Creator can remit if it so pleases Him. And, if He remits it, it is remitted. No one but the great God against whom we have committed the sin can blot out that sin. Therefore, let us see that we go to Him and seek mercy at His hands. Do not let us be led aside by those who would have us confess to them; they have no warrant in the Word of God for their pretensions. Yet even if they were ordained to pronounce absolution in God's name, it would still be better for us to go to the great Lord through Jesus Christ, the Mediator, and seek and find pardon at His hands, since we are sure that this is the right way. Proxy Christianity involves too great a risk. You had better see to your soul's matters yourself and leave them in no man's hands.

Only God can justify the ungodly, but He can do it to perfection. He casts our sins behind His back (Isaiah 38:17); He blots them out (Isaiah 43:25). He says that, although they are sought after, they will not be found (Jeremiah 50:20). With no other reason for it but His own infinite goodness, He has prepared a glorious way by which He can make scarlet sins *"as white as snow"* (Isaiah 1:18). He can remove our transgressions from us *"as far as the east is from the west"* (Psalm 103:12). He says, *"Their sins*

25

and iniquities will I remember no more" (Hebrews 10:17). He goes the length of making an end of sin. One of old called out in amazement, *"Who is a God like unto thee, that pardoneth iniquity, and passeth by the transgression of the remnant of his heritage? he retaineth not his anger for ever, because he delighteth in mercy"* (Micah 7:18).

We are not now speaking of justice, nor of God's dealing with men according to what they deserve. If you profess to deal with the righteous Lord on legal grounds, everlasting wrath threatens you, for that is what you deserve. Blessed be His name, *"He hath not dealt with us after our sins"* (Psalm 103:10), but now He deals with us in terms of free grace and infinite compassion, and He says, "I will receive you graciously and love you freely." (See Hosea 14:2, 4.) Believe it, for it is certainly true that the great God is able to treat the guilty with abundant mercy. Yes, He is able to treat the ungodly as if they had always been godly.

Read carefully the parable of the prodigal son, and see how the forgiving father received the returning wanderer with as much love as if he had never gone away and had never defiled himself with prostitutes. He carried this so far that the elder brother began to grumble at it, but the father never withdrew his love. (See Luke 15:11–32.) However guilty you may be, if you will only come back to your God and Father, He will treat you as if you had never done wrong! He will regard you as just, and deal with you accordingly. What do you say to this?

Do you not see—for I want to clearly bring out what a splendid thing it is—that, as no one but God would think of justifying the ungodly, and no one but God could do it, yet the Lord can do it? See how the apostle puts the challenge: *"Who shall lay any thing to the charge of God's elect? It is God that justifieth"* (Romans 8:33). If God has justified a man, it is well done; it is rightly done; it is justly done; it is everlastingly done.

The Highest Court Can Pronounce You Just

I read a statement in a magazine that is full of venom against the Gospel and those who preach it. It said that we hold some kind of theory by which we imagine that sin can be removed from men. We hold no theory; we publish a fact. The grandest fact under heaven is this: Christ, by His precious blood, does actually put away sin. And God, for Christ's sake dealing with men on terms of divine mercy, forgives the guilty and justifies them—not according to anything that He sees in them or foresees will be in them, but according to the riches of His mercy, which lie in His own heart. This we have preached, do preach, and will preach as long as we live. *"It is God that justifieth"* the ungodly. He is not ashamed of doing it, nor are we of preaching it.

The justification that comes from God Himself must be beyond question. If the Judge acquits me, who can condemn me? If the highest court in the universe has pronounced me just, who will lay anything to my charge? Justification from God is a sufficient answer to an awakened conscience. The Holy Spirit, by His means, breathes peace over our entire nature, and we are no longer afraid. With this justification, we can answer all the roarings and railings of Satan and ungodly men. With this we will be able to die. With this we will boldly rise again and face the last great court of justice.

> Bold shall I stand in that great day,
> For who aught to my charge shall lay?
> While by my Lord absolved I am,
> From sin's tremendous curse and blame.
> —Count Zinzendorf

The Lord can blot out all your sins. I make no shot in the dark when I say this. *"All manner of sin and blasphemy shall be forgiven unto men"* (Matthew 12:31). Though you are steeped up to your throat in crime, He can, with a word, remove the defilement and say, *"I will; be thou clean"* (Mark 1:41). The Lord is a great forgiver.

"I believe in the forgiveness of sins." Do you?

He can even at this hour pronounce the sentence, "Your sins are forgiven; go in peace." If He does this, no power in heaven or earth or under the earth can put you under suspicion, much less under wrath. Do not doubt the power of almighty love. You could not forgive your fellow-man if he offended you as you have offended God. However, you must not measure God's corn with your bushel. His thoughts and ways are as much above yours as the heavens are high above the earth (Isaiah 55:9).

"Well," you say, "it would be a great miracle if the Lord were to pardon me." Indeed, it would be a supreme miracle. Therefore, He is likely to do it, for He does *"great things and unsearchable"* (Job 5:9) that we did not look for.

Look to Jesus

I myself was stricken with a horrible sense of guilt that made my life a misery. Yet when I heard the command, *"Look unto me, and be ye saved, all the ends of the earth: for I am God, and there is none else"* (Isaiah 45:22), I looked, and in a moment the Lord justified me. Jesus Christ, crucified for me, was what I saw, and that sight gave me rest. When those who were bitten by the fiery serpents in the wilderness looked to the serpent of brass, they were healed at once. (See Numbers 21:5–9.) Likewise, I was healed when I looked to the crucified Savior. The Holy Spirit, who enabled me to believe, gave me peace through believing. I felt as sure that I was forgiven as I had felt sure of condemnation before. I had been certain of my condemnation because the Word of God declared it and my conscience bore witness to it. However, when the Lord justified me, I was made equally certain by the same witnesses. The word of the Lord in the Scripture says, *"He that believeth on him is not condemned"* (John 3:18). My conscience bears witness that I believed and that, in pardoning me, God is just. Thus I have the witness of the Holy Spirit and my own conscience, and these two agree. Oh, how I wish you would receive the testimony of God on this matter, for then you also would soon have the witness in yourself!

I venture to say that a sinner justified by God stands on a surer footing than even a righteous man justified by his works, if there is such. Yet, if we were in that situation, we could never be sure that we had done enough works. Our consciences would always be uneasy for fear that, after all, we would fall short and have only the trembling verdict of a fallible judgment to rely on. However, when God Himself justifies, and the Holy Spirit bears witness to this fact by giving us peace with God, then we feel that the matter is sure and settled, and we enter into rest. No tongue can tell the depth of the calm that comes over the soul that has received the *"peace of God, which passeth all understanding"* (Philippians 4:7).

Chapter 5

"Just, and the Justifier"

That he might be just, and the justifier of him
which believeth in Jesus.
—Romans 3:26

W e have seen that the ungodly can be justified, and we have considered the great truth that only God can justify any man. We now come a step further and make the inquiry, How can a just God justify guilty men? We find a full answer in the words of Paul in Romans 3:21–26. We will read these six verses in order to get the main idea of the passage:

> But now the righteousness of God without the law is manifested, being witnessed by the law and the prophets; even the righteousness of God which is by faith of Jesus Christ unto all and upon all them that believe: for there is no difference: for all have sinned, and come short of the glory of God; being justified freely by his grace through the redemption that is in Christ Jesus: whom God hath set forth to be a propitiation through faith in his blood, to declare his righteousness for the remission of sins that are past, through the forbearance of God; to declare, I say, at

this time his righteousness: that he might be just, and
the justifier of him which believeth in Jesus.

Let me give you a bit of personal experience. When I was under the conviction of sin, under the hand of the Holy Spirit, I had a clear and sharp sense of the justice of God. Sin, whatever it might be to other people, became to me an intolerable burden. It was not so much that I feared hell, but that I feared sin. I knew myself to be so horribly guilty that I remember feeling that if God did not punish me for sin, He should do so. I felt that the Judge of all the earth ought to condemn such sin as mine. I sat on the judgment seat and condemned myself to perish, for I confessed that if I had been God, I could have done nothing else than send such a guilty person as I was down to the lowest hell.

All the while, I had on my mind a deep concern for the honor of God's name and the integrity of His moral government. I felt that my conscience would not be satisfied if I could be unjustly forgiven. The sin I had committed must be punished. However, then there was the question of how God could be just and yet justify me who had been so guilty. I asked my heart, "How can He be just and yet be the Justifier?" I was worried and wearied with this question; I could see no answer to it. Certainly, I could never have invented an answer that would have satisfied my conscience.

Christ Is Our Representative and Our Covenant Head

The doctrine of the Atonement is, to my mind, one of the surest proofs of the divine inspiration of Holy Scripture. Who would or could have thought of the just Christ dying for the unjust rebel? This is no teaching of human mythology or dream of poetic imagination. This method of atonement is known among men only because it is a fact.

Fiction could not have devised it. God Himself ordained it; it is not a matter that could have been imagined.

I had heard the plan of salvation by the sacrifice of Jesus from my youth, but I did not know any more about it in my innermost soul than if I had been born and bred a heathen. The light was there, but I was blind. It was necessary for the Lord Himself to make it plain to me. It came to me as a new revelation, as fresh as if I had never read in Scripture that Jesus was declared to be the propitiation for sins so that God might be just (Romans 3:25). I believe that the glorious doctrine of the substitution of the Lord Jesus will have to come as a revelation to every newborn child of God when he sees it. I came to understand that salvation is possible through vicarious sacrifice and that provision had been made in the first constitution and arrangement of things for such a substitution.

I was made to see that He who is the Son of God, coequal and coeternal with the Father, had of old been made the covenant Head of a chosen people so that He might in that capacity suffer for them and save them. Inasmuch as our fall was not at first a personal one, for we fell by the first Adam, it became possible for us to be recovered by a second Representative. We are saved by Him who has undertaken to be the covenant Head of His people in order to be their Second Adam. I saw that before I had actually sinned, I had fallen by my first father's sin. I rejoiced that therefore it became possible in point of law for me to rise by a second Head and Representative. The fall by Adam left a loophole of escape; another Adam could undo the ruin made by the first.

When I was anxious about the possibility of a just God pardoning me, I understood and saw by faith that He who is the Son of God became man. In His own blessed person He bore my sin *"in his own body on the tree"* (1 Peter 2:24). I saw that the chastisement of my peace was laid on Him, and that with His stripes I was healed (Isaiah 53:5). Have you ever seen that? Have you ever understood how God can be just to the fullest extent, not remitting penalty nor blunting the edge of the sword, and yet can be infinitely merciful and can justify the ungodly who turn to Him?

It is because the Son of God, supremely glorious in His matchless person, undertook the vindication of the law by bearing the sentence due to me that God is therefore able to pass by my sin. The law of God was more vindicated by the death of Christ than it would have been had all transgressors been sent to hell. For the Son of God to suffer for sin was a more glorious establishment of the government of God than for the whole race to suffer.

Jesus has borne the death penalty on our behalf. Behold the wonder! There He hangs on the cross! This is the greatest sight you will ever see. There He hangs, Son of God and Son of Man, bearing pains unutterable, the Just for the unjust, to bring us to God. Oh, the glory of that sight! The Innocent punished! The Holy One condemned! The ever blessed One made a curse! The infinitely glorious One put to a shameful death! The more I look at the sufferings of the Son of God, the more I am sure that they must meet my case. Why did He suffer if not to take the penalty away from us? If, then, He took it away by His death, it is surely taken. Those who believe in Him need not fear it. It must be that, since atonement is made, God is able to forgive without disrupting the basis of His throne or in the least degree blotting the statute book. Conscience gets a full answer to her tremendous question.

The wrath of God against iniquity must be terrible beyond all conception. Moses said it well: *"Who knoweth the power of thine anger?"* (Psalm 90:11). Yet when we hear the Lord of glory cry, *"Why hast thou forsaken me?"* (Matthew 27:46), and see Him yielding up His spirit (v. 50), we feel that the justice of God has been abundantly vindicated by the divine Jesus' perfect obedience and terrible death. If God Himself bows before His own law, what more can be done? There is more in the Atonement by way of merit than there is in all human sin by way of demerit.

The great gulf of Jesus' loving self-sacrifice can swallow up the mountains of our sins—all of them. For the sake of the infinite good of this one representative Man, the Lord may well look with favor on other men. He does so, however unworthy they may be in and of themselves. It was a miracle of miracles that the Lord Jesus Christ would stand in our stead and

> Bear that we might never bear
> His Father's righteous ire.

Yet He has done so. *"It is finished"* (John 19:30). God will spare the sinner because He did not spare His Son. God can pass by your transgressions because He laid them upon His only begotten Son nearly two thousand years ago. If you believe in Jesus (that is the point), then your sins were carried away by Him who was the Scapegoat for His people.

Trust Him Wholly and Entirely

What is it to believe in Him? It is not merely to say, "He is God and the Savior," but to trust Him wholly and entirely and take Him for all your salvation from this time forth and forever as your Lord, your Master, your all. If you will have Jesus, He has you already. If you believe in Him, I tell you that you cannot go to hell, for then Christ's death would be in vain. A sacrifice cannot be made and then withheld from the one for whom it was given. If the believing soul could be condemned, then why a sacrifice? If Jesus died in my stead, why should I die, also?

Every believer can claim that the sacrifice was actually made for him. By faith he has laid his hands on it and made it his own, and therefore he may rest assured that he can never perish. The Lord would not receive this offering on our behalf and then condemn us to die. The Lord cannot read our pardon written in the blood of His own Son and then smite us. That would be impossible. Oh, that you may at once have grace given to you to look to Jesus and to begin at the beginning—with Jesus, the Fountainhead of mercy to guilty man!

He *"justifieth the ungodly"* (Romans 4:5). *"It is God that justifieth"* (Romans 8:33). Therefore, and for that reason only, it can be done. He does it through the atoning sacrifice of His divine Son. Therefore, it can be justly done—so justly done that no one will ever question it. It can be so thoroughly done that, in the last tremendous Day, when heaven and earth will pass away, there will be none who deny the validity of the justification. *"Who is he that condemneth? It is Christ that died....Who shall lay any thing to the charge of God's elect? It is God that justifieth"* (Romans 8:34, 33).

Now will you come into this lifeboat just as you are? Here is safety from the wreck! Accept the sure deliverance. "I have nothing with me," you say. You are not asked to bring anything with you. Men who escape for their lives will leave even their clothes behind. Leap for it just as you are.

I will tell you something about myself to encourage you. My sole hope for heaven lies in the full atonement made on Calvary's cross for the ungodly. I firmly rely on that. I do not have a shadow of hope anywhere else. You are in the same condition as I am. Neither of us has anything of our own worth to be a basis of trust. Let us join hands and stand together at the foot of the cross and trust our souls once and for all to Him who shed His blood for the guilty. We will be saved by one and the same Savior. If you perish trusting Him, I must perish, too. What can I do to further prove my own confidence in the Gospel that I set before you?

Chapter 6

Deliverance from Sinning

A new heart also will I give you,
and a new spirit will I put within you.
—Ezekiel 36:26

I would like to say a word or two to those who understand the method of justification by faith that is in
Christ Jesus, but who have a hard time refraining from
sin. We can never be happy, restful, or spiritually healthy
until we become holy. We must get rid of sin. Yet how can
we? This is the life-or-death question of many. The old
nature is very strong, and they have tried to curb and
tame it. However, it will not be subdued. They find themselves, though anxious to be better, if anything, growing
worse than before.

The heart is so hard, the will is so obstinate, the
passions are so furious, the thoughts are so volatile, the
imagination is so ungovernable, the desires are so wild,
that man feels as if he has a den of wild beasts within
him. He feels that they will devour him sooner than they
will be ruled by him. We may say of our fallen nature
what the Lord said to Job concerning Leviathan: *"Wilt*
thou play with him as with a bird? or wilt thou bind him

for thy maidens?" (Job 41:5). A man might as well hope to hold the north wind in the palm of his hand as expect to control, by his own strength, those boisterous powers that exist within his fallen nature. This is a greater feat than any of the fabled labors of Hercules; God is needed here.

"I could believe that Jesus would forgive sin," says one, "but my trouble is that I sin again and that I feel such awful tendencies to evil within me. As surely as a stone flung into the air soon comes down again to the ground, so do I, though I am sent up to heaven by earnest preaching, return again to my insensible state. I am easily fascinated with the spellbinding eyes of sin. I am thus held, as if under a spell, so that I cannot escape from my own folly."

Salvation would be a sadly incomplete promise if it did not deal with this part of our ruined state. We need to be purified as well as pardoned. Justification without sanctification would not be salvation at all. It would call the leper clean and leave him to die of his disease. It would forgive the rebellion and allow the rebel to remain an enemy to his king. It would remove the consequences but overlook the cause, and this would leave an endless and hopeless task before us. It would stop the stream for a time but leave an open fountain of defilement that would sooner or later break forth with increased power. Remember that the Lord Jesus came to take away sin in three ways. He came to remove the penalty of sin, the power of sin, and last, the presence of sin. At once you may reach the second part—the power of sin may immediately be broken—and so you will be on the road to the third—the removal of the presence of sin. We *"know that he was manifested to take away our sins"* (1 John 3:5).

The angel said of our Lord, *"Thou shalt call his name JESUS: for he shall save his people from their sins"* (Matthew 1:21). Our Lord Jesus came to destroy in us the works of the devil. What was said at our Lord's birth was also declared in His death. When the soldier pierced His side, blood and water came out to set forth the double cleansing by which we are delivered from the guilt and the defilement of sin.

If, however, you are troubled about the power of sin and about the tendencies of your nature, as you may well be, here is a promise for you. Have faith in it, for it stands in that covenant of grace that is ordered and sure in all things. God, who cannot lie, has said in Ezekiel 36:26, *"A new heart also will I give you, and a new spirit will I put within you: and I will take away the stony heart out of your flesh, and I will give you an heart of flesh."*

You see, it is all *"I will"* and *"I will." "I will give"* and *"I will take away."* This is the royal style of the King of Kings, who is able to accomplish all His will. No word of His will ever fall to the ground.

God's Power Defeats Sin

The Lord knows very well that you cannot change your own heart and cannot cleanse your own nature. However, He also knows that He can do both. He can cause the Ethiopian to change his skin and the leopard his spots. (See Jeremiah 13:23.) Hear this and be astonished: He can create you a second time; He can cause you to be born again. This is a miracle of grace, but the Holy Spirit will perform it. It would be very wonderful if one could stand at the foot of Niagara Falls and speak a word that would make the Niagara River begin to run upstream and leap up that great precipice over which it now rolls down with stupendous force. Nothing but the power of God could achieve that marvel. Yet that would be more than a fit parallel to what would take place if the course of your nature were altogether reversed.

All things are possible with God (Matthew 19:26). He can reverse the direction of your desires and the current of your life. Instead of going downward from God, He can make your whole being tend upward toward God. In fact, that is what the Lord has promised to do for all who are in the covenant, and we know from Scripture that all believers are in the covenant. Let me read the words again: *"A new spirit will I put within you: and I will take away the stony heart out of your flesh, and I will give you an heart of flesh"* (Ezekiel 36:26).

What a wonderful promise! And it is *"yea"* and *"Amen"* in Christ Jesus to the glory of God (2 Corinthians 1:20). Let us lay hold of it, accept it as true, and appropriate it to ourselves. Then it will be fulfilled in us, and we will, after days and years, sing of that wondrous change that the sovereign grace of God has made in us.

God Will Transform You

It is worth considering that, when the Lord takes away the stony heart, the deed is done. Once that is done, no known power can ever take away the new heart that He gives and the right spirit that He puts within us. *"The gifts and calling of God are without repentance"* (Romans 11:29), that is, without repentance on His part. He does not take away what He once has given. Let Him renew you, and you will be renewed. Man's reformations and cleansings soon come to an end, for the dog returns to his vomit (Proverbs 26:11). However, when God puts a new heart in us, the new heart is there forever, and it will never harden into stone again. He who made it flesh will keep it so. Herein we may rejoice and be forever glad of what God creates in the kingdom of His grace.

To put the matter very simply, did you ever hear of Rowland Hill's illustration of the cat and the sow? I will give it in my own fashion to illustrate our Savior's expressive words, *"Ye must be born again"* (John 3:7). Do you see that cat? What a clean animal she is! How cleverly she washes herself with her tongue and her paws! It is quite a pretty sight! Did you ever see a sow do that? No, you never did. It is contrary to its nature. It prefers to wallow in the mud. Go and teach a sow to wash itself, and see how little success you will have. It would be a great sanitary improvement if swine would be clean. Teach them to wash and clean themselves as the cat has been doing! It is a useless task. You may by force wash that sow, but it quickly runs to the mud and is soon as foul as ever. The only way in which you can get a sow to wash itself is to transform it into a cat. But not until then will it wash itself and be clean.

Suppose that transformation had been accomplished. Then what was difficult or impossible is easy enough— the swine will henceforth be fit for your parlor and your hearth rug. So it is with an ungodly man; you cannot force him to do what a renewed man does most willingly. You may teach him and set him a good example, but he cannot learn the art of holiness because he does not want to. His nature leads him another way. When the Lord makes a new man of him, then all things bear a different mark. So great is this change that I once heard a convert say, "Either all the world is changed, or else I am." The new nature follows after right as naturally as the old nature wanders after wrong. What a blessing to receive such a nature! Only the Holy Spirit can give it.

Did it ever strike you how wonderful it is for the Lord to give a new heart and a right spirit to a man? Perhaps you have seen a lobster that has fought with another lobster and lost one of its claws, and a new claw has grown. That is a remarkable thing. However, it is much more astounding that a man should have a new heart given to him. This, indeed, is a miracle beyond the powers of nature. Imagine a tree. If you cut off one of its limbs, another one may grow in its place. Yet can you change the tree? Can you sweeten sour sap? Can you make the thorn bear figs? You can graft something better into it—that is the analogy that nature gives us of the work of grace—but to absolutely change the vital sap of the tree would be a miracle, indeed. God works such a mystery of power in all who believe in Jesus.

If you yield yourself up to His divine working, the Lord will alter your nature. He will subdue the old nature and breathe new life into you. Put your trust in the Lord Jesus Christ. He will take the stony heart out of your flesh and give you a heart of flesh. Where everything was hard, everything will be tender; where everything was depraved, everything will be virtuous; where everything tended downward, everything will rise upward with impetuous force. The lion of anger will give place to the lamb of meekness. The raven of uncleanness will fly before the dove of purity. The vile serpent of deceit will be trodden under the heel of truth.

I have seen with my own eyes such marvelous changes of moral and spiritual character that I despair of no one. I could, if it were fitting, point out those who were once unchaste women who are now pure, and blaspheming men who now delight everyone around them by their intense devotion. Thieves are made honest, drunkards sober, liars truthful, and scoffers zealous for God. Wherever the grace of God has appeared to a man, it has trained him to deny *"ungodliness and worldly lusts,"* and to *"live soberly, righteously, and godly, in this present world"* (Titus 2:12). It will do the same for you.

"I cannot make this change," says someone. Who said you could? The Scripture that we have quoted does not speak of what man will do, but of what God will do. It is God's promise, and it is for Him to fulfill His own commitments. Trust in Him to fulfill His Word to you, and it will be done.

"But how is it to be done?" What business is that of yours? Must the Lord explain His methods before you will believe Him? The Lord's working in this matter is a great mystery; the Holy Spirit performs it. He who made the promise has the responsibility of keeping the promise; and He is equal to the occasion. God, who promises this marvelous change, will assuredly carry it out in all who receive Jesus. To all of them He gives *"power to become the sons of God"* (John 1:12).

Oh, that you would believe it! Oh, that you would do the gracious Lord the justice to believe that He can and will do this for you, great miracle though it will be! Oh, that you would believe that God cannot lie! Oh, that you would trust Him for a new heart and a right spirit, for He can give them to you! May the Lord give you faith in His promise, faith in His Son, faith in the Holy Spirit, and faith in Him. To Him will be praise and honor and glory forever and ever! Amen.

Chapter 7

By Grace
through Faith

By grace are ye saved through faith;
and that not of yourselves: it is the gift of God.
—Ephesians 2:8

I ask you now to take a moment to adoringly observe the fountainhead of our salvation—the grace of God. *"By grace are ye saved."* God is gracious; therefore, sinful men are forgiven, converted, purified, and saved. It is not because of anything in them or that can ever be in them that they are saved. It is because of the boundless love, goodness, pity, compassion, mercy, and grace of God. Wait a moment, then, at the wellhead. Behold the pure river of life-giving water as it proceeds *"out of the throne of God and of the Lamb"* (Revelation 22:1)!

How immeasurable is the grace of God! Who can calculate its breadth? Who can fathom its depth? Like all the rest of the divine attributes, it is infinite. God is full of love, for *"God is love"* (1 John 4:8). God is full of goodness; the very name *God* is short for "good." Unbounded goodness and love enter into the very essence of the Godhead. It is because His *"mercy endureth for ever"* (Psalm 107:1) that men are not destroyed; because His *"compassions fail not"*

All of Grace

(Lamentations 3:22), sinners are brought to Him and forgiven.

Remember this or you may fall into error by fixing your minds so much on the faith that is the channel of salvation that you will forget the grace that is the fountain and source of faith itself. Faith is the work of God's grace in us. *"No man can say that Jesus is the Lord, but by the Holy Ghost"* (1 Corinthians 12:3). *"No man can come to me,"* said Jesus, *"except the Father which hath sent me draw him"* (John 6:44). So that faith, which is coming to Christ, is the result of divine drawing. Grace is the first and last moving cause of salvation. Faith, essential as it is, is only an important part of the machinery that grace employs. We are saved *"through faith,"* but salvation is *"by grace."* Sound forth those words as with the archangel's trumpet: *"By grace are ye saved."* What glad tidings for the undeserving!

Faith occupies the position of a channel or conduit pipe. Grace is the fountain and the stream. Faith is the aqueduct along which the flood of mercy flows down to refresh the thirsty sons of men. It is a great pity when the aqueduct is broken. It is a sad sight to see the many noble aqueducts around Rome that no longer carry water into the city. They are no longer used because the arches are broken and the marvelous structures are in ruins. The aqueduct must be kept intact to carry the current. Similarly, faith must be true and sound. It must lead right up to God and come right down to ourselves so that it may become a serviceable channel of mercy to our souls.

Still, I remind you again that faith is only the channel or aqueduct, and not the fountainhead. We must not look to it so much that we exalt it above the divine source of all blessing, which lies in the grace of God. Never make a Christ out of your faith, nor think of faith as if it were the independent source of your salvation. Our life is found in *"looking unto Jesus"* (Hebrews 12:2), not in looking to our own faith. By faith all things become possible to us. Yet the power is not in the faith but in the God in whom faith relies. Grace is the powerful engine, and faith is the chain that attaches the carriage of the soul to the great motive power. The righteousness of faith is not the moral excellence of faith but the righteousness of Jesus Christ, which faith grasps and takes as its own. The peace within the soul is not derived from contemplation of our own faith. It comes to us from Him who is our peace. Faith touches the hem of His garment, and virtue comes out of Him into the soul.

See, then, that the weakness of your faith will not destroy you. A trembling hand may receive a golden gift. The Lord's salvation can come to us even though we have faith only as a grain of mustard seed. The power lies in the grace of God and not in our faith. Great messages can be sent along slender wires. The peace-giving witness of the Holy Spirit can reach the heart by means of a threadlike faith that seems almost unable to sustain its own weight. Think more of Him to whom you look than of the look itself. You must look away even from your own looking and see nothing but Jesus and the grace of God revealed in Him.

Chapter 8

What Is Faith?

*By grace are ye saved through faith;
and that not of yourselves: it is the gift of God.*
—Ephesians 2:8

hat is this faith concerning which it is said, *"By grace are ye saved through faith"*? There are many descriptions of faith, but almost all the definitions I have heard have made me understand it less than I did before I heard them. Someone said that after he read the chapter, he would "confound" it. It is very likely that he did so, though he meant to *expound* it. We may explain faith until nobody understands it. I hope I will not be guilty of that fault. Faith is the simplest of all things; perhaps it is the more difficult to explain because of its simplicity.

Three Aspects of Faith

What is faith? It is made up of three things: knowledge, belief, and trust. Knowledge comes first.

Knowledge

"How shall they believe in him of whom they have not heard?" (Romans 10:14). I need to be informed of a fact before I can possibly believe it. *"Faith cometh by hearing"* (v. 17). We must first hear so that we may know what is to

46

be believed. *"They that know thy name will put their trust in thee"* (Psalm 9:10). A measure of knowledge is essential to faith; hence the importance of acquiring knowledge. *"Incline your ear, and come unto me: hear, and your soul shall live"* (Isaiah 55:3). Such was the word of the ancient prophet, and it is still the word of the Gospel. Search the Scriptures and learn what the Holy Spirit teaches concerning Christ and His salvation. Seek to know God, *"for he that cometh to God must believe that he is, and that he is a rewarder of them that diligently seek him"* (Hebrews 11:6). May the Holy Spirit give you *"the spirit of knowledge and of the fear of the LORD"* (Isaiah 11:2)!

Know the Gospel. Know what the Good News is and how it talks of free forgiveness, change of heart, adoption into the family of God, and countless other blessings. Especially know Christ Jesus the Son of God, the Savior of men, united to us by His human nature and yet one with God. Thus He was able to act as Mediator between God and man. He was able to lay His hand on both and be the connecting link between the sinner and the Judge of all the earth. Endeavor to know more and more of Christ Jesus. Endeavor especially to know the doctrine of the sacrifice of Christ, for the main point that addresses saving faith itself is this: *"God was in Christ, reconciling the world unto himself, not imputing their trespasses unto them"* (2 Corinthians 5:19). Know that Jesus was *"made a curse for us: for it is written, Cursed is every one that hangeth on a tree"* (Galatians 3:13). Drink deep of the doctrine of the substitutionary work of Christ, for therein lies the sweetest possible comfort to the guilty sons of men, since the Lord *"made him to be sin for us...that we might be made the righteousness of God in him"* (2 Corinthians 5:21). Faith begins with knowledge.

Belief

The mind goes on to believe that these things are true. The soul believes that God is and that He hears the cries of sincere hearts. The soul believes that the Gospel is from God and that justification by faith is the grand truth that God has revealed in these last days by His Spirit more clearly than before. Then the heart believes that Jesus is verily and in truth our God and Savior, the Redeemer of men, the Prophet, Priest, and King of His people. All this is accepted as sure truth, not to be questioned. I pray that you may at once come to this. Firmly believe that *"the blood of Jesus Christ his* [God's] *Son cleanseth us from all sin"* (1 John 1:7). Believe that His sacrifice is complete and fully accepted by God on man's behalf, so that he who believes in Jesus is not condemned (John 3:17–18). Believe these truths as you believe any other statements, for the difference between ordinary faith and saving faith lies mainly in the subjects in which it is placed. Believe the witness of God just as you believe the testimony of your own father or friend. *"If we receive the witness of men, the witness of God is greater"* (1 John 5:9).

Trust

So far, you have made an advance toward faith; only one more ingredient is needed to complete it—trust. Commit yourself to the merciful God; rest your hope on the gracious Gospel. Trust your soul to the dying and living Savior; wash away your sins in the atoning blood; accept His perfect righteousness, and all will be well. Trust is the lifeblood of faith; there is no saving faith without it. The Puritans were accustomed to explaining faith by the word *recumbency.* It meant leaning upon a thing. Lean with all your weight upon Christ. An even better illustration is this: Fall at full length and lie upon the Rock of Ages. Cast yourself upon Jesus. Rest in Him. Commit yourself to Him. That done, you have exercised saving faith. Faith is not a blind thing, for faith begins with knowledge. It is not a speculative thing, for faith believes facts of which it is sure. It is not an impractical, dreamy thing, for faith trusts and stakes its destiny on the truth of revelation. That is one way of describing what faith is.

Faith Believes in the Person of Christ

Let me try again. Faith is believing that Christ is what He is said to be and that He will do what He has promised to do. Faith expects this of Him. The Scriptures speak of Jesus Christ as being God in human flesh, as being perfect in His character, as being made a sin offering on our behalf, and as bearing *"our sins in his own body on the tree"* (1 Peter 2:24). The Scripture speaks of Him as having finished transgression, made an end of sin, and brought in everlasting righteousness (Daniel 9:24).

The sacred records further tell us that He *"rose again"* (1 Corinthians 15:4) from the dead, and that He *"ever liveth to make intercession for* [us]*"* (Hebrews 7:25). The Scriptures also say that He has gone up into glory and has taken possession of heaven on behalf of His people. He will shortly come again to *"judge the world...with righteousness...and the people with equity"* (Psalm 98:9). We are to believe most firmly that it is so, for this was the testimony of God the Father when He said, *"This is my beloved Son: hear him"* (Luke 9:35). This also is testified by God the Holy Spirit, for the Spirit has borne witness to Christ—in the inspired Word, by many miracles, and by His working in the hearts of men. We are to believe this testimony to be true.

Faith also believes that Christ will do what He has promised. Since He has promised to cast out none who come to Him (John 6:37), it is certain that He will not cast us out if we come to Him. Faith believes that since Jesus said, *"The water that I shall give him shall be in him a well of water springing up into everlasting life"* (John 4:14), it must be true. Faith believes that if we get this living water from Christ, it will abide in us and will well up within us in streams of holy life. Whatever Christ has promised to do, He will do, and we must believe this in order to look for pardon, justification, preservation, and eternal glory from His hands, since He has promised them to believers in Him.

Then comes the next necessary step. Jesus is what He is said to be. Jesus will do what He says He will do. Therefore, we must each trust Him, saying, "He will be to me what He says He is, and He will do to me what He has promised to do. I leave myself in the hands of Him who is appointed to save, so that He may save me. I rest on His promise that He will do even as He has said." This is saving faith, and he who has it has everlasting life. Whatever his dangers and difficulties, whatever his darkness and depression, whatever his infirmities and sins, he who believes thus on Christ Jesus is not condemned and will never come into condemnation.

May that explanation be of some service! I trust it may be used by the Spirit of God to direct you into immediate peace. *"Be not afraid, only believe"* (Mark 5:36). Trust, and be at rest.

Do Not Delay

My fear is that you will rest content with understanding what is to be done and yet never do it. The poorest real faith actually at work is better than the best ideal of it left in the region of speculation. The great matter is to believe on the Lord Jesus at once. Never mind distinctions and definitions. A hungry man eats even though he does not understand the composition of his food, the anatomy of his mouth, or the process of his digestion. He knows that he lives because he eats. Another far more clever person understands thoroughly the science of nutrition, but if he does not eat, he will die with all his knowledge. There are, no doubt, many in hell at this hour who understood the doctrine of faith but did not believe. On the other hand, not one who has trusted in the Lord Jesus has ever been cast out, though he may never have been able to intelligently define his faith. Oh, receive the Lord Jesus into your soul, and you will live forever! *"He that believeth on the Son hath everlasting life"* (John 3:36).

Chapter 9

How May Faith Be Illustrated?

Faith is the substance of things hoped for,
the evidence of things not seen.
—Hebrews 11:1

I will give you a few illustrations to make the matter of faith clearer. Though the Holy Spirit alone can make you see, it is my duty and my joy to furnish all the light I can and to pray to the Divine Lord to open blind eyes. Oh, that you would pray the same prayer for yourself!

Faith Illustrated by the Human Body

The Eye

The faith that saves has its analogies in the human body. It is the *eye* that looks. The eye brings into the mind what is far away. We can bring the sun and the far-off stars into the mind by a glance of the eye. So by trust we bring the Lord Jesus near to us. And though He is far away in heaven, He enters into our hearts. Only look to Jesus, for the hymn is exactly true:

There is life in a look at the Crucified One,
There is life at this moment for thee.

The Hand

Faith is the *hand* that grasps. When a hand takes hold of anything for itself, it does precisely what faith does when it appropriates Christ and the blessings of His redemption. Faith says, "Jesus is mine." Faith hears of the pardoning blood and cries, "I accept it to pardon *me*." Faith calls the legacies of the dying Jesus its own. And they are faith's own, for faith is Christ's heir; He has given Himself and all that He has to faith. Take what grace has provided for you. You will not be a thief, for you have a divine permit: *"Whosoever will, let him take the water of life freely"* (Revelation 22:17). He who may have a treasure simply by grasping it will be foolish indeed if he remains poor.

The Mouth

Faith is the *mouth* that feeds on Christ. Before food can nourish us, it must be received into us. This eating and drinking is a simple matter. We willingly receive food into our mouths, and then we allow it to pass down into our inward parts where it is taken up and absorbed into our bodily frames. Paul said in Romans 10:8, *"The word is nigh thee, even in thy mouth."* Now all that is left to be done is to swallow it, to allow it to go down into the soul. Oh, that men had an appetite! For he who is hungry and sees meat before him does not need to be taught how to eat. "Give me," said one, "a knife and a fork and a chance." He was fully prepared to do the rest. A heart that truly hungers and thirsts after Christ only has to know that He is freely given and at once it will receive Him. If you are in such a case, do not hesitate to receive Jesus. You may be sure that you will never be blamed for doing so, for *"as many as received him, to them gave he power to become the sons of God"* (John 1:12). He never rejects anyone, but He authorizes all who come to remain sons forever.

Faith Illustrated by the Pursuits of Life

The pursuits of life illustrate faith in many ways. The farmer buries good seed in the earth and expects it not only to live but also to multiply. He has faith in the covenant arrangement that *"seedtime and harvest...shall not cease"* (Genesis 8:22). He is rewarded for his faith.

The merchant places his money in the care of a banker and completely trusts the honesty and soundness of the bank. He entrusts his capital to another's hands and feels far more at ease than if he had the solid gold locked up in an iron safe.

The sailor trusts himself to the sea. When he swims, he lifts his feet from the bottom and rests on the buoyant ocean. He could not swim if he did not wholly cast himself upon the water.

The goldsmith puts precious metal into the fire, which seems eager to consume it. However, he receives it back again from the furnace purified by the heat.

You cannot turn anywhere in life without seeing faith in operation between man and man or between man and natural law. Now, just as we trust in daily life, even so are we to trust in God as He is revealed in Christ Jesus.

Faith Illustrated by Its Degrees

Faith exists in different persons in various degrees, according to the amount of their knowledge or growth in grace.

Clinging Faith

Sometimes faith is little more than a simple *clinging* to Christ—a sense of dependence and a willingness to depend. When you are down at the seashore, you will see limpets sticking to the rocks. You can walk softly up to a rock, strike a mollusk a quick blow with a stick, and off he comes. Yet try the next limpet in that way. You have given him warning; he heard the blow with which you struck his neighbor, and he clings with all his might. You will never get him off! Strike and strike again, but you might as well break the rock. The limpet does not know much, but he clings. He is not acquainted with the geological formation of the rock, but he clings. He can cling and has found something to cling to; this is all his stock of knowledge, and he uses it for his security and salvation. It is the limpet's life to cling to the rock, and it is the sinner's life to cling to Jesus. Thousands of God's people have no more faith than this. They know enough to cling to Jesus with all their heart and soul, and this suffices for present peace and eternal safety. Jesus Christ is to them a strong and mighty Savior, a Rock immovable and immutable. They cling to Him for dear life, and this clinging saves them. Can you not cling? Do so at once.

Faith That Trusts in Jesus' Merits and Truth

Another example of faith is when one man relies on another because of a knowledge of the superiority of the other. This is a higher faith—the faith that knows the reason for its dependence and acts on it. I do not think the limpet knows much about the rock, but, as faith grows, it becomes more and more intelligent. A blind man trusts himself with his guide because he knows that his friend can see. Trusting, he walks where his guide conducts him. If the poor man is born blind, he does not know what sight is, but he knows that there is such a thing as sight and that it is possessed by his friend. Therefore, he freely puts his hand into the hand of the seeing one and follows his leadership. *"We walk by faith, not by sight"* (2 Corinthians 5:7). *"Blessed are they that have not seen, and yet have believed"* (John 20:29). This is an excellent image of faith. We know that Jesus has merit and power and blessing that we do not possess, and therefore we gladly trust Him to be to us what we cannot be to ourselves. We trust Him as the blind man trusts his guide. He never betrays our confidence, but He *"of God is made unto us wisdom, and righteousness, and sanctification, and redemption"* (1 Corinthians 1:30).

Every child who goes to school has to exert faith while learning. His teacher teaches him geography and instructs him as to the form of the earth and the existence of certain great cities and empires. The child himself does not know that these things are true, except that he believes his teacher and the books put into his hands. That is what you will have to do with Christ if you are to be saved. You must simply know because He tells you, believe because He assures you it is so, and trust yourself with Him because He promises you that salvation will be the result.

Almost all that you and I know has come to us by faith. A scientific discovery has been made, and we are sure of it. On what grounds do we believe it? On the authority of certain well-known men of learning whose reputations are established. We have never made or seen their experiments, but we believe their witness. You must do the same with regard to Jesus. Because He teaches you certain truths, you are to be His disciples and believe His words. Because He has performed certain acts, you are to be His clients and trust yourselves with Him. He is infinitely superior to you and presents Himself to you as your Master and Lord. If you will receive Him and His words, you will be saved.

Faith That Grows out of Love

Another and a higher form of faith is the faith that grows out of love. Why does a child trust his father? It is because he loves him. Blessed and happy are they who have a sweet faith in Jesus intertwined with deep affection for Him, for this is a restful confidence. These lovers of Jesus are enthralled with His character and delighted with His mission. They are carried away by the loving-kindness that He has manifested. Therefore, they cannot help trusting Him because they so much admire, revere, and love Him.

The way of loving trust in the Savior is illustrated by a lady who is the wife of the most eminent physician of the day. She is seized with a dangerous illness and is afflicted by its power. Yet she is wonderfully calm and quiet because her husband has made this disease his special study and has healed thousands who were similarly afflicted. She is not in the least troubled, for she feels perfectly safe in the hands of one so dear to her and in whom skill and love are blended in their highest forms. Her faith is reasonable and natural; her husband, from every point of view, deserves it from her.

This is the kind of faith that the happiest of believers exercise toward Christ. There is no physician like Him; none can save as He can. We love Him, and He loves us. Therefore, we put ourselves into His hands, accept whatever He prescribes, and do whatever He bids. We feel that nothing can be wrongly ordered while He is the Director of our affairs. He loves us too well to let us perish or suffer a single needless pang.

Faith is the root of obedience, and this truth may be clearly seen in the affairs of life. When a captain trusts a pilot to steer his vessel into port, he manages the vessel according to his direction. When a traveler trusts a guide to conduct him over a difficult pass, he follows the track that his guide points out. When a patient believes in a physician, he carefully follows his prescriptions and directions. Faith that refuses to obey the commands of the Savior is a mere pretense and will never save the soul. We trust Jesus to save us. He gives us directions as to the way of salvation; we follow those directions and are saved. Do not forget this. Trust Jesus and prove your trust by doing whatever He bids you.

Faith That Arises from Assured Knowledge

A notable form of faith rises out of assured knowledge. This comes by growth in grace and is the faith that believes Christ because it knows Him. It trusts Christ because it has proven Him to be infallibly faithful. An old Christian was in the habit of writing *T* and *P* in the margin of her Bible whenever she had tried and proven a promise. How easy it is to trust a tried and proven Savior! You may not do this as yet, but you will do so. Everything must have a beginning. You will rise to strong faith in due time. This matured faith does not ask for signs and tokens, but bravely believes.

Look at the faith of the master mariner; I have often wondered at it. He loosens his cable and steams away from the land. For days, weeks, or even months, he never sees sail or shore. Yet on he goes day and night without fear until one morning he finds himself closely approaching the desired haven toward which he has been steering. How has he found his way over the trackless deep? He has trusted in his compass, his nautical almanac, his glass, and the heavenly bodies. Obeying their guidance, without sighting land, he has steered so accurately that he has not had to change a point to enter into port. It is a wonderful thing to sail or steam without sight.

Spiritually, it is a blessed thing to altogether leave the shores of sight and feeling and to say good-bye to inward feelings, cheering providences, signs, tokens, and so forth. It is glorious to be far out on the ocean of divine love, believing in God and steering straight for heaven by the direction of the Word of God. *"Blessed are they that have not seen, and yet have believed"* (John 20:29). A safe voyage on the way and an abundant entrance at the last will be given to them. Will you put your trust in God, in Christ Jesus? There I rest with joyous confidence. Come with me and believe our Father and our Savior. Come at once.

Chapter 10

Why Are We Saved by Faith?

For by grace are ye saved through faith; and that not of yourselves: it is the gift of God.
—Ephesians 2:8

W hy is faith selected as the channel of salvation? No doubt this inquiry is often made. *"By grace are ye saved **through faith"*** is assuredly the doctrine of Holy Scripture and the ordinance of God, but why is this so? Why is faith selected rather than hope or love or patience?

Faith Is Naturally Adapted as the Receiver

It becomes us to be modest in answering such a question. God's ways are not always to be understood, nor are we allowed to presumptuously question them. Humbly we would reply that, as far as we can tell, faith has been selected as the channel of grace because faith is naturally adapted to be used as the receiver. Suppose that I am about to give a poor man some money. I will put it into his hand. Why? Well, it would hardly be fitting to put it into his ear or to lay it on his foot. The hand seems made on purpose to receive. So, in our mental frame, faith is created on purpose to be a receiver. It is like the hand of a man, and there is a fitness in receiving grace by its means.

Let me put this very plainly. Receiving Christ by faith is as simple an act as when your child receives an apple from you because you hold it out and promise to give him the apple if he comes for it. The belief and the receiving relate only to an apple, but they make up precisely the same act as the faith that deals with eternal salvation. What the child's hand is to the apple, your faith is to the perfect salvation of Christ. The child's hand does not make the apple nor improve the apple nor deserve the apple; it only takes it. And faith is chosen by God to be the receiver of salvation because it does not pretend to create salvation or to help in it, but is content to receive it humbly. "Faith is the tongue that begs pardon, the hand that receives it, and the eye that sees it; but it is not the price that buys it." Faith never makes itself its own plea. It rests all its argument on the blood of Christ. It becomes a good servant to bring the riches of the Lord Jesus to the soul because it acknowledges from where it drew them and admits that grace alone entrusted it with them.

Faith Gives All the Glory to God

Faith is again selected because it gives all the glory to God. *"It is of faith, that it might be by grace"* (Romans 4:16), and it is of grace that there might be no boasting, for God cannot endure pride. *"The proud he knoweth afar off"* (Psalm 138:6). He has no wish to come nearer to them. He will not give salvation in a way that will suggest or foster pride. Paul said, *"Not of works, lest any man should boast"* (Ephesians 2:9). Now, faith excludes all boasting. The hand that receives charity does not say, "I am to be thanked for accepting the gift"; that would be absurd. When the hand gives bread to the mouth, it does not say to the body, "Thank me, for I feed you." It is a very simple thing that the hand does—though very necessary—and it never designates glory to itself for what it does. So God has selected faith to receive the *"unspeakable gift"* (2 Corinthians 9:15) of His grace. It cannot take any credit to itself but must adore the gracious God who is the Giver of all good. Faith sets the crown on the right head. Therefore, the Lord Jesus was accustomed to putting the crown on the head of faith, saying, *"Thy faith hath saved thee; go in peace"* (Luke 7:50).

Faith Is a Sure Method of Linking Man with God

Next, God selects faith as the channel of salvation because it is a sure method of linking man with God. When man confides in God, there is a point of union between them, and that union guarantees blessing. Faith saves us because it makes us cling to God and therefore connects us with Him. I have often used the following illustration. Years ago, a boat was upset above Niagara Falls. Two men were being carried down the current when people on the shore managed to float a rope out to them. Both seized it. One of them held onto it and was safely drawn to the bank. However, the other, seeing a great log come floating by, unwisely let go of the rope and clung to the log, for it was bigger and apparently better to cling to. The log with the man on it went right over the vast abyss because nothing connected the log and the shore. The size of the log was of no benefit to him who grasped it; it needed a connection with the shore to produce safety.

So when a man trusts to his works or to sacraments or to anything of that sort, he will not be saved, because there is no junction between him and Christ. However, faith, though it may seem to be like a slender cord, is in the hands of the great God on the shore. Infinite power pulls in the connecting line between God and faith and thus draws the man from destruction. Oh, the blessedness of faith because it ties us to God!

Faith Touches the Springs of Action

Faith is chosen again because it touches the springs of action. Even in common things faith of a certain sort lies at the root of all. I wonder whether I am wrong if I say that we never do anything except through faith of some sort. If I walk across my study, it is because I believe my legs will carry me. A man eats because he believes in the necessity of food. He goes to his business because he believes in the value of money. He accepts a check because he believes that the bank will honor it. Colombus discovered America because he believed that there was another continent beyond the ocean. The Pilgrim fathers colonized it because they believed that God would be with them on those rocky shores. Most grand deeds have been born of faith. For good or for evil, faith works wonders by the person in whom it dwells.

Faith in its natural form is an all-prevailing force that enters into all manner of human actions. Possibly he who mocks faith in God is the man who in an evil form has the most faith. Indeed, he usually falls into a credulity that would be ridiculous if it were not disgraceful. God gives salvation to faith, because by creating faith in us He thus touches the real mainspring of our emotions and actions. He has, so to speak, taken possession of the battery, and now He can send the sacred current to every part of our nature. When we believe in Christ, and the heart has come into the possession of God, then we are saved from sin and are moved toward repentance, holiness, zeal, prayer, consecration, and every other gracious thing. "What oil is to the wheels, what weights are to a clock, what wings are to a bird, what sails are to a ship, faith is to all holy duties and services." Have faith, and all other graces will follow and continue to hold their course.

Faith Draws the Heart to God

Faith, again, has the power of working by love (Galatians 5:6). It influences the affections toward God and draws the heart after the best things. He who believes in God will beyond all question love God. Faith is an act of understanding, but it also proceeds from the heart. *"With the heart man believeth unto righteousness"* (Romans 10:10). Hence, God gives salvation to faith because it resides next door to the affections and is closely related to love. And love is the parent and the nurse of every holy feeling and act. Love for God is obedience; love for God is holiness. To love God and to love man is to be conformed to the image of Christ, and this is salvation.

Faith Creates Peace and Joy

Moreover, faith creates peace and joy. He who has it rests and is tranquil, glad, and joyous, and this is a preparation for heaven. God gives all heavenly gifts to faith for this reason, among others: Faith works in us the life and spirit that are to be eternally manifested in the upper and better world. Faith furnishes us with armor for this life and education for the life to come. It enables a man both to live and to die without fear; it prepares both for action and for suffering. Hence, the Lord selects it as a most convenient medium for conveying grace to us and thereby securing us for glory.

Certainly, faith does for us what nothing else can do. It gives us joy and peace and causes us to enter into rest. Why do men attempt to gain salvation by other means? An old preacher said,

A silly servant, who is told to open a door, puts his shoulder against it and pushes with all his might, but the door does not stir, and he cannot enter, whatever strength he uses. Another comes with a key, easily unlocks the door, and enters immediately. Those who would be saved by works are pushing at heaven's gate without result, but faith is the key that opens the gate at once.

Will you not use that key? The Lord commands you to believe in His dear Son. Therefore, you may do so, and in doing so you will live. Is this not the promise of the Gospel: *"He that believeth and is baptized shall be saved"* (Mark 16:16)? What can your objection be to a way of salvation that commends itself to the mercy and the wisdom of our gracious God?

Chapter 11

I Can Do Nothing!

When we were yet without strength,
in due time Christ died for the ungodly.
—Romans 5:6

After the anxious heart has accepted the doctrine of atonement and learned the great truth that salvation is by faith in the Lord Jesus, it is often troubled with a sense of inability toward that which is good. Many are groaning, "I can do nothing." They are not using this as an excuse, but they feel it as a daily burden. They would if they could. Each one can honestly say, *"To will is present with me; but how to perform that which is good I find not"* (Romans 7:18).

This feeling seems to make all the Gospel null and void, for what is the use of food to a hungry man if he cannot get at it? Of what avail is the river of the water of life if one cannot drink? There is a story of a doctor and a poor woman's child. The learned practitioner told the mother that her little one would soon be better under proper treatment, but it was absolutely necessary that her boy regularly drink the best wine and spend a season at one of the German spas. This he said to a widow who could hardly get enough bread to eat! Now, it sometimes seems to the troubled heart that the simple Gospel of "Believe and live" is not, after all, so very simple. It asks the poor sinner to do what he cannot do. To the suddenly awakened but half-instructed person, there appears to be a missing link. Yonder is the salvation of Jesus, but how is it to be reached? The soul is without strength and does not know what to do. It lies within sight of the city of refuge, but cannot enter its gate.

Is this lack of strength provided for in the plan of salvation? It is. The work of the Lord is perfect. It begins where we are and asks nothing of us for its completion. When the Good Samaritan saw the traveler lying wounded and half dead, he did not tell him to rise and come to him, mount the donkey, and ride off to the inn. No, he *"went to him"* (Luke 10:34) and ministered to him. He lifted him up onto the animal and took him to the inn. Thus does the Lord Jesus deal with us in our low and wretched state.

We have seen that God justifies, that He *"justifieth the ungodly"* (Romans 4:5), and that He justifies them through faith in the precious blood of Jesus. We now have to see the condition these ungodly ones are in when Jesus works out their salvation. Many people who are newly awakened are troubled not only about their sin, but also about their moral weakness. They have no strength with which to escape from the mire into which they have fallen or to keep out of it in the days to come. They lament not only over what they have done, but also over what they cannot do. They feel powerless, helpless, and spiritually lifeless. It may sound odd to say that they feel dead, yet it is so. They are, in their own opinion, incapable of all good. They cannot travel the road to heaven, for their bones are broken. *"None of the men of might* [strength] *have found their hands"* (Psalm 76:5). In fact, they are *"without strength."* Happily, this truth is written as the commendation of God's love to us: *"When we were yet without strength, in due time Christ died for the ungodly."*

Here we see conscious helplessness helped by the interposition of the Lord Jesus. Our helplessness is extreme. It is not written, "When we were comparatively weak, Christ died for us," or "When we had only a little strength," but the description is absolute and unrestricted: *"When we were yet without strength."* We have no strength whatsoever that can aid in our salvation. Our Lord's words are emphatically true: *"Without me ye can do nothing"* (John 15:5). I will go further than the text and remind you of the great love with which the Lord loved us even when we *"were dead in trespasses and sins"* (Ephesians 2:1). To be dead is even worse than being without strength.

The one thing that the poor strengthless sinner has to fix his mind on and firmly retain as his one ground of hope is the divine assurance that *"in due time Christ died for the ungodly."* Believe this, and all inability will disappear. As it is fabled of Midas that he turned everything into gold by his touch, so it is true of faith that it turns everything it touches into good. Our very needs and weaknesses become blessings when faith deals with them.

Forms of Lack of Strength

Weakness in Thinking and Concentration

Let us consider certain forms of this lack of strength. To begin with, one man will say, "Sir, I do not seem to have the strength to collect my thoughts and keep them fixed on those solemn topics that concern my salvation. A short prayer is almost too much for me. It is partly so, perhaps, through natural weakness, partly because I have injured myself through excessive drinking, and partly because I worry myself with worldly cares so that I am not capable of those high thoughts that are necessary before a soul can be saved."

This is a very common form of sinful weakness. Note this! You are without strength on this point, and there are many like you. They could not carry out a train of consecutive thought to save their lives. Many poor men and women are illiterate and untrained, and they find deep thought to be very hard work. Others are so light and tri-fling by nature that they could no more follow out a long process of argument and reasoning than they could fly. They could never attain to the knowledge of any profound mystery if they spent their whole life in the effort.

You need not, therefore, despair. What is necessary to salvation is not continuous thought but a simple reliance upon Jesus. Hold onto this one fact: *"In due time Christ died for the ungodly."* This truth will not require you to do any deep research or profound reasoning or convincing argument. There it stands: *"In due time Christ died for the ungodly."*

Fix your mind on that, and rest there. Let this one great, gracious, glorious fact lie in your spirit until it per-meates all your thoughts and makes you rejoice even though you are without strength. Rejoice that the Lord Jesus has become your strength and your song; yes, He has become your salvation (Exodus 15:2). According to the Scriptures, it is a revealed fact that *"in due time Christ died for the ungodly"* when they were *"yet without strength."* Maybe you have heard these words hundreds of times, and yet you have never before perceived their mean-ing. There is a wonderful thing about them. Jesus did not die for our righteousness, but He died for our sins. He did not come to save us because we were worth saving, but because we were utterly worthless, ruined, and undone. He did not come to earth out of any reason that was in us, but solely and only because of reasons that He took from the depths of His own divine love.

In due time Jesus died for those whom He describes not as godly but as *"ungodly,"* describing them with as hopeless an adjective as He could have selected. Even if you think little, fasten your mind to this truth, for it is fitted to the smallest capacity and is able to cheer the heaviest heart. Let this text lie under your tongue like a sweet morsel until it dissolves into your heart and flavors all your thoughts. People who have never shone in science nor displayed the least originality of thinking have nevertheless been fully able to accept the doctrine of the Cross and have been saved. Why should you not?

Inability to Repent

I hear another man cry, "Oh, sir, my lack of strength lies mainly in that I cannot repent sufficiently!" What a curious idea men have of what repentance is! Many believe that so many tears are to be shed and so many groans are to be heaved and so much despair is to be endured. Where do they get this unreasonable notion? Unbelief and despair are sins. Therefore, I do not see how they can be constituent elements of acceptable repentance. Yet there are many who regard them as necessary parts of true Christian experience. They are in great error.

Still, I know what they mean, for in the days of my darkness, I used to feel the same way. I desired to repent, but I thought that I could not do it. Yet, all the while, I was repenting. Odd as it may sound, I felt that I could not feel. I used to get into a corner and weep because I could not weep. I was bitterly sorrowful because I could not sorrow for sin. What a jumble it all is when in our unbelieving state we begin to judge our own condition! It is like a blind man looking at his own eyes. My heart was melted within me for fear because I thought that my heart was as hard as stone. My heart was broken to think that it would not break. Now I can see that I was exhibiting the very thing that I thought I did not possess; but *then* I did not know where I was.

Oh, that I could help others into the light that I now enjoy! I would gladly say a word that might shorten the time of their bewilderment. I would say a few plain words and ask the Comforter to apply them to the heart.

Remember that the man who truly repents is never satisfied with his own repentance. We can no more repent perfectly than we can live perfectly. However pure our tears, there will always be some dirt in them; there will be something to be repented of even in our best repentance. Yet listen! To repent is to change your mind about sin and Christ and all the great things of God. There is sorrow implied in this, but the main point is the turning of the heart from sin to Christ. If there is this turning, you have the essence of true repentance, even though no alarm and no despair have ever cast their shadow on your mind.

If you find it difficult to repent, it will greatly help you to firmly believe that *"in due time Christ died for the ungodly."* Think of this again and again. How can you continue to be hardhearted when you know that out of supreme love *"Christ died for the ungodly"*? Let me persuade you to reason with yourself like this: "Ungodly as I am, though this heart of steel will not relent, though I hit my chest in vain, yet He died for such as I am, because He died for the ungodly. Oh, that I may believe this and feel the power of it in my unmerciful heart!"

Blot out every other reflection from your soul; sit down by the hour and meditate deeply on this one resplendent display of unmerited, unexpected, unparalleled love: *"Christ died for the ungodly."* Carefully read over the narrative of the Lord's death as you find it in the four Gospels. If anything can melt your stubborn heart, it will be a view of the sufferings of Jesus and the knowledge that He suffered all this for His enemies.

> O Jesus, sweet the tears I shed,
> While at Thy cross I kneel,
> Gaze on Thy wounded, fainting head,
> And all Thy sorrows feel.
>
> My heart dissolves to see Thee bleed,
> This heart so hard before;
> I hear Thee for the guilty plead,
> And grief o'erflows the more.

> 'Twas for the sinful Thou didst die,
>   And I a sinner stand:
> Convinc'd by Thine expiring eye,
>   Slain by Thy piercèd hand.
>
> —Ray Palmer

Surely, the Cross is that wonder-working rod that can bring water out of a rock. If you understand the full meaning of the divine sacrifice of Jesus, you must repent of ever having been opposed to One who is so full of love. It is written, *"They shall look upon me whom they have pierced, and they shall mourn for him, as one mourneth for his only son, and shall be in bitterness for him, as one that is in bitterness for his firstborn"* (Zechariah 12:10). Repentance will not make you see Christ, but to see Christ will give you repentance. You may not make a christ out of your repentance, but you must look to Christ for repentance. The Holy Spirit, by turning us to Christ, turns us from sin. Look away, then, from the effect to the cause, from your own repenting to the Lord Jesus, who is exalted on high to give repentance.

Tormenting and Blasphemous Thoughts

I have heard another say, "I am tormented with horrible thoughts. Wherever I go, blasphemies steal in on me. Frequently, at my work, a dreadful suggestion forces itself upon me. Even in my bed, I am startled from my sleep by whispers of the evil one. I cannot get away from this horrible temptation." Friend, I know what you mean, for I myself have been hunted by this wolf. A man might as well hope to fight a swarm of flies with a sword as to master his own thoughts when they are set on by the devil. A poor tempted soul, assailed by satanic suggestions, is like a traveler I have read about. His head and ears and whole body were attacked by a swarm of angry bees. He could not keep them off or escape from them. They stung him everywhere and threatened to kill him. I do not wonder that you feel that you have no strength to stop these hideous and abominable thoughts that Satan pours into your soul. Yet I would remind you of the Scripture before us: *"When we were yet without strength, in due time Christ died for the ungodly."*

Jesus knew where we were and where we should be. He saw that we could not overcome *"the prince of the power of the air"* (Ephesians 2:2). He knew that we would be greatly worried by the devil. Yet, even then, when He saw us in that condition, Christ died for the ungodly. Cast the anchor of your faith on this. The devil himself cannot tell you that you are not ungodly.

Believe, then, that Jesus died even for such as you are. Remember Martin Luther's way of cutting the devil's head off with his own sword. "Oh," said the devil to Martin Luther, "you are a sinner." "Yes," said Luther, "Christ died to save sinners." Thus he smote him with his own sword. Hide in this refuge and stay there: *"In due time Christ died for the ungodly."* If you stand on that truth, your blasphemous thoughts, which you do not have the strength to drive away, will go away by themselves, for Satan will see that he is achieving nothing by plaguing you with them.

These thoughts, if you hate them, are not yours but are injections of the devil. He is responsible, and not you. If you strive against them, they are no more yours than are the cursings and falsehoods of rioters in the street. It is by means of these thoughts that the devil wants to drive you to despair, or at least keep you from trusting Jesus. The poor diseased woman could not come to Jesus because of the crowd. You are in much the same condition because of the rush and crowd of these dreadful thoughts. Still, she put forth her finger and touched the fringe of the Lord's garment, and she was healed. (See Mark 5:25–34.) Do the same.

Jesus died for those who are guilty of *"all manner of sin and blasphemy"* (Matthew 12:31). Therefore, I am sure

All of Grace

He will not refuse those who are unwillingly the captives of evil thoughts. Cast yourself upon Him, thoughts and all, and prove that He is mighty to save. He can still those horrible whisperings of the fiend, or He can enable you to see them in their true light so that you will not be worried by them. In His own way, He can and will save you and, at length, give you perfect peace. Only trust Him for this and everything else.

Lack of Power to Believe

The form of inability that lies in a supposed lack of power to believe is sadly perplexing. We are not strangers to the cry,

> Oh, that I could believe,
>   Then all would easy be;
> I would, but cannot; Lord, relieve,
>   My help must come from Thee.

Many remain in the dark for years because they have no strength, they say, to give up all power and rest in the power of Another, the Lord Jesus. Indeed, this whole matter of believing is a very curious thing, for people do not get much help by trying to believe. Believing does not come by trying. If a person were to make a statement of something that happened today, I would not tell him that I would *try* to believe him. If I believed in the truthfulness of the man who told me the incident and said that he saw it, I would accept the statement at once. If I did not think he was a truthful man, I would, of course, disbelieve him. There would be no *trying* in the matter. Now, when God declares that there is salvation in Christ Jesus, I must either believe Him at once or call Him a liar. Surely, you will not hesitate as to which is the right path in this case. The witness of God must be true, and we are bound at once to believe in Jesus.

Yet possibly you have been trying to believe too much. Do not aim at great things. Be satisfied to have a faith that can hold in its hand this one truth: *"When we were yet without strength, in due time Christ died for the ungodly."* He laid down His life for men while they were not yet believing in Him, nor were able to believe in Him. He died for men, not as believers but as sinners. He came to make these sinners into believers and saints, but when He died for them, He viewed them as utterly without strength. If you believe that Christ died for the ungodly, your faith will save you, and you may go in peace. If you will trust your soul to Jesus, who died for the ungodly, even though you cannot believe all things or move mountains or do any other wonderful works, yet you will be saved. It is not great faith but true faith that saves. Salvation lies not in the faith but in the Christ in whom faith trusts. Faith as a grain of mustard seed will bring salvation. It is not the amount of faith but the sincerity of faith that is the point to be considered. Surely, a man can believe what he knows to be true; and as you know Jesus to be true, you can believe in Him.

The cross, which is the object of faith, is also, by the power of the Holy Spirit, the cause of it. Sit down and watch the dying Savior until faith springs up spontaneously in your heart. There is no place like Calvary for creating confidence. The air of that sacred hill brings health to trembling faith. Many a watcher there has said,

> While I view Thee, wounded, grieving,
> Breathless on the cursèd tree,
> Lord, I feel my heart believing
> That Thou suffer'dst thus for me.

Inability to Stop Sinning

"Alas!" cries another, "my trouble is that I cannot quit my sinning. I know that I cannot go to heaven and carry my sin with me." I am glad that you know that, for it is quite true. You must be divorced from your sin, or you cannot be married to Christ. Recall the question that flashed into the mind of young Bunyan while he was playing sports on Sunday: "Wilt thou have thy sins and go to hell, or wilt thou quit thy sins and go to heaven?" That brought him to a dead stop. That is a question that every man will have to answer, for there is no going on in sin and going to heaven. That cannot be. You must quit sin or quit hope.

Do you reply, "Yes, I am willing enough. *'To will is present with me; but how to perform that which* [I would] *I find not'* (Romans 7:18). Sin masters me, and I have no strength." Come, then, if you have no strength; this text is still true: *"When we were yet without strength, in due time Christ died for the ungodly."* Can you still believe that? No matter how many other things may seem to contradict it, will you still believe it? God has said it, and it is a fact; therefore, hold on to it tightly, for your only hope lies there. Believe this, trust Jesus, and you will soon find power with which to slay your sin. However, apart from Him, the armed strongman will hold you forever as his bondslave.

Personally, I could never have overcome my own sinfulness. I tried and failed. My evil tendencies were too much for me until, in the belief that Christ died for me, I cast my guilty soul on Him. And then I received a conquering principle by which I overcame my sinful self. The doctrine of the Cross can be used to slay sin as the old warriors used their huge two-handed swords and mowed down their foes at every stroke. There is nothing like faith in the sinner's Friend; it overcomes all evil. If Christ has died for me—ungodly as I am, without strength as I am—then I can no longer live in sin, but must rouse myself to love and serve Him who has redeemed me. I cannot trifle with the evil that slew my Best Friend. I must be holy for His sake. How can I live in sin when He has died to save me from it?

See what a splendid help this is to you who are without strength—to know and believe that in due time Christ died for such ungodly ones as you are. Have you caught the idea yet? It is, somehow, so difficult for our darkened, prejudiced, and unbelieving minds to see the essence of the Gospel. At times I have thought, when I have finished preaching, that I have presented the Gospel so clearly that the nose on one's face could not be more plain. Yet I perceive that even intelligent hearers have failed to understand what was meant by *"Look unto me, and be ye saved"* (Isaiah 45:22). Converts usually say that they did not know the Gospel until such and such a day, yet they had heard it for years. The Gospel is unknown, not from lack of explanation, but from absence of personal revelation. This the Holy Spirit is ready to give and will give to those who ask Him. Yet, when given, the sum total of the truth revealed lies within these words: *"Christ died for the ungodly."*

The Fear of Man

I hear another person bewailing himself thus: "Oh, sir, my weakness lies in this: I do not seem to keep spiritual things in my mind long! I hear the Word on a Sunday, and I am impressed. Yet, during the week, I meet with an evil companion, and my good feelings are all gone. My fellow workmen do not believe in anything, and they say such terrible things. I do not know how to answer them, so I find myself knocked over." I know this Plastic Pliable very well, and I tremble for him. However, at the same time, if he is really sincere, his weakness can be met by divine grace. The Holy Spirit can cast out the evil spirit of the fear of man. He can make the coward brave.

Remember, my poor vacillating friend, you must not remain in this state. It will never do to be mean and beggarly to yourself. Stand upright and look at yourself. See if you were ever meant to be like a toad under a rotary cultivator, afraid for your life either to move or to stand still. Do have a mind of your own.

This is not a spiritual matter only, but one that concerns ordinary human nature. I would do many things to please my friends, but to go to hell to please them is more than I would venture. It may be very well to do this and that for good fellowship, but it will never do to lose the friendship of God in order to keep on good terms with men. "I know that," says the man, "but still, though I know it, I cannot get enough courage. I cannot show my colors. I cannot stand fast." Well, to you, also, I have the same text to bring: *"When we were yet without strength, in due time Christ died for the ungodly."*

If Peter were here, he would say, "The Lord Jesus died for me even when I was such a poor weak creature that the maid who kept the fire drove me to lie and to swear that I did not know the Lord." (See Matthew 26:69–74.) Yes, Jesus died for those who forsook Him and fled. Take a firm grip on this truth: Christ died for the ungodly while they were yet without strength. This is your way out of your cowardice. Get this thought, "Christ died for me," worked into your soul, and you will soon be ready to die for Him. Believe that He suffered in your stead and offered for you a full, true, and satisfactory atonement. If you believe that fact, you will be forced to feel, "I cannot be ashamed of Him who died for me." A full conviction that this is true will give you fearless courage.

Look at the saints in the martyr age. In the early days of Christianity, when this great thought of Christ's exceeding love was sparkling in all its freshness in the church, men were not only ready to die, but also grew ambitious to suffer and even presented themselves by the hundreds at the judgment seats of the rulers, confessing the Christ. I do not say that they were wise to court a cruel death, but it proves my point that a sense of the love of Jesus lifts the mind above all fear of what man can do to us. Why should it not produce this effect in you? Oh, that it might now inspire you with a brave resolve to come out on the Lord's side and be His follower to the end!

May the Holy Spirit help us to come thus far by faith in the Lord Jesus, and it will be well!

Chapter 12

The Increase of Faith

The apostles said unto the Lord, Increase our faith.
—Luke 17:5

H ow can we increase our faith? This is a very earnest question for many. They say they want to believe but cannot. A great deal of nonsense is said about this subject. Let us be strictly practical in our dealing with it. Common sense is as much needed in Christianity as anywhere else.

Ways to Increase Faith

Believe at Once

"What am I to do in order to believe?" One who was asked the best way to do a certain simple act replied that the best way to do it was to do it at once. We waste time in discussing methods when the action is simple. The shortest way to believe is to believe. If the Holy Spirit has made you candid, you will believe as soon as truth is set before you. You will believe it because it is true. The Gospel command is clear, *"Believe on the Lord Jesus Christ, and thou shalt be saved"* (Acts 16:31). It is idle to evade this truth by questions and quibbles. The order is clear; let it be obeyed.

Ask God to Lead You into the Truth

Yet still, if you have difficulty, take it before God in prayer. Tell God the Father exactly what it is that puzzles you, and beg Him by His Holy Spirit to solve the question. If I cannot believe a statement in a book, I ask the author what he means by it. If he is an honest man, his explanation will satisfy me. The divine explanation of the hard points of Scripture will satisfy the heart of the true seeker much more than this. The Lord is willing to make Himself known. Go to Him and see if it is not so. Go at once to prayer and cry, "O Holy Spirit, lead me into the truth! Teach me what I do not know."

Hear the Gospel Often and Attentively

Furthermore, if faith seems difficult, it is possible that God the Holy Spirit will enable you to believe if you listen often and well to what you are commanded to believe. We believe many things because we have heard them so often. Do you not find that, in everyday life, if you hear a thing fifty times a day, you come to believe it? Some men have come to believe very unlikely statements by this process. Therefore, I can easily understand why the Holy Spirit often blesses this method of hearing the truth and uses it to work faith concerning what is to be believed. It is written, *"Faith cometh by hearing"* (Romans 10:17). Therefore, hear often. If I earnestly and attentively hear the Gospel, one of these days I will find myself believing it because of the blessed workings of the Spirit of God on my mind. Only, be sure you hear the Gospel, and do not be distracted by either hearing or reading what is designed to make you doubt.

Consider the Testimony of Others

If that should seem to be poor advice, I would add this next: Consider the testimony of others. The Samaritans believed because of what the woman told them concerning Jesus. (See John 4:6–30, 39.) Many of our beliefs arise out of the testimony of others. I believe that there is such a country as Japan. I have never seen it, yet I believe that there is such a place because others have been there. I believe that I will die. I have never died, but a great many people whom I once knew have died. Therefore, I believe that I will also die. The experience of many convinces me of that fact.

Listen, then, to those who tell you how they were saved, how they were pardoned, how they were changed in character. If you will look into the matter, you will find that somebody just like yourself has been saved. If you have been a thief, you will find that a thief rejoiced to wash away his sin in the fountain of Christ's blood. If, unhappily, you have been unchaste, you will find that men and women who have fallen in that way have been cleansed and changed. If you are in despair, you need only to get among God's people and inquire a little. You will discover that some of the saints have been equally in despair at times. They will be pleased to tell you how the Lord delivered them. As you listen to one after another who have tried the Word of God and proved it, the Divine Spirit will lead you to believe.

Have you heard of the African who was told by the missionary that water sometimes becomes so hard that a man can walk on it? He declared that he believed a great many things the missionary had told him, but he would never believe that. When he came to England, he saw the river frozen one frosty day, but he would not walk on it. He knew that it was a deep river, and he felt certain that he would be drowned if he walked on it. He could not be induced to walk on the frozen water until his friend and many others went on it. Then he was persuaded and trusted himself where others had safely walked. So, when you see others believing in the Lamb of God and notice their joy and peace, you will be gently led to believe. The experience of others is one of God's ways of helping us to faith. You have either to believe in Jesus or die. There is no hope for you but in Him.

Note the Authority You Are Commanded to Believe

A better plan is this: Note the authority upon which you are commanded to believe, and you will be greatly helped to faith. The authority is not mine, or you might well reject it. However, you are commanded to believe upon the authority of God Himself. He bids you to believe in Jesus Christ, and you must not refuse to obey your Maker.

The foreman of a certain factory had often heard the Gospel, but he was troubled with the fear that Christ might not want him. One day his employer sent him a card at the factory that read, "Come to my house immediately after work." The foreman appeared at his employer's door. The employer came out and said, somewhat roughly, "What do you want, John, troubling me at this time? Work is done; what right have you here?" "Sir," he said, "I had a card from you saying that I was to come after work." "Do you mean to say that merely because you had a card from me you came to my house and called me out after business hours?" "Well, sir," replied the foreman, "I do not understand you, but it seems to me that since you sent for me, I had a right to come." "Come in, John," said his employer. "I have another message that I want to read to you." He sat down and read these words: *"Come unto me, all ye that labour and are heavy laden, and I will give you rest"* (Matthew 11:28). "Do you think that after such a message from Christ you can be wrong in coming to Him?" The poor man saw it all at once and believed in the Lord Jesus for eternal life because he perceived that he had good warrant and authority for believing. So have you! You have good authority for coming to Christ, for the Lord Himself tells you to trust Him.

Consider What You Are to Believe

If that does not bring you faith, think over what it is that you have to believe: The Lord Jesus Christ suffered in the place and stead of sinners and is able to save all who trust Him. Why, this is the most blessed fact that men were ever told to believe. It is the most suitable, the most comforting, the most divine truth that was ever set before mortal minds. I advise you to think much about it and to search out the grace and love that it contains. Study the four Gospels, study Paul's Epistles, and then see if the message is not such a credible one that you are forced to believe it.

Consider the Person of Jesus Christ

If that is not enough, then think about the person of Jesus Christ—think of who He is and what He did and where He is and what He is. How can you doubt Him? It is cruelty to distrust the ever truthful Jesus. He has done nothing to deserve distrust. On the contrary, it should be easy to rely on Him. Why crucify Him again by unbelief? Is this not crowning Him with thorns again and spitting on Him again? What! Is He not to be trusted? What worse insult did the soldiers pour on Him than this? They made Him a martyr, but you make Him a liar, which is far worse. Do not ask, "How can I believe?" Rather, answer another question: "How can you disbelieve?"

Submit to God

If none of these things avails, then there is something wrong with you altogether. My last word to you is this: Submit yourself to God! Prejudice or pride is at the bottom of this unbelief. May the Spirit of God take away your enmity and make you yield. You are a rebel, a proud rebel, and that is why you do not believe your God. Give up your rebellion; throw down your weapons. Yield at discretion; surrender to your King. I believe that every time a soul throws up its hands in self-despair and cries, "Lord, I yield," faith becomes easy to it before long. It is because you still quarrel with God and resolve to have your own will and your own way that you cannot believe. *"How can ye believe,"* said Christ, *"which receive honour one of another?"* (John 5:44). Proud self creates unbelief. Submit. Yield to your God, and then you will sweetly believe in your Savior. May the Holy Spirit now work secretly but effectively in you and bring you at this very moment to believe in the Lord Jesus! Amen.

Chapter 13

Regeneration and the Holy Spirit

Ye must be born again.
—John 3:7

No man can come to me, except the Father which hath sent me draw him.
—John 6:44

Y*e must be born again."* This word of our Lord Jesus has appeared to stand in the way of many, like the drawn sword of the cherub at the gate of Paradise (Genesis 3:24). They have despaired because this change is beyond their utmost effort. The new birth is from above, and therefore it is not in man's power. Now, it is far from my mind to deny or ever to conceal a truth in order to create a false comfort. I freely admit that the new birth is supernatural and that it cannot be done by the sinner's own self. It would be of little help to you if I were wicked enough to try to cheer you by persuading you to reject or forget what is unquestionably true.

Yet is it not remarkable that the very chapter in which our Lord makes this sweeping declaration also contains the most explicit statement as to salvation by faith? Read chapter three of John's Gospel and do not concentrate only on its earlier sentences. It is true that verse three says, *"Jesus answered and said unto him, Verily, verily, I say unto thee, Except a man be born again, he cannot see the kingdom of God."* However, verses fourteen and fifteen say, *"And as Moses lifted up the serpent in the wilderness, even so must the Son of man be lifted up: that whosoever believeth in him should not perish, but have eternal life."*

Verse eighteen repeats the same doctrine in the broadest terms: *"He that believeth on him is not condemned: but he that believeth not is condemned already, because he hath not believed in the name of the only begotten Son of God."*

It is clear that these two statements must agree, since they came from the same lips and are recorded on the same inspired page. Why should we find difficulty where there is none? One statement assures us of the necessity to salvation of something that only God can give. Another assures us that the Lord will save us when we believe in Jesus. Therefore, we may safely conclude that the Lord will give to those who believe all that is declared to be necessary for salvation. The Lord does, in fact, produce the new birth in all who believe in Jesus. Their believing is the surest evidence that they are born again.

We trust in Jesus for what we cannot do ourselves. If it were in our own power, why would we need to look to Him? It is ours to believe; it is the Lord's to create us anew. He will not believe for us; neither are we to do regenerating work for Him. It is enough for us to obey the gracious command. It is for the Lord to work the new birth in us. He who could go so far as to die on the cross for us can and will give us all things necessary for our eternal safety.

"But a saving change of heart is the work of the Holy Spirit." This statement, also, is most true, and let it be far from us to question it or to forget it. Yet the work of the Holy Spirit is secret and mysterious. It can be perceived only by its results. There are mysteries about our natural birth into which it would be an unhallowed curiosity to pry. Still more is this the case with the sacred operations of the Spirit of God. *"The wind bloweth where it listeth, and thou hearest the sound thereof, but canst not tell whence it cometh, and whither it goeth: so is every one that is born of the Spirit"* (John 3:8). This much, however, we do know: The mysterious work of the Holy Spirit cannot be a reason for refusing to believe in Jesus to whom that same Spirit bears witness.

If a man were told to sow a field, he could not excuse his neglect by saying that it would be useless to sow unless God caused the seed to grow. He would not be justified in neglecting tillage because the secret energy of God alone can create a harvest. No one is hindered in the ordinary pursuits of life by the fact that *"except the LORD build the house, they labour in vain that build it"* (Psalm 127:1). It is certain that no man who believes in Jesus will ever find that the Holy Spirit refuses to work in him. In fact, his believing is the proof that the Spirit is already at work in his heart.

God works in providence, but men do not, therefore, sit still. They could not move without the divine power giving them life and strength. Yet they proceed on their way without question, the power being bestowed from day to day by Him in whose hand their breath is, and by Him who guides all their ways. So is it in grace. We repent and believe, though we could do neither if the Lord did not enable us. We forsake sin and trust in Jesus. Then we perceive that the Lord has caused us *"to will and to do of his [own] good pleasure"* (Philippians 2:13). It is idle to pretend that there is any real difficulty in the matter.

Some truths that are hard to explain in words are simple enough in actual experience. There is no discrepancy between the truth that the sinner believes and that his faith is brought about by the Holy Spirit. Only folly can lead men to puzzle themselves about plain matters while their souls are in danger. No man would refuse to enter a lifeboat because he did not know the specific gravity of bodies. Neither would a starving man decline to eat until he understood the whole process of nutrition. If you will not believe until you can understand all mysteries, you will never be saved at all. If you allow self-invented difficulties to keep you from accepting pardon through your Lord and Savior, you will perish in a condemnation that will be richly deserved. Do not commit spiritual suicide through a passion for discussing metaphysical subtleties.

Chapter 14

"My Redeemer Liveth"

I know that my redeemer liveth, and that he shall stand at the latter day upon the earth.
—Job 19:25

I have continually spoken to you concerning Christ crucified, who is the great hope of the guilty. Yet we will be wise to remember that our Lord has risen from the dead and lives eternally.

You are not asked to trust in a dead Jesus but in One who, though He died for our sins, has risen again *"for our justification"* (Romans 4:25). You may go to Jesus at once as to a living and present Friend. He is not a mere memory but a continually existent Person who will hear your prayers and answer them. He lives to carry on the work for which He once laid down His life. He is interceding for sinners at the right hand of the Father; for this reason, He is able to save to the uttermost those who come to God by Him (Hebrews 7:25). Come and try this living Savior if you have never done so before.

This living Jesus is also raised to an eminence of glory and power. He does not now sorrow as "a humble man before his foes," nor labor as "the carpenter's son." He is exalted *"far above all principality, and power,...and every name that is named"* (Ephesians 1:21). The Father has given Him *"all power...in heaven and in earth"* (Matthew 28:18), and He exercises this high endowment in carrying out His work of grace. Hear what Peter and the other apostles testified concerning Him before the high priest and the council:

> *The God of our fathers raised up Jesus, whom ye slew and hanged on a tree. Him hath God exalted with his right hand to be a Prince and a Saviour, for to give repentance to Israel, and forgiveness of sins.*
> (Acts 5:30–31)

The glory that surrounds the ascended Lord should breathe hope into every believer's breast. Jesus is no ordinary Person. He is *"a saviour, and a great one"* (Isaiah 19:20). He is the crowned and enthroned Redeemer of men. The sovereign prerogative of life and death is vested in Him. The Father has put all men under the mediatorial government of the Son so that He can quicken whom He will. He opens and no man shuts (Revelation 3:7). At His word, the soul that is bound by the cords of sin and condemnation can be unloosened in a moment. He stretches out the silver scepter, and whoever touches it lives.

It is a blessing for us that, as sin lives, and the flesh lives, and the devil lives, so Jesus lives. It is also a blessing that, whatever strength these may have to ruin us, Jesus has still greater power to save us.

All His exaltation and ability are on our account. He is exalted both to be and to give. He is exalted to be a Prince and a Savior so that He may give all that is needed to accomplish the salvation of all who come under His rule. Jesus *has* nothing that He will not use for a sinner's salvation, and He *is* nothing that He will not display in the abundance of His grace. He links His princedom with His saviorship, as if He would not have the one without the other. He sets forth His exaltation as designed to bring blessings to men, as if this were the flower and crown of His glory. Could anything be more suitable to raise the hopes of seeking sinners who are looking Christward?

Jesus endured great humiliation, and therefore there was room for Him to be exalted. By that humiliation He accomplished and endured all the Father's will. Therefore, He was rewarded by being raised to glory. He uses that exaltation on behalf of His people. Raise your eyes to these hills of glory, from where your help must come. Contemplate the high glories of the Prince and Savior. Is it not most hopeful for men that a Man is now on the throne of the universe? Is it not glorious that the Lord of all is the Savior of sinners? We have a Friend at court; not only this, but we have a Friend on the throne. He will use all His influence for those who entrust their affairs in His hands. One of our poets sings well:

> He ever lives to intercede
> Before His Father's face;
> Give Him, my soul, thy cause to plead,
> Nor doubt the Father's grace.

Come and commit your cause and your case to those once-pierced hands that are now glorified with the signet rings of royal power and honor. No case that was left with this great Advocate ever failed.

Chapter 15

Repentance Must Go with Forgiveness

*Him hath God exalted with his right hand to be a Prince
and a Saviour, for to give repentance to Israel,
and forgiveness of sins.*
—Acts 5:31

I t is clear from the above text that repentance is linked with the forgiveness of sins. In Acts 5:31, we read that Jesus is exalted to give repentance and forgiveness of sins. These two blessings come from that sacred hand that once was nailed to the tree but is now raised to glory. Repentance and forgiveness are riveted together by the eternal purpose of God. What God has joined together, let no man put asunder.

Repentance must go with remission of sins. You will understand this if you give it some thought. It cannot be that pardon of sin would be given to an impenitent sinner. This would only confirm him in his evil ways and teach him to think little of evil. If the Lord were to say, "You love sin and live in it, and you are going on from bad to worse, but all the same, I forgive you," this would proclaim a horrible license for iniquity. The foundations of social order would be removed, and moral anarchy would follow. I cannot tell what innumerable wrongs would occur if you could divide repentance and forgiveness, and could then pass by the sin while the sinner remained as fond of it as ever.

If we believe in the holiness of God, we cannot be forgiven if we continue to sin and refuse to repent of it. We will reap the consequence of our obstinacy. According to God's infinite goodness, we are promised that if we will forsake our sins, confess them, and by faith accept the grace that is provided in Christ Jesus, God *"is faithful and just to forgive us our sins, and to cleanse us from all unrighteousness"* (1 John 1:9). Yet as long as God lives, there can be no promise of mercy to those who continue in their evil ways and refuse to acknowledge their wrongdoing. Surely, no rebel can expect the King to pardon his treason while he remains in open revolt. No one can be so foolish as to imagine that the Judge of all the earth will put away our sins if we refuse to put them away ourselves.

Moreover, it must be so for the completeness of divine mercy. The mercy that could forgive the sin and yet let the sinner continue in it would be scant and superficial. It would be unequal and deformed mercy, lame in one foot and withered in one of its hands. Which do you think is the greater privilege: cleansing from the guilt of sin or deliverance from the power of sin? I will not attempt to weigh in the scales two mercies so surpassing. Neither of them could have come to us apart from the precious blood of Jesus. However, it seems to me that to be delivered from the dominion of sin and to be made holy—to be made like God—must be esteemed the greater of the two, if a comparison has to be made.

To be forgiven is an immeasurable favor. We make this one of the first notes of our psalm of praise: *"Who forgiveth all thine iniquities"* (Psalm 103:3). Yet if we could be forgiven and then could be permitted to love sin, to riot in iniquity, and to wallow in lust, what would be the use of such a forgiveness? Might it not turn out to be poisoned candy that would most effectually destroy us? To be washed and yet to lie in the dirt, to be pronounced clean and yet to have the leprosy white on one's brow, would be the worst mockery of mercy. What good is it to bring the man out of his grave if you leave him dead? Why lead him into the light if he is still blind?

We thank God that He who forgives our iniquities also heals our diseases. He who washes us from the stains of the past also uplifts us from the foul ways of the present and keeps us from falling in the future. We must joyfully accept both repentance and remission; they cannot be separated. The covenantal heritage is one and indivisible and must not be parceled out. To divide the work of grace would be like cutting a living child in half; and those who would permit this have no interest in it. (See 1 Kings 3:16–27.)

You who are seeking the Lord, would you be satisfied with one of these mercies alone? Would you be content if God would forgive your sin and then allow you to be as worldly and wicked as before? Oh, no! The quickened spirit is more afraid of sin itself than of the penal results of it. The cry of your heart is not, "Who will deliver me from punishment?" but *"O wretched man that I am! who shall deliver me from the body of this death?'* (Romans 7:24). Who will enable me to live above temptation and to become holy, even as God is holy?" Since the unity of repentance with remission agrees with gracious desire, and since it is necessary for the completeness of salvation and for holiness' sake, rest assured that it abides.

Repentance and forgiveness are joined together in the experience of all believers. There never was a person who unfeignedly repented of sin with believing repentance who was not forgiven. On the other hand, there never was a person forgiven who had not repented of his sin. I do not hesitate to say that beneath heaven there never was, there is not, and there never will be any case of sin being washed away unless, at the same time, the heart was led to repentance and faith in Christ. Hatred of sin and a sense of pardon come together into the soul and abide together while we live.

These two things act and react on each other. The man who realizes he is forgiven, therefore repents. The man who repents is also most assuredly forgiven. Remember first that Christ's forgiveness leads to repentance. As we sing, in Hart's words,

> Law and terrors do but harden
> All the while they work alone;
> But a sense of blood-bought pardon
> Soon dissolves a heart of stone.

When we are sure that we are forgiven, then we abhor iniquity. And I suppose that when faith grows into full assurance, so that we are certain beyond a doubt that the blood of Jesus has washed us whiter than snow, it is then that repentance attains its greatest height. Repentance grows as faith grows. Do not make any mistake about it. Repentance is not a thing of days and weeks, a temporary penance to be gotten over as fast as possible! No, it is the grace of a lifetime, like faith itself. God's little children repent, and so do the young men and the fathers. Repentance is the inseparable companion of faith.

All the time that we walk by faith and not by sight, the tear of repentance glistens in the eye of faith. It is not a true repentance that does not come from faith in Jesus. It is not a true faith in Jesus that is not colored with repentance. Faith and repentance, like Siamese twins, are vitally joined together. We repent in proportion to our belief in the forgiving love of Christ. We rejoice in the fullness of Jesus' absolution in proportion to our repentance of sin and our hatred of evil. You will never value pardon unless you feel repentance. You will never taste the deepest portion of repentance until you know that you are pardoned. It may seem like a strange thing, and so it is. The bitterness of repentance and the sweetness of pardon blend in the flavor of every gracious life and make up an incomparable happiness.

These two covenantal gifts are the mutual assurance of each other. If I know that I repent, I know that I am forgiven. How am I to know that I am forgiven except that I also know that I have turned from my former sinful course? To be a believer is to be a penitent. Faith and repentance are but two spokes in the same wheel, two handles of the same plow. Repentance has been well described as a heart broken for sin and from sin. It may equally well be spoken of as turning and returning. It is a change of mind of the most thorough and radical sort. It is attended with sorrow for the past and a resolve of amendment in the future.

> Repentance is to leave
> The sins we loved before;
> And show that we in earnest grieve,
> By doing so no more.

Now, when that is the case, we may be certain that we are forgiven, for the Lord never caused a heart to be broken for sin and broken from sin without pardoning it. If, on the other hand, we are enjoying pardon through the blood of Jesus and are justified by faith and have peace with God through Jesus Christ our Lord (Romans 5:1), we know that our repentance and faith are of the right sort.

Do not regard your repentance as the cause of your remission, but as the companion of it. Do not expect to be able to repent until you are able to see the grace of our Lord Jesus and His readiness to blot out your sin. Keep these blessed things in their places, and view them in their relation to each other. They are the Jachin and

Boaz of a saving experience. I mean that they are comparable to Solomon's two great pillars that stood in the forefront of the house of the Lord and formed a majestic entrance to the holy place. (See 1 Kings 7:21.) No man comes to God properly unless he passes between the pillars of repentance and remission. The rainbow of covenantal grace has been displayed upon your heart in all its beauty when the teardrops of repentance have been shone upon by the light of full forgiveness. Repentance of sin and faith in divine pardon are the intertwining threads of the fabric of real conversion. By these characteristics, you will know a true Israelite.

To come back to the Scripture on which we are meditating, both forgiveness and repentance flow from the same source and are given by the same Savior. The Lord Jesus in His glory bestows both on the same people. You can find neither the remission nor the repentance elsewhere. Jesus has both ready, and He is prepared to bestow them now and to bestow them most freely on all who will accept them at His hands. Never forget that Jesus gives all that is needed for our salvation. It is very important that all seekers after mercy remember this fact. Faith is as much the gift of God as is the Savior upon whom that faith relies. Repentance of sin is as truly the work of grace as the making of an atonement by which sin is blotted out. Salvation, from first to last, is of grace alone.

Do not misunderstand me. It is not the Holy Spirit who repents. He has never done anything for which He should repent. If He could repent, it would not help us. We ourselves must repent of our own sin, or we are not saved from its power. It is also not the Lord Jesus Christ who repents. What should He repent of? We ourselves repent with the full consent of every faculty of our minds. The will, the affections, and the emotions all work together most heartily in the blessed act of repentance for sin. And yet, behind all that is our personal act, there is a secret holy influence that melts the heart, gives contrition, and produces a complete change.

The Spirit of God enlightens us to see what sin is and thus makes it loathsome in our eyes. The Spirit of God also turns us toward holiness. He makes us greatly appreciate, love, and desire it, and thus gives us the impetus by which we are led onward from stage to stage of sanctification. The Spirit of God works in us to will and to do according to God's good pleasure (Philippians 2:13). To that Good Spirit let us submit ourselves at once so that He may lead us to Jesus, who will freely give us the double benediction of repentance and remission, *according to the riches of his grace*" (Ephesians 1:7). *"By grace are ye saved"* (Ephesians 2:8).

Chapter 16

How Repentance Is Given

*Him hath God exalted with his right hand
to be a Prince and a Saviour,
for to give repentance to Israel,
and forgiveness of sins.*
—Acts 5:31

R eturn to the grand text, *"Him hath God exalted with his right hand to be a Prince and a Saviour, for to give repentance to Israel, and forgiveness of sins."* Our Lord Jesus Christ has gone up so that grace may come down. His glory is employed to give greater currency to His grace. The Lord has not taken a step upward except with the design of bearing believing sinners upward with Him. He is exalted to give repentance, and we will see this if we remember a few great truths.

Christ Has Made Repentance Possible, Available, and Acceptable

The work that our Lord Jesus has done has made repentance possible, available, and acceptable. The Old Testament makes no mention of repentance, but says plainly, *"The soul that sinneth, it shall die"* (Ezekiel 18:20). If the Lord Jesus had not died and risen again and gone to the Father, what would our repenting be worth? We might feel remorse with its horrors, but never repentance with its hopes. Repentance, as a natural feeling, is a common duty deserving no great praise. Indeed, it is so generally mingled with a selfish fear of punishment that the kindest estimate makes little of it. Had Jesus not interposed and accomplished a wealth of merit, our tears of repentance would have been so much water spilled on the ground. Jesus is exalted on high so that through the virtue of His intercession, repentance may have a place before God. In this respect, He gives us repentance because He puts repentance into a position of acceptance that otherwise it could never have occupied.

The Holy Spirit Renews Our Nature

When Jesus was exalted on high, the Spirit of God was poured out to work all needful graces in us. The Holy Spirit creates repentance in us by supernaturally renewing our nature and taking the heart of stone out of our flesh. Oh, do not strain those eyes of yours to make impossible tears! Repentance does not come from an unwilling nature, but from free and sovereign grace. Do not go to your room to punish yourself, as if to bring from a heart of stone feelings that are not there. Rather, go to Calvary and see how Jesus died. Look upward to the hills from where your help comes. The Holy Spirit has come with the purpose that He may overshadow men's spirits and breed repentance within them, even as He once brooded over chaos and brought forth order. (See Genesis 1.) Breathe your prayer to Him: "Blessed Spirit, dwell with me. Make me tender and lowly of heart that I may hate sin and unfeignedly repent of it." He will hear your cry and answer you.

The Works of Nature and Providence Are Consecrated for Our Salvation

Remember, too, that, when our Lord Jesus was exalted, He gave us repentance not only by sending forth the Holy Spirit, but also by consecrating all the works of nature and of providence to the great ends of our salvation. In this way, any one of them may call us to repentance, whether it crow like Peter's rooster (see Matthew 26:33–35, 47–58, 69–74) or shake the prison like the jailer's earthquake (Acts 16:23–34). From the right hand of God, our Lord Jesus rules all things here below and makes them work together for the salvation of His redeemed. He uses both bitter and sweet things, trials and joys, so that He may produce in sinners a better mind toward their God. Be thankful for the providence that has made you poor or sick or sad. By all this Jesus works the life of your spirit and turns you to Himself. The Lord's mercy often rides to the door of our hearts on the black horse of affliction. Jesus uses the whole range of our experience to wean us from earth and woo us to heaven. Christ is exalted to the throne of heaven and earth in order that, by all the processes of His providence, He may subdue hard hearts to the gracious softening of repentance.

Christ Has Abundant Ways of Bringing About Repentance

Besides, He is at work this hour by all His whispers in the conscience, by His inspired Book, by those of us who speak out of that Book, and by praying friends and earnest hearts. He can send a word to you that will strike your rocky heart as with the rod of Moses and cause streams of repentance to flow forth. He can bring to your mind some heartbreaking text out of Holy Scripture that will conquer you immediately. He can mysteriously soften you and cause a holy frame of mind to steal over you when you least look for it. Be sure of this: He who is gone into His glory, raised into all the splendor and majesty of God, has abundant ways of working repentance in those to whom He grants forgiveness. Even now, He is waiting to give repentance to you. Ask Him for it at once.

Repentance Is Given to the Most Unlikely People

Observe with great comfort that the Lord Jesus Christ gives this repentance to the most unlikely people in the world. He is exalted *"to give repentance to Israel."* Israel! In the days when the apostles spoke this, Israel was the nation that had most grossly sinned against light and love by daring to say, *"His blood be on us, and on our children"* (Matthew 27:25). Yet Jesus is exalted to give *them* repentance! What a marvel of grace! If you have been brought up in the brightest of Christian light and yet have rejected it, there is still hope. If you have sinned against conscience and against the Holy Spirit and against the love of Jesus, there is still room for repentance. Though you may be as hard as unbelieving Israel of old, softening may yet come to you, since Jesus is exalted and clothed with boundless power. For those who went the furthest in iniquity and sinned with special aggravation, the Lord Jesus is exalted to give to them *"repentance...and forgiveness of sins."* I am happy to have so full a Gospel to proclaim! Happy are you to be allowed to read it!

The hearts of the children of Israel had grown as hard as stone. Luther used to think it impossible to convert a Jew. We are far from agreeing with him. Yet we must admit that the children of Israel have been exceedingly obstinate in their rejection of the Savior during these many centuries. Truly did the Lord say, *"Israel would* [have] *none of me"* (Psalm 81:11). *"He came unto his own, and his own received him not"* (John 1:11). However, on behalf of Israel, our Lord Jesus is exalted for the giving of repentance and remission. You are probably a Gentile, but yet you may have a very stubborn heart that has stood against the Lord Jesus for many years. Even so, our Lord can work repentance in you. It may be that you will feel compelled to write as William Hone did when he yielded to divine love. He was the author of some entertaining volumes called the *Everyday Book,* but he was once an out-and-out atheist. When subdued by sovereign grace, he wrote,

> The proudest heart that ever beat
> Hath been subdued in me;
>> The wildest will that ever rose
>> To scorn Thy cause and aid Thy foes
> Is quell'd my Lord, by Thee.
> Thy will, and not my will be done,
>> My heart be ever Thine;
> Confessing Thee the mighty Word,
> My Savior Christ, my God, my Lord,
>> Thy cross shall be my sign.

The Lord can give repentance to the most unlikely—turning lions into lambs, and ravens into doves. Let us look to Him so that this great change may take place in us.

Meditate on Christ's Sacrificial Death

Assuredly, the contemplation of the death of Christ is one of the surest and speediest methods of gaining repentance. Do not sit down and try to pump up repentance from the dry well of a corrupt nature. It is contrary to the laws of your mind to suppose that you can force your soul into that gracious state. Take your heart in prayer to Him who understands it and say, "Lord, cleanse it. Lord, renew it. Lord, work repentance in it." The more you try to produce penitent emotions in yourself, the more you will be disappointed. However, if you believingly think of Jesus dying for you, repentance will burst forth.

Meditate on the Lord's shedding His heart's blood out of love for you. Set before your mind's eye the agony and bloody sweat, the cross and passion. As you do this, He who was the Bearer of all this grief will look at you. With that look, He will do for you what He did for Peter, so that you also will go out and weep bitterly (Matthew 26:75). He who died for you can, by His gracious Spirit, make you die to sin. He who has gone into glory on your behalf can draw your soul after Him, away from evil and toward holiness.

I will be content if I leave this one thought with you: Do not look beneath the ice to find fire, nor hope in your own natural heart to find repentance. Look to the Living One for life. Look to Jesus for all you need between the gate of hell and the gate of heaven. Never seek elsewhere for any part of what Jesus loves to bestow, but remember that Christ is all.

Chapter 17

The Fear of Final Falling

Now unto him that is able to keep you from falling,
and to present you faultless before the presence
of his glory with exceeding joy.
—Jude 24

A dark fear haunts the minds of many who are coming to Christ. They are afraid that they will not persevere to the end. I have heard the seeker say, "If I were to cast my soul on Jesus, perhaps I would, after all, draw back into perdition. I have had good feelings before now, and they have died away. My goodness has been as the morning cloud and as the early dew. It has come suddenly, lasted for a season, promised much, and then vanished away."

I believe that this fear is often the father of the fact, and that some who have been afraid to trust Christ for all time and eternity have failed because they had a temporary faith that never went far enough to save them. They set out trusting Jesus in a measure, yet looking to themselves for continuance and perseverance in the heavenward way. So they set out faultily and, as a natural consequence, turned back before long. If we trust in ourselves for our holding on, we will not hold on. Even though we rest in Jesus for a part of our salvation, we will fail if we trust in self for anything. No chain is stronger than its weakest link. If Jesus is our hope for everything except one thing, we will utterly fail, because in that one point we will come to nothing.

Look to Christ as Your Strength from Beginning to End

I have no doubt whatever that a mistaken idea about the perseverance of the saints has prevented the perseverance of many who ran well. What hindered them so that they did not continue to run? They trusted in themselves for that running, and so they stopped short. Beware of mixing even a little of self with the mortar with which you build, or you will make it untempered mortar. The stones will not hold together. If you look to Christ for your beginning, beware of looking to yourself for your ending. He is Alpha. See to it that you make Him Omega, also. If you begin in the Spirit, you must not hope to be made perfect by the flesh (Galatians 3:3). Begin as you intend to go on, and go on as you began. Let the Lord be all in all to you. Oh, that God the Holy Spirit may give us a very clear idea of where the strength must come from by which we will be preserved until the Day of our Lord's appearing!

Here is what Paul said on this subject when he was writing to the Corinthians:

Our Lord Jesus Christ...shall also confirm you unto the end, that ye may be blameless in the day of our Lord Jesus Christ. God is faithful, by whom ye were called unto the fellowship of his Son Jesus Christ our Lord. (1 Corinthians 1:7–9)

All of Grace

This language silently admits a great need by telling us how it is provided for. Wherever the Lord makes a provision, we are quite sure that there was a need for it. No superfluities clutter the covenant of grace. Golden shields that hung in Solomon's courts were never used, but there are none such in the armory of God. What God has provided, we will surely need. Between this hour and the consummation of all things, every promise of God and every provision of the covenant of grace will be brought into requisition. The urgent need of the believing soul is confirmation, continuance, final perseverance, preservation to the end. This is the great necessity of the most advanced believers, for Paul was writing to saints at Corinth who were men of a high order, of whom he could say, *"I thank my God always on your behalf, for the grace of God which is given you by Jesus Christ"* (1 Corinthians 1:4).

Such men are the very people who most assuredly feel that they have daily need of a new grace if they are to hold on and hold out and become conquerors at the last. If you were not saints, you would have no grace, and you would feel no need of more grace. However, because you are men of God, you feel the daily demands of the spiritual life. The marble statue requires no food, but the living man hungers and thirsts. He rejoices that his bread and his water are guaranteed for him, or else he would certainly faint by the way. The believer's personal needs make it inevitable that he should draw daily from the great Source of all supplies. What could he do if he could not resort to his God?

This is true of the most gifted of the saints, as it was of those men at Corinth who were *"enriched...in all utterance, and in all knowledge"* (v. 5). They needed to be confirmed to the end (v. 8) or else their gifts and achievements would have proved to be their ruin. If we had the tongues of men and of angels, yet we did not receive fresh grace, where would we be? If we had all experience until we were fathers in the church—if we had been taught by God so as to understand all mysteries—even so, we could not live a single day without the divine life flowing into us from our covenant Head. How could we hope to hold on for a single hour, to say nothing of a lifetime, unless the Lord held on to us? He who began the good work in us must *"perform it until the day of Jesus Christ"* (Philippians 1:6), or it will prove to be a painful failure.

Why We Need Christ to Uphold Us

Fickleness of Heart

The great necessity arises very much from our own selves. In some there is a painful fear that they will not persevere in grace because they know their own fickleness. Certain people are constitutionally unstable. Some men are by nature conservative, not to mention obstinate. Yet others are just as naturally variable and volatile. Like butterflies, they flit from flower to flower until they visit all the beauties of the garden and settle upon none of them. They are never in one place long enough to do any good, not in their business nor in their intellectual pursuits. Such people may well be afraid that ten, twenty, thirty, forty, perhaps fifty years of continuous Christian watchfulness will be too much for them. We see men joining one church and then another until they have tried them all. They do everything in phases and nothing in a long-lasting way. Such people need to pray twice as much that they may be divinely confirmed and may be made not only steadfast but also unmovable (1 Corinthians 15:58). Otherwise, they will not be found *"always abounding in the work of the Lord"* (v. 58).

All of us, even if we have no natural inclination to fickleness, must feel our own weakness if we are really quickened by God. Is there not enough in any one single day to make you stumble? You who desire to walk in perfect holiness and you who have set before yourself a high standard of what a Christian should be, do you not find that before the breakfast things are cleared away from the table you have displayed enough sin to make you ashamed of yourselves? If we were to shut ourselves up in the lone cell of a hermit, temptation would follow us. As long as we cannot escape from ourselves, we cannot escape from incitements to sin. There is within our hearts that which should make us watchful and humble before God. If He does not confirm us, we are so weak that we will stumble and fall—not overturned by an enemy but by our own carelessness. Lord, be our strength. We are weakness itself.

Weariness with Life

Besides that, there is the weariness that comes with a long life. When we begin our Christian profession, we mount up with wings as eagles. Further on, we run without weariness. Yet in our best and truest days, we walk without fainting. (See Isaiah 40:31.) Our pace seems slower, but it is more serviceable and better sustained. I pray God that the energy of our youth may continue with us as long as it is the energy of the Spirit and not the mere energy of proud flesh. He who has been on the road to heaven for a long time finds that there was a good reason why it was promised that his shoes would be iron and brass (Deuteronomy 33:25): The road is rough. He has discovered, as did John Bunyan's famous Pilgrim, that there are Hills of Difficulty and Valleys of Humiliation. He has learned that there is a Valley of the Shadow of Death and, worse still, a Vanity Fair. All these are to be experienced. If there are Delectable Mountains (and, thank God, there are), there are also castles of Giant Despair, the inside of which pilgrims have too often seen. Considering all things, those who hold out to the end in the way of holiness will be *"men wondered at"* (Zechariah 3:8).

"O world of wonders, I can say no less." The days of a Christian's life are like so many Koh-i-noors* of mercy threaded on the golden string of divine faithfulness. In heaven, we will tell angels and principalities and powers the unsearchable riches of Christ that were spent on us and enjoyed by us while we were here below. We have been kept alive on the brink of death. Our spiritual lives have been as a flame burning on in the midst of the sea. They have been as a stone that has remained suspended in the air. It will amaze the universe to see us enter the pearly gates blameless in the Day of our Lord Jesus Christ. We should be full of grateful wonder if we are kept by Him for an hour, and I trust we are.

The Wilderness of the World

If this were all, there would be enough cause for anxiety, but there is far more. We have to think of what a place we live in. The world is a howling wilderness to many of God's people. Some of us are greatly indulged in the providence of God, but others have a stern fight of it. We begin our day with prayer, and many of us very often hear the voice of holy song in our houses. Yet many good people have scarcely risen from their knees in the morning before they are greeted with blasphemy. They go out to work and all day long are distressed, like righteous Lot in Sodom, over having to listen to filthy conversation. Can you even walk the open streets without your ears being afflicted with foul language? The world is no friend to grace. The best we can do with this world is to get through it with Jesus as close to us as possible. We live in an enemy's country. A "robber" lurks in every bush. We need to travel everywhere with a "drawn sword" in our hand (Ephesians

---

* The Koh-i-noor is an Indian diamond, weighing 106 carats, that was acquired by the British. It became the central stone in the crown worn by Elizabeth, the Queen Mother, at the coronation of her husband, George VI, in 1937.

6:17), or at least with that weapon that is called *"all prayer"* (v. 18) at our side. We have to fight for every inch of our way. Make no mistake about this, or you will be rudely shaken out of your fond delusion. O God, help us and confirm us to the end, or where will we be?

He Will Keep You from Falling

True Christianity is supernatural at its beginning, supernatural in its continuance, and supernatural in its close. It is the work of God from first to last. There is great need for the hand of the Lord to be stretched out still. You are feeling that need now, and I am glad that you feel it. Now you will look for your own preservation to the Lord, who alone is able to keep us from falling and glorify us with His Son.

Chapter 18

Confirmation

Christ...shall also confirm you unto the end, that ye may be blameless in the day of our Lord Jesus Christ.
—1 Corinthians 1:7–8

Notice the security that Paul confidently expected for all the saints. He said, *"Christ...shall also confirm you unto the end, that ye may be blameless in the day of our Lord Jesus Christ."* This is the kind of confirmation that is to be desired above all things. It supposes that the people are right, and it proposes to confirm them in the right. It would be an awful thing to confirm a man in ways of sin and error. Think of a confirmed drunkard or a confirmed thief or a confirmed liar. It would be a deplorable thing for a man to be confirmed in unbelief and ungodliness. Divine confirmation can be enjoyed only by those to whom the grace of God has already been manifested. It is the work of the Holy Spirit.

He who gives faith strengthens and establishes it. He who kindles love in us preserves it and increases its flame. What He causes us to know by His first teaching, the Holy Spirit causes us to know with greater clearness and certainty by still further instruction. Holy acts are confirmed until they become habits, and holy feelings are confirmed until they become abiding conditions. Experience and practice confirm our beliefs and our resolutions. Both

113

our joys and our sorrows, our successes and our failures, are sanctified to the same end, even as the tree is helped to take root both by the soft showers and the rough winds. The mind is instructed, and in its growing knowledge it gathers reasons for persevering in the good way. The heart is comforted, and so it is made to cling more closely to the consoling truth. The grip grows tighter, the tread grows firmer, and the man himself becomes more solid and substantial.

This is not merely natural growth, but is as distinct a work of the Spirit as is conversion. The Lord will surely give it to those who are relying on Him for eternal life. By His inward working, He will deliver us from being *"unstable as water"* (Genesis 49:4) and cause us to be *"rooted and grounded"* (Ephesians 3:17). This building us up into Christ Jesus and causing us to abide in Him is a part of the method by which He saves us. You may look for it daily, and you will not be disappointed. He whom you trust will make you to be as a tree planted by the river of water, so preserved that even your leaf will not wither (Psalm 1:3).

What strength a confirmed Christian is to a church! He is a comfort to the sorrowful and a help to the weak. Would you not like to be such? Confirmed believers are pillars in the house of our God (Revelation 3:12). They are not carried away by *"every wind of doctrine"* (Ephesians 4:14), nor overthrown by sudden temptation. They are a great inspiration to others and act as anchors in times of church trouble. You who are beginning the holy life hardly dare to hope that you will become like them. Yet you need not fear; the Good Lord will work in you as well as in them. One of these days, you who are now a "babe" in Christ will be a "father" in the church. Hope for this great thing. Hope for it as a gift of grace and not as the wages of work or as the product of your own energy.

Confirmed to the End

The inspired apostle Paul spoke of these people as those who would be confirmed *"unto the end."* He expected the grace of God to preserve them personally to the end of their lives, or until the Lord Jesus returned. Indeed, he expected that the whole church of God, in every place and in all time, would be kept to the end of the dispensation, until the Lord Jesus as the Bridegroom would come to celebrate the Wedding Feast with His perfected bride. All who are in Christ will be confirmed in Him until that illustrious day. Has He not said, *"Because I live, ye shall live also"* (John 14:19)? He also said, *"I give unto them* [My sheep] *eternal life; and they shall never perish, neither shall any man pluck them out of my hand"* (John 10:28). *"He which hath begun a good work in you will perform it until the day of Jesus Christ"* (Philippians 1:6).

The work of grace in the soul is not a superficial reformation. The life implanted as the new birth comes from a living and incorruptible seed *"which liveth and abideth for ever"* (1 Peter 1:23). And the promises of God made to believers are not of a transient character. They involve, for their fulfillment, the believer's "holding on his way" until he comes to endless glory. We are *"kept by the power of God through faith unto salvation"* (v. 5). *"The righteous also shall hold on his way"* (Job 17:9). Not as the result of our own merit or strength, but as a gift of free and undeserved favor, those who believe are *"preserved in Jesus Christ"* (Jude 1). Jesus will lose none of the sheep of His fold. No member of His body will wither; no gem of His treasure will be missing in the day when He makes up His jewels (Malachi 3:17). The salvation that is received by faith is not a thing of months and years, for our Lord Jesus has *"obtained eternal redemption for us"* (Hebrews 9:12). What is eternal cannot come to an end.

Confirmed Blameless

Paul also declared his expectation that the Corinthian saints would be confirmed *"blameless"* to the end. This blamelessness is a precious part of our keeping. To be kept holy is better than merely to be kept safe. It is a dreadful thing when you see religious people blundering out of one dishonor into another. They have not believed in the power of our Lord to make them blameless. The lives of some professing Christians are a series of stumbles. They are never quite down, yet they are seldom on their feet. This is not a fit thing for a believer. He is invited to walk with God. By faith, he can attain steady perseverance in holiness, and he should do so. The Lord is able not only to save us from hell, but also to keep us from falling (Jude 24). We need not yield to temptation. Is it not written, *"Sin shall not have dominion over you"* (Romans 6:14)? The Lord is able to keep the feet of His saints, and He will do it if we will trust Him to do so. We need not defile our garments; we may by His grace keep them *"unspotted from the world"* (James 1:27). We are bound to do this, for without holiness *"no man shall see the Lord"* (Hebrews 12:14).

The apostle prophesied for these believers what he would have us seek after—that we may be preserved *"blameless in the day of our Lord Jesus Christ."* The *American Standard Version* has *"unreproveable"* instead of *"blameless."* Possibly a better rendering would be "unimpeachable." God grant that in that last great Day we may stand free from all charge, that no one in the whole universe may dare to challenge our claim to be the redeemed of the Lord. We have sins and infirmities to mourn over, but these are not the kind of faults that would prove us to be out of Christ. We will be clear of hypocrisy, deceit, hatred, and delight in sin, for these things would be fatal charges.

Despite our failings, the Holy Spirit can work in us a character spotless before men so that, like Daniel, we will not provide an occasion for accusing tongues, except in the matter of our faith. Multitudes of godly men and women have exhibited lives so transparent, so consistent throughout, that no one could say anything against them. The Lord will be able to say of many a believer, as he did of Job when Satan stood before Him, *"Hast thou considered my servant..., a perfect and an upright man, one that feareth God, and escheweth evil?"* (Job 1:8). This is what you must look for at the Lord's hands. This is the triumph of the saints—to continue to follow the Lamb wherever He goes, maintaining our integrity as before the living God. May we never turn aside into *"crooked ways"* (Psalm 125:5) and give the adversary cause to blaspheme. (See 2 Samuel 12:14.) Of the true believer it is written, *"He...keepeth himself, and that wicked one toucheth him not"* (1 John 5:18). May it be so written concerning us!

If you are just beginning in the divine life, the Lord can give you an irreproachable character. Even though, in your past life, you may have gone far into sin, the Lord can altogether deliver you from the power of former habits and make you an example of virtue. Not only can He make you moral, but He can also make you abhor every false way and follow after all that is saintly. Do not doubt it. The chief of sinners need not be a step behind the purest of the saints. Believe this, and according to your faith it will be unto you.

Oh, what a joy it will be to be found blameless in the Day of Judgment! We do not sing amiss when we join in this charming hymn:

> Bold shall I stand in that great day,
>   For who aught to my charge shall lay?
> While by my Lord absolved I am,
>   From sin's tremendous curse and blame.
>   —Count Zinzendorf

All of Grace

What bliss it will be to enjoy that dauntless courage when heaven and earth will flee from the face of the Judge of all! This bliss will be the portion of everyone who looks only to the grace of God in Christ Jesus and in that sacred power wages continual war with all sin.

Chapter 19

Why Saints Persevere

*God is faithful, by whom ye were called unto
the fellowship of his Son Jesus Christ.*
—1 Corinthians 1:9

We have already seen that the hope that filled Paul's heart concerning the Corinthian saints was a great comfort to those who feared their future. Yet why was it that he believed that the saints would be confirmed unto the end?

I want you to notice that he gave his reasons. Here they are: *"God is faithful, by whom ye were called unto the fellowship of his Son Jesus Christ."*

"God Is Faithful"

The apostle did not say, "You are faithful." The faithfulness of man is very unreliable; it is mere vanity. He did not say, "You have faithful ministers to lead and guide you, and therefore I trust you will be safe." Oh, no! If we are kept by men, we will be badly kept. He said, *"God is faithful."* If we are found faithful, it will be because God is faithful. The whole burden of our salvation must rest on the faithfulness of our covenant God. On this glorious attribute of God the matter hinges. We are as variable as the wind, as frail as a spider's web, as *"weak as water"*

(Ezekiel 7:17; 21:7). No dependence can be placed on our natural qualities or our spiritual attainments, but God remains faithful.

He is faithful in His love; He knows no *"variableness, neither shadow of turning"* (James 1:17). He is faithful to His purpose; He does not begin a work and then leave it undone. He is faithful to His relationships. As a Father He will not renounce His children; as a Friend He will not deny His people; as a Creator He will not forsake the work of His own hands. He is faithful to His promises and will never allow one of them to fail for a single believer. He is faithful to His covenant, which He has made with us in Christ Jesus and ratified with the blood of His sacrifice. He is faithful to His Son and will not allow His precious blood to be spilled in vain. He is faithful to His people, to whom He has promised eternal life and from whom He will not turn away.

This faithfulness of God is the foundation and cornerstone of our hope of final perseverance. The saints will persevere in holiness because God perseveres in grace. He perseveres to bless, and therefore believers persevere in being blessed. He continues to keep His people, and therefore they continue to keep His commandments. This is good solid ground to rest on. It is delightfully consistent with the title of this book, *All of Grace.* Thus, it is free favor and infinite mercy that ring in the dawn of salvation; and the same sweet bells sound melodiously through the whole day of grace.

Reasons the Saints Will Be Confirmed unto the End

What God Has Already Done

You see that the only reasons for hoping that we will be confirmed to the end and be found blameless at the last are found in our God. Yet, in Him, these reasons are exceedingly abundant.

They lie first in what God has done. He has gone so far in blessing us that it is not possible for Him to turn back. Paul reminded us that He has called us *"unto the fellowship of his Son Jesus Christ."* Has He called us? Then the call cannot be reversed, *"for the gifts and calling of God are without repentance"* (Romans 11:29). The Lord never turns from the effectual call of His grace. *"Whom he called, them he also justified: and whom he justified, them he also glorified"* (Romans 8:30). This is the invariable rule of the divine procedure. There is a common call of which it is said, *"Many are called, but few are chosen"* (Matthew 22:14). Yet what we are now thinking of is another kind of call that means special love and necessitates the possession of that to which we are called. In such a case, it is with the called one even as with Abraham's seed, of whom the Lord said, *"Thou whom I have taken from the ends of the earth, and called thee from the chief men thereof, and said unto thee, Thou art my servant; I have chosen thee, and not cast thee away"* (Isaiah 41:9).

Our Fellowship with Jesus Christ

In what the Lord has done, we see strong reasons for our preservation and future glory because the Lord has called us into *"the fellowship of his Son Jesus Christ."* This means into partnership with Jesus Christ, and I want you to carefully consider what this signifies. If you are indeed called by divine grace, you have come into fellowship with the Lord Jesus Christ. You are joint-owner with Him in all things (Romans 8:17). Henceforth, you are one with Him in the sight of the Most High. The Lord Jesus bore your sins *"in his own body on the tree"* (1 Peter 2:24), *"being made a curse for* [you]*"* (Galatians 3:13); at the same time, He has become your righteousness, so that you are justified in Him. You are Christ's and Christ is yours.

All of Grace

As Adam stood for his descendants, so Jesus stands for all who are in Him. As husband and wife are one, so is Jesus one with all those who are united to Him by faith—they are one by a conjugal union that can never be broken. More than this, believers are members of the body of Christ, and so they are one with Him by a loving, living, lasting union. God has called us into this union, this fellowship, this partnership. By this very calling, He has given us the token and pledge of our being confirmed to the end. If we were considered apart from Christ, we would be poor, perishable units, soon dissolved and carried away to destruction. However, because we are one with Jesus, we are made partakers of His nature and are endowed with His immortal life. Our destiny is linked with that of our Lord, and until *He* can be destroyed, it is not possible that we would perish.

Deeply contemplate this partnership with the Son of God unto which you have been called, for all your hope lies there. You can never be poor while Jesus is rich, because you are as in one firm with Him. Want can never assail you, since you are joint-proprietor with Him who is Possessor of heaven and earth. You can never fail. Though one of the partners in the firm is as poor as a church mouse, an utter bankrupt who could not pay even a small amount of his heavy debts, yet the other Partner is inconceivably, inexhaustibly rich. In such a partnership, you are raised above the depression of the times, the changes of the future, and the shock of the end of all things. The Lord has called you into *"the fellowship of his Son Jesus Christ,"* and by that act and deed He has put you into the place of infallible safeguard.

If you are indeed a believer, you are one with Jesus, and therefore you are secure. Do you not see that it must be so? You must be confirmed to the end until the Day of His appearing, if you have indeed been made one with Jesus by the irrevocable act of God. Christ and the believing sinner are in the same boat. Unless Jesus sinks, the believer will never drown. Jesus has taken His redeemed into such connection with Himself that He must first be struck down, overcome, and dishonored before the least of His purchased ones can be injured. His name is at the head of the firm, and because He cannot be dishonored, we are secure against all dread of failure.

Linked with Jesus, Leaning on Jesus

So, then, with the utmost confidence, let us go forward into the unknown future, linked eternally with Jesus. If the men of the world cry, *"Who is this that cometh up from the wilderness, leaning upon her beloved?"* (Song of Solomon 8:5), we will joyfully confess that we do lean on Jesus and that we intend to lean on Him more and more. Our faithful God is an ever flowing well of delight, and our fellowship with the Son of God is a full river of joy. Knowing these glorious things, we cannot be discouraged. Rather, we cry with the apostle, *"Who shall separate us from the love of...God, which is in Christ Jesus our Lord?"* (Romans 8:35, 39).

Chapter 20

Conclusion

As I live, saith the Lord GOD, I have no pleasure
in the death of the wicked; but that the wicked
turn from his way and live: turn ye, turn ye from
your evil ways; for why will ye die?
—Ezekiel 33:11

I f you have not followed me step-by-step as you have read these pages, I am truly sorry. Book reading is of little value unless the truths that pass before the mind are grasped, appropriated, and carried out in a practical way. It is as if one saw plenty of food in a store and yet remained hungry for lack of actually eating some. It is all in vain that you and I have met unless you have actually laid hold of Christ Jesus my Lord. On my part, there was a distinct desire to benefit you, and I have done my best to that end. It pains me if I have not been able to do you good, for I have longed to win that privilege. I was thinking of you when I wrote this page, and I laid down my pen and solemnly bowed in prayer for everyone who would read it.

Why Should You Refuse?

It is my firm conviction that great numbers of readers will get a blessing, even if you refuse to be among them. Yet why should you refuse? If you do not desire the choice blessing that I would have brought to you, at least do me the justice to admit that the blame of your final doom will not lie at my door. When we meet before the Great White Throne, you will not be able to charge me with having idly used the attention that you were pleased to give me while you were reading my book. God knows I wrote each line for your eternal good. I now in spirit take you by the hand with a firm grip. Do you feel my brotherly grasp? The tears are in my eyes as I look at you and say, "Why will you die? Will you not give your soul a thought? Will you perish through sheer carelessness? Oh, do not do so, but weigh these solemn matters and make sure of eternity! Do not refuse Jesus, His love, His blood, His salvation. Why should you do so? Can you do it? I beseech you, do not turn away from your Redeemer!"

Let Jesus Be Your All in All

If, on the other hand, my prayers are heard and you have been led to trust the Lord Jesus and receive from Him salvation by grace, then keep this doctrine and this way of living. Let Jesus be your all in all, and let free grace be the one line in which you live and move. There is no life like that of one who lives in the favor of God. To receive all as a free gift preserves the mind from self-righteous pride and from self-accusing despair. It makes the heart grow warm with grateful love. It thus creates a feeling in the soul that is infinitely more acceptable to God than anything that can possibly come from slavish fear.

Those who hope to be saved by trying to do their best know nothing of that glowing fervor, that hallowed warmth, that devout joy in God that come with salvation freely given according to the grace of God. The slavish spirit of self-salvation is no match for the joyous spirit of adoption. There is more real virtue in the least emotion of faith than in all the efforts of legalistic bondslaves or all the weary machinery of devotees who would climb to heaven by means of ceremonies. Faith is spiritual, and

God, who is a Spirit, delights in it for that reason. Years of saying prayers, and church or chapel going, and ceremonies and performances, may be only an abomination in the sight of Jehovah. Yet a glance from the eye of true faith is spiritual and is therefore dear to Him. *"The Father seeketh such to worship him"* (John 4:23). Look first to the inner man and to the spiritual; the rest will then follow in due course.

If you are saved, be on the watch for the souls of others. Your own heart will not prosper unless it is filled with intense concern to bless your fellowmen. The life of your soul lies in faith; its health lies in love. He who does not long to lead others to Jesus has never been under the influence of love himself. Get busy doing the work of the Lord, the work of love. Begin at home. Visit your neighbors next. Enlighten the town or the street where you live. Scatter the Word of the Lord wherever your hand can reach.

Believe in Jesus Now

Meet me in heaven! Do not go down to hell. There is no coming back again from that abode of misery. Why do you wish to enter the way of death when heaven's gate is open before you? Do not refuse the free pardon, the full salvation, that Jesus grants to all who trust Him. Do not hesitate and delay. You have had enough of resolving; come to action. Believe in Jesus now with full and immediate decision. Take with you words and come to your Lord this day, even this day. Remember, O soul, it may be now or never with you. Let it be now; it would be horrible if it were never.

Again I charge you, meet me in heaven.

Faith

Contents

Introduction

He that believeth on him is not condemned.
—John 3:18

T he way of salvation is stated in Scripture in the very plainest terms. Yet, perhaps, there is no truth about which more errors have been uttered than that concerning the faith that saves the soul. Well has it been proved by experience that all doctrines of Christ are mysterious—mysterious not so much in themselves, but because they are *"hid to them that are lost: in whom the god of this world hath blinded the minds of them which believe not"* (2 Corinthians 4:3–4). Scripture is so plain that one would have said, "He who runs may read." (See Habbakuk 2:2.) However, so dim is man's eye and so marred is his understanding that he distorts and misrepresents the very simplest truth of Scripture.

Indeed, beloved, even those who know what faith is, personally and experientially, do not always find it easy to give a good definition of it. They think they have hit the mark, and then, afterward, they lament that they have failed. Straining themselves to describe one part of faith, they find they have forgotten another. In the excess of their earnestness to clear the poor sinner out of one mistake, they often lead him into a worse error. Thus, I think I may say that, while faith is the simplest thing in all the world, yet it is one of the most difficult about which to write.

Because of its very importance, the soul begins to tremble while speaking of it, and then we are not able to describe it as clearly as we would like.

With God's help, I intend to put together various thoughts on faith, each of which I may have spoken at different times, but which have not been collected before, and which, I have no doubt, have been misunderstood from the lack of their having been put together in their proper order. I will address these points:

1. The object of faith—to what it looks.

2. The reason of faith—why does any man believe, and from where does his faith come?

3. The ground of the sinner's faith—on what ground he dares to believe on the Lord Jesus Christ.

4. The warranty of faith—why it dares to trust in Christ.

5. The result of faith—how it speeds when it comes to Christ.

6. The satisfactory declaration made in Scripture concerning those who have faith.

7. Misapprehensions about faith, by reason of which Christians are often cast down.

8. What this faith includes.

9. What this faith excludes.

—Charles Spurgeon

Chapter 1

The Object of Faith

For ye are all the children of God
by faith in Christ Jesus.
—Galatians 3:26

I am told in the Word of God to believe, but what am I to believe? I am bidden to look, but at what am I to look? What is to be the object of my hope, belief, and confidence? The reply is simple: The object of faith for a sinner is Christ Jesus. How many make a mistake about this and think that they are to believe on God the Father! Belief in God is a result of faith in Jesus. We come to believe in the eternal love of God the Father as the result of trusting the precious blood of the Son.

Many men say, "I would believe in Christ if I knew that I were elect." However, this is the same thing as coming to the Father, and no man can come to the Father except by Christ. (See John 14:6.) It is the Father's work to elect. You cannot come directly to Him. Therefore, you cannot know your election until you have first believed on Christ the Redeemer. Then, through redemption, you can approach the Father and know your election.

Some, too, make the mistake of looking to the work of God the Holy Spirit. They look within to see if they have certain feelings. If they find them, their faith is strong; but if their feelings have departed from them, then their faith is weak. Thus, they look to the work of the Spirit, which is not the object of a sinner's faith.

Look to Christ Alone

Both the Father and the Spirit must be trusted in order to complete redemption, but for the particular mercy of justification and pardon, the blood of the Mediator is the only plea. Christians have to trust the Spirit after conversion. However, the sinner's business, if he would be saved, is not with trusting the Spirit nor with looking to the Spirit, but with looking to Christ Jesus, and to Him alone. I know your salvation depends on the whole Trinity, but yet the first and immediate object of a sinner's justifying faith is neither God the Father nor God the Holy Spirit, but God the Son, incarnate in human flesh and offering atonement for sinners.

Look to Christ as God and Man

Do you have the eye of faith? Then, soul, look to Christ as God. If you would be saved, believe Him to be God over all, blessed forever. Bow before Him, and accept Him as being "very God of very God." If you do not, you have no part in Him.

When you have thus believed, then believe in Him as man. Believe the wondrous story of His incarnation. Rely on the testimony of the evangelists who declare that the Infinite was robed in the infant, that the Eternal was concealed within the mortal, that He who was King of heaven became a Servant of servants and the Son of Man. Believe and admire the mystery of His incarnation, for unless you believe this, you cannot be saved.

Look to Christ's Perfect Righteousness

Then, especially, if you would be saved, let your faith behold Christ in His perfect righteousness. See Him keeping the law without blemish, obeying His Father without error, preserving His integrity without flaw. All this you are to consider as being done on your behalf. You could not keep the law; He kept it for you. You could not obey God perfectly; His obedience stands in the stead of your obedience—by it, you are saved.

Look to Christ's Death

Yet take care that your faith clearly fixes itself upon Christ as dying and as dead. View the Lamb of God as dumb before His shearers. (See Isaiah 53:7.) See Him as the *"man of sorrows, and acquainted with grief"* (v. 3). Go with Him to Gethsemane, and behold Him sweating drops of blood.

Note that your faith has nothing to do with anything within yourself. The object of your faith is not something within you, but something outside of you. Then believe on Him who, on that tree, with nailed hands and feet, poured out His life for sinners. There is the object of your faith for justification—not in yourself, nor in anything that the Holy Spirit has done in you, nor in anything He has promised to do for you. You are to look to Christ, and to Christ alone.

Look to Christ's Resurrection and Reign

Next, let your faith behold Christ as rising from the dead. See Him—He has borne the curse, and now He receives the justification. He dies to pay the debt. He rises that He may nail the handwriting of that discharged debt to the cross. See Him ascending on high, and behold Him this day pleading before the Father's throne. He is there today pleading for His people, offering up His authoritative petition for all who come to God by Him. And He—as God, as man, as living, as dying, as rising, and as reigning above—He, and He alone, is to be the object of your faith for the pardon of sin.

In nothing else must you trust. Christ is to be the only prop and pillar of your confidence. Everything else you add will be a wicked antichrist, a rebellion against the sovereignty of the Lord Jesus. However, take care, if your faith is to save you, that while you look to Christ in all these matters, you view Him as being your Substitute.

Look to Christ as Your Substitute

This doctrine of substitution is so essential to the whole plan of salvation that I must explain it here for the thousandth time. God is just—He must punish sin. God is merciful—He wills to pardon those who believe in Jesus. How is this to be done? How can He be just and exact the penalty, but still be merciful and accept the sinner? He does it in this way: He takes the sins of His people and actually transfers them from His people to Christ. They can then stand innocent, as though they had never sinned, and Christ is looked on by God as though He had been all the sinners in the world rolled into one. His people's sins were taken from their persons, really and actually—not typically and metaphorically—and truly laid on Christ. Then God came forth with His fiery sword to meet the sinner and to punish him. He met Christ. Christ was not a sinner Himself, but the sins of His people were all imputed to Him. Justice, therefore, met Christ as though He had been the sinner, punished Christ for His people's sins, punished Him as far as its rights could go, exacted from Him the last atom of the penalty, and left not a dreg in the cup.

Now, the person who can see Christ as being his Substitute, and puts his trust in Him, is thereby delivered from *"the curse of the law"* (Galatians 3:13). Friend, when you see Christ obeying the law, your faith is to say, "He obeys that for His people." When you see Him dying, you are to count the burgundy drops and say, "Thus He took my sins away." When you see Him rising from the dead, you are to say, "He rises as the Head and Representative of all His elect." And when you see Him sitting at the right hand of God, you are to view Him there as the pledge that all for whom He died will most surely sit at the Father's right hand.

Learn to look on Christ as being in God's sight as though He were the sinner. *"In him is no sin"* (1 John 3:5). *"For Christ also hath once suffered for sins, the just for the unjust"* (1 Peter 3:18). He was the Righteous, but He stood in the place of the unrighteous. All that the unrighteous ought to have endured, Christ has endured *"once for all"* (Hebrews 10:10) and put away their sins forever by the sacrifice of Himself.

This is the great object of faith. I pray you, do not make any mistake about this, for a mistake here will be dangerous, if not fatal. By your faith, see Christ, in His life, death, sufferings, and resurrection, as being the Substitute for all whom His Father gave Him—the vicarious sacrifice for the sins of all those who will trust Him with their souls. Thus set forth, Christ, then, is the object of justifying faith.

In What Are You Placing Your Faith?

Now, let me further remark that there are some who may read this who will no doubt say, "Oh, I would believe and I would be saved if..." If what? If Christ had died? "Oh no, sir, my doubt is nothing about Christ." I thought so. Then what is the doubt? "Why, I would believe if I felt this or if I had done that." So you think you would. Yet I tell you that you would not believe in Jesus if you felt that way or if you had done whatever, for then you would believe in yourself and not in Christ. That is the plain truth of it.

If you were So-and-So, then you could have confidence. Confidence in what? Why, confidence in your feelings and confidence in your actions, which is clearly contrary to confidence in Christ.

Faith is not to infer from something good within me that I will be saved. Rather, it is to say, determinedly and despite all feelings, "I am guilty in the sight of God and deserve His wrath. Yet I do nevertheless believe that *'the blood of Jesus Christ his Son cleanseth* [me] *from all sin'* (1 John 1:7). Although my present consciousness condemns me, yet my faith overpowers my consciousness, and I do believe, *'He is able also to save them to the uttermost that come unto God by him'* (Hebrews 7:25)."

To come to Christ as a saint is very easy work. To trust a doctor to cure you when you believe you are getting better is very easy. However, to trust your physician when you feel as if the sentence of death were in your body, to bear up when the disease is rising in your skin and when the ulcer is gathering its venom, to believe even then in the efficacy of the medicine—that is faith.

Saving Faith

And so, when sin masters you, when you feel that the law condemns you, then—even then, as a sinner—to trust Christ is the most daring feat in all the world. The faith that shook down the walls of Jericho, the faith that raised the dead, the faith that stopped the mouths of lions, was not greater than that of a poor sinner who dares to trust the blood and righteousness of Jesus Christ when he is in the jaws of all his sins. Do this, soul, and you are saved, whoever you may be.

The object of saving faith, then, is Christ as the Substitute for sinners. God in Christ, but not God apart from Christ, nor any work of the Spirit alone, but the work of Jesus, must be viewed by you as the foundation of your hope.

Chapter 2

The Reason of Faith

Faith cometh by hearing.
—Romans 10:17

G ranted that faith comes by hearing, but of all people who hear, do not many still remain unbelieving? How, then, does anyone come by his faith?

A Sense of Need

To his own experience, his faith comes as the result of a sense of need. The man feels himself needing a Savior. He finds Christ to be just such a Savior as he needs. Therefore, because he cannot help himself, he believes in Jesus. Having nothing of his own, he feels he must take Christ or else perish. Thus, he does it because he cannot help doing it. He is boxed into a corner, and there is but this one way of escape, namely, by the righteousness of Another. He feels he cannot escape by any good deeds or sufferings of his own. Thus, he comes to Christ and humbles himself because he cannot do without Christ and must perish unless he lays hold of Him.

The Work of God and the Spirit

To carry the question further back, where does that man get his sense of need? How is it that he, rather than another, feels his need of Christ? It is certain he has no more necessity for Christ than others. How does he come to know that he is lost and ruined? And how is it that he is driven by the sense of ruin to take hold of Christ, the Restorer?

The reply is this: It is the gift of God; it is the work of the Spirit. *"No man can come to me* [Christ], *except the Father...draw him"* (John 6:44); and the Father through the Spirit draws people to Christ by shutting them up under the law to a conviction that, if they do not come to Christ, they must perish. Then by sheer stress of weather, they tack about and run into this heavenly port. Salvation by Christ is so disagreeable to our carnal minds, so inconsistent with our love of human merit, that we never would take Christ to be our all in all if the Spirit did not convince us that we were nothing and did not so compel us to lay hold of Christ.

All Whom the Father Gives Will Come

Yet, then, the question goes even further back. How is it that the Spirit of God teaches some people their need and not others? Why is it that some of you were driven to Christ by your sense of need, while others go on in their self-righteousness and perish? There is no answer to be given but this: *"Even so, Father: for so it seemed good in thy sight"* (Matthew 11:26). In the end, it comes down to divine sovereignty. The Lord has *"hid these things from the wise and prudent, and hast revealed them unto babes"* (Luke 10:21).

The way in which Christ put it was this: *"My sheep hear my voice....Ye believe not, because ye are not of my sheep, as I said unto you"* (John 10:27, 26). Some clergymen would like this to read, "You are not My sheep, because you do not believe," as if believing made us the sheep of Christ. However, it says, *"Ye believe not, because ye are not of my sheep."*

Faith

"All that the Father giveth me shall come to me" (John 6:37). If they don't come, it is a clear proof that they were never given. Those who were given to Christ in eternity past, chosen by God the Father and then redeemed by God the Son—these are led by the Spirit, through a sense of need, to come and lay hold of Christ.

No man ever did, or ever will, believe in Christ unless he feels his need of Him. No man ever did, or will, feel his need of Christ unless the Spirit makes him feel it; and the Spirit will make no man feel his need of Jesus savingly unless it is written in that eternal book in which God has surely engraved the names of His chosen.

So, then, I hope I am not to be misunderstood on this point: The reason of faith, or why people believe, is God's electing love working through the Spirit, by a sense of need, to bring them to Christ Jesus.

Chapter 3

The Basis of the Sinner's Faith

For all have sinned, and come short of the glory of God.
—Romans 3:23

My dear friends, I have already said that no man will believe in Jesus unless he feels his need of Him. However, I have often said, and I repeat it again, that I do not come to Christ pleading that I feel my need of Him. My reason for believing in Christ is not that I feel my need of Him, but that I have a need of Him.

Come as Nothing but a Sinner

The basis on which a man comes to Jesus is not as a sensible sinner, but as a sinner, and nothing but a sinner. He will not come unless he is awakened. Yet when he comes, he does not say, "Lord, I come to You because I am an awakened sinner. Save me." Rather, he says, "Lord, I am a sinner. Save me." Not his awakening, but his sinnership, is the means and the way by which he dares to come.

You will, perhaps, perceive what I mean, for I cannot exactly explain myself just now. In reference to the preaching of a great many Calvinistic clergymen, they will say to a sinner, "Now, if you feel your need of Christ, if you have repented so much, if you have been chastened by the law to such and such a degree, then you may come to Christ on the grounds that you are an awakened sinner." I say that is false. No one may come to Christ on the basis of his being an awakened sinner. A person must come to Him as a sinner.

When I come to Jesus, I know I cannot come unless I am awakened; but, nevertheless, I do not come as an awakened sinner. I do not stand at the foot of His cross to be washed because I have repented. I bring nothing but sin when I come. A sense of need is a good feeling, but when I stand at the foot of the cross, I do not believe in Christ because I have good feelings; rather, I believe in Him whether I have good feelings or not.

> Just as I am without one plea,
> But that Thy blood was shed for me,
> And that Thou bidst me come to Thee,
> O Lamb of God, I come.

Do Not Rely on Feelings

Mr. Roger, Mr. Sheppard, Mr. Flavell, and several excellent ministers of the Puritan age, and especially Richard Baxter, used to give descriptions of what a man must feel before he would dare to come to Christ. Now, I say, in the language of Mr. Fenner, another of those clergymen, who said he was but a babe in grace when compared to the others,

> I dare to say it, that all this is not scriptural. Sinners do feel these things before they come, but they do not come on the ground of having felt it; they come on the ground of being sinners, and on no other ground whatever.

The gate of mercy is opened, and over the door it is written, *"This is a faithful saying, and worthy of all acceptation, that Christ Jesus came into the world to save sinners"* (1 Timothy 1:15). Between that word *"save"* and the next word, *"sinners,"* there is no adjective. It does not say "penitent sinners," "awakened sinners," "sensible sinners," "grieving sinners," or "alarmed sinners." No, it says only *"sinners."*

I know this: When I come, I come to Christ today, for I feel it is as much a necessity of my life to come to the cross of Christ today as it was to come ten years ago. When I come to Him, I dare not come as a conscious sinner or an awakened sinner, but I still have to come as a sinner with nothing in my hands. I saw an aged man lately in the vestry of a chapel in Yorkshire. I had preached something to this effect. The old man had been a Christian for years, and he said, "I never saw it put exactly so, but still I know that is just the way I come. I say,

> Nothing in my hands I bring,
> Simply to Thy cross I cling;
> > Naked, look to Thee for dress;
> > Helpless, come to Thee for grace;
> Black ["Black enough!"] I to the fountain fly,
> Wash me, Savior, or I die.

Faith is getting out of yourself and getting into Christ. I know that many hundreds of poor souls have been troubled because the minister has said, "If you feel your need, you may come to Christ." "But," they say, "I do not feel my need, at least not enough. I am sure I do not."

I have received scores of letters from those with poor troubled consciences who have written, "I would venture to believe in Christ to save me if I had a tender conscience, if I had a soft heart. But my heart is like a rock of ice that will not melt. I cannot feel as I would like to feel, and therefore I must not believe in Jesus." Oh, away with this wicked antichrist spirit! It is not your soft heart that entitles you to believe. You are to believe in Christ to renew your hard heart, and come to Him with nothing about you but sin.

The basis on which a sinner comes to Christ is that he is black, not that he knows he is black; that he is dead, not that he knows he is dead; that he is lost, not that he knows he is lost. I know he will not come unless he does know it, but that is not the true basis on which he comes. It is the secret reason why, but it is not the public, positive ground that he understands.

Year after year, I was afraid to come to Christ because I thought I did not feel enough. I used to read that hymn of Cowper's about being insensible as steel:

> If aught is felt, 'tis only pain
> To find I cannot feel.

When I believed in Christ, I thought I did not feel at all. Now, when I look back, I find that, all the time, I had been feeling most acutely and intensely, and most of all because I thought I did not feel.

Generally, the people who repent the most think they are impenitent. People feel their need most when they think they do not feel at all, for we are no judges of our feelings. Hence the Gospel invitation is not put upon the ground of anything of which we can be a judge. It is put on the basis of our being sinners, and nothing but sinners.

Says one, "The Bible says, 'Come unto me, all ye that [are weary] and are heavy laden, and I will give you rest' (Matthew 11:28). Then we must be weary and heavy laden." So it is in that text, but another says, "'Whosoever will, let him [come and] take the water of life freely' (Revelation 22:17)." That does not say anything about being "weary and heavy laden."

144

Besides, while the invitation is given to the weary and heavy laden, you will perceive that the promise is not made to them as weary and heavy laden, but it is made to them as coming to Christ. They did not know that they were weary and burdened when they came. They thought they were not. They really were, but part of their weariness was that they could not be as weary as they would have liked to have been, and part of their load was that they did not feel their load enough. They came to Christ just as they were. He saved them, not because there was any merit in their weariness or any efficacy in their being loaded down, but He saved them as sinners and nothing but sinners. So they were washed in His blood and made clean.

Christ Will Receive You

My dear reader, do let me put this truth home to you: If you will come to Christ as nothing but a sinner, He will not cast you out. Old Tobias Crisp said in one of his sermons upon this very point, "I dare to say it, but if you do come to Christ, whosoever you may be, if He does not receive you, then He is not true to His word, for He says, *'Him that cometh to me I will in no wise cast out'* (John 6:37)."

If you come to Christ, never mind qualification or preparation. He needs no qualification of duties or of feelings, either. You are to come just as you are. If you are the biggest sinner from hell, you are as fit to come to Christ as if you were the most moral and excellent of men. There is a bath: Who is fit to be washed? A man's blackness is no reason why he should not be washed, but the clearer reason why he should be. When our city magistrates gave relief to the poor, nobody said, "I am so poor that I am not fit to have relief." Your poverty is your preparation. The black is the white here. What a strange contradiction!

The only thing you can bring to Christ is your sin and your wickedness. All He asks is that you will come

Faith

empty-handed, except for your sin. If you have anything of your own, you must leave it all before you come. If there is anything good in you, you cannot trust Christ. You must come with nothing in your hand. Take Him as your all in all. That is the only ground upon which a poor soul can be saved—as a sinner, and nothing but a sinner.

Chapter 4

The Warranty of Faith

Believe on the Lord Jesus Christ,
and thou shalt be saved.
—Acts 16:31

I s it not foolhardy for any man to trust Christ to save him, especially when he has nothing good whatever in himself? Is it not an arrogant presumption for any man to trust Christ? No, dear ones, it is not. It is a grand and noble work of God the Holy Spirit for a man to give the lie to all his sins, and still to believe and affirm that God is true and to believe in the virtue of the blood of Jesus.

I ask you now, "But why does any man dare to believe in Christ?" "Well," says one man, "I summoned faith to believe in Christ because I felt there was a work of the Spirit in me." Then you do not believe in Christ at all. "Well," says another, "I thought that I had a right to believe in Christ because I felt somewhat." You do not have any right to believe in Christ at all on such a surety as feelings.

Christ's Word Is Our Warrant

Then what is a man's authorization for believing in Christ? Here it is: Christ tells him to do it—that is his warrant. Christ's word is the license of the sinner for believing in Christ—not what he feels, nor what he is, nor what he is not, but that Christ has told him to do it. The Gospel goes like this: *"Believe on the Lord Jesus Christ, and thou shalt be saved." "He that believeth not shall be damned"* (Mark 16:16).

Faith in Christ, then, is a commanded duty as well as a blessed privilege. What a mercy it is that it is a duty, because there never can be any question that a man has a right to do his duty. Now, on the basis that God commands me to believe, I have a right to believe, whoever I may be. The Gospel is sent to every creature. (See Mark 16:15.) Well, I belong to that tribe: I am one of the "every creatures." That same Gospel commands me to believe, and I do it. I cannot have done wrong in doing it, for I was commanded to do so. I cannot be wrong in obeying a command of God.

It is a command of God given to every creature that he should believe on Jesus Christ, whom God has sent. This is your authorization, sinner; and a blessed warrant it is, for it is one that hell cannot refute and heaven cannot withdraw. You need not search within to look for the misty confirmation in your experience. You need not look to your works or your feelings to get some dull and insufficient surety for your confidence in Christ. You may believe Christ because He tells you to do so. That is sure ground to stand on, and one that admits no doubt.

Suppose that we are all starving: The city has been under siege and shut down, there has been a long famine, and we are ready to die of hunger. An invitation comes to us to journey at once to the palace of some great prince, there to enjoy a great feast. Yet we have grown foolish and will not accept the invitation. Suppose now that some hideous madness has gotten hold of us, so that we prefer to die and would rather starve than go.

Suppose the king's herald should say, "Come and feast, poor hungry souls. And because I know you are unwilling to come, I add this threat: If you do not come, my warriors will be upon you; they will make you feel the sharpness of their swords." I think, my dear friends, we would say, "We bless the great man for that threat, because now we cannot say, 'I may not come,' when the fact is that we must not stay away. Now I need not say I am not fit to come, for I am commanded to come, and I am threatened if I do not come. I will go."

That awful sentence, *"He that believeth not shall be damned"* (Mark 16:16), was added not out of anger, but because the Lord knew our silly madness and that we would refuse our own mercies unless He thundered at us to make us come to the feast. *"Compel them to come in"* (Luke 14:23) was the word of the Master of old. That warning is part of the carrying out of the exhortation to *"compel them to come in."*

Sinner, you cannot be lost by trusting Christ, but you will be lost if you do not trust Him, and lost for not trusting Him. Sinner, not only may you come, but, I pray you, do not defy the wrath of God by refusing to come. The gate of mercy stands wide open. Why will you not come? Why will you not? Why be so proud? Why will you still refuse His voice and perish in your sins?

Note this well: If you perish, any one of you, your blood lies not at God's door, nor Christ's door, but at your own. Christ can say about you, *"Ye* [would] *not come to me, that ye might have life"* (John 5:40). Poor trembling soul, if you are willing to come, there is nothing in God's Word to keep you from coming, but there are both threats to drive you and powers to draw you.

Still I hear you say, "I must not trust Christ." You may, for every creature under heaven is commanded to do it, and what you are commanded to do, you may do. "Well," says one, "I still do not feel that I may." There you are again. You say you won't do what God tells you because of some stupid feelings of your own. You are not told to trust

Christ because you feel anything, but simply because you are a sinner.

Christ Is Able to Save to the Uttermost

Now, you know you are a sinner. "I am," says one. "And that is my sorrow." Why your sorrow? That is some sign that you do feel. "Yes," someone says, "but I do not feel enough. That is why I sorrow. I do not feel as deeply as I should." Well, suppose you do feel, or suppose you do not; you are still a sinner. *"This is a faithful saying, and worthy of all acceptation, that Christ Jesus came into the world to save sinners"* (1 Timothy 1:15).

"Oh, but I am such an old sinner. I have been sixty years in sin." Where is it written that after sixty you cannot be saved? Sir, Christ could save you at a hundred years old—yes, if you were a Methuselah in guilt. *"The blood of Jesus Christ his Son cleanseth us from all sin"* (1 John 1:7). *"Whosoever will, let him* [come and] *take the water of life freely"* (Revelation 22:17). *"He is able also to save them to the uttermost that come unto God by him"* (Hebrews 7:25). "Yes, but I have been a drunkard, a swearer, lascivious, profane," someone protests. Then you are a sinner. You have not gone further than the uttermost, and He is able to save you still.

"Yes," says another, "but you do not know how my guilt has been aggravated." That only proves you to be a sinner, and that you are commanded to trust Christ and be saved. Yet another cries, "But you do not know how often I have rejected Christ." That only makes you all the more a sinner. "You do not know how hard my heart is." Perhaps not, but that only proves that you are a sinner, and still proves you to be one whom Christ came to save.

"Sir, I have not any good thing. If I had, you know, I should have something to encourage me." The fact of your not having any good thing just proves to me that you are the man I am sent to witness to. Christ came *"to save that which was lost"* (Luke 19:10), and all you have said only proves that you are lost. Therefore, He came to save you. Do trust Him. Do trust Him.

"But if I am saved," says one, "I will be the biggest sinner who ever was saved." Then the greater the music will be in heaven when you get there. The more glory to Christ, for the bigger the sinner, the more honor to Christ when at last he is brought home. "But my sin has abounded." His *"grace did much more abound"* (Romans 5:20). "But my sin has even reached to heaven." Yes, but His mercy reaches above the heavens (Psalm 108:4). "But my guilt is as broad as the world." Yes, but His righteousness is broader than a thousand worlds. "But my sin is scarlet." Yes, but His blood is more scarlet than your sins and can wash the scarlet out by a richer scarlet. "But I deserve to be lost, and death and hell cry for my damnation." Yes, and so they may, but the blood of Jesus Christ can cry louder than either death or hell; and it cries today, "Father, let the sinner live."

Oh, how I wish I could get this thought out of my own mouth and into your heads: When God saves you, it is not because of anything in you; it is because of something in Himself! God's love has no reason except in His own heart. God's reason for pardoning a sinner is found in His own heart, and not in the sinner. There is as much reason in you why you should be saved as why another should be saved, namely, no reason at all. There is no reason in you why He should have mercy on you; but there is no reason necessary, for the reason lies in God, and in God alone.

Chapter 5

The Result of Faith

If the Son therefore shall make you free,
ye shall be free indeed.
—John 8:36

There is a man who has just this moment believed. He is not condemned, though he has spent fifty years in sin and has plunged into all manner of vice. "[His] *sins, which are many, are forgiven"* (Luke 7:47). He stands now in the sight of God as innocent as though he had never sinned.

The One Who Believes Is Not Condemned

The power of Jesus' blood is such that *"he that believeth on him is not condemned"* (John 3:18). Do these words relate to what is to happen at the Day of Judgment? I ask you, look at God's Word, and you will find that it does not say, "He that believeth shall not be condemned," but that it says, *"is not condemned"*—he is not condemned at the present moment. If he is not condemned now, then it follows that he never will be. Having believed in Christ, that promise still stands, *"He that believeth...is not condemned."* I believe that today I am not condemned; in fifty years' time that promise will be just the same: *"He that believeth...is not condemned."*

Thus, the moment a man puts his trust in Christ, he is freed from all condemnation—past, present, and future. From that day on, he stands in God's sight as though he were without *"spot, or wrinkle, or any such thing"* (Ephesians 5:27). "But he still sins," you say. He does, indeed, but his sins are not laid to his charge. They were already laid to the charge of Christ, and God can never charge the offense to two—first to Christ, and then to the sinner.

Someone objects, "Yes, but he often falls into sin." That may be possible. However, if the Spirit of God is in him, he does not sin as he was accustomed to. He sins by reason of infirmity, not by reason of his love for sin, for now he hates it. Note this truth. You can object or question in any way you will, and I will still answer, "Yes, but though he sins, yet he is no longer guilty in the sight of God. All his guilt has been taken from him and put on Christ—positively, literally, and actually lifted off him and put on Jesus Christ."

Christ Has Taken Away Our Sins Forever

Imagine the Israelites in the wilderness. A scapegoat is brought out. The high priest confesses the sin of the people over the scapegoat's head. All the sin is gone from the people and laid upon the scapegoat. Away goes the scapegoat into the wilderness. (See Leviticus 16:5–22.) Is there any sin left on the people? If there is, then the scapegoat has not carried it away. It cannot be both here and there; it cannot be carried away and left behind, too. "No," you say, "Scripture says the scapegoat carried away the sin; there was none left on the people when the scapegoat had taken away the sin."

And so, when by faith we put our hands upon the head of Christ, does Christ take away our sin or does He not? If He does not, then our believing in Him is of no use. Yet if He really does take away our sin, then our sin cannot be on Him and on us, too. If it is on Christ, we are free, clear, accepted, justified. This is the true doctrine of justification by faith. As soon as a man believes in Christ Jesus, his sins are gone from him, and gone away forever. They are blotted out now.

Consider a man who owed a hundred pounds. If he has a receipt for it, he is free. The debt is blotted out. An erasure has been made in the book, and the debt is gone. Although a man commits sin, he is no longer a debtor to the law of God, the debt having been paid even before the debt was incurred.

Pure and Perfect in God's Sight

Does not Scripture say that God has *"cast all their* [His people's] *sins into the depths of the sea"* (Micah 7:19)? Now, if they are in the depths of the sea, they cannot be on His people, too. Blessed be His name, in the day when He casts our sins into the depths of the sea, He views us as pure in His sight, and we stand *"accepted in the beloved"* (Ephesians 1:6). Then He says, *"As far as the east is from the west, so far hath he removed our transgressions from us"* (Psalm 103:12). They cannot be removed and be here still.

Then, if you believe in Christ, you are no longer a sinner in the sight of God. You are accepted as though you were perfect, as though you had kept the law—for Christ has kept it, and His righteousness is yours. You have broken it, but your sin is His, and He has been punished for it. Do not mislead yourselves any longer; you are no longer what you were. When you believe, you stand in Christ's place, even as Christ long ago stood in your stead. The transformation is complete; the exchange is positive and eternal. Those who believe in Jesus are as much accepted by God the Father as His Eternal Son is accepted. And those who do not believe, let them do what they will, they can try to work out their own righteousness, but they abide under the law and are still under the curse. Now, you who believe in Jesus, walk up and down the earth in the glory of this great truth. You are sinners in yourselves, but you are washed in the blood of Christ.

David said, *"Wash me, and I shall be whiter than snow"* (Psalm 51:7). You have seen the snow come down. How clear! How white! What could be whiter? Why, the Christian is whiter than that. You say, "He is black." I know he is as black as anyone, as black as hell. Yet when the blood-drop of Christ falls on him, he is white, *"whiter than snow."* The next time you see the snow-white crystals falling from heaven, look on them and say, "Though I must confess in myself that I am unworthy and unclean, yet, since I have believed in Christ, He has given me His righteousness so completely that I am even whiter than the snow as it descends from the treasury of God."

Victory over Doubts and Fears

Oh, may we have faith to lay hold of this! Oh, for an overpowering faith that will get the victory over doubts and fears! Oh, for a faith that will make us enjoy *"the liberty wherewith Christ hath made us free"* (Galatians 5:1). You who believe in Christ, go to your beds this night and say, "If I die in my bed, I cannot be condemned." Should you wake the next morning, go into the world and say, "I am not condemned." When the devil howls at you, tell him, "Ah, you may accuse, but I am not condemned." And if sometimes your sins rise, say, "I know you, but you are all gone forever; I am not condemned." And when your turn does come to die, shut your eyes in peace.

> Bold shall you stand
>   In that great day,
> For who aught to
>   Your charge can lay?

Faith

In the end, you will be found fully absolved by grace; all sin's tremendous curse and blame will be taken away, though not because of anything you have done. I pray that you do all you can for Christ out of gratitude; but even when you have done all, do not rest there. Rest quietly in the substitution and the sacrifice. Be what Christ was in His Father's sight. When your conscience bothers you, you can tell it that Christ was everything that you ought to have been, that He has suffered all your penalty. Now neither mercy nor justice can strike you, since justice has clasped hands with mercy in a firm covenant to save the man whose faith is in the Cross of Christ.

Chapter 6

The Satisfactory Declaration

There is therefore now no condemnation to them
which are in Christ Jesus.
—Romans 8:1

Y ou are aware that in our courts of law, a verdict of "not guilty" amounts to an acquittal, and the prisoner is immediately discharged. So it is in the language of the Gospel: A sentence of "not condemned" implies the justification of the sinner. It means that the believer in Christ receives a present justification. Faith does not produce its fruits by-and-by, but now. So far as justification is the result of faith, it is given to the soul in the moment the soul comes to Christ and accepts Him as its all in all.

Are they who now stand before the throne of God justified today? So are we as truly and as clearly justified as they who walk in white robes and sing praises above. The thief on the cross was justified the moment that he turned his eye of faith to Jesus, who was just then hanging by his side. The aged Paul, after years of service, was not more justified than was the thief with no service at all.

Innocent Forever in the Sight of God

We are today *"accepted in the beloved"* (Ephesians 1:6), today absolved from sin, today innocent in the sight of God. Oh, what a soul-transporting thought! Some clusters of this vine we will not be able to gather until we go to heaven, but this is one of the first ripe clusters, and it may be plucked and eaten here. This is not like the corn on the land, which we cannot eat until we cross the Jordan. Rather, this is part of the manna in the wilderness and part, too, of our daily clothing with which God supplies us in our journeying here.

We are now—even now—pardoned. Even now our sins are put away. Even now we stand in the sight of God as though we had never been guilty; as innocent as Adam when he stood in integrity before he had eaten of the forbidden fruit; as pure as though we had never received the taint of depravity in our veins. *"There is therefore now no condemnation to them which are in Christ Jesus."*

There is not a sin in God's Book, even now, against one of His people. There is nothing laid to their charge. There is neither speck, nor spot, nor wrinkle, nor any such thing remaining upon any single believer in the matter of justification in the sight of the Judge of all the earth.

Further, there is not simply present, but also continual, justification. In the moment when you and I believed, it was said of us, "He is not condemned." Many days have passed since then; many changes we have seen, but it is still true of us today, "He is not condemned."

The Lord alone knows how long our appointed days will be—how long before we fulfill our time and flee away like a shadow. Yet this we know, since every word of God is assured and because *"the gifts and calling of God are without repentance"* (Romans 11:29): Though we should live another fifty years, yet would it still be written here, *"He that believeth on him is not condemned"* (John 3:18).

If by some mysterious dealing in providence our lives should be lengthened to ten times the usual limit of man and we should live for the nine hundred years of Methuselah, the truth would still stand the same: "He that believeth on him is not condemned."

"I give unto them [My sheep] *eternal life; and they shall never perish, neither shall any man pluck them out of my hand"* (John 10:28). *"The just shall live by faith"* (Galatians 3:11). *"He that believeth on him shall not be confounded"* (1 Peter 2:6). All these promises go to show that the justification that Christ gives to our faith is a continual one, which will last as long as we live.

Remember, it will last in eternity as well as in time. We will not wear any other clothing in heaven but that which we wear here. Today the righteous stand clothed in the righteousness of Christ. They will wear the same wedding dress at the great Wedding Feast. Yet what if it should wear out? What if that righteousness should lose its virtue in the eternity to come? Oh, beloved, we entertain no fear about that. Heaven and earth will pass away, but His righteousness will never wax old. No moth will chew it; no thief will steal it; no weeping hand of lamentation will tear it in two.

It must be eternal, even as Christ Jesus our righteousness is. Because He is our righteousness, the self-existent, the everlasting, the immutable Jehovah, of whose years there is no end and whose strength does not fail, therefore our righteousness has no end; and there will never be any termination of its perfection and beauty. I think Scripture very clearly teaches us that the person who believes in Christ has received forever a continual justification.

Justified Completely

Again, think for a moment: This justification is complete. *"He that believeth on him is not condemned"* (John

159

Faith

3:18). That is to say, not in any measure or in any degree. I know some people think it is possible for us to be in such a state as to be half-condemned and half-accepted. They mistakenly think that to the extent we are sinners is the extent to which we are condemned, and to the degree we are righteous is the degree to which we are accepted. Beloved, there is nothing like that in Scripture. It is altogether apart from the doctrine of the Gospel. *"If by grace, then is it no more of works....But if it be of works, then is it no more grace"* (Romans 11:6). Works and grace cannot mix and mingle any more than fire and water can. It is either one or the other; it cannot be both. The two can never be allied. There can be no mixture of the two, no dilution of one with the other.

He who believes is free from all iniquity, guilt, and blame. Though the devil brings an accusation, it is a false one. He is free even from accusation, since it is boldly challenged, *"Who shall lay any thing to the charge of God's elect?"* (Romans 8:33). It does not say, "Who shall prove it?" but *"Who shall lay any thing to [his] charge?"* He is so completely freed from condemnation that not a shadow of a spot can be found on his soul; there is not even the slightest passing by of iniquity to cast its black shadow on him. He stands before God not as half-innocent, but as perfectly so; not as half-washed, but as *"whiter than snow"* (Psalm 51:7). His sins are not simply erased, but they are blotted out (Isaiah 43:25); not simply put out of sight, but *"cast...into the depths of the sea"* (Micah 7:19); not merely gone, and gone *"as far as the east is from the west"* (Psalm 103:12), but gone forever, *"once for all"* (Hebrews 10:10).

You know, beloved, that the Jew in his ceremonial purification never had a conscience free from sin. After one sacrifice, he needed still another, because these offerings could never make those who came there perfect. The next day's sins needed a new lamb, and the next year's iniquity needed a new victim for an atonement. *"But this man, after he had offered one sacrifice for sins for ever, sat down on the right hand of God"* (Hebrews 10:12). No more burnt offerings are needed. There is no longer a need for washing, blood, atonement, or sacrifice. Hear the dying Savior cry, *"It is finished"* (John 19:30). Your sins have sustained their deathblow; the robe of your righteousness has received its last thread. It is done, complete, perfect. It needs no addition; it can never suffer any diminution.

Oh, Christian, grasp this precious thought! I may not be able to state it except in weak terms, but do not let my weakness prevent your comprehending its glory and its preciousness. This thought is enough to make a man leap, though his legs were chained with irons, and to make him sing, though his mouth were gagged. We are perfectly accepted in Christ, and our justification is not partial. It does not go to a limited extent, but it goes the whole way. Our unrighteousness is covered. We are entirely and irrevocably free from condemnation.

An Effectual Justification

Further, the non-condemnation is effectual justification. The royal privilege of justification will never miscarry. It will be brought home to every believer.

In the reign of King George III, the son of a member of my church lay under sentence of death for forgery. My predecessor, Dr. Rippon, after incredible exertions, obtained a promise that his sentence would be remitted. By a singular occurrence, the present senior deacon—then a young man—learned from the governor of the jail that the reprieve had not been received, and the unhappy prisoner was to have been executed the next morning. Dr. Rippon went hastily to Windsor, obtained an interview with the monarch in his bedchamber, and received from the king's own hand a copy of that reprieve, which had been negligently put aside by a thoughtless officer. "I charge you, Doctor," said his majesty, "to make good speed." "Trust me, Sire, for that," responded the doctor, and he returned to London just in time, for the prisoner was being marched with many others onto the scaffold. That pardon had been given, and yet the man might have been executed if it had not been effectually carried out.

However, blessed be God, our non-condemnation is an effectual thing. It is not a matter of letter; rather, it is a matter of fact. Friends, you know that condemnation is a matter of fact. When we suffered in our souls and were brought under the heavy hand of the law, we felt that its curses were not mock thunders, like the wrath of the Vatican, but that they were real. We felt that the anger of God was indeed a thing to tremble at—a real, substantial fact.

Just as real as the condemnation that justice brings is the justification that mercy bestows. You are not nominally guiltless, but you are really so, if you believe in Christ. You are not nominally put into the place of the innocent, but you are really put there the moment you believe in Jesus. It does not only say that your sins are gone; they are truly gone. God does not look on you only as though you were accepted; you are accepted.

It is a matter of fact to you, as much a matter of fact as the reality that you sinned. You do not doubt that you have sinned—you cannot doubt that. Likewise, do not doubt, then, that when you believe, your sins are put away. As certain as the black spot fell on you when you sinned, so certainly and so surely was it all washed away when you were bathed in that "fountain filled with blood," which was "drawn from Immanuel's veins."

Come, my friend, and think about this. You are actually and effectually cleared from guilt. You are led out of your prison. You are no longer in chains as a bond slave. You are delivered now from the bondage of the law. You are freed from sin, and you can walk at large as a free man. Your Savior's blood has procured your full discharge.

Guiltless before God

Come, beloved; you have a right now to come to your Father's feet. No flames of vengeance are there to scare you now, no fiery sword. Justice cannot smite the innocent. Come, believer; your disabilities are taken away. You were once unable to see your Father's face, but you can see it now. You could not speak with Him, nor He with you, but now you have bold *"access by faith into this grace wherein we stand"* (Romans 5:2). Once there was a fear of hell upon you; there is no hell for you now. How can there be punishment for the guiltless? He who believes is guiltless; he is not condemned and cannot be punished. No frowns of an avenging God exist now. If God is viewed as a Judge, how could He frown on the guiltless? How could the Judge frown on an absolved one?

All the Blessings and Privileges—and More

More than all the privileges you might have enjoyed if you had never sinned belong to you now that you are justified. All the blessings that you could have had if you had kept the law, and more, are yours today because Christ has kept it for you. All the love and acceptance that a perfectly obedient being could have obtained from God belong to you because Christ was perfectly obedient on your behalf. This imputed all His merits to your account so that you might be exceedingly rich through Him who for your sake became exceedingly poor (2 Corinthians 8:9).

Oh, that the Holy Spirit would enlarge our hearts so that we might take in the sweetness of these thoughts! There is no condemnation. Moreover, there never will be any condemnation. The forgiveness is not partial, but perfect. It is so effectual that it delivers us from all the penalties of the law, gives to us all the privileges of obedience, and puts us actually high above where we would have been if we had never sinned. It fixes our standing more securely than it was before we fell. We are not now where Adam was, for Adam could fall and perish. We are, rather, where Adam would have been if we could suppose God had put him into the Garden for seven years and said, "If you are obedient for seven years, your time of probation will be over, and I will reward you."

In one sense, the children of God may be said to be in a state of probation; in another sense, there is no probation. There is no probation as to whether the child of God will be saved. He is saved already; his sins are washed away; his righteousness is complete. If that righteousness could endure probation for a million years, it would never be defiled. In fact, it always stands the same in the sight of God, and must do so forever and ever.

Chapter 7

Misapprehensions about Faith

He that believeth...is not condemned.
—John 3:18

What simpletons we are! Whatever our natural age might be, how childish we are in spiritual things! What great simpletons we are when we first believe in Christ! We think that our being pardoned involves a great many things that, afterward, we find have nothing whatever to do with our pardon. For instance, we think we will never sin again. We fancy that the battle is all fought, that we have come into a safe field, with no more war to wage. We believe, in fact, we have won the victory and have only to stand up and wave the palm branch because it is all over. We imagine that God has only to call us up to Himself and we will enter heaven without having to fight any enemies on earth.

We Imagine That Our Faith Will Not Be Tried

Now, all these ideas are obvious mistakes. Observe that, although it is asserted, *"He that believeth...is not condemned,"* Scripture never says that he who believes will not have his faith exercised. Your faith will be exercised. An untried faith is no faith at all. God never gave men faith without intending to try it. Faith is received for the purpose of developing endurance.

Just as our rifle corps friends put up a target with the intention of shooting at it, so God gives faith with the intention of letting trials and troubles, and sin and Satan, aim all their darts at it. When you have faith in Christ, it is a great privilege; but remember that it involves a great trial. When you asked for great faith, did you consider that you asked for great troubles, also? You cannot have great faith just to store it up and allow it to rust.

Mr. Great-Heart, in John Bunyan's *The Pilgrim's Progress,* was a very strong man; but then, what strong work he had to do! He had to go with all those women and children many scores of times up to the Celestial City and back again. He had to fight all the giants, drive back all the lions, slay the giant Slay-good, and knock down Doubting Castle, the castle of Giant Despair. If you have a great measure of faith, you will have need to use it all. You will never have a single scrap to spare. You will be like the virgins in our Lord's parable: Even though you are a wise virgin, you will have to say to others who might borrow from you, *"Not so; lest there be not enough for* [me] *and you"* (Matthew 25:9).

Yet when your faith is exercised with trials, do not think you are brought into judgment for your sins. Oh, no, believer, there is plenty of exercise, but that is not condemnation. There are many trials, but we are still justified. We may often be buffeted, but we are never accursed. We may often be cast down, but the sword of the Lord never can and never will smite us to the heart.

We Imagine That Our Faith Will Not Wane

Moreover, our faith may not only be exercised, but it may also come to a very low ebb. Still we are not condemned. When your faith gets so small that you cannot see it, even then you are not condemned. If you have ever believed in Jesus, your faith may be like the sea when it goes out a very long way from the shore, leaving a vast track of mud—when some might even say the sea had dried up—but you are not condemned when your faith is almost dried up. And I dare to say, when your faith is at the flood tide, you are not more accepted than when your faith is at the lowest ebb. Your acceptance does not depend upon the quantity of your faith; it depends upon only its reality.

If you are really resting in Christ, though your faith may be but a spark, and a thousand devils may try to quench that one spark, yet you are not condemned—you stand accepted in Christ. Though your comforts will necessarily decay as your faith declines, yet your acceptance does not decay. Though faith rises and falls like the thermometer, though faith is like the mercury in the bulb because all weathers change it, yet God's love is not affected by the weather of earth or the changes of time. Until the perfect righteousness of Christ can be a mutable thing—a football to be kicked about by the feet of fiends—your acceptance with God can never change. You are, you must be, perfectly *"accepted in the beloved"* (Ephesians 1:6).

We Imagine That We Will Always Feel Close to God

There is another thing that often tries the child of God. He at times loses the light of his Father's countenance. Now, remember, it is not said, "He who believes will not lose the light of God's countenance." That may happen, but God's child will not be condemned for it. You may walk not only for days, but also for months, in such a state that you have little fellowship with Christ, very little communion with God of a joyous sort. The promises may seem broken to you; the Bible may afford to you but little comfort. When you turn your eyes to heaven, you may only have to feel all the more the smarting that is caused by your Father's rod. You may have vexed and grieved His Spirit, and He may have turned away His face from you. Nevertheless, you are not condemned for all of that. Note well this testimony: *"He that believeth...is not condemned."*

Even when your Father smites you and leaves a welt at every stroke and brings blood at every blow, there is not a particle of condemnation in any of His lashes. He does not smite you in His anger, but in His dear covenant love. There is as unmixed and unalloyed affection in every love stroke of chastisement from your Father's hand as there is in the kisses of Jesus Christ's lips. Oh, believe this. It will tend to lift up your heart. It will cheer you when neither sun nor moon appear. It will honor your God; it will show you where your acceptance really lies. When His face is turned away, believe Him still and say, *"'He abideth faithful'* (2 Timothy 2:13), though He hides His face from me."

I will go a little further still. The child of God may be so assaulted by Satan that he may nearly give up to despair, and yet he is not condemned. Devils may beat the great hell-drum in his ear, until he thinks he is on the very brink of perdition. He may read the Bible and think that every threat is against him and every promise shuts its mouth and will not cheer him. He may at last sink so low into despondency that he is ready to break the harp that has so long been hanging on the willow. (See Psalm 137:1–4.) He may say, "The Lord has quite forsaken me. My God will be gracious no more," but it is not true. He may be ready to swear a thousand times that God's mercy is gone forever and His faithfulness will fail forever, but it is not true! A thousand liars swearing to a falsehood could not make it true, and our doubts and fears are all liars. If there were ten thousand of them, and they all professed the same, it is still a falsehood that God ever forsook His people or that He ever cast from Himself an innocent man. You are innocent, remember, when you believe in Jesus.

"But," you say, "I am full of sin." "Yes," I respond, "but that sin has been laid on Christ." "Oh," you reply, "but I sin daily." "Yes," say I, "but that sin was laid on Him years ago, before you committed it. It is not yours. Christ has taken it away *'once for all'* (Hebrews 10:10). You are a righteous man by faith, and God will not forsake the righteous, nor will He cast away the innocent."

Therefore, I say that the faith of the child of God may be at a low ebb. He may lose the light of his Father's countenance. He may even get into thorough despair. Yet all these things cannot disprove God's word: *"He that believeth...is not condemned."*

We Imagine We Will Be Cast Off When We Sin

"But," you say, "what if the child of God should sin?" It is a deep and tender subject, yet we must touch it and be bold here. I would not mince God's truth, lest any should make a bad use of it. I know there are some, not the people of God, who will say, "Let us sin, that grace may abound." Their condemnation is just. (See Romans 6:1; 3:7–8.) I cannot abide the perversion of truth. There are always men who will take the best of food as though it were poison and make the best of truth into a lie, thus damning their own souls.

You ask, "What if a child of God should fall into sin?" I answer that the child of God does fall into sin. Every day, he mourns and groans because, when he would do good, evil is present with him. (See Romans 7:21.) Yet though he falls into sins, he is not condemned—not by one of them, nor by all of them put together—because his acceptance does not depend upon himself, but upon the perfect righteousness of Christ. That perfect righteousness is not invalidated by any sins of his. He is perfect in Christ; and until Christ is imperfect, the imperfections of the creature do not mar the justification of the believer in the sight of God.

If he falls into some glaring sin—O God, keep us from it!—if he falls into some glaring sin, he will go with broken bones, but he will reach heaven for all that. Although, in order to try him and let him see his vileness, he is allowed to go far astray, yet He who bought him will not lose him; He who chose him will not cast him away. He will say unto him, *"I, even I, am he that blotteth out thy transgressions for mine own sake, and will not remember thy sins"* (Isaiah 43:25). David may go ever so far away, but David is not lost. He comes back and cries, *"Have mercy upon me, O God"* (Psalm 51:1). And so it will be with every believing soul—Christ will bring him back. Though he slip, he will be kept, and all the chosen seed will meet around the throne.

If it were not for this last truth—though some may chafe at it—what would become of some of God's people? They would be given up to despair. If, dear reader, you are a backslider, I pray that you will not make bad use of what I have said. Let me say to you, poor backslider, that your Father yearns over you. He has not erased your name out of the registry. Come back, come back now to Him, and say, "Receive me graciously and love me freely." He will say, "I will put you among the children." He will pass by your backsliding and will heal your iniquities. You will yet stand once more in His favor and know that you are still accepted in the Redeemer's righteousness and saved by His blood.

Justified Forever

God does not mean that His child will not be tried, or that he will not sometimes even fall under the trial. Yet He

170

does mean this, once and for all: *"He that believeth on him* [Christ] *is not condemned"* (John 3:18). At no time, by no means, is he under the sentence of condemnation, but is forever justified in the sight of God.

Chapter 8

What This Faith Includes

There is therefore now no condemnation
to them which are in Christ Jesus,
who walk not after the flesh, but after the Spirit.
For the law of the Spirit of life in
Christ Jesus hath made me free from
the law of sin and death.
—Romans 8:1–2

I f we are not condemned, then at no time does God ever look upon His children, when they believe in Christ, as being guilty. Are you surprised that I should put it so? I put it so again: From the moment you believe in Christ, God ceases to look upon you as being guilty, because He never looks upon you apart from Christ. You often look upon yourself as guilty, and you fall upon your knees, as you should do, weeping and lamenting. Yet even then, while you are weeping over inbred and actual sin, He is still saying out of heaven, "As far as your justification is concerned, you are all fair and lovely." You are as black as the tents of Kedar—that is you by nature. You are as fair as the curtains of Solomon—that is you in Christ. (See Song of Solomon 1:5.) You are *"black"* (v. 5)—that is you in the first Adam—*"but comely"* (v. 5)—that is you in the Second Adam.

Always Pleasing and Perfect

Oh, think of that! You are always pleasing in God's sight, always lovely in God's sight, always as though you were perfect in God's sight. For you are *"complete"* in Christ Jesus, and *"perfect"* in Christ Jesus, as the apostle put it in Colossians 4:12. You always stand completely washed and fully clothed in Christ. Remember this truth. It is certainly included in the words, *"He that believeth on him is not condemned"* (John 3:18).

Never Liable to Punishment— Only Loving Chastisement

Another great thought is this: You are never liable as a believer to receive punishment for your sins. You will be chastised on account of them, as a father chastises his child—that is a part of the Gospel dispensation—but you will not be smitten for your sins as the lawgiver smites the criminal. Your Father may often punish you as He punishes the wicked, but never for the same reason.

The ungodly stand on the ground of their own demerits. Their sufferings are awarded as their due deserts. However, your sorrows do not come to you as a matter of desert—they come to you as a matter of love. God knows that, in one sense, your sorrows are such a privilege that you may count them as a blessing you do not deserve. I have often thought of that when I have been sorely troubled. I know that some people say, "You deserved the trouble." Yes, my friends, but there is not enough merit in all the Christians put together to deserve such a good thing as the loving rebuke of our heavenly Father.

Perhaps you cannot see this truth. You cannot think that a trouble can come to you as a real blessing in the covenant. Yet I know that the rod of the covenant is as much the gift of grace as the blood of the covenant. It is not a matter of desert or merit. It is given to us because we need it. But question whether we were ever good enough to deserve it. We were never able to get up to so high a standard as to deserve so rich, so gracious, a providence as this covenant blessing—the rod of our chastening God. Never at any time in your life has a law-stroke fallen on you. Since you believed in Christ, you are out of the law's jurisdiction.

The law of England cannot touch a Frenchman while he lives under the protection of his own ruler. *"For ye are not under the law, but under grace"* (Romans 6:14). The law of Sinai cannot touch you, for you are out of its jurisdiction. You are not in Sinai or in Arabia. You are not the son of Hagar or the son of a handmaid. You are the child of Sarah; you have come to Jerusalem and are free. You are out of Arabia and have come to God's own happy land. You are not under Hagar, but under Sarah, under God's covenant of grace. You are a child of promise, and you will have God's own inheritance. (See Galatians 4:22–31.)

Believe this: Never will a law-stroke fall on you. Never will God's anger in a judicial sense drop on you. He may give you a chastising stroke, not as the result of sin, but rather as the result of His own rich grace, which would get the sin out of you so that you may be perfected in sanctification, even as you are now perfect and complete before Him in the blood and righteousness of Jesus Christ.

Chapter 9

What This Faith Excludes

*For by grace are ye saved through faith; and that
not of yourselves: it is the gift of God: not of works,
lest any man should boast.*
—Ephesians 2:8–9

W hat does faith exclude? Well, I am sure it
excludes boasting. *"He that believeth...is not
condemned"* (John 3:18). Oh, if it said, "He who
works is not condemned," then you and I might boast in
unlimited quantity. Yet when it says, *"He that believeth,"*
there is no room for us to say half a word for the old
self.

Faith Excludes Boasting in Ourselves

No, Lord, if I am not condemned, it is because of Your
free grace, for I have deserved to be condemned a thousand times since I sat down to write this. When I am on
my knees and I am not condemned, I am sure it must be
sovereign grace, for even when I am praying, I deserve to
be condemned. Even when we are repenting, we are sinning, and adding to our sins while we are repenting of
them.

Every act we do as the result of the flesh is again sin, and our best performances are so stained with sin that it is hard to know whether they are good works or bad works. Inasmuch as they are our own works, they are bad; and inasmuch as they are the works of the Spirit, they are good. Yet, then, the goodness is not ours; it is the Spirit's, and only the evil remains to us. Ah, then, we cannot boast! Be gone, pride! Be gone!

The Christian must be humble. If he lifts up his head to say something, then he is nothing, indeed. When he once begins to boast as though his own right hand had gotten him the victory, He does not know where he is or where he stands. Quit boasting, Christian. Live humbly before your God, and never let a word of self-congratulation escape your lips. Sacrifice self, and let your song be before the throne, *"Not unto us, O LORD, not unto us, but unto thy name* [we] *give glory"* (Psalm 115:1).

Faith Excludes Doubts and Fears

What else does it exclude? I think it ought to exclude —now I am about to smite myself—it ought to exclude doubts and fears. *"He that believeth...is not condemned"* (John 3:18). How dare you and I draw such long faces and go about as we do sometimes, as though we had a world of cares upon our backs? What I would have given ten or eleven years ago if I could have known that verse was assured to me, that I was not condemned! Why, I thought if I had to live on bread and water, be locked up in a dungeon, and every day be flogged with a cat-o'-nine-tails, I would gladly have accepted it if I could have once felt my sins were forgiven.

Now, you are forgiven; and yet are you cast down? Oh, shame on you! No condemnation, and yet miserable? Fie, Christian! Get up and wipe the tears from your eyes. If there were a person lying in jail now who was to be executed next week, and if you could go to him and say, "You are pardoned," would he not spring up with delight from his seat? Although he might have lost his goods, and though it would be possible for him after the pardon to have to suffer many things, yet, as long as his life was spared, what would all that be to him? He would feel that it was less than nothing.

Now, Christian, you are pardoned; all your sins are forgiven. Christ has said to you, "[Your] *sins, which are many, are forgiven*" (Luke 7:47). Are you yet miserable? Well, if we must be so sometimes, let us be so for as short a time as we can. If we must sometimes be cast down, let us ask the Lord to lift us up again. I am afraid that some of us get into bad habits and have come to make it a matter of practice to be downcast.

Christian, understand that it will grow on you—this peevish spirit. If you do not resist this sinfulness at first, it will get worse with you. If you do not go to God to banish these doubts and fears from you, they will soon swarm upon you like flies in Egypt. When you are able to kill the first great doubt, you will perhaps kill a hundred; for one great doubt will breed a thousand, and to kill the mother is to kill the whole brood.

Therefore, look with both eyes against the first doubt, lest you should become confirmed in your despondency and grow into sad despair. *"He that believeth on him is not condemned"* (John 3:18). If this excludes boasting, it ought to exclude doubts, too.

Faith Excludes Sinning Any Longer

Finally, faith excludes sinning any longer. My Lord, have I sinned against You so many times, and yet have You freely forgiven me all? What stronger motive could I have for keeping me from sinning again? Ah, there are some who are saying that this is licentious doctrine. The man who can find any licentiousness here must be a thousand devils rolled into one. What! Go and sin because I am forgiven? Go and live in iniquity because Jesus Christ took my guilt and suffered in my place instead of me? Human nature is bad enough, but I think the very worst state of human nature is when it tries to draw an argument for sin from the free grace of God.

Bad as I am, I do feel this: It is hard to sin against a pardoning God. It is far harder to sin against the blood of Christ and against a sense of pardon than it is to sin against the terrors of the law and the fears of hell itself. I know that when my soul is most alarmed by a dread of the wrath of God, I can sin with comfort compared with what I can tolerate when I have a sense of His love shed abroad in my heart (Romans 5:5).

What is more monstrous than to know that your title is clear and yet to sin? Oh, vile reprobate! You are on the border of the deepest hell. Yet I am sure, if you are a child of God, that you will say the following when you have discovered that your title is clear and feel yourself justified in Christ Jesus:

> Now, for the love I bear His name,
>   What was my gain, I count my loss;
> My former pride I call my shame,
>   And nail my glory to His cross.

Yes, I must and will *"count all things but loss for the excellency of the knowledge of Christ Jesus my Lord"* (Philippians 3:8). May my soul be found in Him, perfect in His righteousness!

This will make you live near to Him. This will make you like Him. Do not think that dwelling on this doctrine will make you think lightly of sin. It will make you think of it as a hard and stern executioner for putting Christ to death, as an awful load that could never be lifted from you except by the eternal arm of God. Then you will come to hate it with all your soul, because it is rebellion against a loving and gracious God. You will, by this means, far better than by any Arminian* doubts or any legal quibbles, be led to walk in the footsteps of your Lord Jesus and to follow the Lamb wherever He goes.

I think that this little work, though I have written it for the children of God, is meant for sinners, too. Sinner, I would desire that you did say so. If you know that *"he that believeth...is not condemned"* (John 3:18), then, sinner, if you believe, you will not be condemned. May all that I have said help you to this belief in your soul.

Oh, but you ask, "May I trust Christ?" As I said, it is not a question of whether you may or may not; you are commanded to do so. The Scripture commands the Gospel to be preached to every creature (Mark 16:15). The Gospel is, *"Believe on the Lord Jesus Christ, and thou shalt be saved"* (Acts 16:31). I know you will be too proud to do it, unless God by His grace should humble you. Yet if you feel that you are nothing and have nothing of your own, I think you will be very glad to take Christ as your all in all. If you can say, with poor Jack the Huckster, "I'm a poor sinner and nothing at all," you may go on and say with him, "But Jesus Christ is my all in all."

God grant that it may be so, for His name's sake.

---

* Dutch theologian Jacob Arminius [1560–1609] opposed the Calvinists' beliefs in absolute predestination, irresistible grace, and the inability to fall from grace. Arminians believe in a conditional predestination, man's ability to resist or respond to grace out of his free will, and the possibility of salvation for all.

Spurgeon on the Holy Spirit

Contents

Chapter 1

The Work of the Holy Spirit

Are ye so foolish? having begun in the Spirit,
are ye now made perfect by the flesh?
—Galatians 3:3

Yes, in response to the question in our text, we are this foolish. Folly is bound up not only in the heart of a child, but even in the heart of a child of God; and though the rod may be said to bring folly out of a child (Proverbs 22:15), it will take many repetitions of the rod of affliction upon the shoulders of a Christian before that folly is taken out of him.

I suppose all of us are very sound on this point as a matter of theory. If any should ask us how we hope to have our salvation worked in us, we would, without the slightest hesitation, state our belief that *"salvation is of the LORD"* (Jonah 2:9) alone, and we would declare that, as the Holy Spirit first of all began our piety in us, we look to His might alone to continue, preserve, and at last perfect the sacred work (Philippians 1:6).

I say we are sound enough on this point as a matter of theory, but we are all very heretical and unsound as a matter of practice. Sadly, you will not find a Christian who does not have to mourn over his self-righteous tendencies. You will not discover a believer who has not, at certain periods in his life, needed to groan because the spirit of self-confidence has risen in his heart and prevented him from feeling the absolute necessity of the Holy Spirit. This dependence on self has led him to put his confidence in the mere strength of nature, the strength of good intentions, or the strength of strong resolutions, instead of relying on the might of God the Holy Spirit alone. This one thing I know, friends: While, as a preacher, I can tell you that the Holy Spirit must work all our works in us, and that without Him we can do nothing, yet as a man, I find myself tempted to deny my own preaching—not in my words but in fact, by endeavoring to do deeds without looking first to the Holy Spirit.

While I would never be unsound in the teaching part of it, in that part that concerns the working out of it, in common with all who love the Lord Jesus but who are still subject to the infirmities of flesh and blood, I have to admit with sorrow that I repeatedly find myself *"having begun in the Spirit,"* seeking to be *"made perfect by the flesh."*

Yes, we are as foolish as that; and, beloved, it is well for us if we have a consciousness that we are foolish, for when a man is foolish and knows it, there is the hope that he will one day be wise. To know one's self to be foolish is to stand upon the doorstep of the temple of wisdom; to understand the wrongness of any position is halfway toward amending it; to be quite sure that our self-confidence is a heinous sin and folly and an offense toward God, and to have that thought burned into us by God's Holy Spirit, is going a great length toward the absolute casting of our self-confidence away and the bringing of our souls, in practice, as well as in theory, to rely wholly upon the power of God's Holy Spirit.

However, I will diverge from my text somewhat. Having just in a few words endeavored to explain the meaning of the whole sentence, I intend to dwell upon only the doctrine that, incidentally, the apostle Paul taught. He taught us that we begin in the Spirit: *"Having begun in the Spirit."* I have already illustrated the whole text sufficiently for our understanding, if God the Holy Spirit will enlighten us. I will now confine myself to the thought that Christians begin in the Spirit; that the early part of Christianity is of God's Spirit, and of God's Spirit only, while it is equally true that all the way through we must lean upon the same power and depend upon the same strength.

I have selected this text for this reason: We have a very large influx of young believers, month after month, week after week. Every week, we receive additions to the church in a considerable number. Month after month, these hands baptize into a profession of faith in the Lord Jesus many of those who are yet young in the faith of the Gospel.

Now, I am astonished to find those persons who thus come before me so well instructed in the doctrines of grace and so sound in all the truths of the covenant, insomuch that I may think it my boast and glory, in the name of Jesus, that I do not know of any members whom we have received into the church who do not give their full assent and consent to all the doctrines of the Christian religion. Doctrines that others are accustomed to laugh at as being high doctrinal points are those that these new Christians most readily receive, believe, and rejoice in. I find, however, that the greatest deficiency lies in this point: forgetfulness of the work of the Holy Spirit.

I find them very easily remembering the work of God the Father. They do not deny the great doctrine of election; they can see clearly the great sentence of justification passed by the Father upon the elect through the vicarious sacrifice and perfect righteousness of Jesus. Additionally, they are not backward in understanding the work of Jesus, either. They can see how Christ was the Substitute for His people and stood in their place. Neither do they for one moment impugn any doctrine concerning God's Spirit, but they are not clear about the aforementioned point. They can talk about the other points better than they can about those that more particularly concern the blessed work of that all-adorable person of the Godhead, God the Holy Spirit.

I thought, therefore, that I would preach as simply as ever I could about the work of the Holy Spirit and begin at the beginning. I hope, at other times, as God the Holy Spirit will guide me, to enter more fully into the subject of the work of the Spirit from the beginning to the end.

However, let me say that it is no use your expecting me to preach a series of sermons. I know a great deal better than that. I don't believe God the Holy Spirit ever intended men to publish three months beforehand lists of sermons that they were going to preach because there always will arise changes in providence, and different states of mind both in the preacher and the hearer, and he will be a very wise man who has an Old Moore's Almanack* correct enough to let him know what would be the best sort of sermon to preach three months ahead. He had better leave it to his God to give him in the same hour what he will speak and look for his sermons as the Israelites looked for the manna, day by day. (See Exodus 16:14–27.) However, we now begin by endeavoring to narrate the different points of the Spirit's work in the beginning of salvation.

Salvation Begins with the Work of the Holy Spirit

Not by Means of Grace Alone

First, let me start by asserting that salvation is not begun in the soul by the means of grace apart from the

---

* Authored by Francis Moore [1657–1715]. First edition was published in 1697.

Holy Spirit. No man in the world is at liberty to neglect the means that God has appointed. If a house is built for prayer, no man must expect a blessing who neglects to tread its floor. If a pulpit is erected for the ministry of the Word, no man must expect (although we do sometimes get more than we expect) to be saved except by the hearing of the Word. If the Bible is printed in our own native language, and we can read it, he who neglects the Holy Scripture and ceases from its study has lost one great and grand opportunity of being blessed. There are many means of grace, and let us speak as highly of them as ever we can. We would be far from depreciating them, for they are of the highest value. Blessed are the people who have them, and happy is the nation that is blessed with the means of grace. Yet, my friends, no one was ever saved by the means of grace apart from the Holy Spirit.

You may hear the sermons of the man whom God delights to honor; you may select from all your Puritan clergy the writings of the man whom God has blessed with a double portion of His Holy Spirit; you may attend every meeting for prayer; you may turn over the leaves of the blessed Book; but in all this, there is no life for the soul apart from the breath of the Divine Spirit. Use these means; we exhort you to use them, and use them diligently, but recollect that in none of these means is there anything that can benefit you unless God the Holy Spirit will own and crown them. These are like the conduit pipes of the marketplace. When the fountainhead flows with water, then they are full, and we derive a blessing from them; but if the stream is blocked, if the fountainhead ceases to give forth its current, then these are wells without water, clouds without rain. You may go to ordinances as an Arab turns to his skin bottle when it is dry, and with your parched lips you may suck the wind and drink the whirlwind, but receive neither comfort, blessing, nor instruction from the means of grace.

Not through Ministers or Priests

Nor is the salvation of any sinner begun in him by a minister or a priest. God forgive the man who ever calls himself a priest or allows anyone else to call him that since the days of our Lord Jesus. The other morning, at family prayer, I read the case of King Uzziah, who, because he was the king, thrust himself into the tabernacle of the Lord to take the place of the priests. You remember how the priests opposed him and said, *"It appertaineth not unto thee, Uzziah, to burn incense unto the* Lord, *but to the priests the sons of Aaron, that are consecrated to burn incense"* (2 Chronicles 26:18). Remember how he seized the censer and angrily insisted on burning incense as a priest before the Lord God. While he was still speaking, leprosy appeared on his face, and he went out a leper, as white as snow, from the house of God.

Oh, my friends, it is no small offense against God for any man to call himself a priest. All the saints have a priestly office through Christ Jesus, but when any man asserts the idea that he has a calling that elevates him above his fellowman, and he claims to be a priest among men, he commits a sin before God. Even though it is a sin of ignorance, it is indeed great and grievous and leads to many deadly errors, the guilt of which must lie partly upon the head of the man who gave a basis for those errors by allowing the title to be applied to himself.

Well, there is no man—call him priest if you like, by way of ill courtesy—who can begin the work with us—no, not in the use of the ceremony. The Papist may tell us that grace begins in the heart at the dropping of the water upon the child's brow; but he tells a lie, a lie before God, that does not have even so much as the shadow of truth to justify the liar. There is no power in man, even if he was ordained by one who could most assuredly claim succession from the apostles, even if he was endowed with miraculous gifts, or even if he was the apostle Paul himself. If he asserted that he had in himself the power to convert or the power to regenerate, let him be accursed, for he has denied the truth, and Paul himself would have declared him *"Anathema ["accursed,"* NJKV]*"* (1 Corinthians 16:22) for having departed from the everlasting Gospel, one cardinal point of which is that regeneration is the work of God the Holy Spirit; the new birth is a thing that is from above.

Not by Self-Efforts

And, my brothers and sisters, it is quite certain that no man ever begins the new birth himself. The work of salvation never started with the efforts of any man. God the Holy Spirit must begin it. Now, the reasons why no man ever started the work of grace in his own heart are very apparent: first, because he cannot; second, because he won't. The best reason of all is that he cannot; he is dead. The dead may be made alive, but the dead cannot make themselves alive, for the dead can do nothing. Besides, the new thing to be created as yet has no being. The uncreated cannot create. Yet you say, "Man can create." Well, if hell can create heaven, then sin can create grace.

What! Will you tell me that fallen human nature, which has come almost to a level with the beasts, is competent to rival God? Can it emulate the Divinity in working as great marvels and in imparting as divine a life as God Himself can give? It cannot. Besides, it is a creation; we are created anew in Christ Jesus (2 Corinthians 5:17). Let any man create a fly, and afterward let him create a new heart in himself; until he has done the lesser thing, he cannot do the greater. Besides, no man will. If any man could convert himself, there is no man who would. If any man says that he would, if that is true, he is already converted, for the will to be converted is in great part conversion. The will to love God, the desire to be in unison with

Christ, is not to be found in any man who has not already been brought to be reconciled with God through the death of His Son. There may be a false desire, a desire grounded upon a misrepresentation of the truth, but a true desire after true salvation by the true Spirit is a certain indication that the salvation already is there in the germ and in the bud, and needs only time and grace to develop itself. It is certain that man neither can nor will save himself—being on the one hand utterly helpless and dead, and on the other hand utterly depraved and unwilling, hating the change when he sees it in others, and most of all despising it in himself. Be certain, therefore, that God the Holy Spirit must begin the work, since no one else can do so.

What the Holy Spirit Does

And now, my brothers and sisters, I must enter into the subject very briefly by showing what the Holy Spirit does in the beginning. Permit me to say that, in describing the work, the true work of salvation in the soul, you must not expect me to exhibit any critical distinction in judgment. We have heard of an assembly of clergymen who once debated whether men repented first or believed first. After a long discussion, someone wiser than the rest suggested another question: whether in the newborn child the lungs inflated first or the blood circulated first. "Now," said he, "when you find the answer to the one, you may be able to know the answer to the other."

You will not know which comes first—repenting or believing; they are, very likely, begotten in us at the same moment. We are not able, when we mention these things in order, exactly to declare and testify that these all happen according to the order in which we mention them. However, according to the judgment of men and to my own experience, I seek now to set forth what is the usual way that God the Holy Spirit acts in the work of salvation.

Regenerates the Soul

The first thing, then, that God the Holy Spirit does in the soul is to regenerate it. We must always learn to distinguish between regeneration and conversion. A man may be converted a great many times in his life, but regenerated only once. Conversion is a thing that is caused by regeneration, but regeneration is the very first act of God the Spirit in the soul. You ask, "Does regeneration come before conviction of sin?" Most certainly; there could be no conviction in the dead sinner. Now, regeneration quickens the sinner and makes him live. He is not competent to have true spiritual conviction worked in him until, first of all, he has received life. It is true that one of the earliest developments of life is conviction of sin, but before any man can see his need of a Savior, he must be a living man. Before he can really, I mean, in a spiritual position, in a saving, effective manner, understand his own deep depravity, he must have eyes with which to see the depravity; he must have ears with which to hear the sentence of the law. He must have been quickened and made alive; otherwise, he could not be capable of feeling, seeing, or discerning at all.

I believe, then, that the first thing the Spirit does is this: He finds the sinner dead in sin, just where Adam left him; He breathes into him a divine influence. The sinner knows nothing about how it is done, nor do any of us understand it. As the Scripture says,

> The wind bloweth where it listeth, and thou hearest the sound thereof, but canst not tell whence it cometh, and whither it goeth: so is every one that is born of the Spirit. (John 3:8)

Now, none of us can tell how the Holy Spirit works in men. I do not doubt there have been some who have sat in church, and in the middle of a sermon or in prayer or in singing—they did not understand how it happened—the Spirit of God was in their hearts. He had entered their souls, and they were no longer dead in sin, no longer without thought, without hope, without spiritual capacity, but they had begun to live. And I believe this work of regeneration, when it is done effectively—and God the Spirit would not do it without doing it effectively—is done mysteriously, often suddenly, and it is done in various ways, but still it always has this mark about it: The man, although he may not understand how it is done, feels that something is done. The what, the how, he does not know, but he knows that something is done, and he now begins to think thoughts he never thought before. He begins to feel as he never felt before. He is brought into a new state; there is a change worked in him—as if a dead post standing in the street were suddenly to find itself possessed of a soul and to hear the sound of the passing carriages, to listen to the words of the passengers. There is something quite new about it.

The fact is, the man does have a spirit; he never had one before; he was nothing but a body and a soul; but now, God has breathed into him the third great principle, the new life, the Spirit, and he has become a spiritual man. Now, he is not only capable of mental exercise, but also of spiritual exercise.

Having a soul, he could repent, and he could believe. As a mere mental exercise, he could think thoughts of God and have some desires after Him, but he could not have one spiritual thought or one spiritual wish or desire, for he has no powers that could elicit these things. Yet now, in regeneration, he has something given to him, and being given, you soon see its effects. The man begins to feel that he is a sinner. Why did he not feel that before? Ah, my brothers and sisters, he could not. He was not in a state to feel; he was a dead sinner. And though he used to tell you, and tell God, by way of a compliment, that he was a sinner, he did not know anything about it. He said he was a sinner, but he talked about being a sinner just as the blind man talks about the stars that he has never seen, as he talks about the light, the existence of which he would not know unless he were told of it; but now it is a deep reality. You may laugh at him, you who have not been regenerated, but now he has something that really puts him beyond your laughter. He begins to feel the exceeding weight and evil of transgression; his heart trembles, his very flesh quivers—in some cases, his whole frame is affected. The man is sick by day and night. The flesh on his bones creeps for fear. His appetite fails him, and he cannot eat. He cannot bear the sound of melody and mirth. All his fleshly spirits are dried up. He cannot rejoice. He is unhappy, miserable, downcast, distressed, and, in some cases, almost ready to go mad. Although, in the majority of cases, it takes a less intense form, and there are the gentle whispers of the Spirit; even then, the pangs and pains caused by regeneration while the new life reveals the sin and evil of the past condition of the man are things that are not to be well described or mentioned without tears. This is all the work of the Spirit.

Reveals Man's Inability to Save Himself

Having brought the soul thus far, the next thing the Holy Spirit does is to teach the soul that it is utterly incapable of saving itself. The man knew that before, perhaps, if he sat under a Gospel ministry, but he heard it only with his ears and understood it with his mind. Now, it has become part of his very life. He feels it; it has entered into his soul, and he knows it to be true. Once he thought he would be good and thought that would save him. The Holy Spirit just knocks the brains out of that thought. "Then," he says, "I will try ceremonies and see whether I cannot gain merit in that way." God the Holy Spirit shoots the arrow right through the heart of that thought, and it falls dead before him. He cannot bear the sight of the carcass, so that, like Abraham said of Sarah, he exclaims, "Bury the dead out of my sight." (See Genesis 23:2–11.) Though once he loved it dearly, now he hates the sight thereof. He thought once that he could believe; he had an Arminian* notion in his head that he could believe when he liked and repent when he liked. Now God the Spirit has brought him to such a condition that he says, "I can do nothing." He begins to discover his own death, now that he is made alive. He did not know anything about it before. He now finds that he has no hand of faith to lift, though the minister tells him to do it. He now discovers, when he is told to pray, that he wants to, but he cannot. He now finds that he is powerless, and he dies in the hand of God like clay in the hand of the potter, and is made to cry out, "O Lord, my God, unless You save me, I am damned for all eternity, for I cannot lift a finger in this matter until first of all You give me strength." And if you urge him to do anything, he longs to be doing, but he is so afraid that it would be only fleshly doings, and not the doings of the Spirit, that he meditates, stops, and waits, until he groans and cries. Feeling that these groans and cries are the real work of the Spirit and proof that he has spiritual life, he then begins in earnest to look to Jesus Christ, the Savior. Note that all these things are caused by the Spirit, and none of them can ever be produced in the soul of any man or woman, apart from the divine influence of God the Holy Spirit.

Applies the Blood

This being done, the soul, weaned from all confidence, despairing, and brought to its last standing place, lies

---

* Dutch theologian Jacob Arminius [1560–1609] opposed the Calvinists' beliefs in absolute predestination, irresistible grace, and the inability to fall from grace. Arminians believe in a conditional predestination, man's ability to resist or respond to grace out of his free will, and the possibility of salvation for all.

prostrate on the ground. The rope is tied about its neck, and the ashes and sackcloth are on its head. God the Holy Spirit next applies the blood of Jesus to the soul, gives it the grace of faith whereby it lays hold of Jesus, and gives it an anointing of holy consolation and unction of assurance, whereby, casting itself wholly on the blood and righteousness of Jesus, it receives joy, knows itself to be saved, and rejoices in pardon.

Yet note, that is the work of the Spirit. Some preachers will tell their people, "Believe; only believe." Yes, it is right that they should tell them so, but they should remember that it is also right to tell them that even this must be the work of the Spirit. For although we say, "Only believe," that is the greatest only in the world. What some men say is so easy is just what those who want to believe find to be the hardest thing in all the world. It is simple enough for a man who has the Spirit in him to believe, when he has the written Word before him and the witness of the Spirit in him; that is easy enough. However, for the poor, tried sinner who cannot see anything in the Word of God but thunder and threatening—for him to believe—ah, my brothers and sisters, it is not such a little matter as some make it to be. The fullness of the power of God's Spirit is needed to bring any man to such faith as that.

Avails the Soul of Blessings

When the sinner has thus believed, then the Holy Spirit brings all the precious things to him. There is the blood of Jesus. The blood can never save my soul unless God the Spirit takes it and sprinkles it upon my conscience. There is the perfect, spotless righteousness of Jesus. It is a robe that will fit me and adorn me from head to foot, but it is no use to me until I have put it on, and I cannot put it on myself. God the Holy Spirit must put the robe of Jesus' righteousness on me. There is the covenant of adoption, whereby God gives me the privileges of a son, but I cannot rejoice in my adoption until I receive *"the Spirit of adoption, whereby [I] cry, Abba, Father"* (Romans 8:15). So, beloved, you see—I might enlarge on these truths, but my time fails me—you see that every point that is brought out in the experience of the newborn Christian, every point in that part of salvation that we may call its beginning in the soul, has to do with God the Holy Spirit.

No step can be taken without Him. Nothing can be accomplished right without Him. Even though you had the best of means, the rightest of ceremonies, the most orthodox of truths; though you exercised your minds upon all these things; though the blood of Jesus Christ were shed for you, and God Himself had ordained you from before the foundation of the world to be saved, still that one link always must be inserted in the golden chain of the plan of salvation; for without that, it would all be incomplete. You must be quickened by the Spirit; you must be called out of darkness into light; you must be made *"a new creature"* (2 Corinthians 5:17) in Christ Jesus.

Excuses Fall Short

Now, I wonder how many of you know anything about this. That is the practical part of it. My friend, do you understand this? Perhaps you are exceedingly wise, and you turn on your heel with a sneer. You say, "Supernaturalism in one of its phases—these Methodists are always talking about supernatural things." You are very wise, no doubt, but it seems to me that Nicodemus of old had gotten as far as you, and you have gone no further than he. He asked, *"How can a man be born when he is old?"* (John 3:4). And though every Sunday school child has had a smile at the expense of Nicodemus's ignorance, you are not wiser. And yet you are a Rabbi, sir, and you would teach us, would you? (See verse 10.) You would teach us about these things, and yet you sneer about supernaturalism. Well, the day may come—I pray it may come to you before the day of your death and your doom—when the Christ of the supernaturalists will be the only Christ for you; when you will come into the floods of death, where you will need something more than nature. Then you will be crying for a work within your heart that is supernatural. It may be that, then, when you first of all awake to know that your wisdom was but one of the methods of madness, you may perhaps have to cry in vain, having for your only answer, "I called, and you refused; I stretched out my hands, and no man regarded. I also will mock at your calamity and laugh when your fear comes." (See Proverbs 1:24, 26.)

I hear another of you say, "Well, sir, I know nothing of this work of God the Holy Spirit in my heart. I am just as good as other people. I never make a profession of religion; it is very rarely that I go into a place of worship at all, but I am as good as the saints, any of them. Look at some of them—very fine fellows, certainly."

Stop, now. Religion is a thing between you and your Maker, and you have nothing to do with those very fine fellows you have spoken of. Suppose I make a confession that a large number of those who are called saints deserve a great deal more to be called sinners double-dyed and then whitewashed. Suppose I make a confession of that. What has that to do with you? Your religion must be for yourself, and it must be between you and your God. If all the world were hypocrites, that would not exonerate you before your God. When you came before the Master, if you were still at enmity with Him, could you venture to plead such an excuse as this: "All the world was full of hypocrites"? "Well," He would say, "what did that have to do with you? So much the more why you should have been an honest man. If you say the church was drifting away into quicksand through the evil conduct and folly of the members thereof, so much the more why you should have helped to make it sound, if you thought you could have done so."

Another cries, "Well, I do not see that I need it. I am as moral a man as I can be. I never break the Sabbath. I am one of the most conscientious of Christians. I always go to church twice on Sunday. I listen to a thoroughly evangelical minister, and you would not find fault with him." Perhaps another says, "I go to a Baptist chapel. I am always found there, and I am scrupulously correct in my conduct. I am a good father, a good husband. I do not know that any man can find fault with me in business." Well, certainly, that is very good, and if you will be so good tomorrow morning as to go into Saint Paul's and wash one of those statues until you make it alive, then you will be saved by your morality. However, since you, even you, are *dead in trespasses and sins*" (Ephesians 2:1), without the Spirit you may wash yourself ever so clean, but you cannot wash life into you any more than those statues, by all your washing, could be made to walk or think or breathe. You must be quickened by the Holy Spirit, for you are dead in trespasses and sins.

Yes, my lovely young woman, you who are everything excellent; you who are not to be blamed in anything; you who are affectionate, tender, kind, and dutiful, your very life seems to be so pure that all who see you think that you are an angel. Yet even you, unless you are born again, cannot see the kingdom of God. The golden gate of heaven must grind upon its hinges with a doleful sound and shut you out forever unless you are the subject of a divine change, for this requirement permits no exception.

And, you, vilest of the vile, you who have wandered farthest from the paths of righteousness, *"ye must be born again"* (John 3:7); you must be quickened by a divine life. It is comforting for you to remember that the very same power that can awaken the moral man, that can save the righteous and honest man, is able to work in you, is able to change you. This power can turn a lion into a lamb, and a raven into a dove.

Oh, my readers, ask yourselves, are you the subjects of this change? If you are, rejoice with joy unspeakable, for happy is that mother's child, and full of glory, who can say, "I am born of God." Blessed is that man. God and the holy angels call him blessed who has received the quickening of the Spirit and is born of God. For him there may be many troubles, but there is *"a far more exceeding and eternal weight of glory"* (2 Corinthians 4:17) to counterbalance all his woe; for him there may be wars and fightings, but let him wait. There are trumpets of victory, there are better wreaths than the laurels of conquerors, there is a crown of immortal glory, there is bliss unfading, there is acceptance in the heart of God and perpetual fellowship with Jehovah. Yet, oh, if you are not born again, I can but tremble for you and lift my heart in prayer to God and pray for you that He may now, by His Divine Spirit, make you alive, show you your need of Him, and then direct you to the Cross of Jesus.

However, if you know your need of a Savior, if you are conscious of your death in sin, listen to the Gospel. The Lord Jesus Christ died for you. Do you know yourself to be guilty, not as the hypocrite pretends to know it, but do you know it consciously, sensitively? Do you weep over it? Do you lament it? Do you feel that you cannot save yourself? Are you sick of all fleshly ways of saving? Can you say, right now, "Unless God reaches out His hand of mercy, I know I deserve to be lost forever, and I am"? Then, as the Lord my God lives, before whom I stand, my Master bought you with His blood; and those whom He bought with His blood, He will have; from the fangs of the lion and the jaws of the bear He will pluck them. He will save you, for you are a part of His bloody purchase. He has taken your sins upon His head; He suffered in your place. He has been punished for you. You will not die; "your sins, which are many, are all forgiven." (See Luke 7:47.) I am the Master's glad herald to tell you what His Word tells you, also: You may rejoice in the fullness of faith, for *"Christ Jesus came into the world to save sinners"* (1 Timothy 1:15), and *"this is a faithful saying, and worthy of all acceptation"* (v. 15). May the Lord now be pleased to add His blessing, for Jesus' sake.

Chapter 2

The Necessity of the Work of the Spirit

I will put my spirit within you.
—Ezekiel 36:27

T he miracles of Christ are remarkable, in part, because none of them were unnecessary. The pretended miracles of Muhammad, and of the Church of Rome, even if they had been miracles, would have been acts of folly. Suppose that St. Denis* *had* walked with his head in his hand after it had been cut off; what practical purpose would have been served by that? He would certainly have been quite as well off in his grave, for any practical good he could have conferred on men.

The miracles of Christ were never unnecessary. They were not capricious demonstrations of power. It is true that they were displays of power, but all of them had a practical end. The same thing may be said of the promises of God. Not one promise in the Scripture may be regarded as a mere whim of grace. As every miracle was necessary, absolutely necessary, so is every promise that is given in

---

* Italian missionary to Paris, France. He was beheaded circa A.D. 258, and his body was thrown into the Seine River. A legend that came out of his martyrdom was that he carried his severed head some distance beyond his execution site.

the Word of God. Hence, from the text that is before us, may I draw, and I think I may very conclusively, the argument that, if God in His covenant made with His people has promised to put His Spirit within them, it must be absolutely necessary that this promise should have been made, and it must be absolutely necessary also to our salvation that every one of us should receive the Spirit of God.

This topic will be the subject of my discourse. I will not hope to make it very interesting, except to those who are anxiously longing to know the way of salvation.

We start, then, by laying down this proposition: that the work of the Holy Spirit is absolutely necessary to us, if we would be saved.

Consider Man's Nature

In endeavoring to prove our need of the Holy Spirit, I would first of all state that the need is very obvious if we remember what man is by nature. Some say that man may, through his own efforts, attain salvation—that if he hears the Word, it is in his power to receive it, to believe it, and to have a saving change worked in him by it.

To this we reply, You do not know what man is by nature; otherwise, you would never have ventured to make such an assertion. Holy Scripture tells us that man by nature is *"dead in trespasses and sins"* (Ephesians 2:1). It does not say that he is sick; that he is faint; that he has grown callous, hardened, and seared, but it says he is absolutely dead. Whatever the term *death* means in connection with the body, it also means in connection with man's soul, viewing it in its relation to spiritual things. When the body is dead, it is powerless. It is unable to do anything for itself. And when the soul of man is dead, in a spiritual sense, it must be, if there is any meaning in the comparison, utterly and entirely powerless and unable to

203

do anything of itself or for itself. When you see dead men raising themselves from their graves, unwinding their own shrouds, opening their own coffin lids, and walking down the streets alive and animate as the result of their own powers, then perhaps you will believe that souls that are dead in sin may turn to God, may recreate their own natures, and may make themselves heirs of heaven, though before they were heirs of wrath. But note, not until then.

The substance of the Gospel is that man is dead in sin and that divine life is God's gift. You must go contrary to the whole meaning before you can suppose that a man is brought to know and love Christ apart from the work of the Holy Spirit.

The Spirit finds men as destitute of spiritual life as Ezekiel's dry bones. He brings bone to bone, fits the skeletons together, and then comes from the four winds and breathes into the slain, and they live and stand upon their feet, an exceeding great army, and worship God. (See Ezekiel 37:4–10.) Yet apart from that, apart from the vivifying influence of the Spirit of God, men's souls must lie in the valley of dry bones, dead, and dead forever.

Scripture not only tells us that man is dead in sin, but also something worse than this, namely, that he is utterly and entirely averse to everything that is good and right. *"The carnal mind is enmity against God: for it is not subject to the law of God, neither indeed can be"* (Romans 8:7).

Look all through Scripture, and you will find continually that the will of man is described as being contrary to the things of God. What did Christ say to those who imagined that men would come to God without divine influence? He said, first, *"No man can come to me, except the Father which hath sent me draw him"* (John 6:44). However, He said something even stronger: *"Ye will not come to me, that ye might have life"* (John 5:40).

No one will come. Here lies the deadly trouble; man is not only powerless to do good, but also powerful enough to do what is wrong, and his will is desperately set against everything that is right. Men will not come. They will never come of themselves. You cannot induce them to come. You cannot force them to come by all your clamorous warnings, nor can you entice them to come by all your gentle invitations. They will not come to Christ that they may have life. Until the Spirit draws them, neither will they come, nor can they come.

Therefore, from the fact that man's nature is hostile to the Divine Spirit, that he hates grace, that he despises the way in which grace is brought to him, that it is contrary to his own proud nature to stoop to receive salvation by the deeds of another, it is necessary that the Spirit of God should operate to change the will, to correct the bias of the heart, to set man on a right track and then give him strength to run on it. Oh, if you read men and understand them, you cannot help being sound on the point of the necessity of the Holy Spirit's work.

It has been well said by a noted writer that he never knew a man who believed any great theological error who did not also support a doctrine that diminished the depravity of man. It is true that the Arminian believes that man is fallen, but then he says that man has the power of his free will left, and that he can raise himself. He diminishes the desperate character of the fall of man.

On the other hand, the Antinomian says that man cannot do anything. However, he also says that man is not at all responsible and is not bound to do it. It is not his duty to believe or to repent. Thus, you see, he also diminishes the sinfulness of man and does not have the right view of the Fall.

Once you understand the correct view, that man is utterly fallen, powerless, guilty, defiled, lost, condemned, then you must be sound on all points of the great Gospel of

Jesus Christ. Once you believe man to be what Scripture says he is—once you believe that his heart is depraved, his affections perverted, his understanding darkened, his will perverse—you must hold that, if such a wretch as that is saved, it must be as a result of the work of the Spirit of God, and of the Spirit of God alone.

Consider the Means of Salvation

Salvation must be the work of the Spirit in us because the means used in salvation are of themselves inadequate to accomplish the work. And what are the means of salvation?

Preaching

First and foremost stands the preaching of the Word of God. More men are brought to Christ by preaching than by anything else, for it is God's chief and first instrument. The Word is the *"sword of the Spirit"* (Ephesians 6:17), *"quick, and powerful, and sharper than any twoedged sword, piercing even to the dividing asunder of soul and spirit, and of the joints and marrow"* (Hebrews 4:12). *"It pleased God by the foolishness of preaching to save them that believe"* (1 Corinthians 1:21).

Yet what is there in preaching, by which souls are saved, that looks as if it would be the means of saving souls? I could point you to various churches and chapels into which you might step and say, "Here is an educated minister; indeed, he is a man who would instruct and enlighten the intellect." You sit down and say, "Well, if God means to work a great work, he will use a learned man like this."

However, do you know any learned men who are used as the means of bringing souls to Christ, to any great degree? Go around to your churches, if you please, and look at them, and then answer the question. Do you know any great men—men great in learning and wisdom—who have become spiritual fathers in our Israel? Is it not a fact that stares us in the face that our fashionable preachers, our eloquent preachers, our learned preachers, are nearly useless for the winning of souls to Christ?

And where are souls born to God? Why, in the house around which the jeers and the scoffing and the sneers of the world have long gathered. Sinners are converted under the man whose eloquence is rough and homely, the one who has nothing to commend him to his fellowmen, who daily has to fall on his knees and confess his own folly. When the world speaks worst of him, he feels that he deserves it all, since he is nothing but an earthen vessel in which God is pleased to put His heavenly treasure (2 Corinthians 4:7). I will dare to say that, in every age of the world, the most despised ministry has been the most useful. Today, I could show you poor Primitive Methodist preachers, who can scarcely speak correct English, who have been the fathers of more souls and who have brought to Christ more people than any one bishop on the bench. Why, the Lord has always been pleased to make it so. He will clothe the weak and the foolish with power, but He will not clothe with power those who, if good were done, might be led to ascribe the excellence of the power to their learning, their eloquence, or their position. Like the apostle Paul, it is every minister's business to glory in his infirmities (2 Corinthians 12:9).

The world says, "Pshaw on your oratory! It is rough, rude, and eccentric." Yet, even so, we are content, for God blesses it. Then so much the better that it has infirmities in it, for now it will be plainly seen that it is not of man or by man, but the work of God, and of God alone.

It is said that once upon a time a man was exceedingly curious to see the sword with which a mighty hero had fought some desperate battles. Casting his eye along the blade, he said, "Well, I don't see much in this sword."

"No," said the hero, "but you have not examined the arm that wields it."

And so, when men come to hear a successful minister, they are apt to say, "I do not see anything in him." No, but you have not examined the eternal arm that reaps its harvest with this sword of the Spirit. If you had looked at the jawbone of the ass in Samson's hand (see Judges 15:15–17), you would have said, "What! You cannot accomplish anything with this! Bring out some polished blade; bring forth the Damascus steel!"

No, for God would have all the glory; therefore, not with polished steel, but with a jawbone, Samson won the victory. So it is with ministers. Usually, God has blessed the weakest to do the most good. Does it not follow from this observation that it must be the work of the Spirit? If there is nothing in the instrument that can lead to the ends, is it not the work of the Spirit when the thing is accomplished?

Let me put it to you this way. Under the ministry, dead souls are quickened, sinners are made to repent, the vilest of sinners are made holy, and men who came determined not to believe are compelled to believe. Now, who does this? If you say the ministry does it, then I say farewell to your reason, because there is nothing in the successful ministry that would support your position. It must be that the Spirit works in man through the ministry or else such deeds would never be accomplished. You might as well expect to raise the dead by whispering in their ears, as hope to save souls by preaching to them, if it were not for the agency of the Spirit.

Melanchthon went out to preach, you know, without the Spirit of the Lord, and he thought he would convert all the people, but he found out at last that old Adam was too strong for young Melanchthon. He had to go back and ask for the help of the Holy Spirit before he ever saw a soul saved.

I say, the fact that the ministry is blessed proves, since there is nothing in the ministry, that salvation must be the work of a Higher Power.

Baptism and the Lord's Supper

Other means, however, are used to bless men's souls. For instance, the two ordinances of baptism and the Lord's Supper are a rich means of grace. Yet let me ask you: Is there anything in baptism that can possibly bless anybody? Can immersion in water have the slightest tendency to be blessed to the soul? And then with regard to the eating of bread and the drinking of wine at the Lord's Supper, can it by any means be conceived by any rational man that there is anything in the mere piece of bread that we eat or in the wine that we drink? And yet, undoubtedly, the grace of God does go with both ordinances for the confirming of the faith of those who receive them, and even for the conversion of those who look upon the ceremonies. There must be something, then, beyond the outward ceremony; there must, in fact, be the Spirit of God, witnessing through the water, witnessing through the wine, witnessing through the bread, or otherwise none of these things could be the means of grace to our souls. They could not edify; they could not help us to commune with Christ; they could not tend to the conviction of sinners or to the establishment of saints. There must, then, from these facts, be a higher, unseen, mysterious influence—the influence of the divine Spirit of God.

Consider the Works of God the Father and God the Son

Let me remind you, in the third place, that the absolute necessity of the work of the Holy Spirit in the heart may be clearly seen in that all that has been done by God the Father, and all that has been done by God the Son, must be ineffectual to us unless the Spirit reveals these things to our souls.

First, we believe that God the Father elects His people. From *"before the foundation of the world"* (Ephesians 1:4), He has chosen us to Himself, but let me ask you: What effect does the doctrine of election have on any man until the Spirit of God enters into him? How do I know whether God has chosen me from *"before the foundation of the world"*? How can I possibly know? Can I climb to heaven and read the roll? Is it possible for me to force my way through the thick mists that hide eternity, open the seven seals of the Book (Revelation 5:1), and read my name recorded there?

Ah, no! Election is a dead letter both in my consciousness and in any effect that it can produce upon me, until the Spirit of God calls me *"out of darkness into his marvellous light"* (1 Peter 2:9). And then, through my calling, I see my election, and, knowing that I have been called by God, I know that I have been chosen by God from *"before the foundation of the world."*

It is a precious thing—this doctrine of election—to a child of God. Yet what makes it precious? Nothing but the influence of the Spirit. Until the Spirit opens the eyes to read, until the Spirit imparts the mystical secret, no heart can know its election. No angel ever revealed to any man that he was chosen by God, but the Spirit does it. He, by His divine workings, bears an infallible witness with our spirits that we are born of God (Romans 8:16). Then we are enabled to "read our title clear to mansions in the skies."

Look, again, at the covenant of grace. We know that there was a covenant made with the Lord Jesus Christ by His Father from before the foundation of the world, and that, in this covenant, the persons of all His people were given to Him and were secured. Yet of what use, or of what avail, is the covenant to us, until the Holy Spirit brings the blessings of the covenant to us? The covenant is, as it were, a holy tree, laden with fruit. If the Spirit does not shake that tree and make the fruit fall from it so that it comes within our reach, how can we receive it?

Bring any sinner here and tell him that there is a covenant of grace. Of what advantage is that knowledge to him? "Ah," he says, "I may not be included in it. My name may not be recorded there. I may not be chosen in Christ." However, let the Spirit of God dwell in his heart richly, by the faith and the love that is in Christ Jesus, and that man sees the covenant, *"ordered in all things, and sure"* (2 Samuel 23:5), and he cries with David, *"This is all my salvation, and all my desire"* (v. 5).

Take, again, the redemption of Christ. We know that Christ stood in the room, place, and stead of all His people, and that all those who will appear in heaven will appear there as an act of justice as well as of grace, seeing that Christ was punished in their stead, and that it would be unjust if God punished them, seeing that He had punished Christ for them. We believe that since Christ paid all their debts, they have a right to their freedom in Christ— that since Christ covered them with His righteousness, they are entitled to eternal life as much as if they themselves had been perfectly holy. Yet of what avail is this to me, until the Spirit takes of the things of Christ and shows them to me?

What is Christ's blood to any of you until you have received the Spirit of grace? You have heard the minister preach about the blood of Christ a thousand times, but you passed by; it was nothing to you that Jesus died. You know that He atoned for sins that were not His own, but you regarded this knowledge as only a tale, perhaps, even an idle tale. However, when the Spirit of God led you to the Cross, opened your eyes, and enabled you to see Christ crucified, ah, then, there was something in the blood, indeed. When His hand dipped the hyssop in the blood, and when it applied that blood to your spirit, then there was a joy and peace in believing, such as you had never known before. Yet, my friend, Christ's dying is nothing to you unless you have a living Spirit within you. Christ brings you no advantage—saving, personal, and lasting—unless the Spirit of God has baptized you in the fountain filled with Christ's blood and washed you from head to foot therein.

I mention only these few, out of the many blessings of the covenant, just to prove that they are, none of them, of any use to us unless the Holy Spirit gives them to us. There hang the blessings on the nail—on the nail, Christ Jesus; but we are short of stature. We cannot reach them. The Spirit of God takes them down and gives them to us, and there they are; they are ours. They are like the manna in the skies, far out of mortal reach; but the Spirit of God opens the windows of heaven, brings down the bread, puts it to our lips, and enables us to eat. Christ's blood and righteousness are like wine stored in a wine vat that we cannot get to. The Holy Spirit dips our containers into this precious wine, and then we drink. Without the Spirit, we would die and perish, even though the Father elected and the Son redeemed, as though the Father never had elected, and as though the Son never had bought us with His blood. The Spirit is absolutely necessary. Without Him, the works of neither the Father nor the Son are of any avail to us.

Consider the Experiences of Christians

This brings us to another point. The experience of the true Christian is a reality, but it can never be known and felt without the Spirit of God. For what is the experience of the Christian? Let me give just a brief picture of some of its scenes.

Recognizing His Lost State

A person comes into church one morning. He is one of the most reputable men in London. He has never committed any outward vice; he has never been dishonest. He is known as a staunch, upright tradesman. Now, to his astonishment, he is informed that he is a condemned, lost sinner, and just as surely lost as the thief who died for his crimes upon the cross.

Do you think that man will believe it? Suppose, however, that he does believe it, simply because he reads it in the Bible. Do you think he will ever be made to feel it? I know you say, "Impossible!" Some of you, even now, perhaps, are saying, "Well, I never would!" Can you imagine that honorable, upright businessman saying, *"God be merciful to me a sinner"* (Luke 18:13)—while he stands side by side with the prostitute and the swearer? Can you imagine him feeling in his own heart that he was as guilty as they, and using the same prayer and saying, "Lord, save, or I perish"?

You cannot conceive it, can you? It is contrary to nature that a man who has been as good as he should put himself down among the chief of sinners. Yet that will be done before he will be saved; he must feel that guilty before he can enter heaven. Now, I ask, who can bring him to such a leveling experience as that, except for the Spirit of God? You know very well that his proud nature will not stoop to it. We are all aristocrats in our own righteousness; we do not like to bend down and come among common sinners. If we are brought there, it must be the Spirit of God who casts us to the ground.

Why, I know that if anyone had told me that I would ever cry to God for mercy and confess that I had been the vilest of the vile, I would have laughed in his face. I would have said, "Why, I have not done anything particularly wrong. I have not hurt anybody." And yet I know this very day that I can take my place on the lowest form, and if I can get inside heaven, I will feel happy to sit among the chief of sinners and praise the almighty love that has saved even me from my sins.

Now, what works this humiliation of heart? Grace. It is contrary to nature for an honest and upright man in the eyes of the world to consider himself to be a lost sinner. It must be the Holy Spirit's work, or else it never will be done.

Relying on Christ's Righteousness

After a man has been brought to this place, can you conceive that man at last conscience-stricken and led to believe that his past life deserves the wrath of God? His first thought would be, "Well, now, I will live better than I have ever lived." He would say, "Now I will try to play the hermit, pinch myself here and there, deny myself, and do penance; in that way, by paying attention to the outward ceremonies of religion, together with a high moral character, I do not doubt that I will blot out whatever slurs and stains there have been against me."

Can you imagine that man feeling that, if he ever gets to heaven, he will have to get there through the righteousness of another? "Through the righteousness of another?" he asks. "I don't want to be rewarded for what another man does—not I. If I go there, I will go there and take my chance. I will go there through what I do myself. Tell me something to do, and I will do it. I will be proud to do it, however humiliating it may be, so that I may at last win the love and esteem of God."

Now, can you conceive such a man as that brought to feel that he can do nothing—that, as good as he thinks he is, he cannot do anything whatsoever to merit God's love and favor? Do you think he will understand that, if he goes to heaven, he must go on the merits of what Christ did? Just the same as the drunkard must go there through the sacrifice of Christ, so this moral man must enter into life having nothing about him but Christ's perfect righteousness, and having been washed in the blood of Jesus. We say that this is so contrary to human nature, so diametrically opposed to all the instincts of our poor fallen humanity, that nothing but the Spirit of God can ever bring a man to strip himself of all self-righteousness, and of all reliance on his own strength, and compel him to rest and lean simply and wholly upon Jesus Christ the Savior.

Depending on God during Trials

These two examples would be sufficient to prove the necessity of the Holy Spirit to make a man a Christian. Yet now let me describe a Christian as he is after his conversion. Trouble comes, storms of trouble, and he looks the tempest in the face and says, "I know that all things work together for my good." (See Romans 8:28.) His children die, the partner of his heart is carried to the grave, and he says, "The Lord gave and the Lord has taken away; blessed be the name of the Lord." (See Job 1:21.) His farm fails, his crop is blighted, his business prospects are clouded, all his wealth seems to vanish, and he is left in poverty. He says,

> *Although the fig tree shall not blossom, neither shall fruit be in the vines; the labour of the olive shall fail, and the fields shall yield no meat; the flock shall be cut off from the fold, and there shall be no herd in the stalls: yet I will rejoice in the LORD, I will joy in the God of my salvation.* (Habakkuk 3:17–18)

Next, you see him laid upon a sick bed himself, and when he is there, he says, *"It is good for me that I have been afflicted; that I might learn thy statutes"* (Psalm 119:71). You see him approaching at last the dark valley of the shadow of death, and you hear him cry, *"Yea, though I walk through the valley of the shadow of death, I will fear no evil: for thou art with me; thy rod and thy staff they comfort me"* (Psalm 23:4).

Spurgeon on the Holy Spirit

I ask you, what makes this man calm in the midst of all these varied trials and personal troubles, if it is not the Spirit of God? Oh, you who doubt the influence of the Spirit, produce the same results without the Spirit. Go and live as Christians live, and die as Christians die. If you can show the same calm resignation, the same quiet joy, and the same firm belief that adverse things will, nevertheless, work together for good, then we may be, perhaps, at liberty to concede the point, but not until then. The high and noble experience of a Christian in times of trials and suffering proves that there must be the operation of the Spirit of God.

Delighting in God

Yet look at the Christian, too, in his joyous moments. He is rich. God has given him all his heart's desire on earth. Look at him. He says, "I do not value these things at all, except as they are the gifts of God. I hold to them loosely. Notwithstanding this house and home, and all these comforts, I am willing to depart and *'be with Christ; which is far better'* (Philippians 1:23). It is true that I lack nothing here on earth, but still, I feel that to die would be gain to me (v. 21), even though I would leave all these things behind." He holds earth loosely; he does not grasp it with a tight hand, but looks upon it all as dust—a thing that is to pass away. He takes but little pleasure therein, saying, "I've no abiding city here. I seek a city out of sight."

Note that man. He has plenty of room for pleasures in this world, but he drinks out of a higher cistern. His pleasure springs from things unseen. His happiest moments are when he can shut out all these good things and come to God as a poor guilty sinner. He delights in coming to Christ and entering into fellowship with Him, rising into nearness of access and confidence, and boldly approaching the throne of heavenly grace.

The Necessity of the Work of the Spirit

Now, what is it that keeps a man who has all these mercies from setting his heart upon the earth? It is a wonder, indeed, that a man who has gold and silver, flocks and herds, would not make these his god, but that he would still say,

> There's nothing round this spacious earth
> That suits my large desire;
> To boundless joy and solid mirth
> My nobler thoughts aspire.

"These are not my treasure; my treasure is in heaven, and in heaven only." What can do this? No mere moral virtue. No Stoic doctrine ever brought a man to such a place as this. No, it must be the work of the Spirit, and the work of the Spirit alone, that can lead a man to live in heaven while there is a temptation for him to live on earth.

I do not wonder that a poor man looks forward to heaven; he has nothing to look upon on earth. When there is a thorn in the nest, I do not wonder that the lark flies up, for there is no rest for him below. When you are beaten and chafed by trouble, no wonder you say,

> Jerusalem! my happy home!
> Name ever dear to me;
> When will my labors have an end,
> In joy, and peace, and thee?

Yet the greatest wonder is that, if you line the Christian's nest ever so softly, if you give him all the mercies of this life, you still cannot keep him from saying,

> To Jesus, the crown of my hope,
> My soul is in haste to be gone;
> Oh, bear me, ye cherubim, up,
> And waft me away to His throne.

Consider the Actions of a Christian

And now, last of all, the actions, the acceptable acts, of the Christian's life cannot be performed without the Spirit; hence, again, we need the Spirit of God.

Repentance

The first act of the Christian's life is repentance. Have you ever tried to repent? If so, if you tried without the Spirit of God, you know that to urge a man to repent without the promise of the Spirit to help him, is to urge him to do the impossible. A rock might as soon weep, and a desert might as soon blossom, as a sinner repent of his own accord. If God should offer heaven to man, simply upon the terms of repentance of sin, heaven would be as impossible to gain as it is by good works, for a man can no more repent by himself than he can perfectly keep God's law.

Repentance involves the very principle of perfect obedience to the law of God. It seems to me that in repentance there is the whole law solidified and condensed; and if a man can repent by himself, then there is no need of a Savior; he may as well try to reach heaven by climbing up the steep sides of Mount Sinai itself.

Faith

Faith is the next act in the divine life. Perhaps you think faith is very easy to exercise, but if you are ever brought to feel the burden of sin, you would not find it quite so light a labor. If you are ever brought into deep mire, where there is no possibility of standing, it is not so easy to put your feet on a rock, when the rock does not seem to be there. I find faith the easiest thing in the world to have when there is nothing in which to believe; but when I have room to exercise my faith, then I do not find I have as much strength to accomplish it.

Strength

As I talked one day with a countryman, he used this description: "In the middle of winter, I sometimes think how well I could mow; and in early spring, I think, oh, how I would like to reap! I feel ready for it. But when mowing time comes, and when reaping time comes, I find I do not have any strength to spare." In the same way, when you have no troubles, couldn't you mow them down at once? When you have no work to do, couldn't you do it? Yet when work and trouble come, you find how difficult they are.

Many Christians are like the stag who talked to itself, saying, "Why should I run away from the dogs? Look what a fine pair of horns I've got, and look what heels I've got, too. I might do these hounds some mischief. Why not stand and show them what I can do with my antlers? I can keep off any quantity of dogs." No sooner did the dogs bark than the stag took off running.

So it is with us. "Let sin arise," we say, "and we will soon rip it up and destroy it. Let trouble come, and we will soon get over it." However, when sin and trouble come, we then find what our weakness is. Then we have to cry for the help of the Spirit. Through Him, we can do all things (see Philippians 4:13); without Him, we can do nothing at all. In all the actions of the Christian's life, whether it is the act of consecrating oneself to Christ; the act of daily prayer; the act of constant submission, preaching the Gospel, ministering to the needs of the poor, or comforting the despondent—in all these things, the Christian finds his weakness and his powerlessness, unless he is clothed with the Spirit of God.

Effective Service

Why, I have been to see the sick at times, and I have thought how I would like to comfort them, but I could not get out a word that was worth their hearing, or worth my saying. My soul has been in agony to be the means of comforting a poor, sick, despondent brother, but I could do nothing. I left his room half wishing I had never been to see a sick person in my life. I have learned the lesson of my own inadequacy.

Often, this same lesson is learned in preaching. You prepare a sermon and study it, but then make the greatest mess in delivering it that can possibly be made. Then you say, "I wish I had never preached at all." Yet all this is to show us that neither in comforting nor in preaching can we do anything right, unless the Spirit works in us *to will and to do of his good pleasure"* (Philippians 2:13). Moreover, everything that we do without the Spirit is unacceptable to God. Whatever we do under His influence, however we may despise it, is not despised by God. He never despises His own work or looks upon what He works in us with any other view than that of satisfaction and delight. If the Spirit helps me to groan, then God must accept the groaner. If you could pray the best prayer in the world without the Spirit, God would have nothing to do with it. However, if your prayer is broken, lame, and limping, if the Spirit made it, God will look upon it and say, as He did upon the works of creation, "It is very good," and He will accept it.

Final Considerations

Let me conclude by asking this question: Do you have the Spirit of God in you? You have some religion, most of you, I daresay. Well, of what kind is it? Is it a homemade article? Did you make yourself what you are? If so, you are a lost person up to this moment. If, my friend, you have gone no further than you have walked yourself, you are not on the road to heaven yet; your face is turned the wrong way. However, if you have received something that neither flesh nor blood could reveal to you, if you have been led to do the very thing that you once hated, and to love the thing that you once despised, and to despise that on which your heart and your pride were once set, then, soul, if this is the Spirit's work, rejoice; for where He has begun the good work, He will carry it on (Philippians 1:6).

And you may know whether it is the Spirit's work by this: Have you been led to Christ, and away from self? Have you been led away from all feelings, from all doings, from all willings, from all prayings, as the ground of your trust and your hope, and have you been brought nakedly to rely upon the finished work of Christ? If so, this is more than human nature ever taught any man; this is a height to which human nature never climbed. The Spirit of God has done this, and He will never leave what He has once begun, but you will *go from strength to strength* (Psalm 84:7), and you will stand among the bloodwashed throng, at last complete in Christ, and *accepted in the beloved* (Ephesians 1:6). Yet if you do not have the Spirit of Christ, you are none of His.

May the Spirit lead you to a quiet place where you can weep, repent, and look to Christ. May you now have a divine life implanted, which neither time nor eternity will be able to destroy. God, hear this prayer, and bless us for Jesus' sake. Amen.

Chapter 3

The Chief Office of the Holy Spirit

He shall glorify me: for he shall receive of mine, and
shall show it unto you. All things that the Father hath
are mine: therefore said I, that he shall take of mine,
and shall show it unto you.
—John 16:14–15

It is the chief office of the Holy Spirit to glorify Christ. He does many things, but this is what He aims at in all of them: to glorify Christ. Brothers and sisters, what the Holy Spirit does must be right for us to imitate; therefore, let us endeavor to glorify Christ. To what higher end can we devote ourselves than to something to which God the Holy Spirit devotes Himself? Let this be, then, your fervent prayer: "Blessed Spirit, help me ever to glorify the Lord Jesus Christ!"

Observe that the Holy Spirit glorifies Christ by showing the things of Christ to us. It is a great marvel that there should be any glory given to Christ by showing Him to such poor creatures as we. What! Does making us see Christ glorify Him? For our weak eyes to behold Him, for our trembling hearts to know Him and to love Him, does this glorify Him? Yes, it is so, for the Holy Spirit chooses this as His principal way of glorifying the Lord Jesus. He takes of the things of Christ, not to show them to angels, not to write them in letters of fire across the brow of night, but to show them to us.

Within the little temple of a sanctified heart, Christ is praised, not so much by what we do or think, as by what we see. This puts great value on meditation, on the study of God's Word, and on silent thought under the teaching of the Holy Spirit, for Jesus says, *"He shall glorify me: for he shall receive of mine, and shall show it unto you."*

Here is a Gospel word at the very outset of our sermon: Poor sinner, conscious of your sin, it is possible for Christ to be glorified by His being shown to you. If you look to Him, if you see Him to be a suitable Savior, an all-sufficient Savior, if your mind's eye takes Him in, if He is effectually shown to you by the Holy Spirit, He is thereby glorified. Sinner, as you are, apparently unworthy to become the arena of Christ's glory, you will yet be a temple in which the King's glory will be revealed, and your poor heart, like a mirror, will reflect His grace.

> Come, Holy Spirit, heavenly Dove,
> With all Your quickening powers.

Show Christ to the sinner so that Christ may be glorified in the sinner's salvation!

If that great work of grace is really done at the beginning of the sermon, I will not mind if I never finish this message. God the Holy Spirit will have accomplished more without me than I could possibly have done myself, and to the Triune Jehovah will be all the praise. Oh, that the name of Christ may be glorified in every one of you! Has the Holy Spirit shown you Christ, the Sin-Bearer, the one Sacrifice for sin, exalted on high to give repentance and remission? If so, then the Holy Spirit has glorified Christ, even in you.

Now proceeding to examine the text a little in detail, my first observation is this: The Holy Spirit is our Lord's Glorifier: *"He shall glorify me."* Second, Christ's own things are His best glory: *"He shall glorify me: for he shall receive of mine, and shall show it unto you."* Third, Christ's glory is His Father's glory: *"All things that the Father hath are mine: therefore said I, that he shall take of mine, and shall show it unto you."*

The Holy Spirit Is Our Lord's Glorifier

I want you to keep this truth in your mind and never forget it: What does not glorify Christ is not of the Holy Spirit, and what is of the Holy Spirit invariably glorifies our Lord Jesus Christ.

In All Comforts

First, then, have an eye to this truth in all comforts. If a comfort that you think you need, and that appears to you to be very sweet, does not glorify Christ, look very suspiciously at it. If, in conversing with an apparently religious man, he chatters about truth that he says is comforting, but that does not honor Christ, do not have anything to do with it. It is a poisonous sweet; it may charm you for a moment, but it will ruin your soul forever if you partake of it.

Yet blessed are those comforts that smell of Christ; those consolations in which there is a fragrance *"of myrrh, and aloes, and cassia"* (Psalm 45:8), out of the King's palace; the comfort drawn from His person, His work, His blood, His resurrection, and His glory; the comfort directly derived from that sacred spot where He trod *"the wine-press alone"* (Isaiah 63:3). This is wine of which you may drink and forget your misery and be unhappy no more.

However, always look with great suspicion on any comfort offered to you, either as a sinner or a saint, that does not come distinctly from Christ. Say, "I will not be comforted until Jesus comforts me. I will refuse to lay aside my despondency until He removes my sin. I will not go to Mr. Civility or Mr. Legality for the unloading of my burden. No hands will ever lift the load of conscious sin from my heart but those that were nailed to the cross, when Jesus Himself bore my *"sins in his own body on the tree"* (1 Peter 2:24). Please carry this truth with you wherever you go, as a kind of spiritual litmus paper by which you may test everything that is presented to you as a help or comfort. If it does not glorify Christ, let it not console or please you.

In All Ministries

In the next place, have an eye to this truth in all ministries. There are many ministries in the world, and they are very different from one another, but this truth will enable you to judge which are right out of them all. The ministries that make much of Christ are of the Holy Spirit, and the ministries that discredit Him, ignore Him, or put Him in the background in any degree are not of the Spirit of God.

Any doctrine that magnifies man, but not man's Redeemer, any doctrine that denies the depth of the Fall, and consequently detracts from the greatness of salvation, any doctrine that makes man sinless, and therefore makes Christ's work less—away with it, away with it! This will be an infallible test as to whether it is of the Holy Spirit or not, for Jesus says, *"He shall glorify me."*

It would be better to speak five words to the glory of Christ than to be the greatest orator who ever lived or to neglect or dishonor the Lord Jesus Christ. We who are preachers of the Word have but a short time to live; let us dedicate all that time to the glorious work of magnifying Christ.

Longfellow says in his poem "A Psalm of Life," "Art is long," but longer still is the great art of lifting up the

Crucified before the eyes of the sin-bitten sons of men. Let us keep to that one employment. If we have but this one string upon which we can play, we may create such music on it that would ravish angels and would save men; therefore, again, I say, let us keep to that alone. *"Cornet, flute, harp, sackbut, psaltery, dulcimer, and all kinds of music"* (Daniel 3:5) called the people to worship Nebuchadnezzar's golden image; but, as for worshipping our God, our one harp is Christ Jesus. We will touch every string of that wondrous instrument, even though it is with trembling fingers, and marvelous will be the music we will evoke from it.

All ministries, therefore, must be subjected to this test: If they do not glorify Christ, they are not of the Holy Spirit.

In All Religious Movements

We should also have an eye to this truth in all religious movements and judge them by this standard. If they are of the Holy Spirit, they glorify Christ. There are great movements in the world every now and then. We are inclined to look upon them hopefully, for any stir is better than stagnation, but, before long, we begin to fear with a holy jealousy what their effects will be. How will we judge them? To what test will we put them? Always to this test: Does this movement glorify Christ? Is Christ preached? Then therein I rejoice, yes, and will rejoice.

Are men pointed to Christ? Then this is the ministry of salvation. Is He preached as First and Last? Are men invited to be justified by faith in Him, and then to follow Him and copy His divine example? It is well.

I do not believe that any man ever lifted up the Cross of Christ in a hurtful way. If only the Cross is seen, it is the sight of the Cross, not of the hands that lift it, that will bring salvation.

Some modern movements are heralded with great noise, and some come quietly, but if they glorify Christ, it is well. However, dear friends, if it is some new theory that is propounded, if it is some old error revived, if it is something very glittering and fascinating that attracts the multitudes for a while, think nothing of it; unless it glorifies Christ, it is not for you and me. "Aliquid Christi," as one of the old fathers said, "Anything of Christ," and I love it. Yet if something has nothing of Christ, or something against Christ, then it may be very fine and flowery, and it may be very fascinating and charming, highly poetical, and in harmony with the spirit of the age, but we say of it, *"Vanity of vanities; all is vanity"* (Ecclesiastes 1:2) where there is no Christ."

Where He is uplifted, there is all that is needed for the salvation of a guilty race. Judge every movement, then, not by those who adhere to it, nor by those who admire and praise it, but by this word of our Lord, *"He shall glorify me."* The Spirit of God is not in it if it does not glorify Christ.

In Physical, Mental, or Spiritual Weakness

Once again, brothers and sisters, I pray that you would consider this truth when you are under a sense of great weakness, either physical, mental, or spiritual. You have finished preaching a sermon, you have completed a time of distributing tracts, or you have ended your Sunday school work for another Sabbath. You say to yourself, "I fear that I have done very poorly." You groan as you go to your bed because you think that you have not glorified Christ. It is good for you to groan if that is the case. I will not forbid it, but I will relieve the bitterness of your distress by reminding you that it is the Holy Spirit who is to glorify Christ: *"He shall glorify me."*

Spurgeon on the Holy Spirit

If I preach and the Holy Spirit is with me, Christ will be glorified; but if I were able to *"speak with the tongues of men and of angels"* (1 Corinthians 13:1), yet without the power of the Holy Spirit, Christ would not be glorified. Sometimes, our weakness may even help to make way for the greater display of the might of God. If so, we may glory in infirmity, *"that the power of Christ may rest upon* [us]" (2 Corinthians 12:9). It is not merely we who speak, but the Spirit of the Lord who speaks through us.

There is *"a sound of abundance of rain"* (1 Kings 18:41) outside the tabernacle; oh, that there were also the sound of abundance of rain within our hearts! May the Holy Spirit come at this moment, and come at all times whenever His servants are trying to glorify Christ. May He do what must always be His own work!

How can you and I glorify anybody, much less glorify Him who is infinitely glorious? However, the Holy Spirit, being Himself the glorious God, can glorify the glorious Christ. It is a work worthy of God, and it shows us, when we think of it, the absolute need of our crying to the Holy Spirit that He would take us in His hand and use us as a workman uses his hammer. What can a hammer do without the hand that grasps it, and what can we do without the Spirit of God?

In Trials

I will make only one more observation upon this first point. If the Holy Spirit is to glorify Christ, I beg you to have an eye to this truth amid all oppositions, controversies, and contentions. If we alone had the task of glorifying Christ, we might be beaten; but since the Holy Spirit is the Glorifier of Christ, His glory is in very safe hands.

"Why do the heathen rage, and the people imagine a vain thing?" (Psalm 2:1). The Holy Spirit is still on the front lines. The eternal purpose of God to set His King upon the

throne and to make Jesus Christ reign forever and ever must be fulfilled, for the Holy Spirit has undertaken to see it accomplished. Amid the surging tumults of the battle, the result of the conflict is never in doubt for a moment. It may seem as though the fate of Christ's cause hung in the balance, and that the scales were in equilibrium, but it is not so. The glory of Christ never wanes; it must increase from day to day, as it is made known in the hearts of men by the Holy Spirit; and the day will come when Christ's praise will go up from all human tongues. Every knee will bow to Him (Philippians 2:10), and *"every tongue [will] confess that Jesus Christ is Lord, to the glory of God the Father"* (v. 11). Therefore, *"lift up the hands which hang down, and the feeble knees"* (Hebrews 12:12).

If you have failed to glorify Christ by your speech as you have wanted, there is Another who has done it, and who will still do it, according to Christ's words, *"He shall glorify me."* My text seems to be a silver bell, ringing sweet comfort into the dispirited Christian worker's ear. *"He shall glorify me."* That is the first point, that the Holy Spirit is our Lord's Glorifier. Keep that truth before your mind's eye under all circumstances.

Christ's Own Things Are His Best Glory

When the Holy Spirit wants to glorify Christ, what does He do? He does not go abroad for anything; He goes to Christ Himself for that which will be for Christ's own glory: *"He shall glorify me: for he shall receive of mine, and shall show it unto you."* No glory can be added to Christ; it must be His own glory, which He has already, which is made more apparent to the hearts of God's chosen by the Holy Spirit.

Nothing New Is Needed

First of all, Christ needs no new inventions to glorify Him. "We have invented a new line of things," says one.

Have you? "We have discovered something very wonderful." I daresay you have, but Christ, *"the same yesterday, and to day, and for ever"* (Hebrews 13:8), needs none of your inventions, discoveries, or additions to His truth. A plain Christ is forever the loveliest Christ. Dress Him up, and you have deformed Him and defamed Him. Bring Him out just as He is, the Christ of God, nothing else but Christ, unless you bring in His Cross, for *"we preach Christ crucified"* (1 Corinthians 1:23). Indeed, you cannot have Christ without the Cross; but preach Christ crucified, and you have given Him all the glory that He desires. The Holy Spirit does not reveal in these last times any fresh laws or any novel doctrines or any new evolutions. He simply brings to mind the things that Christ Himself spoke. He brings Christ's own things to us, and in that way glorifies Him.

His Person

Think for a minute of Christ's person as revealed to us by the Holy Spirit. What can more glorify Him than for us to see His person, as "very God of very God," and yet as truly man? What a wondrous being, as human as ourselves, but as divine as God! Was there ever another like Him? Never. Think of His incarnation, His birth at Bethlehem. There was greater glory among the oxen in the stall than ever was seen where those born in marble halls were swathed in purple and fine linen. Was there ever another baby like Christ? Never. I am not surprised that the wise men fell down to worship Him.

His Life

Look at His life, the standing wonder of all ages. Men who have not worshipped Him have admired Him. His life is incomparable, unique; there is nothing like it in all the history of mankind. Imagination has never been able to invent anything approximating the perfect beauty of the life of Jesus Christ.

His Death

Think of His death. There have been many heroic deaths and martyrdoms, but there is not one that can be set side by side with Christ's death. He did not pay the debt of nature as others do, and yet He paid our nature's debt. He did not die because He had to; He died because He would. The only "must" that came upon Him was a necessity of all-conquering love. The Cross of Christ is the greatest wonder of fact or fiction; fiction invents many marvelous things, but nothing that can be compared for a moment with the Cross of Christ.

His Resurrection

Think of our Lord's resurrection. If this is one of the things that is taken and shown to you by the Holy Spirit, it will fill you with holy delight. I am sure that I could go into that sepulchre where John and Peter went and spend a lifetime in revering Him who broke down the barrier of the tomb and made it a passageway to heaven. Instead of its being a dungeon and a cul-de-sac, into which all men seem to go but could never come out of, Christ has, by His resurrection, made a tunnel right through the grave. Jesus, by dying, has killed death for all believers.

His Ascension

Then think of His ascension. Yet why do I need to take you over all these scenes with which you are blessedly familiar? What a wondrous fact that, when the cloud received Him out of the disciples' sight, the angels came to accompany Him to His heavenly home!

> They brought His chariot from above,
>   To bear Him to His throne;
> Clapp'd their triumphant wings, and cried,
>   "The glorious work is done."

His Second Coming

Think of Him now, at His Father's right hand, adored by all the heavenly host. Then let your mind fly forward to the glory of His Second Advent, the final Judgment with its terrible terrors, the Millennium with its indescribable bliss, and the heaven of heavens with its endless and unparalleled splendor. If these things are shown to you by the Holy Spirit, the beatific vision will indeed glorify Christ, and you will sit down and sing with the blessed Virgin, *"My soul doth magnify the Lord, and my spirit hath rejoiced in God my Saviour"* (Luke 1:46).

Thus you see that the things that glorify Christ are all in Christ; the Holy Spirit brings nothing from abroad, but He takes of the things of Christ and shows them to us. The glory of kings lies in their silver and gold, their silk and gems, but the glory of Christ lies in Himself.

If we want to glorify a man, we bring Him presents; if we wish to glorify Christ, we must accept presents from Him. Thus we take the cup of salvation, calling on the name of the Lord, and, in so doing, we glorify Christ.

The Spirit Must Reveal Christ

Notice next that these things of Christ's are too bright for us to see until the Spirit shows them to us. We cannot see them because of their excessive glory, until the Holy Spirit tenderly reveals them to us, until He takes the things of Christ and shows them to us.

He Enlightens the Ability to Understand

What does this mean? Does it not mean, first, that He enlightens our understanding? It is wonderful how the Holy Spirit can take a fool and cause him to know the wonder of Christ's dying love; He makes him know it very quickly when He begins to teach him. Some of us have been very slow learners, yet the Holy Spirit has been able to teach something even to us. He opens the Scriptures, and He also opens our minds; and when these two openings are together, what a wonderful opening it is! It becomes like a new revelation. The first is the revelation of the letter, which we have in the Book; the second is the revelation of the Spirit, which we receive in our own spirits. Friend, if the Holy Spirit has ever enlightened your understanding, you know what it is for Him to show the things of Christ to you!

He Touches the Soul

He does this by a work upon the whole soul. I mean this: When the Holy Spirit convinces us of sin, we become equipped to see Christ, and so the blessed Spirit shows Christ to us. When we are conscious of our feebleness, then we see Christ's strength; thus, the Holy Spirit shows Him to us. Often the operations of the Spirit of God may not seem to include directly showing Christ to us, but as they prepare us for seeing Him, they are a part of the work.

He Brings Truth to Life

The Holy Spirit sometimes shows Christ to us by His power of vivifying the truth. I have sometimes seen a truth differently from what I have ever seen it before. I knew it long ago. I owned it as part of the divine revelation. However, now I realize it, grip it, grasp it; or what is better, it seems to get a grip on me and hold me in its mighty hands. Have you not sometimes been overjoyed with a promise that never seemed anything to you before? Or has a doctrine that you believed, but never fully appreciated, suddenly become to you a gem of the purest luster, a very Koh-i-noor,* which means "mountain of light"? The Holy

---

* The Koh-i-noor is an Indian diamond, weighing 106 carats, that was acquired by the British. It became the central stone in the crown worn by Elizabeth, the Queen Mother, at the coronation of her husband, George VI, in 1937.

Spirit has a way of focusing light, and when it falls in this special way upon a certain point, then the truth is revealed to us. He will take the things of Christ and show them to you. Have you never felt ready to jump for joy, ready to rise from your seat, ready to sit up in your bed at night and sing praises to God through the overpowering influence of some grand old truth that has seemed to be all at once quite new to you?

He Uses Life Experience

The Holy Spirit also shows to us the things of Christ in our experiences. As we journey on in life, we pass up hill and down dale, through bright sunlight and through dark shadows, and in each of these conditions, we learn a little more of Christ, a little more of His grace, a little more of His glory, a little more of His sin-bearing, a little more of His glorious righteousness. Blessed is the life that is one long lesson on the glory of Christ. I think that is what every Christian's life should be. "Every dark and bending line" in our experience should meet in the center of Christ's glory and should lead us nearer and nearer to the power of enjoying the bliss at His right hand forever and ever. Thus the Holy Spirit takes of the things of Christ and shows them to us, and so glorifies Christ.

Respond to the Holy Spirit's Leadings

Beloved, the practical lesson for us to learn is this: Let us try to abide under the influence of the Holy Spirit. To that end, let us think very reverently of Him. Some never think of Him at all. How many sermons there are without even an allusion to Him! Shame on the preachers of such discourses! If any hearers come without praying for the enlightenment of the Holy Spirit, shame on such hearers! We know and we confess that He is everything to our spiritual lives. Then why do we not remember Him with greater love, worship Him with greater honor, and think of Him continually with greater reverence?

Beware of committing the sin against the Holy Spirit. If you feel any gentle touches of His power when you are hearing a sermon, beware lest you harden your heart against them. Whenever the sacred fire comes as but a spark, *"quench not the Spirit"* (1 Thessalonians 5:19), but pray that the spark may become a flame.

And you, Christian people, cry to Him that you may not read your Bibles without His light. Do not pray without being helped by the Spirit. Above all, may you never preach without the Holy Spirit! It seems a pity when a man asks to be guided by the Spirit in his preaching, and then pulls out a manuscript and reads it. The Holy Sprit may bless what the minister reads, but He cannot very well guide him when he has tied himself down to what he has written. And it will be the same with the speaker if he only repeats what he has learned and leaves no room for the Spirit to give him a new thought or a fresh revelation of Christ. How can he hope for the divine blessing under such circumstances? Oh, it would be better for us to sit still until some of us were moved by the Spirit to get up and speak than for us to prescribe the methods by which He should speak to us, and even to write down the very words we mean to utter! What room is there for the Spirit's operations then?

"Come, Holy Spirit, heavenly Dove." I cannot help breaking out into that prayer. "Blessed Spirit, abide with us. Take of the things of Christ and show them to us so that Christ may be glorified."

Christ's Glory Is His Father's Glory

The last point is a very deep one, much too deep for me. I am unable to take you into the depths of my text. I will not pretend to do so. I believe that there are meanings here that we will probably never understand until we get to heaven. *"Thou knowest not now; but thou shalt know hereafter"* (John 13:7). However, this is the point: *"All things that the Father hath are mine: therefore said I, that he shall take of mine, and shall show it unto you."*

Christ Has All the Father Has

First, Christ has all that the Father has. Think about that. No more can any man dare to say, *"All things that the Father hath are mine."* All the Godhead is in Christ; not only all the attributes of it, but also the essence of it. The Nicene Creed puts it well, and it is not too strong to say it this way, "Light of Light, very God of very God," for Christ has all that the Father has. When we come to Christ, we come to omnipotent, omnipresent omniscience; we come to almighty immutability; we come, in fact, to the eternal Godhead. The Father has all things, and all power is given to Christ in heaven and on earth, so that He has all that the Father has.

God Is Glorified in Christ's Glory

Further, the Father is glorified in Christ's glory. Never let us fall into the false notion that if we magnify Christ, we are depreciating the Father. If any lips have ever spoken concerning the Christ of God so as to depreciate the God of Christ, let those lips be covered with shame. We never preached Christ as merciful, and the Father as only just, or Christ as moving the Father to be gracious. That is a slander that has been cast upon us, but there is not an atom of truth in it. We have known and believed what Christ Himself said, *"I and my Father are one"* (John 10:30).

The more glorious Christ is, the more glorious the Father is; and when men, professedly Christians, begin to cast off Christ, they cast off God the Father, to a large extent. Irreverence toward the Son of God soon becomes irreverence toward God the Father Himself. However, dear friends, we delight to honor Christ, and we will continue to do so. Even when we stand in the heaven of heavens, before the burning throne of the infinite Jehovah, we will sing praises to Him and to the Lamb, putting the Two evermore in that divine conjunction in which They are always to be found.

Thus, you see, Christ has all that the Father has, and when He is glorified, the Father is also glorified.

The Holy Spirit Must Reveal the Truth to Us

Next, the Holy Spirit must lead us to see this truth, and I am sure that He will. If we give ourselves up to His teaching, we will fall into no errors. It will be a great mystery, but we will know enough so that it will never trouble us. If you sit down and try to study the mystery of the Eternal, well, I believe that the longer you look, the more you will be like people who look into the sea from a great height, until they grow dizzy and are ready to fall and to be drowned.

Believe what the Spirit teaches you, and adore your divine Teacher; then His instruction will become easy to you. I believe that, as we grow older, we come to worship God as Abraham did—as Jehovah, the great I AM. Jesus does not fade into the background, but the glorious Godhead seems to become more and more apparent to us. As our Lord's words to His disciples state, *"Ye believe in God, believe also in me"* (John 14:1). And as we come to full confidence in the glorious Lord, the God of nature, of providence, of redemption, and of heaven, the Holy Spirit helps us to know more of the glories of Christ.

I have talked with you as well as I could about this sublime theme. If I did not know that the Holy Spirit glorifies Christ, I would be miserable, for I have not been able to glorify my Lord as I wish I could. Yet I know that the Holy Spirit can take what I have said out of my very heart, can put it into your hearts, and can add to it whatever I have omitted. Go, you who love the Lord, and glorify Him. Try to do it by your lips and by your lives. Go and preach Him, preach more of Him, and lift Him up higher, higher, and higher.

I heard of an old lady who made a mistake in what she said, yet there was a truth behind her blunder. She had been to a little Baptist chapel, where a high Calvinist preached. On leaving, she said that she liked "high Calvary" preachers best. So do I. Give me a "high Calvary" preacher, one who will make Calvary the highest of all the mountains. I suppose it was not a hill at all, but only a mound; still, let us lift it higher and higher, and say to all other hills, *"Why leap ye, ye high hills? this is the hill which God desireth to dwell in; yea, the* LORD *will dwell in it for ever"* (Psalm 68:16).

The crucified Christ is wiser than all the wisdom of the world. The Cross of Christ has more newness in it than all the fresh things of the earth. Oh, believers and preachers of the Gospel, glorify Christ! May the Holy Spirit help you to do so! And you, poor sinners, who think that you cannot glorify Christ at all, come and trust Him. "Come naked, come filthy, come just as you are," and believe that He will receive you, for that will glorify Him. Believe, even now, O sinner at death's door, that Christ can make you live, for your faith will glorify Him! Look up out of the awful depths of hell into which conscience has cast you, and believe that He can pluck you out of the *"horrible pit, out of the miry clay, and set* [your] *feet upon a rock"* (Psalm 40:2), for your trust will glorify Him! It is in the power of the sinner to give Christ the greatest glory, if the Holy Spirit enables him to believe in the Lord Jesus Christ. You may come, you who are more leprous, more diseased, more corrupt, than any other; if you look to Him, and He saves you, oh, then you will praise Him! You will be of the mind of the one I have spoken of many times, who said to me,

"Sir, you say that Christ can save me. Well, if He does, He will never hear the last of it." No, and He never will hear the last of it. Blessed Jesus,

> I will love Thee in life, I will love Thee in death,
> And praise Thee as long as Thou lendest me breath;
> And say when the death-dew lies cold on my brow,
> If ever I loved Thee, my Jesus, 'tis now.
>
> In mansion of glory and endless delight,
> I'll ever adore Thee in heaven so bright;
> I'll sing with the glittering crown on my brow,
> If ever I loved thee, my Jesus, 'tis now.

We will do nothing else but praise Christ and glorify Him, if He will but save us from sin. God grant that it may be so with every one of us, for the Lord Jesus Christ's sake!

Chapter 4

The Personality of the Holy Spirit

*And I will pray the Father, and he shall give you
another Comforter, that he may abide with you for ever;
even the Spirit of truth; whom the world cannot receive,
because it seeth him not, neither knoweth him:
but ye know him; for he dwelleth with you,
and shall be in you.*
—John 14:16–17

After reading the text, you will be surprised to know that I do not intend to say anything about the Holy Spirit as the Comforter. In this message, I will endeavor to explain and enforce certain other doctrines, which I believe are plainly taught in this text, and which I hope God the Holy Spirit may make profitable to our souls. Old John Newton once said that there were some books that he could not read. They were good and sound enough, but he said,

> They are books of halfpence; you have to take so
> much in quantity before you have any value; there
> are other books of silver, and others of gold; but I
> have one book that is a book of banknotes; and every
> leaf is a banknote of immense value.

I have found this to be true with this text. I have a banknote of so large a sum that I could not tell its whole worth in this one message. I would have to write many chapters before I could unfold to you the whole value of this precious promise—one of the last that Christ gave to His people.

I invite your attention to this passage because we will find in it some instruction on four points: first, concerning the true and proper personality of the Holy Spirit; second, concerning the united agency of the glorious Three Persons in the work of our salvation; third, something to establish the doctrine of the indwelling of the Holy Spirit in the souls of all believers; fourth, the reason why the carnal mind rejects the Holy Spirit.

The Person of the Holy Spirit

We are so accustomed to talking about the influence of the Holy Spirit and His sacred operations and graces that we are apt to forget that the Holy Spirit is truly and actually a person—that He is a subsistence—an existence, or, as we Trinitarians usually say, one person in the essence of the Godhead.

I am afraid that, though we do not know it, we have acquired the habit of regarding the Holy Spirit as an emanation flowing from the Father and the Son, but not as being actually a person Himself. I know it is not easy to carry around in our minds the idea of the Holy Spirit as a person.

I can think of the Father as a person, because His acts are such as I can understand. I see Him hang the world in ether. I behold Him swaddling a newborn sea in bands of darkness. I know it is He who formed the drops of hail, who led forth the stars by their hosts and called them by their names. I can conceive of Him as a person, because I can observe His operations.

241

Spurgeon on the Holy Spirit

I can realize that Jesus, the Son of Man, is a real person, because He is bone of my bone and flesh of my flesh. It takes no great stretch of my imagination to picture the babe in Bethlehem, or to behold the *"man of sorrows,...acquainted with grief"* (Isaiah 53:3) or the King of martyrs, as He was persecuted in Pilate's hall or nailed to the accursed tree for our sins. Neither do I find it difficult at times to realize the person of my Jesus sitting on His throne in heaven or encircled with clouds and wearing the diadem of all creation, calling the earth to judgment and summoning us to hear our final sentences.

Yet when I come to deal with the Holy Spirit, His operations are so mysterious, His doings are so secret, His acts are so removed from everything that is of sense, and of the body, that I cannot so easily grasp the idea of His being a person—but a person He is. God the Holy Spirit is not an influence, an emanation, a stream of something flowing from the Father, but He is as much an actual person as either God the Son or God the Father. I will attempt to establish the doctrine, and to show you the truth of it, that God the Holy Spirit is actually a person.

Baptism

We will gather the first proof from the pool of holy baptism. Let me take you down, as I have taken others, into the pool, now concealed, but which I wish were always open to your view. Let me take you to the baptismal font, where believers put on the name of the Lord Jesus, and you will hear me pronounce the solemn words, *"I baptize thee in the name"*—note, *"in the name,"* not names—*"of the Father and of the Son and of the Holy Spirit."* Everyone who is baptized according to the true form laid down in Scripture must be a Trinitarian; otherwise, his baptism is a farce and a lie, and he himself is found to be a deceiver and a hypocrite before God.

The Personality of the Holy Spirit

As the Father is mentioned, and as the Son is mentioned, so is the Holy Spirit; and the whole is summed up as being a Trinity in unity, by its being said, not the names, but *"the name,"* the glorious name, the Jehovah name, *"of the Father and of the Son and of the Holy Spirit."*

Benediction

Let me remind you that the same thing often occurs when you are dismissed from the house of prayer. In pronouncing the solemn closing benediction, the minister invokes on your behalf the love of Jesus Christ, the grace of the Father, and the fellowship of the Holy Spirit. Thus, according to the apostolic manner, he makes a manifest distinction among the persons, showing that we believe the Father to be a person, the Son to be a person, and the Holy Spirit to be a person. Were there no other proofs in Scripture, I think these would be sufficient for every sensible man. He would see that if the Holy Spirit were a mere influence, He would not be mentioned in conjunction with Two whom we all confess to be actual and proper persons.

Appearances

Another argument arises from the fact that the Holy Spirit has actually made different appearances on earth. The Great Spirit has manifested Himself to man. He has put on a form, so that, while He has not been seen by mortal men, He has been so veiled in appearance that He has been seen, as far as that appearance was concerned, by the eyes of all beholders. Imagine Jesus Christ our Savior at His baptism. There is the river Jordan, with its shelving banks and its willows weeping at its side. Jesus Christ, the Son of God, descends into the stream, and the holy Baptist, John, plunges Him into the waves. The doors of heaven are opened. A miraculous appearance presents itself. A bright light shines from the sky, brighter than

the sun in all its grandeur, and down in a flood of glory
descends something that you recognize to be a dove. It
rests on Jesus. It sits upon His sacred head, and as the
old painters put a halo around the brow of Jesus, so did
the Holy Spirit shed a resplendence around the face of Him
who came to fulfill all righteousness, and therefore commenced with the ordinance of baptism. The Holy Spirit
was seen as a dove, to mark His purity and His gentleness,
and He came down like a dove from heaven to show that it
is from heaven alone that He descends.

Neither was this the only time when the Holy Spirit
has been manifest in a visible shape. Can you envision
that company of disciples gathered together in an upper
room? They are waiting for some promised blessing, and,
before long, it will come. Listen! There is a sound *"as of a
rushing mighty wind"* (Acts 2:2). It fills all the house where
they are sitting (v. 2); and astonished, they look around
them, wondering what will come next. Soon a bright light
appears, shining upon the heads of each. Cloven tongues
of fire rest upon them (v. 3). What were these marvelous
appearances of wind and flame but a display of the Holy
Spirit in His proper person? The fact of an appearance
manifests that He must be a person. An "influence" could
not appear; an "attribute" could not appear. We cannot
see attributes, and we cannot behold influences. The Holy
Spirit must, then, be a person, since He was beheld by
mortal eyes, and He came under the cognizance of mortal
sense.

Human Characteristics

Another proof is that personal qualities are, in Scripture, ascribed to the Holy Spirit.

Understanding

First, let us consider a text in which the Holy Spirit is
spoken of as having understanding.

The Personality of the Holy Spirit

But as it is written, Eye hath not seen, nor ear heard, neither have entered into the heart of man, the things which God hath prepared for them that love him. But God hath revealed them unto us by his Spirit: for the Spirit searcheth all things, yea, the deep things of God. For what man knoweth the things of a man, save the spirit of man which is in him? even so the things of God knoweth no man, but the Spirit of God.

(1 Corinthians 2:9–11)

Here you see an understanding—a power of knowledge is ascribed to the Holy Spirit. Now, if there are any people whose minds are of so preposterous a complexion that they would ascribe one attribute to another, and would speak of a mere influence as having understanding, then I give up all the argument. However, I believe every rational man will admit that, when anything is spoken of as having an understanding, it must be an existence. It must, in fact, be a person.

Will

In the same epistle, you find a will ascribed to the Holy Spirit. *"But all these worketh that one and the selfsame Spirit, dividing to every man severally as he will"* (1 Corinthians 12:11). So it is plain that the Spirit has a will. He does not come from God simply at God's will, but He has a will of His own, which is always in keeping with the will of the infinite Jehovah; nevertheless, it is distinct and separate. Therefore, I say He is a person.

Power

In another text, power is ascribed to the Holy Spirit, and power is something that can be ascribed only to an existence. Romans 15:13 reads, *"Now the God of hope fill you with all joy and peace in believing, that ye may abound in hope, through the power of the Holy Ghost."* I need not insist upon it, because it is self-evident, that wherever you find understanding, will, and power, you must also find an existence. It cannot be a mere attribute. It cannot be a metaphor. It cannot be a personified influence. It must be a person. However, I have a proof that, perhaps, will be more telling upon you than any other.

Actions and Deeds

Actions and deeds are ascribed to the Holy Spirit; therefore, He must be a person. You read in the first chapter of the book of Genesis that the Spirit hovered over the surface of the earth, when it was as yet all disorder and confusion (v. 2). This world was once a mass of chaotic matter with no order. It was like the valley of darkness and of the shadow of death. God the Holy Spirit spread His wings over it. He sowed the seeds of life in it. The seeds from which all beings sprang were implanted by Him. He impregnated the earth so that it became capable of life.

Now, it must have been a person who brought order out of confusion. It must have been an existence who hovered over this world and made it what it is now. Yet do we not read in Scripture something more of the Holy Spirit? Yes, we are told that *"holy men of God spake as they were moved by the Holy Ghost"* (2 Peter 1:21). When Moses penned the Pentateuch, the Holy Spirit moved his hand. When David wrote the Psalms and created sweet music on his harp, it was the Holy Spirit who gave his fingers their seraphic motion. When Solomon dropped from his lips the words of the proverbs of wisdom, or when he hymned the canticles of love, it was the Holy Spirit who gave him the words of knowledge and hymns of rapture. Ah, what fire was it that touched the lips of the eloquent Isaiah? What hand was it that came upon Daniel? What might was it that made Jeremiah so plaintive in his grief? What was it that lifted Ezekiel and made him fly like an eagle, soaring aloft into mysteries and seeing the mighty unknown beyond our reach? Who was it that made Amos, the herdsman, a prophet? Who taught the rugged Haggai to pronounce his thundering sentences? Who showed Habakkuk the horses of Jehovah marching through the waters? Who kindled the burning eloquence of Nahum? Who caused Malachi to close his book with the mention of the word "curse"? Who was it in each of these cases, except the Holy Spirit?

Must it not have been a person who spoke in and through these ancient witnesses? We must believe it. We cannot avoid believing it when we read that *"holy men of God spoke as they were moved by the Holy Spirit."*

And when has the Holy Spirit ceased to have an influence on men? We find that He still deals with His ministers and with all His saints. Turn to the book of Acts, and you will find that the Holy Spirit said, *"Separate me Barnabas and Saul for the work"* (Acts 13:2). I never heard of an attribute saying such a thing. The Holy Spirit said to Peter, "Go to the centurion, and do not call common or unclean what I have cleansed." (See Acts 10.) The Holy Spirit *"caught away Philip"* after he had baptized the eunuch and carried Philip away to another place (Acts 8:38–40). The Holy Spirit said to Paul *"that he should not go up to Jerusalem"* (Acts 21:4). And we know that the Holy Spirit was lied to by Ananias and Sapphira, when Peter said, *"Thou hast not lied unto men, but unto God"* (Acts 5:4). Again, that power that those of us who are called to preach feel every day; that wondrous spell that makes our lips so potent; that power that gives us thoughts that are like birds from a far-off region, not the natives of our soul; that influence that I sometimes strangely feel, which, if it does not give me poetry and eloquence, gives me a might I never felt before and lifts me above my fellowman; that majesty with which He clothes His ministers, until, in the midst of the battle, they cry "Aha!" like the war horse of Job, and move themselves like leviathans in the water;

that power that gives us might over men and causes them to sit and listen as if their ears were chained, as if they were entranced by the power of some magician's wand—that power must come from a person; it must come from the Holy Spirit.

Is it not said in Scripture, and do we not feel it, dear friends, that it is the Holy Spirit who regenerates the soul? It is the Holy Spirit who quickens us. *"You hath he quickened, who were dead in trespasses and sins"* (Ephesians 2:1). It is the Holy Spirit who imparts the first germ of life, convincing us of sin, of righteousness, and of judgment to come (John 16:8). And is it not the Holy Spirit who, after that flame is kindled, still fans it with the breath of His mouth and keeps it alive? Its Author is its Preserver. Oh, can it be said that it is the Holy Spirit who strives in men's souls, that it is the Holy Spirit who brings them into the sweet place that is called Calvary? Can it be said that He does all these things, and yet is not a person? It may be said, but it must be said by fools; for one can never be a wise man who can consider that these things can be done by any other than a glorious person—a divine existence.

Emotions

Allow me to give you one more proof. Certain feelings are ascribed to the Holy Spirit that can be understood only on the supposition that He actually is a person. Ephesians 4:30 states that the Holy Spirit can be grieved: *"Grieve not the holy Spirit of God, whereby ye are sealed unto the day of redemption."* In Isaiah 63:10, we read that the Holy Spirit can be vexed: *"But they rebelled, and vexed his holy Spirit: therefore he was turned to be their enemy, and he fought against them."* Acts 7:51 tells us that the Holy Spirit can be resisted: *"Ye stiffnecked and uncircumcised in heart and ears, ye do always resist the Holy Ghost: as your fathers did, so do ye."* And in Acts 5:9, we find that the Holy Spirit may be tempted. We are informed that

248

Peter said to Ananias and Sapphira, *"How is it that ye have agreed together to tempt the Spirit of the Lord?"*

Now, these things could not be emotions that might be ascribed to a quality or an emanation. They must be understood to relate to a person. An influence could not be grieved; it must be a person who can be grieved, vexed, or resisted. And now, dear ones, I think I have fully established the point of the personality of the Holy Spirit.

Please permit me now, most earnestly, to impress upon you the absolute necessity of being sound on the doctrine of the Trinity. I knew a man, a good minister of Jesus Christ he is now, and I believe he was before he turned his eyes to heresy. He began to doubt the glorious divinity of our blessed Lord, and for years he preached the unorthodox doctrine, until one day he happened to hear a very eccentric old minister preaching from the text,

> *But there the glorious* LORD *will be unto us a place of broad rivers and streams; wherein shall go no galley with oars, neither shall gallant ship pass thereby....Thy tacklings are loosed; they could not well strengthen their mast, they could not spread the sail.*
> (Isaiah 33:21, 23)

"Now," said the old minister, "you give up the Trinity, and your tacklings are loosed; you cannot strengthen your masts. Once you give up the doctrine of the Three Persons, and your tacklings are all gone, your mast, which ought to be a support to your vessel, is a rickety one, and it shakes."

A Gospel without the Trinity! It is a pyramid built upon its apex. A Gospel without the Trinity! It is a rope of sand that cannot hold together. A Gospel without the Trinity! Then, indeed, Satan can overturn it. However, give me a Gospel with the Trinity, and the might of hell cannot prevail against it. No man can overthrow it any more than a bubble could split a rock or a feather break a mountain in two.

Grasp the thought of the Three Persons, and you have the marrow of all divinity. Only know the Father and know the Son and know the Holy Spirit to be one, and all things will appear clear. This is the golden key to the secrets of nature. This is the silken clue of the labyrinths of mystery, and he who understands this truth will soon understand as much as mortals can ever know.

The United Agency of the Trinity

Now we come to our second point: the united agency of the Three Persons in the work of our salvation. Look at the text, and you will find all three persons of the Trinity mentioned. "I"—that is the Son—"will pray the Father, and he shall give you another Comforter." There the Three Persons are mentioned, all of them doing something for our salvation. "I will pray," says the Son. "I will send," says the Father. "I will comfort," says the Holy Spirit.

Now, let us, for a few moments, focus on this wondrous theme: the unity of the Three Persons with regard to the great purpose of the salvation of the elect. When God first made man, He said, *"Let **us** [not "let Me"] make man"* (Genesis 1:26, emphasis added). The covenant Elohim said to each other, "Let Us unitedly become the creator of man."

So, when in the eternal ages of long ago, they said, "Let Us save man," it was not the Father who said, "Let Me save man," but the Three Persons conjointly who said, with one consent, "Let Us save man." It is a source of sweet comfort to me to think that it is not only one person of the Trinity who is engaged for my salvation, it is not simply one person of the Godhead who vows that He will redeem me, but it is a glorious trio of Divine Ones, and the Three declare, unitedly, "We will save man."

The Personality of the Holy Spirit

Now, observe here that each person is spoken of as performing a separate office. "I will pray," says the Son; that is intercession. "I will send," says the Father; that is donation. "I will comfort," says the Holy Spirit; that is supernatural influence. Oh, if it were possible for us to see the three persons of the Godhead, we would behold one of them standing before the throne, with outstretched hands, crying day and night, "O Lord, how long?" We would see him girded with Urim and Thummim, precious stones on which are written the twelve names of the tribes of Israel. We would behold Him, crying unto His Father, "Do not forget Your promises or Your covenant." We would hear Him make mention of our sorrows and speak of our griefs on our behalf, for He is our Intercessor. And if we could see the Father, we would not see Him as a listless, idle spectator of the intercession of the Son, but we would see Him with attentive ear, listening to every word of Jesus and granting every petition.

Where is the Holy Spirit all the while? Is He idle? Oh, no! He is floating over the earth, and when He sees a weary soul, He says, "Come to Jesus; He will give you rest." When He beholds eyes filled with tears, He wipes away the tears and bids the mourner look for comfort at the Cross. When He sees the tempest-tossed believer, He takes the helm of his soul and speaks words of consolation. He helps the broken in heart and binds up their wounds. And, ever on His mission of mercy, He flies around the world, being present everywhere. Behold how the Three Persons work together.

Do not say, then, "I am grateful to the Son." Yes, you ought to be, but God the Son saves you no more than God the Father. Do not imagine that God the Father is a great tyrant, and that God the Son had to die to make Him merciful. It was not to make the Father love His people. Oh, no! One loves as much as the other; the Three are conjoined in the great purpose of rescuing the elect from damnation.

But notice another thing in the text that shows the blessed unity of the Three: The one person promised for the other. The Son said, *"I will pray the Father."* "Very well," the disciples may have said; "we can trust You for that." "And He will send you," Jesus continued. You see, here was the Son signing a bond on behalf of the Father. *"He shall give you another Comforter."* There is a bond on behalf of the Holy Spirit, too. "And He will abide with you forever."

One person spoke for the other; how could they, if there were any disagreement among them? If one wished to save, and the other did not, they could not promise on each other's behalf. But whatever the Son says, the Father listens to; whatever the Father promises, the Holy Spirit works; and whatever the Holy Spirit injects into the soul, God the Father fulfills. So the Three together mutually promise on one another's behalf. There is a bond with three names attached—Father, Son, and Holy Spirit. By three immutable things, the Christian is secured beyond the reaches of death and hell. The Christian has a trinity of securities because there is a Trinity in God.

The Indwelling of the Holy Spirit

Our third point is the indwelling of the Holy Spirit in believers. Now, beloved, my first two points have been matters of pure doctrine; this point, however, is the subject of experience. The indwelling of the Holy Spirit is a subject so profound, and so having to do with the inner man, that no soul will be able truly and really to comprehend what I say, unless it has been taught by God.

I heard of an old minister who told a fellow of one of the Cambridge colleges that he understood a language that he never learned in all his life. "I have not," he said, "even a smattering of Greek, and I know no Latin. However, thank God, I can talk the language of Canaan, and that is more than you can." So, beloved, I will now have to talk a little of the language of Canaan. If you cannot comprehend me, I am afraid it is because you are not of Israelite extraction; you are neither a child of God nor an inheritor of the kingdom of heaven.

We are told, in the text, that Jesus would send the Comforter, who would abide with the saints forever. He would dwell with them and be in them. Old Ignatius, the martyr, used to call himself Theophorus, or Godbearer, because, he said, "I bear about with me the Holy Spirit." And truly, every Christian is a Godbearer. *"Know ye not that ye are the temple of God, and that the Spirit of God dwelleth in you?"* (1 Corinthians 3:16).

A man is no Christian who does not have the Holy Spirit dwelling within him. He may speak well and understand theology. He may be a sound Calvinist. He may be a child of nature finely dressed, but not a child of the living God. He may be a man of so profound an intellect, so gigantic a soul, so comprehensive a mind, and so lofty an imagination that he may dive into all the secrets of nature. He may know the path that the eagle's eye has not seen and go into depths where the understanding of mortals does not reach, but he will not be a Christian, even with all his knowledge; he will not be a son of God, with all his studies, unless he understands what it is to have the Holy Spirit dwelling and abiding in him forever.

Some people call this viewpoint fanaticism, and they say, "You are a Quaker; why not follow George Fox?" Well, we would not mind that much. We would follow anyone who followed the Holy Spirit. Even Fox, with all his eccentricities, I do not doubt, was, in many cases, actually inspired by the Holy Spirit; and, whenever I find a man in whom there rests the Spirit of God, the Spirit within me leaps to hear the Spirit within him, and we feel that we are one. The Spirit of God in one Christian soul recognizes the Spirit in another.

Spurgeon on the Holy Spirit

I remember talking with a good man, as I believe he was, who insisted that it was impossible for us to know whether we had the Holy Spirit within us or not. I would like to read this verse to him, *"But ye know him; for he dwelleth with you, and shall be in you."*

Ah, do you think you cannot tell whether you have the Holy Spirit or not? Can I tell whether I am alive or not? If I were shocked by electricity, could I tell whether I was or not? I am sure I could! The shock would be strong enough to make me know where I stood. So, if I have God within me—if I have Deity tabernacling in my breast—if I have God the Holy Spirit resting in my heart and making a temple of my body, do you think I will know it? Call it fanaticism if you will, but I trust that there are some of us who know what it is to be always, or generally, under the influence of the Holy Spirit—always in one sense, generally in another. When we have difficulties, we ask the direction of the Holy Spirit. When we do not understand a portion of Holy Scripture, we ask God the Holy Spirit to shine upon us. When we are depressed, the Holy Spirit comforts us.

You cannot explain the wondrous power of the indwelling of the Holy Spirit—how it pulls back the hand of the saint when he would touch a forbidden thing; how it prompts him to make a covenant with his eyes; how it binds his feet, lest they should fall in a slippery way; how it restrains his heart and keeps him from temptation. Oh, you who know nothing of the indwelling of the Holy Spirit, do not despise it. Despise not the Holy Spirit, for that is the unpardonable sin.

> *Whosoever speaketh a word against the Son of man, it shall be forgiven him: but whosoever speaketh against the Holy Ghost, it shall not be forgiven him, neither in this world, neither in the world to come.*
> (Matthew 12:32)

Thus says the Word of God. Therefore, tremble, lest in anything you despise the influences of the Holy Spirit.

Before closing this point, there is one little word that pleases me very much, and that is forever. You knew I would not miss that; you were certain I could not let it go without a comment. *"Abide with you for ever."* I wish I could get an Arminian here to finish my sermon. I imagine him taking that word forever. He would stumble and say, "for...forever"; he would have to stammer and stutter, for he could never get it out all at once. At last, though, he would have to say, "The translation is wrong." And I suppose the poor man would have to prove that the original was wrong, too.

Ah, but blessed be God, we can read it! *"That he may abide with you for ever."* Give me the Holy Spirit, and I will never lose Him until *"for ever"* has run out, until eternity has spun its everlasting rounds.

Why the Holy Spirit Is Rejected by Some

Our text reads, *"Whom the world cannot receive, because it seeth him not, neither knoweth him."* You know what is sometimes meant by *"the world"*: those whom God in His wondrous sovereignty passed over when He chose His people—not the reprobates who were condemned to damnation by some awful decree, but those passed over by God when He chose His elect. These cannot receive the Spirit. Again, it means that all in a carnal state are not able to procure this divine influence for themselves; thus, it is true, *"Whom the world cannot receive."*

The World Does Not See Him

The unregenerate world of sinners despises the Holy Spirit, *"because it seeth him not."* Yes, I believe this is the great secret why many laugh at the idea of the existence of the Holy Spirit—because they do not see Him. You tell the worldling, "I have the Holy Spirit within me." He says, "I cannot see it." He wants it to be something tangible, something he can recognize with his senses.

Have you ever heard the argument used by a good old Christian against an infidel doctor? The doctor said there is no soul, and asked, "Did you ever see a soul?"

"No," said the Christian.

"Did you ever hear a soul?"

"No."

"Did you ever smell a soul?"

"No."

"Did you ever taste a soul?"

"No."

"Did you ever feel a soul?"

"Yes," said the man. "I feel I have one within me."

"Well," said the doctor, "there are four senses against one; you have only one on your side."

"Very well," said the Christian. "Did you ever see a pain?"

"No."

"Did you ever hear a pain?"

"No."

"Did you ever smell a pain?"

"No."

"Did you ever taste a pain?"

"No."

"Did you ever feel a pain?"

"Yes."

"And that is quite enough, I suppose, to prove there is a pain?"

"Yes."

The Personality of the Holy Spirit

So the worldling says there is no Holy Spirit because he cannot see it. Fine, but we feel Him. You say that is fanaticism, and that we have never felt it. Suppose you tell me that honey is bitter. I reply, "No, I am sure you cannot have tasted it; taste it and try." So it is with the Holy Spirit. If you but once felt His influence, you would no longer say there is no Holy Spirit because you cannot see it.

Are there not many things, even in nature, that we cannot see? Did you ever see the wind? No, but you know there is wind when you watch a hurricane tossing the waves about or tearing down homes; or when, in the soft evening breeze, it kisses the flowers and makes dewdrops hang in pearly coronets around the rose.

Have you ever seen electricity? No, but you know there is such a thing, for it travels along the wires for thousands of miles and carries our messages. Although you cannot see the thing itself, you know there is such a thing. In the same way, you must believe there is a Holy Spirit working in us, *"both to will and to do of his good pleasure"* (Philippians 2:13), even though He is beyond our senses.

The World Does Not Know Him

Another reason why worldly men laugh at the doctrine of the Holy Spirit is because they do not know Him. If they knew Him through heartfelt experiences; if they recognized His work in their souls; if they had ever been touched by Him; if they had ever trembled under a sense of sin; if they had had their hearts melted, then they would never have doubted the existence of the Holy Spirit.

Words to the Saints

And now, beloved, our text says, *"He dwelleth with you, and shall be in you."* I will conclude with that sweet recollection—the Holy Spirit dwells in all believers and will be with them.

One word of comment and advice to the saints of God and to sinners, and I will be done. Saints of the Lord, you have heard that God the Holy Spirit is a person. You have had it proved to your souls. What should follow the understanding of this truth? Why, it follows how earnest you should be in prayer to the Holy Spirit, as well as for the Holy Spirit. You should lift up your prayers to the Holy Spirit. You should cry earnestly to Him, for He is *"able to do exceeding abundantly above all that we ask or think"* (Ephesians 3:20).

Look at the mass of people in this church.* What is to convert it? See this crowd? Who is to make my influence permeate through the mass? You know this place now has a mighty influence, and, God blessing us, it will have an influence not only upon this city, but also upon England at large, for we now employ the printing press as well as the pulpit. Certainly, I should say, before the close of the year, more than two hundred thousand of my productions will be scattered through the land—words uttered by my lips or written by my pen.

Yet how can this influence be rendered for good? How will God's glory be promoted by it? Only by incessant prayer for the Holy Spirit, by constantly calling down the influence of the Holy Spirit upon us. We want Him to rest upon every page that is printed and upon every word that is uttered. Let us, then, be doubly earnest in pleading with the Holy Spirit that He would come and own our labors, that the whole church at large may be revived thereby. May not only we share in the benefit, but also the whole world.

Words to the Sinners

To the ungodly, I have this one closing word to say. Ever be careful how you speak of the Holy Spirit. I do not

---

* Spurgeon delivered this message to the congregation at New Park Street Chapel, Southwark, a borough of London, England, on January 21, 1855.

know what the unpardonable sin is, and I do not think any man understands it, but it is something like this: "He who speaks a word against the Holy Spirit, it will never be forgiven him." I do not know what that means, but tread carefully!

There is danger. There is a pit that our ignorance has covered by sand. Tread carefully. You may be in it before the next hour! If there is any strife in your heart today, perhaps you will go to a barroom and forget it. Perhaps there is some voice speaking in your soul, and you will put it away. I do not know if you will be resisting the Holy Spirit and committing the unpardonable sin, but it is somewhere there.

Be very careful. There is no crime on earth as black as the crime against the Holy Spirit! You may blaspheme the Father, and you will be damned for it unless you repent. You may blaspheme the Son, and hell will be your portion unless you are forgiven. Yet blaspheme the Holy Spirit, and thus says the Lord:

All manner of sin and blasphemy shall be forgiven unto men: but the blasphemy against the Holy Ghost shall not be forgiven unto men. And whosoever speaketh a word against the Son of man, it shall be forgiven him: but whosoever speaketh against the Holy Ghost, it shall not be forgiven him, neither in this world, neither in the world to come.

(Matthew 12:31–32)

I cannot tell you what it is. I do not profess to understand it, but there it is. It is the danger signal: Stop, man, stop! If you have despised the Holy Spirit, if you have laughed at His revelations and scorned what Christians call His influence, I beg you, stop! Take time right now to deliberate seriously. Perhaps some of you have actually committed the unpardonable sin; stop! Let fear stop you;

sit down. Do not drive on so rashly as you have done, Jehu! (See 2 Kings 9:20.) Oh, slacken your reins! You who are such a profligate in sin, you who have uttered such hard words against the Trinity, stop! Ah, this warning makes us all stop! It makes us all draw up and say, "Have I perhaps done so?" Let us think of this; and let us not at any time stifle the Holy Spirit of God either with our words or actions.

Chapter 5

The Intercession of the Holy Spirit

Likewise the Spirit also helpeth our infirmities:
for we know not what we should pray for as we
ought: but the Spirit itself maketh intercession for us
with groanings which cannot be uttered. And he that
searcheth the hearts knoweth what is the mind of the
Spirit, because he maketh intercession for the saints
according to the will of God.
—Romans 8:26–27

T he apostle Paul wrote to a tried and afflicted people, and one of his purposes was to remind them of the rivers of comfort that were flowing near at hand.

Rivers of Comfort

The Comfort of Sonship

First of all, he stirred up their pure minds by reminding them of their sonship, for he said, *"As many as are led by the Spirit of God, they are the sons of God"* (Romans 8:14). They were, therefore, encouraged to side with Christ, the Elder Brother, with whom they had become *"joint-heirs"* (v. 17). They were exhorted to *"suffer with him"* (v.

17) so that afterward they might be glorified with Him. All that they endured came from the Father's hand, and this truth was to comfort them. A thousand sources of joy are opened in that one blessing of adoption. *"Blessed be the God and Father of our Lord Jesus Christ"* (1 Peter 1:3), by whom we have been begotten into the family of grace (vv. 3–4).

The Comfort of Hope

After Paul had alluded to that consoling subject, he turned to the next ground of comfort, namely, that we are to be sustained by hope during our present trials. There is an amazing glory reserved for us, and though as yet we cannot enter into it, but in harmony with the whole creation must continue to groan and travail (Romans 8:22), yet the hope of this itself should minister strength to us and enable us patiently to bear *"our light affliction, which is but for a moment"* (2 Corinthians 4:17).

This truth is full of sacred refreshment: Hope sees a crown in reserve (2 Timothy 4:8), mansions in readiness, and Jesus Himself preparing a place for us (John 14:2); and by this rapturous sight, hope sustains the soul under the sorrows of the hour. Hope is the grand anchor by whose means we ride out the present storm.

The Comfort of His Abiding Presence

The apostle then turned to a third source of comfort, namely, the abiding of the Holy Spirit in and with the Lord's people. He used the word *"likewise"* to intimate that, in the same manner as hope sustains the soul, the Holy Spirit strengthens us under trial. Hope operates spiritually upon our spiritual faculties, and so does the Holy Spirit. In some mysterious way, He divinely operates upon the newborn faculties of the believer, so that he is sustained under his infirmities. In His light, we will see light. I pray, therefore, that we may be helped by the Spirit while we consider His mysterious operations, so that we may not fall into error or miss precious truths through the blindness of our hearts.

The text speaks of *"our infirmities,"* or—as many translators put it in the singular—of "our infirmity." By this is meant our affliction and the weakness that trouble reveals in us. The Holy Spirit helps us to bear the infirmity of our bodies and of our minds; He helps us to bear our cross, whether it is physical pain, mental depression, spiritual conflict, slander, poverty, or persecution. He helps our infirmity, and with a Helper so divinely strong, we do not need to fear the result. God's grace will be sufficient for us; His *"strength is made perfect in weakness"* (2 Corinthians 12:9).

I think, dear friends, you will all admit that if a man can pray, his troubles are at once lightened. When we feel that we have power with God and can obtain anything we ask for from His hands, then our difficulties cease to oppress us. We take our burdens to our heavenly Father and express them in the accents of childlike confidence; we come away quite content to bear whatever His holy will may lay upon us.

Prayer is a great outlet for grief; it draws up the sluices and abates the swelling flood that otherwise might be too strong for us. We bathe our wounds in the lotion of prayer, and the pain is lulled, the fever removed. Our minds may become so disturbed and our hearts so perplexed that we do not know how to pray. We see the mercy seat, and we perceive that God will hear us. We have no doubt about that, for we know that we are His own favored children, yet we hardly know what to desire. We fall into such heaviness of spirit and complexity of thought that the one remedy of prayer, which we have always found to be unfailing, appears to be taken from us. Here, then, in the nick of time, as *"a very present help in trouble"* (Psalm 46:1), comes the Holy Spirit. He draws near to teach us how to pray, and in this way He helps our infirmity, relieves our suffering, and enables us to bear the heavy burden without fainting under the load.

At this time, let us consider, first, the help that the Holy Spirit gives; second, the prayers that He inspires; and third, the success that such prayers are certain to obtain.

The Help the Holy Spirit Gives

First, the help that the Holy Spirit gives meets the weakness that we deplore. If, in times of trouble, a man can pray, his burden loses its weight. If the believer can take anything and everything to God, then he learns to glory in infirmities (2 Corinthians 12:9) and to rejoice in tribulation, but sometimes we are in such confusion of mind that *"we know not what we should pray for as we ought."*

Knowing What to Pray For

In a measure, through our ignorance, we never know what we should pray for until we are taught by the Spirit of God, but there are times when this beclouding of the soul is dense indeed, and we do not even know what would help us out of our trouble if we could obtain it.

The Holy Spirit sees the disease, but we do not even know the name of the medicine we need. We look over the many things that we might ask for from the Lord, and we feel that each of them would be helpful, but that none of them would precisely meet our case. We could ask with confidence for spiritual blessings that we know to be according to the divine will, but perhaps these would not meet our specific circumstances. There are other things for which we are allowed to ask, but we scarcely know whether, if we had them, they would really meet our needs, and we also feel a reluctance to pray for them.

In praying for temporal things, we plead with measured voices, ever referring our petition for revision to the will of the Lord. Moses was not permitted to enter Canaan, for God denied him. (See Numbers 20:8–12; Deuteronomy 34:4.) The man who was healed begged the Lord to be able to go with Him, but Jesus gave him this answer: *"Go home to thy friends"* (Mark 5:19). Regarding future events, we pray about such matters with this reserve: "Nevertheless, not what I want, but as You desire." (See Matthew 26:39.) At times, this very spirit of resignation appears to increase our spiritual difficulty, for we do not wish to ask for anything that would be contrary to the mind of God, and yet we must ask for something. We are reduced to such straits that we must pray, but what will be the particular subject of prayer we cannot for a while make out. Even when ignorance and perplexity are removed, we still do not know *"what we should pray for as we ought."*

How to Pray

When we know the matter of prayer, we often fail to pray in the right manner. We ask, but we are afraid that we will not receive, because we do not exercise the thought or the faith that we judge to be essential to prayer. At times, we cannot command the earnestness that is the life of supplication. A lethargy steals over us, our hearts are chilled, our hands are numbed, and we cannot wrestle with the angel. (See Genesis 32:24–29.)

We know what material objects to pray for, but we do not know what to pray for *"as we ought."* It is the manner of the prayer that perplexes us, even when the matter is decided upon. How can I pray? My mind wanders; I trumpet like a whooping crane; I roar like a beast in pain; I moan in the brokenness of my heart, but, oh, I do not know what my inmost spirit needs. Or, if I know it, I do not know how to frame my petition properly before Him. I do not know how to open my lips in His majestic presence. I am so troubled that I cannot speak. My spiritual distress robs me of the power to pour out my heart before my God. Now, beloved, it is in such a plight as this that the Holy Spirit aids us with His divine help. Hence, He is *"a very present help in trouble"* (Psalm 46:1).

Instruction

Coming to our aid in our bewilderment, He instructs us. This is one of His frequent operations upon the mind of the believer: *"He shall teach you all things"* (John 14:26). He instructs us as to our need and as to the promises of God that refer to that need. He shows us where our deficiencies are, what our sins are, and what our needs are. He sheds light on our condition and makes us feel deeply our helplessness, sinfulness, and dire poverty. Then He casts the same light on the promises of the Word and lays home to the heart that very text that was intended to meet the occasion—the precise promise that was framed with the foresight of our present distress. In that light, He makes the promise shine in all its truthfulness, certainty, sweetness, and suitability, so that we, poor trembling sons of men, dare to take that Word into our mouths that first came out of God's mouth, and then come with it as an argument and plead it before the throne of the heavenly grace. Our power in prayer lies in the plea, "Lord, do as You have said."

How greatly we ought to value the Holy Spirit, because when we are in the dark, He gives us light, and when our perplexed spirit is so befogged and beclouded that it cannot see its own need and cannot find the appropriate promise in the Scriptures, the Spirit of God comes in, teaches us all things, and brings to our remembrance everything that our Lord has told us (John 14:26).

Guidance

He guides us in prayer; thus, He helps our infirmities. However, the blessed Spirit does more than this; He will often direct the mind to the special subject of prayer. He dwells within us as our Counselor and points out to us what it is we should seek at the hands of God. We do not know why it is so, but we sometimes find our minds carried as by a strong undercurrent into a particular line of prayer for some definite purpose. It is not merely that our judgment leads us in that direction, though usually the Spirit of God acts upon us by enlightening our judgment, but we often feel an unaccountable and irresistible desire rising within our hearts. This so presses upon us that we not only utter the desire before God at our ordinary times for prayer, but also feel it crying in our hearts all the day long, almost to the supplanting of all other considerations. At such times, we should thank God for direction and give our desire a clear road: The Holy Spirit is granting us inward direction as to how we can count on good success in our pleadings. The Spirit will give such guidance to each of you if you will ask Him to illuminate you.

He will guide you both negatively and positively. Negatively, He will forbid you to pray for certain things, just as Paul tried *"to go into Bithynia: but the Spirit suffered* [him] *not"* (Acts 16:7). On the other hand, He will cause you to hear a cry within your soul that will guide your petitions, even as He made Paul to hear the cry from Macedonia, saying, *"Come over into Macedonia, and help us"* (v. 9).

The Spirit teaches wisely, as no other teacher can do. Those who obey His promptings will not walk in darkness. He leads the spiritual eye to take good and steady aim at the very center of the target, and thus we hit the mark in our pleadings.

Intercession

Neither is this all, for the Spirit of God is not sent merely to guide and help our devotion, but He also *"maketh intercession for the saints according to the will of God."* This expression does not mean that the Holy Spirit groans or personally prays, but that He excites intense desire and creates inexpressible groanings in us, and these are ascribed to Him. Solomon built the temple because he superintended and ordained it all, yet I do not know that he ever fashioned a timber or prepared a stone. Likewise, the Holy Spirit prays and pleads within us by leading us to pray and plead. This He does by awakening our desires.

The Holy Spirit has a wonderful power over renewed hearts, as much power as the skillful musician has over the strings on which he lays his experienced hand. The influences of the Holy Spirit at times pass through the soul like winds through an aeolian harp, creating and inspiring sweet notes of gratitude and tones of desire, to which we would have been strangers if it had not been for His divine visitation.

He can wake us from our lethargy; He can warm us out of our lukewarmness; and He can enable us, when we are on our knees, to rise above the ordinary routine of prayer into that victorious importunity against which nothing can stand. He can lay certain desires so pressingly upon our hearts that we can never rest until they are fulfilled. He can make the zeal for God's house to eat us up (Psalm 69:9; John 2:17), and the passion for God's glory to be like *"a burning fire shut up in* [our] *bones"* (Jeremiah 20:9); inspiring our prayers is one part of that process by which He helps our infirmity. True Advocate is He, and Comforter most effectual. Blessed be His name.

Strength

The Holy Spirit also divinely operates in the strengthening of the faith of believers. At first, that faith is of

His creating, and afterward, it is of His sustaining and increasing. Oh, brothers and sisters, have you not often felt your faith rise in proportion to your trials? Have you not, like Noah's ark, mounted toward heaven as the flood deepened around you? You have felt as sure about the promise as you felt about the trial. The affliction was, as it were, in your very bones, but the promise was also in your heart. You could not doubt the affliction, for you smarted under it, but you also could not doubt the divine help, for your confidence was firm and unmoved.

Only the greatest faith is what God has a right to expect from us, yet we never exhibit it unless the Holy Spirit strengthens our confidence and opens up before us the covenant with all its seals and securities. It is He who leads our souls to cry, *"Although my house be not so with God; yet he hath made with me an everlasting covenant, ordered in all things, and sure"* (2 Samuel 23:5). Blessed be the Divine Spirit, then, that since faith is essential to prevailing prayer, He helps us in supplication by increasing our faith. Without faith, prayer cannot speed, for he who wavers *"is like a wave of the sea driven with the wind and tossed"* (James 1:6), and such a person may not expect *"any thing of the Lord"* (v. 7). Happy are we when the Holy Spirit removes our wavering and enables us, like Abraham, to believe without staggering, knowing full well that He who has promised is *"able also to perform"* (Romans 4:20–21).

Using three examples, I will endeavor to describe the work of the Spirit of God in this matter, though they all fall short, and indeed all that I can say must fall infinitely short of the glory of His work. The actual mode of His working upon the mind we may not attempt to explain; it remains a mystery, and it would be an unholy intrusion to attempt to remove the veil. There is no difficulty in our believing that as one human mind operates upon another mind, so does the Holy Spirit influence our spirits. We are forced to use words if we would influence our fellowmen, but the Spirit of God can operate upon the human mind more directly and communicate with it in silence. Into that matter, however, we will not dive lest we intrude where our knowledge would be drowned by our presumption.

Like a Prompter

My illustrations do not touch the mystery, but set forth the grace. The Holy Spirit acts to His people somewhat as a prompter to a reciter. A man has to deliver a piece that he has learned, but his memory is treacherous. Therefore, somewhere out of sight, there is a prompter, so that when the speaker is at a loss and might use a wrong word, a whisper is heard that suggests the right one. When the speaker has almost lost the thread of his speech, he turns his ear, and the prompter gives him the word and aids his memory. If I may be allowed the simile, I would say that this represents, in part, the work of the Spirit of God in us, suggesting to us the right desire and bringing all things to our remembrance, whatever Christ has told us (John 14:26).

In prayer, we would often come to a dead end, but He incites, suggests, inspires, and so we go forward. In prayer, we might grow weary, but the Comforter encourages and refreshes us with encouraging thoughts. When we are, in our bewilderment, almost driven to give up prayer, the whisper of His love drops a live coal from off the altar into our souls, and our hearts glow with greater ardor than before. Regard the Holy Spirit as your prompter, and let your ears be opened to His voice. Yet He is much more than this.

Like an Advocate

Let me attempt a second simile: The Holy Spirit is like an advocate to one in peril with the law. Suppose that a poor man had a great lawsuit concerning his whole estate, and he was forced personally to go into court to plead his own cause and speak up for his rights. If he were an uneducated man, he would be in a poor plight. An adversary in the court might plead against him and overthrow him, for he could not answer him. This poor man knows very little about the law and is quite unable to meet his cunning opponent.

Suppose one who was perfect in the law would take up his cause warmly and come and live with him. He would use all his knowledge so as to prepare his case for him, draw up his petitions, and fill his mouth with arguments. Would this not be a grand relief?

This counselor would suggest the line of pleading, arrange the arguments, and put them into proper legal language. When the poor man was baffled by a question asked in court, he would run home and ask his adviser. His friend would tell him exactly how to meet the objector. Suppose, too, that when he had to plead with the judge himself, this advocate at home would teach him how to behave and what to present, and encourage him to hope that he would prevail. Would this not be a great blessing?

Who would be the pleader in such a case? The poor client would plead, but still, when he won the suit, he would trace it all to the advocate who lived at his home and gave him counsel. Indeed, it would be the advocate pleading for him, even while he pleaded himself. This is an instructive symbol of a great fact. Within this narrow house of my body, this tenement of clay, if I am a true believer, the Holy Spirit dwells; and when I desire to pray, I may ask Him what I should pray for as I ought, and He will help me. He will write the prayers that I ought to offer upon the tablets of my heart, and I will see them there, and so I will be taught how to plead. It will be the Spirit's own Self pleading in me, by me, and through me, before the throne of grace. What a happy man in his lawsuit would such a poor man be, and how happy are you and I that we have the Holy Spirit to be our Counselor!

Like a Father

Yet one more illustration. It is that of a father helping his son. Suppose it is a time of war centuries ago. Old English warfare to a great extent was then conducted by bowmen. Here is a youth who is to be initiated in the art of archery; therefore, he carries a bow. It is a strong bow and very hard to draw; indeed, it requires more strength than the youth can summon to bend it.

See how his father teaches him. "Put your right hand here, my boy, and place your left hand so. Now pull." As the youth pulls back, his father's hands are on the boy's hands, and the bow is drawn. The lad draws the bow, but it is quite as much his father's strength that is pulling the bow as it is the boy's.

We cannot draw the bow of prayer alone. Sometimes a bow of steel is not broken by our hands, for we cannot even bend it. Then the Holy Spirit puts His mighty hand over ours and covers our weakness so that we draw; and then, what a splendid drawing of the bow it is! The bow bends so easily we wonder how that could be. Away flies the arrow, and it pierces the very center of the target, for He who gives has won the day; but it was His secret might that made us strong, and to Him be the glory of it. Thus have I tried to set forth the encouraging fact that the Spirit helps the people of God.

The Prayer the Holy Spirit Inspires

Our second subject is that part of prayer that is especially and distinctively the work of the Spirit of God. The text says, *"The Spirit itself maketh intercession for us with groanings which cannot be uttered."* It is not the Spirit who groans, but we who groan; however, as I have shown you, the Spirit excites the emotion that causes us to groan. It is clear, then, that the prayers that are composed in us by the Spirit of God are those that arise from our inmost souls. A man's heart is moved when he groans.

A groan is a matter about which there is no hypocrisy. A groan comes not from the lips, but from the heart. A groan, then, is a part of prayer that we owe to the Holy Spirit, and the same is true of all the prayer that wells up from the deep fountains of our inner lives. The prophet Jeremiah cried, *"My bowels, my bowels! I am pained at my very heart; my heart maketh a noise in me"* (Jeremiah 4:19). This deep ground swell of desire, this tidal motion of the life-floods, is caused by the Holy Spirit. His work is never superficial, but always deep and inward.

Prayers of Anguish

Such prayers will rise within us when the mind is far too troubled to let us speak. We do not know *"what we should pray for as we ought,"* and it is then that we groan or utter some other inarticulate sound. Hezekiah said, *"Like a crane or a swallow, so did I chatter"* (Isaiah 38:14). The psalmist said, *"I am so troubled that I cannot speak"* (Psalm 77:4), and *"I have roared by reason of the disquietness of my heart"* (Psalm 38:8); but he added, *"Lord, all my desire is before thee; and my groaning is not hid from thee"* (v. 9). The sighing of the prisoner surely comes up into the ears of the Lord. There is real prayer in these *"groanings which cannot be uttered."*

It is the power of the Holy Spirit in us that creates all real prayer, even that which takes the form of a groan, because the mind is incapable, by reason of its bewilderment and grief, of clothing its emotion in words. I pray that you will never think lightly of the supplications of your anguish. Rather, judge that such prayers are like Jabez, of whom it is written, *"And Jabez was more honourable than his brethren: and his mother called his name Jabez, saying, Because I bare him with sorrow"* (1 Chronicles 4:9). What is brought forth from the depth of the soul when it is stirred with a terrible tempest is more precious than pearl or coral, for it is the intercession of the Holy Spirit.

Prayers Expressing Great Need

These prayers are sometimes *"groanings which cannot be uttered"* because they concern such great things that they cannot be spoken. I am in need, my Lord! I need, I need. I cannot tell you what I need, but I seem to need so many things. If it were just a little thing, my narrow capacity could comprehend and describe it, but I need all Your covenant blessings. You know what I need before I ask You (Matthew 6:8); and although I cannot explain each item of my need, I know it to be very great, and more than I myself can ever estimate.

I groan, for I can do no more. Prayers that are the offspring of great desires, sublime aspirations, and elevated designs are surely the work of the Holy Spirit, and their power within a man is frequently so great that he cannot find expression for them. Words fail, and even the sighs that try to embody them cannot be uttered.

Inarticulate Prayers

It may be, beloved, that we groan because we are conscious of the littleness of our desires and of the narrowness of our faith. The trial itself may seem too insignificant to pray about. I have known what it is to feel as if I could not pray about a certain matter, and yet I have been obliged to groan about it. A *"thorn in the flesh"* (2 Corinthians 12:7) may be as painful a thing as a sword in the bones, and yet we may go and beseech the Lord three times about it (see verse 8), and, getting no answer, we may feel that *"we know not what we should pray for as we ought"*; and yet it makes us groan. Yes, and with that natural groan there may go up an unutterable groaning of the Holy Spirit.

Beloved, what a different view of prayer God has from what men think to be the correct one. You may have seen very beautiful prayers in print, and you may have heard very charming compositions from the pulpit, but I trust you have not fallen in love with the sound of them. Judge these things rightly. I pray that you will never think well of fine prayers, for before the thrice-holy God, it is unbecoming for a sinful suppliant to play the orator.

We have heard of a certain clergyman who was said to have prayed "the finest prayer ever offered to a Boston audience." Just so! The Boston audience received the prayer, and there it ended. We want the mind of the Spirit in prayer, and not the mind of the flesh. (See Romans 8:5.) The tail feathers of pride should be pulled out of our prayers, for they need only the wing feathers of faith. The peacock feathers of poetical expression are out of place before the throne of God. Someone says, "What remarkably beautiful language he used in prayer! What an intellectual treat his prayer was!" Yes, yes, but God looks at the heart (1 Samuel 16:7). To Him, fine language is *as sounding brass, or a tinkling cymbal*" (1 Corinthians 13:1), but a groan has music in it.

We do not like groans. Our ears are much too delicate to tolerate such dreary sounds, but not so the great *"Father of spirits"* (Hebrews 12:9). A Methodist brother cries, "Amen," and you say, "I cannot bear such Methodistic noise." No, but if it comes from the man's heart, God can bear it. When you go upstairs to your room this evening to pray and find you cannot pray, but have to moan, "Lord, I am too full of anguish and too perplexed to pray; hear the voice of my roaring," though you reach to nothing else, you will be really praying. When we can say, like David, *"I opened my mouth, and panted"* (Psalm 119:131), we are by no means in a bad state of mind.

All flowery language in prayer, and especially all intoning or performing of prayers, must be abhorrent to God; it is little short of profanity to offer solemn supplication to God after the manner called "intoning." The sighing of a true heart is infinitely more acceptable, for it is the work of the Spirit of God.

Prayers of Knowledge

We may say of the prayers that the Holy Spirit works in us that they are prayers of knowledge. Notice, our difficulty is that we do not know what we should pray for, but the Holy Spirit does know; therefore, He helps us by enabling us to pray intelligently, knowing what we are asking for, as far as this knowledge is needful to valid prayer. The text speaks of *"the mind of the Spirit."* What a mind this must be! It is the mind of the Spirit who arranged all the order that now pervades this earth! There once was chaos and confusion, but the Holy Spirit brooded over all, and His mind is the originator of that beautiful arrangement that we so admire in the visible creation. What a mind this must be!

The Holy Spirit's mind is seen in our intercessions when, under His sacred influence, we present our cases before the Lord and plead with holy wisdom for things proper and necessary. What wise and admirable desires must those be that the Spirit of Wisdom Himself works in us!

Acceptable Prayers

Moreover, the Holy Spirit's intercession creates prayers offered in a proper manner. I showed you that the difficulty is that *"we know not what we should pray for as we ought,"* and that the Spirit meets that difficulty by making intercession for us in a right manner. The Holy Spirit works in us humility, earnestness, intensity, importunity, faith, resignation, and all else that is acceptable to

God in our supplications. We do not know how to mingle these sacred spices in the incense of prayer. If left to ourselves, at our very best, we get too much of one ingredient or another and spoil the sacred compound; but the Holy Spirit's intercessions have in them such a blessed blending of all that is good that they come up as a sweet perfume before the Lord.

Spirit-taught prayers are offered as they ought to be. They are His own intercession, in some respects, for we read that the Holy Spirit not only helps us to intercede but also *"maketh intercession."* It is stated twice in our text that He *"maketh intercession"* for us. I tried to show the meaning of this when I described a father putting his hands upon his child's hands. This is something more than helping us to pray, something more than encouraging us or directing us, but I venture no further, except to say that He puts such force of His own mind into our poor weak thoughts and desires and hopes that He Himself *"maketh intercession for us,"* working in us to will and to pray according to *"his good pleasure"* (Philippians 2:13).

Prayers for the Saints

Notice, however, that these intercessions of the Spirit are only in the saints. *"The Spirit...maketh intercession for us,"* and *"He maketh intercession for the saints."* Does He do nothing for sinners, then? Yes, He quickens sinners into spiritual life, and He strives with them to overcome their sinfulness and to turn them into the right way. However, in the saints, He works with us and enables us to pray after His mind and according to the will of God.

His intercession is not in or for the unregenerate. Oh, unbelievers, you must first be made saints, or you cannot feel the Spirit's intercession within you. What need we have to go to Christ for the blessing of the Holy Spirit. It can be ours only by faith in Christ Jesus! *"But as many as received him, to them gave he power to become the sons of God"* (John 1:12). *"The Spirit of adoption"* (Romans 8:15) and all His helping grace comes to the children of God alone. Unless we are the children of God, the Holy Spirit's indwelling will not be ours. We are shut out from the intercession of the Holy Spirit and from the intercession of Jesus, too, for He has said, *"I pray not for the world, but for them which thou hast given me"* (John 17:9). Thus I have tried to show you the kind of prayers that the Spirit inspires.

The Sure Success of Inspired Prayers

Our third and last point is that all of the prayers that the Spirit of God inspires in us must succeed.

God Understands Our Prayers

First, there is a meaning in our prayers that God reads and approves. When the Spirit of God writes a prayer on a man's heart, the man himself may be in such a state of mind that he does not altogether know what the prayer is. His interpretation of it is a groan, and that is all. Perhaps he does not get even as far as that in expressing the mind of the Spirit, but he feels *"groanings which cannot be uttered."* He cannot find a door of utterance for his inward grief.

Yet our heavenly Father, who looks immediately upon the heart, reads what the Spirit of God has written there and does not need even our groans to explain the meaning. He reads the heart itself. He *"knoweth,"* says the text, *"what is the mind of the Spirit."* The Spirit is one with the Father, and the Father knows what the Spirit means.

The desires that the Spirit prompts may be too spiritual for such babes in grace as we are to actually describe or express, yet the Spirit writes the desire on the renewed mind, and the Father sees it. Now, what God reads in the heart and approves of—for the word *"knoweth"* in this case includes approval as well as the act of omniscience—what God sees and approves of in the heart must succeed. Did Jesus not say, *"Your heavenly Father knoweth that ye have need of all these things"* (Matthew 6:32)? Did He not tell us this as an encouragement to believe that we will receive all necessary blessings? So it is with those prayers that are all broken up, wet with tears, and discordant with those sighs and inarticulate expressions, heavings of the chest and sobbings of the heart, and anguish and bitterness of spirit. Our gracious Lord reads them as a man reads a book, and they are written in a character that He fully understands.

To give a simple example: If I were to come into your house, I might find a little child there who cannot yet speak plainly. He cries for something, and he makes very odd and objectionable noises, combined with signs and movements, which are almost meaningless to a stranger, but his mother understands him and attends to his little pleadings. A mother can translate baby talk. She comprehends incomprehensible noises. Even so does our Father in heaven know all about our poor baby talk, for our prayers are not much better than that. He knows and comprehends the cryings, meanings, sighings, and chatterings of His bewildered children. Yes, a tender mother knows her child's needs before the child knows what he wants. Perhaps the little one stutters, stammers, and cannot get his words out, but the mother sees what he wants to say and understands the meaning. Likewise, we know this concerning our Great Father:

> He knows the thoughts we mean to speak,
> Ere from our opening lips they break.

Rejoice in this truth, because the prayers of the Spirit are known and understood by God; therefore, they will be sure to succeed.

God Agrees with Prayers Prompted by the Holy Spirit

The next argument for making us sure that our prayers will go forth is this: They are *"the mind of the Spirit."* God the Ever Blessed is one, and there can be no division among the Father, the Son, and the Holy Spirit. These Divine Persons always work together. There is a common desire for the glory of each blessed person of the Divine Trinity. Therefore, it cannot be conceived, without being profane, that anything could be the mind of the Holy Spirit and not be the mind of the Father and the mind of the Son, as well.

The mind of God is one and harmonious; if, therefore, the Holy Spirit dwells in you, and He moves you to any desire, then His mind is in your prayers, and it is not possible that the eternal Father would reject your petitions. The prayer that came from heaven will certainly go back to heaven. If the Holy Spirit prompts it, the Father must and will accept it, for it is not possible that He would slight the ever blessed and adorable Spirit.

Prayers from the Spirit Are according to the Will of God

One more word completes the argument, namely, that the work of the Spirit in the heart is not only *"the mind of the Spirit"* that God knows, but it is also according to the will or mind of God, for the Holy Spirit never makes intercession in us other than is consistent with the divine will.

Now, the divine will or mind may be viewed in two ways. First, there is the will declared in the proclamations of holiness in the Ten Commandments. The Spirit of God never prompts us to ask for anything that is unholy or inconsistent with the precepts of the Lord. Second, there is the secret mind of God, the will of His eternal predestination and decree, of which we know nothing; however, we do know this: The Spirit of God never prompts us to ask anything that is contrary to the eternal purpose of God.

Reflect on this for a moment: The Holy Spirit knows all the purposes of God, and when they are about to be fulfilled, He moves the children of God to pray about them, and so their prayers keep touch and tally with the divine decrees. Oh, would you not pray confidently if you knew that your prayers corresponded with the sealed book of destiny? We may safely entreat the Lord to do what He has ordained to do.

A carnal man draws the inference that, if God has ordained an event, we need not pray about it. However, faith obediently draws the inference that the God who secretly ordained to give the blessing has openly commanded that we should pray for it, and therefore, faith obediently prays.

Coming events cast their shadows before them, and when God is about to bless His people, His coming favor casts the shadow of prayer over the church. When He is about to favor an individual, He casts the shadow of hopeful expectation over his soul. Let men laugh at our prayers as they will, and say there is no power in them. These prayers are the indicators of the movement of the wheels of Providence.

Believing supplications are forecasts of the future. He who prays in faith is like the seer of old; he sees what is to be. His holy expectancy, like a telescope, brings distant objects near to him. He is bold to declare that he has the petition that he has asked of God, and he therefore begins to rejoice and to praise God, even before the blessing has actually arrived. So it is: Prayer prompted by the Holy Spirit is the footfall of the divine decree.

My dear friends, I conclude by saying this: See the absolute necessity of the Holy Spirit, for if the saints *"know not what* [they] *should pray for as* [they] *ought,"* if consecrated men and women, with Christ suffering in them, still feel their need of the instruction of the Holy Spirit, how much more do you who are not saints, and have never given yourselves up to God, require divine teaching! Oh, that you would know and feel your dependence on the Holy Spirit so that He may prompt the once crucified but now ascended Redeemer, in order that this gift of the Spirit, this promise of the Father, may be shed abroad upon men.

May He who comes from Jesus lead you to Jesus. And then, people of God, let this last thought stay with you: What condescension that the Divine Person would dwell in you forever, and that He would be with you to help your prayers! Listen to me for a moment. If I read in the Scriptures that, in the most heroic acts of faith, God the Holy Spirit helps His people, I can understand it; if I read that, in the sweetest music of their songs when they worship best and sing their loftiest strains before the Most High God, the Spirit helps them, I can understand it; and even if I hear that, in their wrestling prayers and prevalent intercessions, God the Holy Spirit helps them, I can understand it. However, I bow with reverent amazement, my heart sinking into the dust with adoration, when I reflect that God the Holy Spirit helps us when we cannot speak, but only groan. Yes, and when we cannot even utter our groanings, He not only helps us but also claims as His own particular creation the *"groanings which cannot be uttered."* This is condescension, indeed!

In deigning to help us in the grief that cannot even vent itself in groaning, He proves Himself to be a true Comforter. "O God, my God, You have not forsaken me. You are not far from me or from the voice of my roaring. (See Psalm 22:1.) You left the Firstborn for a while when He was made a curse for us, so that He cried in agony, *'Why hast thou forsaken me?'* (Matthew 27:46), but You will not leave one of the *'many brethren'* (Romans 8:29) for whom He died. The Spirit will be with them, and when they cannot so much as groan, He will make intercession for them with *'groanings which cannot be uttered.'*"

God bless you, my beloved brothers and sisters, and may you feel the Spirit of the Lord working in you and with you.

Chapter 6

Adoption—The Spirit and the Cry

*And because ye are sons, God hath sent forth the Spirit
of his Son into your hearts, crying, Abba, Father.*
—Galatians 4:6

W
e do not find the doctrine of the unity of the Trinity set forth in Scripture in formal terms, such as those employed in the Athanasian Creed, which states, in part, "We worship one God in Trinity, and Unity....The Father is God, the Son God: and the Holy Ghost is God. And yet they are not three Gods: but one God." However, the truth of the triune God is continually taken for granted, as if it were a well-known fact in the church of God. If not expressed very often, in so many words, it is everywhere held in truth. It is mentioned incidentally, in connection with other truths, in a way that renders it quite as distinct as if it were expressed in a set formula. In many passages, it is brought before us so prominently that we must be willfully blind if we do not see it.

In our text, for instance, we have distinct mention of each of the three Divine Persons. *"God,"* that is the Father, *"sent forth the Spirit,"* that is the Holy Spirit; and He is here called *"the Spirit of his Son."*

Neither have we the names alone, for each sacred person is mentioned as acting in the work of our salvation. Note Galatians 4:4, which says, *"God sent forth his Son."* Then note the fifth verse, which speaks of the Son as redeeming those who were under the law; and then the text itself reveals the Spirit as coming into the hearts of believers and *"crying, Abba, Father."* Inasmuch as you have not only the mention of the separate names, but also certain special operations ascribed to each, it is plain that you have here the distinct personality of each.

Neither the Father, the Son, nor the Spirit can be an influence, or a mere form of existence, for each one acts in a divine manner, but with a special sphere and a distinct mode of operation. The error of regarding a certain Divine Person as a mere influence, or emanation, mainly assails the Holy Spirit; but its falseness is seen in the words, *"crying, Abba, Father."* An influence cannot cry; the act requires a person to perform it.

Though we may not understand the wonderful truth of the undivided unity and the distinct personality of the triune Godhead, nevertheless, we see this truth revealed in the Holy Scriptures; therefore, we accept it as a matter of faith.

The divinity of each of these sacred persons is also to be gathered from the text and its connection. We do not doubt the loving union of all in the work of deliverance. We reverence the Father, without whom we would not have been chosen or adopted.

> *Blessed be the God and Father of our Lord Jesus Christ, which according to his abundant mercy hath begotten us again unto a lively hope by the resurrection of Jesus Christ from the dead.* (1 Peter 1:3)

We love and reverence the Son, by whose most precious blood we have been redeemed, and with whom we are one in a mystical and everlasting union. We adore and love the Divine Spirit, for it is by Him that we have been regenerated, illuminated, quickened, preserved, and sanctified; and it is through Him that we receive the seal and witness within our hearts by which we are assured that we are indeed the sons of God.

God said, *"Let us make man in our image, after our likeness"* (Genesis 1:26). In the same way, the Divine Persons take counsel together, and all unite, in the new creation of the believer. We must not fail to bless, adore, and love each one of the exalted persons, but we must diligently bow in lowliest reverence before the one God—Father, Son, and Holy Spirit.

> Glory be to the Father,
> And to the Son,
> And to the Holy Spirit;
> As it was in the beginning,
> Is now, and ever will be,
> World without end. Amen.

Having noted this most important fact, let us come to the text itself, hoping to enjoy the doctrine of the Trinity while we are talking about our adoption, this wonder of grace in which They each have a share. Under the teaching of the Divine Spirit, may we be drawn into sweet communion with the Father through His Son Jesus Christ, to His glory and to our benefit.

Three things are very clearly set forth in the text. The first is the dignity of believers—*"Ye are sons."* The second is the consequent indwelling of the Holy Spirit—*"Because ye are sons, God hath sent forth the Spirit of his Son into your hearts."* The third is the filial cry—*"Crying, Abba, Father."*

The Dignity of Believers

First, adoption gives us the rights of children, and regeneration gives us the nature of children. We are partakers of both of these, for we are sons.

Adoption Is a Gift Received by Faith

Let us observe that this sonship is a gift of grace received by faith. In the sense meant here, we are not the sons of God by nature. We are in a sense *"the offspring of God"* (Acts 17:29) by nature, but this is very different from the sonship described in the text, which is the particular privilege of those who are born again.

The Jews claimed to be of the family of God, but as their privileges came to them by way of their fleshly birth, they are likened to Ishmael, who was born after the flesh, but who was cast out as the son of the bondwoman and compelled to give way to the son of the promise. We have a sonship that does not come to us by nature, for we are *"born, not of blood, nor of the will of the flesh, nor of the will of man, but of God"* (John 1:13). Our sonship comes by promise, by the operation of God as a special gift to a particular seed, set apart unto the Lord by His own sovereign grace, as Isaac was. This honor and this privilege come to us by faith. Note well the twenty-sixth verse of the preceding chapter: *"For ye are all the children of God by faith in Christ Jesus"* (Galatians 3:26). As unbelievers, we know nothing of adoption. While we are under the law, as self-righteous, we know something of servitude, but we know nothing of sonship. It is only after faith has come that we cease to be under the schoolmaster (vv. 24–25) and rise out of our minority to take the privileges of the sons of God.

Faith Brings Us Justification

Faith works in us the *"spirit of adoption"* (Romans 8:15), and our consciousness of sonship, in this way: First, it brings us justification. Galatians 3:24 says, *"The law was our schoolmaster to bring us unto Christ, that we might be justified by faith."* An unjustified man stands in the condition of a criminal, not of a child. His sin is laid to his charge; he is reckoned as unjust and unrighteous, as indeed he really is; and he is, therefore, a rebel against his king, and not a child enjoying his father's love.

Yet when faith realizes the cleansing power of the blood of the Atonement and lays hold of the righteousness of God in Christ Jesus, then the justified man becomes a son and a child. Justification and adoption always go together. *"Whom he called, them he also justified"* (Romans 8:30), and the calling is a call to the Father's house and to a recognition of sonship. Believing brings forgiveness and justification through our Lord Jesus; it also brings adoption, for it is written, *"But as many as received him, to them gave he power to become the sons of God, even to them that believe on his name"* (John 1:12).

Faith Frees Us from the Bondage of the Law

In the next place, faith brings us into the realization of our adoption by setting us free from the bondage of the law. *"After that faith is come, we are no longer under a schoolmaster"* (Galatians 3:25). When we groaned under a sense of sin and were shut up by it as in a prison, we feared that the law would punish us for our iniquity, and our lives were made bitter with fear. Moreover, we strove in our own blind, self-sufficient manner to keep that law, and this brought us into yet another bondage, which became harder and harder as failure gave way to more failure. We sinned and stumbled more and more, to our soul's confusion.

However, now that faith has come, we see the law fulfilled in Christ, and ourselves justified and accepted in Him. This changes the slave into a child, and duty into choice. Now we delight in the law, and by the power of the

Spirit, we walk in holiness to the glory of God. Thus it is that by believing in Christ Jesus, we escape from Moses, the taskmaster, and come to Jesus, the Savior. We cease to regard God as an angry Judge and view Him as our loving Father. The system of merit and command, punishment and fear, has given way to the rule of grace, gratitude, and love, and this new principle of government is one of the grand privileges of the children of God.

Faith Is the Mark of Our Sonship

Now, faith is the mark of sonship in all who have it, whoever they may be, *"for ye are all the children of God by faith in Christ Jesus"* (Galatians 3:26). If you are believing in Jesus, whether you are a Jew or Gentile, bond or free, you are a son of God. If you have believed in Christ recently and have only for the past few weeks been able to rest in His great salvation, even now, beloved, you are a child of God. It is not an after-privilege, granted to assurance or growth in grace; it is an early-blessing and belongs to him who has the smallest degree of faith and is no more than a babe in grace. If a man is a believer in Jesus Christ, his name is in the registry of the great family above, *"for ye are all the children of God by faith in Christ Jesus."*

Yet if you have no faith, no matter what zeal, no matter what works, no matter what knowledge, no matter what pretensions to holiness you may possess, you are nothing, and your religion is in vain. Without faith in Christ, you are *"as sounding brass, or a tinkling cymbal"* (1 Corinthians 13:1), for *"without faith it is impossible to please him [God]"* (Hebrews 11:6). Faith, then, wherever it is found, is the infallible token of a child of God, and its absence is fatal to the claim.

This, according to the apostle Paul, is further illustrated by our baptism, for, in baptism, if there is faith in the soul, there is an open "putting on" of the Lord

Jesus Christ. *"For as many of you as have been baptized into Christ have put on Christ"* (Galatians 3:27). In baptism, you professed to be dead to the world, and you were therefore buried into the name of Jesus. The meaning of that burial, if it had any right meaning to you, was that you professed yourself henceforth to be dead to everything but Christ, and, from that point on, your life was to be in Him. You were to be as one *"raised up from the dead...[to] walk in newness of life"* (Romans 6:4). Of course, the outward form avails nothing to the unbeliever, but to the one who is in Christ, it is a most instructive ordinance.

The spirit and essence of the law lie in the soul's entering into the symbol, in the man's knowing not only the baptism into water, but also the baptism into the Holy Spirit and into fire. As many of you as know that inward mystical baptism into Christ know also that henceforth you have put on Christ and are covered by Him as a man is covered by his clothes. Henceforth, you are one with Christ. You wear His name, you live in Him, you are saved by Him, and you are altogether His.

Now, if you are one with Christ, since He is the Son of God, you are sons, also. If you have put on Christ, God sees you not in yourself but in Christ, and what belongs to Christ belongs also to you. *"If ye be Christ's, then are ye Abraham's seed, and heirs according to the promise"* (Galatians 3:29).

As the Roman youth put on the toga when he came of age and was admitted to the rights of citizenship, so the putting on of Christ is the token of our admission into the position of sons of God. Thus are we actually admitted to the enjoyment of our glorious heritage. Every blessing of the covenant of grace belongs to those who are Christ's, and every believer is on that list. Thus, then, according to the teaching of the passage, we receive adoption by faith as the gift of grace.

Adoption Comes to Us by Redemption

Again, adoption comes to us by redemption. Read the passage that precedes the text:

> But when the fulness of the time was come, God sent forth his Son, made of a woman, made under the law, to redeem them that were under the law, that we might receive the adoption of sons. (Galatians 4:4–5)

Beloved, prize redemption, and never listen to teaching that would destroy its meaning or lower its importance. Remember that you were not redeemed with *"silver and gold,...but with the precious blood of Christ, as of a lamb without blemish"* (1 Peter 1:18–19).

You were under the law and subject to its curse, for you had broken it most grievously. You were subject to its penalty, for it is written, *"The soul that sinneth, it shall die"* (Ezekiel 18:4); and yet again, *"Cursed is every one that continueth not in all things which are written in the book of the law to do them"* (Galatians 3:10).

You were also under the terror of the law, for you feared its wrath. You were under its provoking power, for often when the commandment came, sin within you revived, and you died (Romans 7:9). Yet now you are redeemed from all that. As the Holy Spirit says, *"Christ hath redeemed us from the curse of the law, being made a curse for us: for it is written, Cursed is every one that hangeth on a tree"* (Galatians 3:13). Now, you *"are not under the law, but under grace"* (Romans 6:14), because Christ came under the law and kept it both by His active and His passive obedience, fulfilling all its commands and bearing all its penalty on your behalf and in your stead. Henceforth, you are the redeemed of the Lord and enjoy a liberty that comes by no other way but that of the eternal ransom.

Remember this glorious truth, and whenever you feel most assured that you are a child of God, praise the redeeming blood. Whenever your heart beats highest with love for your Great Father, bless the *"firstborn among many brethren"* (Romans 8:29). For your sakes, He came under the law, was circumcised, kept the law in His life, and bowed His head to it in His death. He honored and magnified the law, and He made the justice and righteousness of God to be more conspicuous by His life than it would have been by the holiness of all mankind, and God's justice to be more fully vindicated by His death than it would have been if all the world of sinners had been cast into hell. Glory be to our redeeming Lord, by whom we have received the adoption!

We Now Enjoy the Privilege of Sonship

Again, we further learn from the passage that we now enjoy the privilege of sonship. According to the context of the passage, the apostle meant not only that we are children, but also that we are full-grown sons. *"Because ye are sons"* means that because the time appointed by the Father has come, and you are of age, you are no longer under tutors and governors. As minors, we are under the authority of the schoolmaster; under the regimen of ceremonies; under types, figures, shadows; learning our ABCs by being convinced of sin. However, when faith comes, we are no longer under the schoolmaster, but come to a more free condition. Until faith comes, we are under *"tutors and governors"* (Galatians 4:2), like mere boys; but after faith comes, we take our rights as sons of God.

The Jewish people of old were under the yoke of the law: Its sacrifices were continual and its ceremonies endless; new moons and feasts had to be kept; jubilees had to be observed and pilgrimages made. In fact, the yoke was too heavy for feeble flesh to bear. The law followed the Israelite into every corner and dealt with him on every point.

It had to do with his clothing, his food, his drink, his bed, his board, and everything about him. It treated him like a boy at school who has a rule for everything.

Now that faith has come, we are full-grown sons; therefore, we are free from the rules that govern the child. We are under law to Christ, even as the full-grown son is still under the discipline of his father's house; but this is a law of love and not of fear, of grace and not of bondage. *"Stand fast therefore in the liberty wherewith Christ hath made us free, and be not entangled again with the yoke of bondage"* (Galatians 5:1). Do not return to the *"beggarly elements"* (Galatians 4:9) of a merely outward religion, but keep close to the worship of God in spirit and in truth, for this is the liberty of the children of God.

Now, by faith, we are no longer like servants. The apostle said that *"the heir, as long as he is a child, differeth nothing from a servant, though he be lord of all; but is under tutors and governors until the time appointed of the father"* (vv. 1–2). However, beloved, now you are the sons of God, and you have come to your majority. Now you are free to enjoy the honors and blessings of the Father's house. Rejoice that the free spirit dwells within you and prompts you to holiness; this is a power far superior to the merely external command and the whip of threatening. Now you are no longer in bondage to outward forms, rites, and ceremonies, but the Spirit of God teaches you all things and leads you into the inner meaning and substance of the truth.

Now, also, said the apostle, we are heirs: *"Wherefore thou art no more a servant, but a son; and if a son, then an heir of God through Christ"* (Galatians 4:7). No man living has ever realized to the full what this means. Believers are at this moment heirs, but what is the estate? It is God Himself! We are heirs of God—not only of the promises, of the covenant engagements, and of all the blessings that belong to the chosen seed, but heirs of God Himself! *"The*

LORD *is my portion, saith my soul"* (Lamentations 3:24).
"This God is our God for ever and ever" (Psalm 48:14).
We are not only heirs to God, to all that He gives to His
firstborn, but also heirs of God Himself. David said, *"The
LORD is the portion of mine inheritance and of my cup"*
(Psalm 16:5). As God said to Abraham, *"Fear not, Abram:
I am thy shield, and thy exceeding great reward"* (Genesis
15:1), so He says to every man who is born of the Spirit.
These are His own words: *"I will be to them a God, and they
shall be to me a people"* (Hebrews 8:10).

Why, then, believer, are you poor? All riches are yours.
Why, then, are you sorrowful? The ever blessed God is
yours. Why do you tremble? Omnipotence waits to help
you. Why do you distrust? His immutability will abide
with you even to the end and make His promise steadfast. All things are yours, for Christ is yours, and Christ
is God's. (See 1 Corinthians 3:22–23.) Although there are
some things that at present you cannot actually grasp in
your hand, or even see with your eyes, namely, the things
that are laid up for you in heaven, still, by faith, you can
enjoy even these, for God has *"raised us up together, and
made us sit together in heavenly places in Christ Jesus"*
(Ephesians 2:6), *"in whom also we have obtained an inheritance"* (Ephesians 1:11), so that *"our conversation* [citizen-
ship] *is in heaven"* (Philippians 3:20). Even now, we enjoy
the pledge and guarantee of heaven in the indwelling of
the Holy Spirit. Oh, what privileges belong to those who
are the sons of God!

One of the Consequences of Sonship Is Opposition

I would like to make one more point regarding the
believer's dignity. We are already tasting one of the inevitable consequences of being the sons of God: the opposition of the children of the bondwoman. (See Galatians
4:22–29.) No sooner had the apostle Paul preached the liberty of the saints than immediately there arose certain

teachers who said, "This will never do; you must be circumcised. You must come under the law." (See Acts 15:1–31; Galatians 5:11.) Their opposition was to Paul an indication that he was of the freewoman, for note that the children of the bondwoman singled him out for their virulent opposition. You will find, dear friend, that if you enjoy fellowship with God, if you live in the spirit of adoption, if you are brought near to the Most High, so as to be a member of the divine family, immediately all those who are under bondage to the law will quarrel with you. Thus, the apostle said, *"As then he that was born after the flesh persecuted him that was born after the Spirit, even so it is now"* (Galatians 4:29).

The child of Hagar was found by Sarah to be mocking Isaac, the child of promise (Genesis 21:8–9). Ishmael would have been glad to have shown his enmity to the hated heir by blows and personal assault, but there was a superior power to check him, so that he could get no further than *"mocking."* So it is now.

There have been periods in which the enemies of the Gospel have gone a great deal further than mocking, for they have been able to imprison and burn alive the lovers of the Gospel. However, now, thank God, we are under His special protection as to life and limb and liberty, and are as safe as Isaac was in Abraham's house. They can mock us, but they cannot go any further, or else some of us would be publicly tried. Yet trials of cruel mocking are still to be endured: Our words are twisted, our sentiments are misrepresented, and all sorts of horrible things are imputed to us, things that we know not, all to which we would reply with Paul, *"Am I therefore become your enemy, because I tell you the truth?"* (Galatians 4:16). This is the old way of the Hagarenes. The child according to the flesh is still doing his best to mock him who is born according to the Spirit. Do not be astonished, neither be grieved in the least degree, when this happens to any of you, but let this also establish your confidence and confirm your faith in Christ Jesus, for long ago He told you, *"If ye were of the world, the world would love his own: but because ye are not of the world, but I have chosen you out of the world, therefore the world hateth you"* (John 15:19).

The Consequent Indwelling of the Holy Spirit

"God hath sent forth the Spirit of his Son into your hearts." Here is a divine act of the Father. The Holy Spirit proceeds from the Father and the Son, and God has sent Him forth into your hearts. If He had come only knocking at your hearts and asking your permission to enter, He would never have entered. However, when Jehovah sent Him, He made His way, without violating your will, yet with irresistible power. Where Jehovah sent Him, there He will abide and never leave.

The Spirit of Christ

Beloved, I have no time to dwell on the words of the following Scripture, but I want you to turn them over in your thoughts, for they contain great depth. As surely as God sent His Son into the world to dwell among men, so that His saints beheld His glory, the *"(glory as of the only begotten of the Father,) full of grace and truth"* (John 1:14), so surely has God sent forth the Spirit to enter into men's hearts, to take up His residence there, that in Him, also, the glory of God may be revealed. Bless and adore the Lord who has sent you such a Visitor as this.

Now, note the style and title under which the Holy Spirit comes to us: He comes as the Spirit of Jesus. The words are *"the Spirit of his Son,"* by which is not meant the character and disposition of Christ—though that is quite true, for God sends these to His people—but the Holy Spirit.

Why, then, is He called the Spirit of His Son, or the Spirit of Jesus? May we not give these reasons? It was by the Holy Spirit that the human nature of Christ was born of the Virgin. By the Spirit, our Lord was attested at His baptism, when the Holy Spirit descended upon Him like a dove and abode upon Him. In Him, the Holy Spirit dwelt without measure, anointing Him for His great work, and by the Spirit He was anointed with the oil of gladness above His fellows.

The Spirit was also with Him, attesting His ministry by signs and wonders. The Holy Spirit is our Lord's great gift to the church; it was after His ascension that He bestowed the gifts of Pentecost, and the Holy Spirit descended upon the church to abide with the people of God forever. The Holy Spirit is the Spirit of Christ because He is Christ's witness here below, as well; for *"there are three that bear witness in earth, the Spirit, and the water, and the blood"* (1 John 5:8). For these, and many other reasons, He is called *"the Spirit of his Son,"* and it is He who comes to dwell in believers.

I would urge you to consider very solemnly and gratefully the wondrous condescension that is here displayed. God Himself, the Holy Spirit, takes up His residence in believers. I never know which is more wonderful, the incarnation of Christ or the indwelling of the Holy Spirit. Jesus dwelled here for a while in human flesh, untainted by sin, *"holy, harmless, undefiled, separate from sinners"* (Hebrews 7:26); but the Holy Spirit dwells continually in the hearts of all believers, though as yet they are imperfect and prone to evil. Year after year, century after century, He still abides in the saints, and will do so until the elect are all in glory. While we adore the incarnate Son, let us also adore the indwelling Spirit whom the Father has sent.

The Spirit's Residence

Now notice the place wherein He takes up His residence: *"God hath sent forth the Spirit of his Son into your hearts."* Note that it does not say that God has sent His Spirit into your heads or your brains. The Spirit of God undoubtedly illuminates the intellect and guides the judgment, but this is not the beginning or the main part of His work. He comes chiefly to the affections; He dwells with the heart, *"for with the heart man believeth unto righteousness"* (Romans 10:10), and *"God hath sent forth the Spirit of his Son into your hearts."*

Now, the heart is the center of our being; therefore, the Holy Spirit occupies this place of strategic advantage. He comes into the central fortress and universal citadel of our nature, and thus takes possession of the whole. The heart is the vital part; we speak of it as the chief residence of life. The Holy Spirit enters it, and as the living God, dwells in the living heart, taking possession of the very core and marrow of our being. It is from the heart and through the heart that life is diffused. The blood is sent even to the extremities of the body by the pulsing of the heart, and when the Spirit of God takes possession of the affections, He operates upon every power, faculty, and member of our entire personhood. *"Out of* [the heart] *are the issues of life"* (Proverbs 4:23); from the affections sanctified by the Holy Spirit, all other faculties and powers receive renewal, illumination, sanctification, strengthening, and ultimate perfection.

The Spirit's Blessing

This wonderful blessing is ours *"because* [we] *are sons."* It is fraught with marvelous results. Sonship sealed by the indwelling Spirit brings us peace and joy. It leads to nearness to God and fellowship with Him. It excites trust, love, and vehement desire and creates in us reverence, obedience, and actual likeness to God. All this occurs, and much more, because the Holy Spirit has come to dwell in us. Oh, matchless mystery! Had it not been revealed, it would never have been imagined. Now that it is revealed, it would never have been believed if it had not become a matter of actual experience to those who are in Christ Jesus.

Many who profess to know Christ know nothing of this reality. They listen to us with bewilderment, as if we told them an idle tale, for the carnal mind does not know the things that are of God; they are spiritual and can only be spiritually discerned. Those who are not sons, or who come in as sons only under the law of nature, like Ishmael, know nothing of this indwelling Spirit, and are up in arms at us for daring to claim so great a blessing. Yet it is ours, and none can deprive us of it.

The Filial Cry

Now I come to the third portion of our text. This point is deeply interesting, and I think it will be profitable to you if your minds enter into it. Where the Holy Spirit enters, there is a cry: *"God hath sent forth the Spirit of his Son... crying, Abba, Father."*

The Spirit Cries

Now, notice, it is the Spirit of God who cries—a most remarkable fact. Some are inclined to view the expression as a Hebraism, and read it, He "makes us to cry"; but, beloved, the text does not say this, and we are not at liberty to alter it upon such a pretense. We are always right in keeping to what God says, and here we plainly read of the Spirit in our hearts that He is crying, *"Abba, Father."* In Romans 8:15, the apostle said, *"Ye have received the Spirit of adoption, whereby we cry, Abba, Father,"* but here he described the Spirit Himself as *"crying, Abba, Father."* We are certain that when he ascribed the cry of *"Abba, Father"* to us, he did not wish to exclude the Spirit's cry, because in the twenty-sixth verse of the famous eighth chapter of Romans, he said,

Likewise the Spirit also helpeth our infirmities: for we know not what we should pray for as we ought: but the Spirit itself maketh intercession for us with groanings which cannot be uttered.

The Spirit Groans

Thus he represented the Spirit Himself as groaning with unutterable groanings within the child of God, so that, when he wrote to the Romans, he had on his mind the same thought that he here expressed to the Galatians—that it is the Spirit Himself who cries and groans in us *"Abba, Father."* How is this possible? Is it not ourselves who cry? Yes, assuredly; and yet the Spirit cries, also. The expressions are both correct. The Holy Spirit prompts and inspires the cry. He puts the cry into the heart and mouth of the believer. It is His cry because He suggests it, approves of it, and educates us to it. We would never have cried thus, if He had not first taught us the way. As a mother teaches her child to speak, so He puts this cry of *"Abba, Father"* into our mouths; yes, it is He who forms the desire after our Father God and keeps it there in our hearts. He is the Spirit of adoption, and the Author of adoption's special and significant cry.

The Spirit Cries for Us

He not only prompts us to cry but also works in us a sense of need that compels us to cry, and a spirit of confidence that emboldens us to claim such relationship to the great God. Neither is this all, for He assists us in some mysterious manner so that we are able to pray correctly. He puts His divine energy into us so that we cry *"Abba, Father"* in an acceptable manner. There are times when we cannot cry at all, and then He cries in us. There are seasons when doubts and fears abound and suffocate us with their fumes, so that we cannot even raise a cry. Then the indwelling Spirit represents us, speaks for us, and makes intercession for us, crying in our name, and making intercession for us according to the will of God. Thus does the cry *"Abba, Father"* rise up in our hearts even when we feel as if we could not pray and dare not think of ourselves as God's children. Then we may each say, "I live, yet not I, but the Spirit who dwells in me." (See Galatians 2:20.)

On the other hand, at times, our souls give such a sweet assent to the Spirit's cry that it becomes ours, also. However, then we more than ever own the work of the Spirit and still ascribe to Him the blessed cry, *"Abba, Father."*

It Is the Cry of the Son

I want you now to notice a very sweet fact about this cry, namely, that it is literally the cry of the Son. God has sent the Spirit of His Son into our hearts, and that Spirit cries in us exactly according to the cry of the Son. If you turn to Mark 14:36, you will find what you will not discover in any other gospel (for Mark was always the man for the striking points and the memorable words). He recorded that our Lord prayed in the Garden, *"Abba, Father, all things are possible unto thee; take away this cup from me: nevertheless not what I will, but what thou wilt."* Therefore, this cry in us copies the cry of our Lord to the letter—*"Abba, Father."*

The Cry Is in His Native Tongue

I daresay that you have heard these words *"Abba, Father"* explained at considerable length at other times, and if so, you know that the first word is Syrian or Aramaic; or, roughly speaking, *Abba* is the Hebrew word for "father." The second word is in Greek and is the Gentile word *pates,* or *pater,* which also signifies father. It is said that these two words are used to remind us that Jews and Gentiles are one before God. They do remind us of this, but this cannot have been the principal reason for their use. Do you think that, when our Lord was in His agony in the Garden, He said *"Abba, Father"* because Jews and Gentiles are one? Why would He have thought of that doctrine, and why would He have needed to mention it in prayer to His Father? Some other reason must have suggested it to Him.

It seems to me that our Lord said *"Abba"* because it was His native tongue. When a Frenchman prays, if he has learned English, he may ordinarily pray in English, but if he ever falls into an agony, he will pray in French, as surely as he prays at all. Our Welsh brethren tell us that there is no language like Welsh. I suppose that is true for them. Now, they will speak English when they talk about their ordinary business, and they can pray in English when everything goes comfortably with them. However, I am sure that if a Welshman is in a great fervency of prayer, he flies to his Welsh tongue to find full expression. Our Lord in His agony used His native language, and as born of the seed of Abraham, He cried in His own tongue, *"Abba."* Even thus, my brothers and sisters, we are prompted by the Spirit of adoption to use our own language, the language of the heart, and to speak to the Lord freely in our own tongue.

It Is the Cry of a Child

Besides, to my mind, the word *Abba* is of all words in all languages the most natural word for father. I must try to pronounce it so that you see the natural childishness of it. "Ab...ba," "Ab...ba." Is this not just what your children say, "Ab...ab...ba...ba," as soon as they try to talk? It is the sort of word that any child would say, whether Hebrew or Greek or French or English. Therefore, *Abba* is a word worthy of introduction into all languages. It is truly a child's word, and our Master felt, I have no doubt, in His agony, a love for a child's words.

Adoption—The Spirit and the Cry

Dr. Guthrie, when he was dying, said, "Sing a hymn," but he added, "Sing me one of the bairns' hymns." When a man comes to die, he wants to be a child again and longs for bairns' hymns and bairns' words. Our blessed Master in His agony used the bairns' word, *"Abba,"* and it is equally becoming in the mouth of each one of us.

I think this sweet word *Abba* was chosen to show us that we are to be very natural with God, and not stilted and formal. We are to be very affectionate, come close to Him, and not merely say "Pater," which is a cold Greek word, but *"Abba,"* which is a warm, natural, loving word, fit for one who is a little child with God, who boldly lies on His bosom and looks up into His face and speaks with holy boldness. *"Abba"* is not a word, somehow, but a babe's lisping. Oh, how near we are to God when we can use such speech! How dear He is to us and how dear we are to Him when we may thus address Him, saying, like the great Son Himself, *"Abba, Father."*

The Cry Is Childlike in Nature

This leads me to observe that this cry in our hearts is exceedingly near and familiar. I have shown you that the sound of it is childlike, but the tone and manner of the utterance are equally so. Note that it is a cry. If we obtain audience with a king, we do not cry. We speak then in measured tones and set phrases, but the Spirit of God breaks down our measured tones and takes away the formality that some hold in great admiration, and He leads us to cry, which is the very reverse of formality and stiffness. When we cry, we cry, *"Abba."*

Even our very cries are full of the Spirit of adoption. A cry is a sound that we are not anxious that every passerby should hear, yet what child minds his father hearing him cry? So when our heart is broken and subdued, we do not feel as if we could speak fine language at all, but the Spirit in us sends forth cries and groans, and of these we are not ashamed, nor are we afraid to cry before God. I know some of you think that God will not hear your prayers because you cannot pray grandly like such-and-such a minister. Oh, but the Spirit of His Son cries, and you cannot do better than cry, too. Be satisfied to offer to God broken language, words salted with your griefs, wetted with your tears. Go to Him with holy familiarity, and do not be afraid to cry in His presence, *"Abba, Father."*

The Cry Is Earnest

But then how earnest it is, for a cry is an intense thing. The word implies fervency. A cry is not a flippant utterance, or a mere thing of the lips; it comes up from the soul. Has not the Lord taught us to cry to Him in prayer with fervent importunity that will not take a denial? Has He not brought us so near to Him that sometimes we say, *"I will not let thee go, except thou bless me"* (Genesis 32:26)? Has He not taught us so to pray that His disciples might almost say of us, as they did of one of long ago, *"Send her away; for she crieth after us"* (Matthew 15:23)? We do cry after Him; our hearts and our flesh cry out for God, for the living God, and this is the cry: "Abba, Father, I must know You. I must taste Your love. I must dwell under Your wing. I must behold Your face. I must feel Your great fatherly heart overflowing and filling my heart with peace." We cry, *"Abba, Father."*

The Cry Comes from the Heart

In closing, note that most of this crying is kept within the heart and does not come out of the lips. Like Moses, we cry when we do not say a word. God has sent forth the Spirit of His Son into our hearts, *"whereby we cry, Abba, Father."* You know what I mean. It is not alone in your little room, by the old armchair, that you cry to God, but you call Him *"Abba, Father"* as you go about the streets or work in the shop. The Spirit of His Son is crying *"Abba,*

Father" when you are in a crowd or at your table among the family. I see it is alleged as a very grave charge against me that I speak as if I were familiar with God. If it is so, I boldly say that I speak only as I feel. Blessed be my heavenly Father's name. I know I am His child, and with whom should a child be familiar but with his father? Strangers to the living God, be it known to you that, if this is vile, I purpose to be viler still, as He will help me to walk more closely with Him. We feel a deep reverence for our Father in heaven that bows us to the very dust. However, for all that, we can say, *"Truly our fellowship is with the Father, and with his Son Jesus Christ"* (1 John 1:3).

No stranger can understand the nearness of the believer's soul to God in Christ Jesus. Because the world cannot understand it, it finds it convenient to sneer; but what of that? Abraham's tenderness to Isaac made Ishmael jealous and caused him to laugh, but Isaac had no cause to be ashamed of being ridiculed, since the mocker could not rob him of the covenant blessing.

Yes, beloved, the Spirit of God makes you cry, *"Abba, Father,"* but the cry is mainly within your heart, and there it is so commonly uttered that it becomes the habit of your soul to be crying to your heavenly Father. The text does not say that the Spirit had cried, but rather, it uses the word "crying." It is a present participle, indicating that He cries every day, *"Abba, Father."*

Live in the Father's Love

Friends, live in the spirit of sonship. When you wake up in the morning, let your first thought be, "My Father, my Father, be with me this day." When you go out into business, and things perplex you, let this be your resort: "My Father, help me in this hour of need." When you go to your home, and there meet with domestic anxieties, let your cry still be, "Help me, my Father." When alone, you are not alone, because the Father is with you; in the midst of the crowd, you are not in danger, because the Father Himself loves you. What a blessed word this is: The Father Himself loves you!

Go and live as His children. Take heed that you reverence Him, for if He is your Father, where is your respect and awe for Him? Go and obey Him, for this is right. *"Be ye therefore followers of God, as dear children"* (Ephesians 5:1). Honor Him, wherever you are, by adorning His doctrine in all things. Go and live upon Him, for you will soon live with Him. Go and rejoice in Him. Go and cast all your cares upon Him. Go, henceforth, and whatever men may see in you, may they be compelled to admit that you are the children of the Highest. *"Blessed are the peacemakers: for they shall be called the children of God"* (Matthew 5:9). May you be such henceforth and evermore. Amen and amen.

Chapter 7

Grieving the Holy Spirit

And grieve not the holy Spirit of God, whereby ye are sealed unto the day of redemption.
—Ephesians 4:30

T here is something very touching in this admonition, *"Grieve not the holy Spirit of God."* It does not say, "Do not make Him angry." A more delicate and tender term is used—*"Grieve not."* There are some men of so hard a character that to make another person angry does not give them much pain; indeed, there are many of us who are scarcely moved by the information that someone is angry with us. Yet where is the heart so hard that it is not moved when it knows that it has caused others grief?

Grief is a sweet combination of anger and love. It is anger, but all the bitterness is taken from it. Love sweetens the anger and turns the edge of it not against the person, but against the offense. We all know how we use the two terms in contradistinction to each other. When I commit any offense, some friend who has but little patience suddenly loses his temper and is angry with me. The same offense is observed by a loving father, and he is grieved. There is anger in his heart, but he is angry and sins not (Ephesians 4:26). He is angry against my sin, yet there is love to neutralize and modify the anger toward me. Instead of wishing me ill as the punishment for my sin, he looks on my sin itself as being the problem. He grieves to think that I am already injured, from the fact that I have sinned. I say grief is a heavenly compound, more precious than all the ointment of the merchants. There may be the bitterness of myrrh, but there is all the sweetness of frankincense, in this sweet term "to grieve."

I am certain, my readers, I do not flatter you when I declare that I am sure that most of you would grieve if you thought you were hurting anyone else. Perhaps you would not care much if you had made anyone angry without a cause; but to grieve him, even though it was done without a cause and without intention, would nevertheless cause you distress of heart. You would not rest until this grief had subsided, until you had made some explanation or apology, or had done your best to alleviate the pain and take away the grief.

When we see anger in another, we at once begin to feel hostility. Anger begets anger, but grief begets pity. Pity is similar to love, and we love those whom we have caused to grieve. Now, is this not a very sweet expression: "Grieve not the holy Spirit"? Of course, the language is be to understood as speaking after the manner of men. The Holy Spirit of God knows no passion or suffering; nevertheless, His emotion is described here in human language as being that of grief. And is it not a tender and touching thing that the Holy Spirit should direct His servant Paul to have said to us, "Grieve not the holy Spirit," that is, do not excite His loving anger, do not vex Him, and do not cause Him to mourn? He is a dove; do not cause Him to mourn because you have treated Him harshly and ungratefully.

Now, the purpose of my sermon will be to exhort you not to grieve the Spirit. I will divide it into three sections: First, I will focus on the love of the Spirit; second, on the seal of the Spirit; third, on the grieving of the Spirit.

The Love of the Spirit

The few words I have to say about the love of the Spirit will be pressing us forward to my great goal: to stir you up not to grieve the Spirit. When we are persuaded that someone loves us, we find at once a very potent reason why we should not grieve him.

How will I describe the love of the Spirit? Surely it needs a songster to sing it, for love is to be spoken of only in words of song. The love of the Spirit! Let me tell you of His early love for us. He loved us without beginning. In the eternal covenant of grace, He was one of the high contracting parties in the divine contract whereby we are saved.

All that can be said of the love of the Father and of the love of the Son may be said of the love of the Spirit: It is eternal, infinite, sovereign, and everlasting. It is a love that cannot be dissolved, decreased, or removed from those who are the objects of it.

He Seeks

Permit me, however, to refer you to His acts, rather than His attributes. Let me tell you of the love of the Spirit for you and me. Oh, how early was that love that He manifested toward us, even in our childhood! My friends, we can well remember how the Spirit was inclined to reach us. We went astray from the womb, speaking lies, but how early did the Spirit of God stir up our consciences and solemnly correct us because of our youthful sins!

How frequently since then has the Spirit wooed us! How often under the ministry has He compelled our hearts to melt and tears to run down our cheeks! He has sweetly whispered in our ears, "My child, give Me your heart. Go to your room, shut the door behind you, confess your sins, and seek the Savior's love and blood."

Oh—let us blush to tell it—how often have we done malice to Him! When we were unregenerate, how we were

309

inclined to resist Him! We quenched the Spirit. He sought us, but we fought Him. Yet blessed be His dear name, and let Him have everlasting songs, for He would not let us go! We would not be saved, but He would save us. We sought to thrust ourselves into the fire, but He sought to pluck us from the burning. We would dash ourselves from the precipice, but He wrestled with us and held us fast. He would not let us destroy our souls.

Oh, how we mistreated Him! How we discounted His counsel! How we scorned and scoffed at Him! How we despised the laws that would lead us to Christ! How we violated that holy cord that was gently drawing us to Jesus and His Cross! I am sure, my friends, as you remember the persevering struggles of the Spirit with you, you must be stirred up to love Him.

How often He restrained you from sin when you were about to plunge headlong into a course of vice! How often did He constrain you to good when you would have neglected it! You, perhaps, would not have been in the right place at all, and the Lord would not have met you, if it had not been for that sweet Spirit, who would not let you become a blasphemer, who would not permit you to forsake the house of God, and who would not allow you to become a regular attendant at immoral establishments.

Instead, He checked you and held you in, as it were, with bit and bridle. Though you were like a young bull, unaccustomed to the yoke, He would not let you have your way. Though you struggled against Him, He would not throw the reins on your neck. Instead, He said, "I will have him. I will have him against his will. I will change his heart. I will not let him go until I have made him a trophy of My mighty power to save."

Then think of the love of the Spirit after that:

> Dost mind the time, the spot of land,
> Where Jesus did thee meet?

Where He first took thee by the hand,
Thy bridegroom's love—how sweet!

He Guides

Ah, then, in that blest hour, dear to memory, was it not
the Holy Spirit who guided you to Jesus? Do you remember the love of the Spirit, when, after having quickened
you, He took you aside and showed you Jesus on the tree?
Who was it that opened your blind eyes to see a dying
Savior? Who was it that opened your deaf ears to hear
the voice of pardoning love? Who opened your clasped and
palsied hands to receive the tokens of a Savior's grace?
Who was it that broke your hard heart and made a way
for the Savior to enter and dwell therein? Oh, it was that
precious Spirit, that same Spirit, to whom you had done
so much malice, whom in the days of your flesh you had
resisted!

What a mercy it was that He did not say, "I will swear
in My wrath that they will not enter into My rest, for they
have vexed Me. I will take My everlasting flight from them."
And since that time, my beloved, how sweetly has the
Spirit proved His love for you and me. How much have
we owed to His instruction—not only in His first endeav-
ors, and then His divine quickenings, but also in all His
actions that have followed!

We have been dull students with the Word before
us. It is so plain and simple that he who reads it may
understand. Yet how small a portion of His Word has
our memory retained; how little progress have we made
in the school of God's grace! We are still but learners,
unstable, weak, and apt to slide, but what a blessed
Instructor we have! Has He not led us into many truths
and taken the things of Christ and applied them to us?
Oh, when I think how stupid I have been, I wonder that
He has not given up on me. When I think what a dolt
I have been, when He would have taught me the things

of the kingdom of God, I marvel that He should have had such patience with me.

It is amazing that Jesus would become a baby. Is it not equally amazing that the Spirit of the living God would become a teacher of babes? It is a marvel that Jesus would lie in a manger; is it not an equal marvel that the Holy Spirit would become an assistant teacher in the sacred school, to teach fools and make them wise? It was condescension that brought the Savior to the Cross, but is it not equal condescension that brings the mighty Spirit of grace down to dwell among stubborn, unruly, perverse men, to teach them the mystery of the kingdom and make them know the wonders of a Savior's love?

He Gives Comfort

Furthermore, do not forget how much we owe to the Spirit's consolation. How much has He manifested His love for you in preserving you in all your sicknesses, assisting you in all your work, and comforting you in all your troubles! He has been a blessed Comforter to me, I can testify. When every other comfort fails, when the promise itself seems empty, when the ministry is void of power, it is then that the Holy Spirit has proved a rich comfort to my soul and filled my poor heart with *"joy and peace in believing"* (Romans 15:13).

How many times would your heart have broken if the Spirit had not bound it up? How often has He who is your Teacher also become your Physician? He has closed the wounds of your poor bleeding spirit and bound up those wounds with the healing balm of the promise. Thus, He has stopped the bleeding and has given you back your spiritual health once more. It does seem miraculous that the Holy Spirit should become a Comforter, for comforting is, to many minds, an inferior work in the church, though really it is not so. To teach, to preach, to command with authority, how many are willing to do these things because they are honorable work? Yet to sit down and bear with the infirmities of a weak person, to deal with the deceit of unbelievers, to find a way of peace for a soul in the midst of seas of trouble—these things require being compassionate as God is compassionate.

How wonderful that the Holy Spirit should stoop from heaven to become a Comforter of disconsolate spirits. What! Must He Himself bring the medicine? Must He wait upon His sick child and stand by his bed? Must He make his bed for him in his afflictions? Must He carry him in his infirmity? Must He continually breathe into him His very breath? Does the Holy Spirit become a waiting-servant of the church? Does He become a lamp to illuminate? Does He become a staff on which we may lean? All this, I say, should move us to love the Holy Spirit, for we have in it abundant proofs of His love for us.

He Helps Our Weaknesses

Do not stop here, beloved, for there are larger fields beyond, now that we are speaking of the love of the Spirit. Remember how much He loves us when He helps our infirmities (Romans 8:26). He not only helps our infirmities, but also teaches us how to pray when we do not know what to pray for. When *"we ourselves groan within ourselves"* (v. 23), then the Spirit Himself intercedes for us *"with groanings which cannot be uttered"* (v. 26)—groans as we should groan, but more audibly, so that our prayers, which otherwise would have been silent, reach the ears of Christ and are then presented before the Father's face.

To help our infirmities is a mighty example of love. When God overcomes infirmity altogether, or removes it, there is something very noble, grand, and sublime in the deed. When He permits the infirmity to remain and yet works with the infirmity, this is tender compassion, indeed. When the Savior heals the lame man, you see His Godhead, but when He walks with the lame man, limping though his gait may be; when He sits with the beggar; when He talks with the publican; when He carries the baby close to His heart, then this helping of infirmities is a manifestation of love almost unequalled.

Except for Christ's bearing our infirmities and *"our sins in his own body on the tree"* (1 Peter 2:24), I know of no greater or more tender instance of divine love than when it is written, *"Likewise the Spirit also helpeth our infirmities"* (Romans 8:26). Oh, how much you owe to the Spirit when you have been on your knees in prayer! You know, my brothers and sisters, what it is to be dull and lifeless there; to groan for a word, and yet you cannot find it; to wish for a word, and yet the very wish is weak; to long to have desires, and yet all the desire you have is a desire that you may be able to desire.

Oh, have you not sometimes, when your desires have been kindled, longed to grasp hold of the promises by the hand of faith? "Oh," you have said, "if I could but plead the promises, all my needs would be removed, and all my sorrows would be lessened." Sadly, the promise was beyond your reach. If you touched it with the tip of your finger, you could not grasp it as you desired, you could not plead it, and therefore you came away without the blessing.

However, when the Spirit has helped our infirmities, how we have prayed! Why, there have been times when you and I have so grasped the knocker of the gate of mercy, and have let it fall with such tremendous force, that it seemed as if the very gate itself shook and tottered. There have been seasons when we have laid hold of the angel, have overcome heaven by prayer, and have declared we would not let Jehovah Himself go unless He would bless us. (See Genesis 32:24–26.) We have, and we say it without blasphemy, moved the arm that moves the world. We have brought down upon us the eyes that look upon the universe. All this we have done, not by our own strength, but by the might and by the power of the

Spirit. Seeing He has so sweetly enabled us, though we have so often forgotten to thank Him; seeing that He has so graciously assisted us, though we have often taken all the glory to ourselves instead of crediting it to Him; must we not admire His love, and must it not be a fearful sin indeed to grieve the Holy Spirit by whom we are sealed?

He Lives Within

Another token of the Spirit's love remains, namely, His indwelling in the saints. We sing in one of our hymns, "Dost Thou not dwell in all the saints?" We ask a question that can have only one answer. He does dwell in the hearts of all God's redeemed and blood-washed people. And what a condescension this is, my friend, that He whom the heaven of heavens cannot contain dwells in your heart. Although that heart is often covered with rags or agitated with anxious cares and thoughts, although it is too often defiled with sin, He dwells there. The Holy Spirit has made the little narrow heart of man His palace. Though it is but a cottage, a very hovel, and all unholy and unclean, yet the Holy Spirit condescends to make the hearts of His people His continual home. Oh, my friends, when I think how often you and I have let the devil in, I wonder why the Spirit has not withdrawn from us.

The final perseverance of the saints is one of the greatest miracles on record; in fact, it is the sum total of miracles. The perseverance of a saint for a single day is a multitude of miracles of mercy. When you consider that the Spirit is of purer eyes than to behold iniquity, yet He dwells in the heart where sin often intrudes, a heart out of which come blasphemies, murders, and all manner of evil thoughts and sexual desires (Matthew 15:19), what if sometimes He is grieved and retires and leaves us to ourselves for a season? It is a marvel that

He is there at all, for He must be daily grieved with these evil guests, these false traitors, these base intruders who thrust themselves into that little temple that He has honored with His presence, the temple of the heart of man.

I am afraid, dear friends, that we are too much in the habit of talking about the love of Jesus, without thinking about the love of the Holy Spirit. Now, I would not wish to exalt one person of the Trinity above another. However, I do feel that because Jesus Christ was a man, bone of our bone and flesh of our flesh (see Genesis 2:23), and because there was therefore something tangible in Him that could be seen with the eyes and handled with the hands, we more readily think of Him and fix our love on Him than we do upon the Spirit.

Yet why should this be? Let us love Jesus with all our hearts, and let us love the Holy Spirit, too. Let us have songs for Him, gratitude for Him. Just as we do not forget Christ's Cross, let us not forget the Spirit's operations. We do not forget what Jesus has done for us; therefore, let us always remember what the Spirit does in us. Why do you talk of the love, grace, tenderness, and faithfulness of Christ, when you do not say the same things about the Spirit? Was ever love like His, that He should visit us? Was ever mercy like His, that He should bear with our bad manners, though we repeatedly do the same things? Was ever faithfulness like His, that multitudes of sins cannot drive Him away? Was ever power like His, which overcomes all our iniquities, and yet leads us safely on, though hosts of foes within and without would rob us of our Christian life?

> Oh, the love of the Spirit I sing
> By whom is redemption applied.

And unto His name be glory forever and ever.

The Seal of the Spirit

This brings me to the second point. Here we have another reason why we should not grieve the Spirit: It is by the Holy Spirit that we are sealed. By the Spirit, we "are sealed unto the day of redemption." I will be very brief here. The Spirit Himself is expressed as the seal, even as He Himself is directly said to be the pledge of our inheritance (Ephesians 1:14). The sealing, I think, has a three-fold meaning.

A Seal of Confirmation

It is a sealing of attestation or confirmation. I want to know whether I am truly a child of God. The Spirit Himself also bears witness with my spirit that I am born of God (Romans 8:16). I have the writings, the title deed of the inheritance that is to come. I want to know whether they are valid, whether they are true, or whether they are mere counterfeits written by that old scribe of hell, Master Presumption and Carnal Security.

How am I to know? I look for the seal. After we have believed on the Son of God, the Father seals us as His children, by the gift of the Holy Spirit. *"Now he which...hath anointed us, is God; who hath also sealed us, and given the earnest of the Spirit in our hearts"* (2 Corinthians 1:21–22). No faith is genuine that does not bear the seal of the Spirit. No love, no hope, can ever save us, unless it is sealed with the Spirit of God, for whatever does not have His seal upon it is false. Faith that is unsealed may be a poison or a presumption, but faith that is sealed by the Spirit is true, real, genuine faith.

Never be content, my dear readers, unless you are sealed, unless you are assured by the inward witness and testimony of the Holy Spirit that you have been *"begotten...again unto a lively hope by the resurrection of Jesus Christ from the dead"* (1 Peter 1:3). It is possible for a man

317

to know infallibly that he is secure of heaven. He may not only hope so, but also know beyond a doubt, and he may know it by being able with the eyes of faith to see the seal, the broad stamp of the Holy Spirit, set upon his own character and experience. It is a seal of attestation.

A Seal of Appropriation

In the next place, it is a sealing of appropriation. When men put their mark upon an article, it is to show that it is their own. The farmer marks his tools so that they will not be stolen. They are his. The shepherd brands his sheep so that they may be recognized as belonging to his flock. The king himself puts his broad arrow upon everything that is his property. So the Holy Spirit puts the broad arm of God upon the hearts of all His people. He seals us. You will *"be mine, saith the LORD of hosts, in that day when I make up my jewels"* (Malachi 3:17).

A Seal of Inheritance

And then the Spirit puts God's seal upon us to signify that we are God's reserved inheritance, His special people, the portion in which His soul delights. However, again, by sealing is meant preservation. Men seal up what they wish to have preserved; and when a document is sealed, it becomes valid henceforth. Now, it is by the Spirit of God that the Christian is sealed, that he is kept, preserved, *"sealed unto the day of redemption,"* sealed until Christ comes fully to redeem the bodies of His saints by raising them from the dead, and fully to redeem the world by purging it from sin and making it a kingdom unto Himself in righteousness.

If we maintain our position in Christ, we will be saved. The chosen seed cannot be lost; they must be brought home at last, but how? By the sealing of the Spirit. Apart from that, they perish; they are undone. When the last general fire blazes out, everything that does not have the seal of the Spirit on it will be burned up. Yet the men upon whose forehead is the seal will be preserved. They will be safe "amid the wreck of matter and the crash of worlds." Their spirits, mounting above the flames, will dwell with Christ eternally, and with that same seal on their foreheads, they will sing the everlasting song of gratitude and praise upon Mount Zion. This is the second reason why we should love the Spirit and why we should not grieve Him.

The Grieving of the Spirit

I come now to the third part of my message, namely, the grieving of the Spirit: How can we grieve Him, what will be the sad result of grieving Him, and if we have grieved Him, how can we bring Him back again?

Through Inward and Outward Acts of Sin

How can we grieve the Spirit? I am now, mark you, speaking of those who love the Lord Jesus Christ. The Spirit of God is in your hearts, and it is easy, indeed, to grieve Him. Sin is as easy as it is wicked. You may grieve Him by impure thoughts. He cannot bear sin. If you indulge in lewd expressions, or even if you allow your imagination to dwell on any impure act, if your heart is covetous, if you set your heart upon anything that is evil, the Spirit of God will be grieved. I hear Him speaking, "I love this man. I want to have his heart, and yet he is entertaining these filthy lusts. His thoughts, instead of running after Me, after Christ, and after the Father are running after the temptations that are in the world through lust." And then His Spirit is grieved. He sorrows in His soul because He knows what sorrow these things must bring to our souls.

We grieve Him still more if we indulge in outward acts of sin. Then sometimes He is so grieved that He takes His flight for a season, for the Dove will not dwell in our hearts if we take loathsome carrion there. The Holy Spirit, the Dove, is a pure being, and we must not strew the place that the Dove frequents with filth and mire. If we do, He will fly elsewhere.

If we commit sin, if we openly bring disgrace upon our religion, if we tempt others to go into iniquity by our evil examples, it is not long before the Holy Spirit will begin to grieve. Again, if we neglect prayer, if our prayer closet is cobwebbed, if we forget to read the Scriptures, if the pages of our Bible are almost stuck together by neglect, if we never seek to do any good in the world, if we live merely for ourselves and not for Christ, then the Holy Spirit will be grieved, for thus He has said, *"They have forsaken me the fountain of living waters, and hewed them out cisterns, broken cisterns, that can hold no water"* (Jeremiah 2:13).

I think I now see the Spirit of God grieving when you sit down to read a novel, and there is your Bible, unread. Perhaps you take down some travel book, and you forget that you have a more precious travel book in the Acts of the Apostles and in the story of your blessed Lord and Master. You have no time for prayer, but the Spirit sees you very active about worldly things, having many hours to spare for relaxation and amusement. And then He is grieved because He sees that you love worldly things better than you love Him. His Spirit is grieved within Him. Take care that He does not go away from you, for it will be a pitiful thing for you if He leaves you to yourself.

Through Ingratitude

Again, ingratitude tends to grieve Him. Nothing cuts a man to the heart more than after having done his utmost to help another, that person turns around and repays him with ingratitude or insult. If we do not want to be thanked, at least we want to know that there is thankfulness in the heart on which we have conferred a blessing. And when the Holy Spirit looks into our souls and sees little love for

Christ and no gratitude to Him for all He has done for us, then He is grieved.

Through Unbelief

Again, the Holy Spirit is exceedingly grieved by our unbelief. When we distrust the promise He has given and applied, when we doubt the power or the affection of our blessed Lord, then the Spirit says within Himself, "They doubt My fidelity; they distrust My power. They say Jesus is not able to save to the uttermost." (See Hebrews 7:25.) Thus, again, is the Spirit grieved.

Oh, I wish the Spirit had an advocate here who could express these thoughts in better terms than I can. I have a theme that overmasters me. I seem to grieve for Him, but I cannot make you grieve or express the grief I feel. In my own soul, I keep saying, "Oh, this is just what you have done; you have grieved Him." Let me make a full and frank confession before you all. I know that too often, I, as well as you, have grieved the Holy Spirit. Much within us has made that sacred Dove to mourn, and my marvel is that He has not taken His flight from us and left us utterly to ourselves.

What Happens When the Spirit Is Grieved?

Now suppose the Holy Spirit is grieved. What is the effect produced upon us? When the Spirit is grieved, first, He bears with us. He is grieved again and again, and again and again, and still He bears with it all. However, at last, His grief becomes so excessive that He says, "I will suspend My operations; I will depart. I will leave life behind Me, but My own actual presence I will take away."

When the Spirit of God goes away from us and suspends all His operations, what a miserable state we are in. He suspends His instructions; we read the Word, but we cannot understand it. We go to our commentaries, but they cannot tell us the meaning. We fall on our knees and ask to be taught, but we get no answer; we learn nothing. He suspends His comfort. We used to dance like David before the ark. (See 2 Samuel 6:13–16.) Now we sit like Job among the ashes and scrape our boils with a potsherd. (See Job 2:7–8.)

There was a time when His candle shone round about us, but now He is gone; He has left us in the blackness of darkness. Now He takes from us all spiritual power. Once we could *"do all things"* (Philippians 4:13); now we can do nothing. We could slay the Philistines and lay them heaps upon heaps, but now Delilah can deceive us, and our eyes are put out and we are made to grind in the mill. (See Judges 15:14–17; 16:4–21.)

We preach, but there is no pleasure in preaching, and no good results come from it. We distribute tracts and attend Sunday school, but we almost might as well be at home. We go through the motions of being a Christian, but there is no love. There is the intention to do good, or perhaps not even that, but alas, there is no power to accomplish the intention. The Lord has withdrawn Himself, His light, His joy, His comfort, His spiritual power; all are gone. And then all our graces flag.

Our graces are much like the flower called the hydrangea; when it has plenty of water, it blooms, but as soon as moisture fails, the leaves drop down at once. And so when the Spirit goes away, faith shuts up its flowers; no perfume is released. Then the fruit of our love begins to rot and drops from the tree; then the sweet buds of our hope become frostbitten, and they die. Oh, what a sad thing it is to lose the Spirit. Have you never, my beloved, been on your knees and been conscious that the Spirit of God was not with you? What awful work it has been to groan, to cry, to sigh, and yet go away again. No light shines on the promises, not so much as a ray of light through the chink of the dungeon. All forsaken, forgotten, and forlorn, you are almost driven to despair. You sing with Cowper,

> What peaceful hours I once enjoyed,
>   How sweet their memory still!
> But they have left an aching void,
>   The world can never fill.
>
> Return, Thou sacred Dove, return,
>   Sweet Messenger of rest,
> I hate the sins that made Thee mourn,
>   And drove Thee from my breast.
>
> The dearest idol I have known,
>   Whate'er that idol be,
> Help me to tear it from its throne,
>   And worship only Thee.

It is sad enough to have the Spirit withdraw from us, but I am about to say something with the utmost love, which, perhaps, may sound severe; nevertheless, I must say it. The churches of the present day are very much in the position of those who have grieved the Spirit of God, for the Spirit deals with churches just as He does with individuals.

In recent years, how little has God worked in the midst of His churches. Throughout England, at least some four or five years ago, an almost universal lethargy had fallen upon the visible body of Christ. There was a little action, but it was spasmodic; there was no real vitality. Oh, how few sinners were brought to Christ. How empty had our places of worship become. Our prayer meetings were dwindling away to nothing, and our church meetings were mere matters of farce. You know very well that this is the case with many London churches to this day, and there are some who do not mourn about it. They go to their accustomed places of worship, the ministers pray, the people either sleep with their eyes or else with their hearts, they go out, and there is never a soul saved. The pool of baptism is seldom stirred. Yet the saddest part of all is this: The churches are willing to have it so. They are not earnest to have a revival of religion.

We have been doing something; the church at large has been doing something. I will not just now put my finger on what the sin is, but something has been done that has driven the Spirit of God from us. He is grieved, and He is gone.

Yet He is present with us here, thank His name. He is still visible in our midst. He has not left us. Though we have been as unworthy as others, yet He has given us a long outpouring of His presence. These last five years or more, we have had a revival that is not to be exceeded by any revival upon the face of the earth. Without cries or shoutings, without fallings down or swooning, steadily God adds to this church numbers upon numbers. Your minister's heart is ready to break with joy when he thinks how manifestly the Spirit of God is with us, but we must not be content with this. We want to see the Spirit poured out on all churches.

Look at the great gatherings that there were in St. Paul's, Westminster Abbey, Exeter Hall, and other places. How was it that no good was done, or so very little? I have watched with anxious eye, and I have never from the time of those gatherings heard but of one conversion—and that was in St. James' Hall—from all these services. It seems strange. The blessing may have come in larger measure than we know, but not in so large a measure as we might have expected if the Spirit of God had been present with all the ministers. Oh, would that we may live to see greater things than we have ever seen yet. Go home to your houses and humble yourselves before God, members of Christ's church. Cry aloud that He will visit His church, that He would open the windows of heaven and pour out

His grace upon His thirsty hill of Zion, that nations may be born in a day, that sinners may be saved by the thousands, and that Zion may travail and may bring forth children.

Oh, there are signs and tokens of a coming revival. We have heard recently of a good work among the Ragged School* boys at St. Giles's, and our souls have been glad on account of that. The news from Ireland comes to us like good tidings, not from a far country, but from a sister province of the kingdom. Let us cry aloud to the Holy Spirit, who is certainly grieved with His church, and let us purge our churches of everything that is contrary to His Word and to sound doctrine. Then the Spirit will return, and His power will be manifest.

In conclusion, there may be some of you who have lost the visible presence of Christ with you—who have, in fact, so grieved the Spirit that He has gone. It is a mercy for you to know that the Spirit of God never leaves His people forever; He leaves them for chastisement, but not for damnation. He sometimes leaves them so that they may benefit from knowing their own weaknesses, but He will not leave them finally to perish.

Are you in a state of backsliding, falling away, and coldness? Listen to me for a moment, and may God bless these words. Friend, do not remain for a moment in a condition so perilous. Do not rest easy for a single second in the absence of the Holy Spirit. I beseech you to use every means by which the Spirit may be brought back to you.

Once more, let me tell you distinctly what the means are. Search out the sin that has grieved the Spirit, give it up, and slay that sin upon the spot. Repent with tears and sighs. Continue in prayer, and never rest satisfied until the Holy Spirit comes back to you. Faithfully attend an

---

* Schools started in the late eighteenth century in England to provide free education and other opportunities for poor children.

earnest ministry. Spend much time with sincere saints. But above all, be much in prayer to God, and let your daily cry be, "Return, return, Holy Spirit; return, and dwell in my soul."

Oh, I beseech you not to be content until that prayer is heard, for you have become weak as water, and faint and empty, while the Spirit has been away from you. It may be that there are some reading this message with whom the Spirit has been striving during the past week. Yield to Him; do not resist Him. Do not grieve Him, but yield to Him.

Is the Holy Spirit saying to you now, "Turn to Christ"? Listen to Him. Obey Him, and He will direct you. I beg you, do not despise Him. Have you resisted Him many times? Then take care that you do not resist Him again, for there may come a last time when the Spirit may say, "I will go to My rest; I will not return to him. The ground is accursed; it will be given up to barrenness."

Hear the word of the Gospel, for the Spirit speaks earnestly to you now in this short sentence: *"Repent ye therefore, and be converted, that your sins may be blotted out, when the times of refreshing shall come from the presence of the Lord"* (Acts 3:19). And hear this solemn sentence: *"He that believeth and is baptized shall be saved; but he that believeth not shall be damned"* (Mark 16:16). May the Lord grant that we may not grieve the Holy Spirit.

Chapter 8

The Holy Spirit and the One Church

*These be they who separate themselves, sensual,
having not the Spirit.*
—Jude 1:19

W hen a farmer comes to thrash his wheat and prepare it for market, he desires two things: that
there will be plenty of the right type of grain,
and that he will have a pure grain to sell. He does not look
upon the quantity alone, for of what worth is the chaff to
the wheat? He would rather have a smaller amount of a
good-quality product than a great heap containing a vast
quantity of chaff.

On the other hand, he would not so winnow his wheat
as to drive away any of the good grain, and thus make
the quantity less than it needs to be. He wants to have as
much as possible—to have as little loss as possible in the
winnowing, and yet to have it as well winnowed as it may
be.

Now, that is what I desire for Christ's church, and what
every Christian should desire. We want Christ's church
to be as large as possible. God forbid that, by any of our
winnowing, we would ever cast away one of the precious

sons of Zion. When we rebuke sharply, we should be concerned lest the rebuke would fall where it is not needed and bruise and hurt the feelings of any whom God has chosen.

On the other hand, we have no wish to see the church multiplied at the expense of its purity. We do not wish to have a charity so large that it takes in chaff as well as wheat. We want to be charitable enough to use the fan thoroughly to purge God's floor, yet charitable enough to pick up the most shriveled ear of wheat and preserve it for the Master's sake, who is the Husbandman.

I trust that God will help me to discern between the precious and the vile so that I may say nothing uncharitable that would cut off any of God's people from being part of His true and living and visible church. At the same time, I pray that I may not speak so loosely, and so without God's direction, as to embrace any in the arms of Christian affection whom the Lord has not received in the eternal covenant of His love.

Our text suggests to us three things: first, an inquiry: Do we have the Spirit?; second, a caution: If we do not have the Spirit, we are sensual; third, a suspicion: Many people separate themselves. Our suspicion concerning them is that notwithstanding their exceptional profession of faith, they are sensual, not having the Spirit, for our text says, *"These be they who separate themselves, sensual, having not the Spirit."*

The Inquiry

First, then, our text suggests this question: Do we have the Spirit? This inquiry is so important that the philosopher may well suspend all his investigations to find an answer to it on his own account. All the great debates of politics, all the most engrossing subjects of human discussion, may well stop today and give us pause to ask ourselves this solemn question: Do I have the Spirit? For this question does not deal with any externals of religion, but it deals with religion in its most vital point. He who has the Spirit, although he is wrong in fifty things, being right in this, is saved. He who does not have the Spirit, even if he is ever so orthodox, even if his creed is as correct as Scripture and his morals are outwardly as pure as the law, is still unsaved. He is destitute of the essential part of salvation—the Spirit of God dwelling in him.

To help us answer this question, I will try to set forth the effects of the Spirit in our hearts by using several scriptural metaphors. To the question, "Do I have the Spirit?" I reply, "What is the operation of the Spirit? How am I to discern it?" Now, the Spirit operates in various ways, all of them mysterious and supernatural, all of them bearing the real marks of His own power and having certain signs following whereby they may be discovered and recognized.

The Spirit Is like the Wind

The first work of the Spirit in the heart is a work during which the Spirit is compared to the wind. You remember that, when our Savior spoke to Nicodemus, He represented the first work of the Spirit in the heart as being like the wind, which *"bloweth where it listeth"* (John 3:8). Jesus said, *"So is every one that is born of the Spirit"* (v. 8).

Now, you know that the wind is a most mysterious thing; and although certain definitions of it pretend to be explanations of the phenomenon, they certainly leave unanswered the great questions of how the wind blows, what the cause of its blowing in a certain direction is, and where it was before. The breath within us, the wind outside us, and all motions of air are mysterious to us. And the renewing work of the Spirit in the heart is exceedingly mysterious.

It is possible that, at this moment, the Spirit of God may be breathing into someone who is reading these words. Yet it would be blasphemous if anyone would ask, "Which way did the Spirit go from God to that person's heart? How did He enter there?"

It would be foolish for a person who is under the operation of the Spirit to ask how He operates. You do not know where thunder is stored; you do not know where the clouds are balanced; neither can you know how the Spirit goes forth from the Most High and enters into the heart of man.

It may be that, during a sermon, two men are listening to the same truth. One listens as attentively as the other and remembers as much of what he heard as the other man remembers. The other man is moved to tears or filled with solemn thoughts. Yet the one who was equally attentive sees nothing in the sermon, except, perhaps, certain important truths well presented. As for the other, his heart is broken within him, and his soul is melted.

How is it that the same truth has an effect on the one and not on his fellowman? It is because the mysterious Spirit of the living God goes with the truth to one heart and not to the other. The one feels only the force of truth, and that may be strong enough to make him tremble, like Felix. (See Acts 24.) However, the other feels the Spirit going with the truth, and that renews and regenerates the man, and causes him to pass into that gracious condition called salvation.

This change takes place instantaneously. It is as miraculous a change as any miracle of which we read in Scripture. It is supremely supernatural. It may be mimicked, but no imitation of it can be true and real. Men may pretend to be regenerated, but without the Spirit, they cannot be. It is a change so marvelous that the highest attempts of man can never reach it. We may reason as long as we please, but we cannot reason ourselves into regeneration. We may meditate until our hairs are gray with study, but we cannot meditate ourselves into the new birth. That is worked in us by the sovereign will of God alone.

> The Spirit, like some heavenly wind,
>   Blows on the sons of flesh,
> Inspires us with a heavenly mind,
>   And forms the man afresh.

Yet ask the man how, and he cannot tell you. Ask him when, and he may recognize the time, but as to the manner thereof, he knows no more of it than you do. It is a mystery to him.

You remember the story of the valley of vision. Ezekiel saw dry bones lying scattered here and there in the open valley. The command came to Ezekiel to prophesy to the bones, telling them what God had said—that He would breathe life into them again, and they would live and know that He is the Lord. Ezekiel prophesied, *"and the bones came together, bone to his bone...and the flesh came up upon them"* (Ezekiel 37:7–8), but as yet they did not live. Then God said to Ezekiel,

> *Prophesy unto the wind, prophesy, son of man, and say to the wind, Thus saith the Lord God; Come from the four winds, O breath, and breathe upon these slain, that they may live.* (v. 9)

They looked as though they were alive. They had flesh and blood, and eyes, hands, and feet. However, when Ezekiel spoke the second time, there was a mysterious something given that men call life. It was given in an inexplicable way, like the blowing of the wind.

It is just like that today. Unconverted and ungodly people may be very moral and outstanding individuals, but they are like the dry bones that are put together and clothed with flesh and blood. To make them live spiritually, they need the divine inspiration from the breath of the Almighty, the divine pneuma, the Divine Spirit. If the divine wind would blow on them, then they would live.

My reader, have you ever had any supernatural influence on your heart? If not, my words may seem to be harsh to you, but I am faithful. If you have never had more than nature in your heart, you are *"in the gall of bitterness, and in the bond of iniquity"* (Acts 8:23). Do not scoff at that statement. It is as true as the Bible, for it was taken from the Bible. Here is the proof: *"Except a man be born again* [from above], *he cannot see the kingdom of God"* (John 3:3). *"Except a man be born of water and of the Spirit, he cannot enter into the kingdom of God"* (v. 5).

What do you say to that? It is in vain for you to talk of making yourself be born again. You cannot be born again except by the Spirit, and you will perish unless you are. You see, then, the first effect of the Spirit, and by that you may answer the question, Do you have the Spirit?

The Spirit Is like Fire

Second, the Spirit in the Word of God is often compared to fire. After the Spirit, like the wind, has made the dead sinner live, then comes the Spirit like fire. Now, fire has a searching and tormenting power. It is purifying, but it purifies by a terrible process. After the Holy Spirit has given us the life of Christ, immediately a burning begins in our hearts. The Lord searches and tries our minds and lights a candle within our spirits that reveals the wickedness of our nature and the loathsomeness of our iniquities. My friend, do you know anything about that fire in your heart? For if not, you have not yet received the Spirit.

To explain what I mean, let me tell something of my own experience, by way of illustrating the fiery effects of the Spirit. I lived carelessly and thoughtlessly. I could indulge in sin as well as others, and did do so. Sometimes my conscience pricked me, but not enough to make me cease from vice. I could indulge in transgression, and I could love it—not as much as others loved it because my early training would not let me do that, but still enough to prove that my heart was debased and corrupt.

One time, something more than conscience pricked me. I did not know then what it was. I was like Samuel when the Lord called him (see 1 Samuel 3:3–7); I heard the voice, but I did not know from where it came. A stirring began in my heart, and I began to feel that in the sight of God I was a lost, ruined, and condemned sinner. I could not shake off that conviction.

Do what I might, it followed me. If I sought to amuse my mind and distract it from serious thoughts, it was of no use. I was still obliged to carry around with me a heavy burden on my back. I went to my bed, and there I dreamed about hell and about *"the wrath to come"* (Matthew 3:7). I woke up, and this dreary nightmare, this incubus, still brooded on me. What could I do?

First, I renounced one vicious habit, then another. That did not help. All my efforts were like pulling one firebrand from a flame that fed itself with blazing forests. Do what I might, my conscience found no rest. I went to the house of God to hear the Gospel, but there was no Gospel for me. The fire burned all the more fiercely, and the very breath of the Gospel seemed to fan the flame.

I went to my room to pray. The heavens were like brass, and the windows of the sky were barred against me. I could get no answer. The fire burned more vehemently. Then I thought, "I will not always be alive. I wish to God that I had never been born!" I dared not die, for I would be in hell when I was dead; but I dared not live, for life had become intolerable. Still the fire blazed vehemently, until at last I came to this resolve: If there is salvation in Christ,

I will have it. I have nothing of my own in which to trust. I do this hour, O God, renounce my sin, and renounce my own righteousness, too.

The fire blazed again and burned up all my good works, yes, and my sins with them. And then I saw that all this burning was to bring me to Christ. Oh, the joy and gladness of my heart when Jesus came and sprinkled water on the flame and said, "I have bought you with My blood. Put your trust in Me. I will do for you what you cannot do for yourself. I will take your sins away. I will clothe you with a spotless robe of righteousness. I will guide you all your journey through and land you at last in heaven."

My dear reader, do you know anything about the Spirit of burning? For, if not, again, I say—I am not harsh, but I am telling the truth—if you have never felt this, you do not know the Spirit.

The Spirit Is like Oil

To proceed a little further, when the Spirit has thus quickened the soul and convinced it of sin, then we can use the simile of oil to understand the Spirit's work. In the Scriptures, the Holy Spirit is frequently compared to oil. *"Thou anointest my head with oil; my cup runneth over"* (Psalm 23:5). Oh, friends, though the beginning of the Spirit is by fire, it does not end there. We may be first of all convinced and brought to Christ by misery, but when we get to Christ, there is no misery in Him; our sorrows result from not getting close enough to Him.

The Holy Spirit comes, like the Good Samaritan, and pours in the oil and the wine. (See Luke 10:30–35.) And, oh, what oil it is with which He anoints our heads, and with which He heals our wounds! How soothing the ointment that He gently applies to our bruises! How blessed the salve with which He anoints our eyes! How heavenly the balm with which He binds up our sores, wounds, and bruises, and makes us whole. He sets our feet on a rock and establishes our goings (Psalm 40:2).

The Spirit, after He has convinced, begins to comfort, and you who have felt the comforting power of the Holy Spirit will bear witness that there is no comforter like the Paraclete. Oh, bring the music, the singing voices, and the sound of harps to this place. They are medicine to the one who has a heavy heart. Bring me the enchantments of the magic world, and all the enjoyments of its pleasures. They only torment the soul and prick it with many thorns. Yet, oh, Spirit of the living God, when You blow upon the heart, there is not a wave of that tempestuous sea that does not sleep forever when You command it to be still. Not one single breath of the proud hurricane and tempest does not cease to howl and does not lie still when You say to it, "Peace be unto you; your sins are forgiven."

Do you know the workings of the Spirit that are like oil? Have you felt Him at work in your spirit, comforting you, anointing your head, making you glad, and causing you to rejoice?

There are many people who have never felt this joy. They hope they are religious, but their religion never makes them happy. Scores of people profess to be Christians who have just enough religion to make them miserable. Let them be afraid that they have any religion at all, for religion makes people happy. When it has its full sway with man, it makes him glad. It may begin in agony, but it does not end there. Tell me, have you ever had your heart leap for joy? Have your lips ever sung songs of ecstatic praise? Do your eyes ever flash with the fire of joy? If these things have not happened to you, I fear that you are still without God and without Christ; for where the Spirit comes, His fruits are joy in the Spirit, peace, love, confidence, and assurance forever.

Spurgeon on the Holy Spirit

The Spirit Is like Water

Bear with me once more. I want to make one more comparison of the Spirit, and by that, also, you will be able to ascertain whether you are under His operation. When the Spirit has acted like wind, fire, and oil, He then acts like water. We are told that we are *"born of water and of the Spirit"* (John 3:5). Now I do not think you are foolish enough to need me to say that no water, either of immersion or of sprinkling, can in the least degree operate in the salvation of a soul.

There may be some few poor creatures, whose heads were put on their shoulders the wrong way, who still believe that a few drops of water from a priest's hands can regenerate souls. There may be a few, but I hope that their race will soon die out. We trust that the day will come when all those gentleman will have no *"other gospel"* (Galatians 1:6) to preach. We desire that the terrible stain upon the Protestant Church, called Puseyism,* will be cut out like a cancer and torn out by its very roots. The sooner we get rid of that doctrine, the better. Whenever we hear of any of them seceding to Catholicism, we say, "Let them go."

But when the Holy Spirit comes into the heart, He comes like water. That is to say, He comes to purify the soul. He who today lives as wickedly as he did before his pretended conversion is a hypocrite and a liar. He who this day loves sin and lives in it just as he was prone to do before, let him know that the truth is not in him, but that he has received the strong delusion to believe a lie.

God's people are a holy people. God's Spirit works by love and purifies the soul. Once His Spirit comes into our hearts, it will have no rest until it has turned every sin

---

* A religious movement among Anglican clergy at Oxford University in the 1830s. Named after Edward Bouverie Pusey, a professor of Hebrew at Oxford, Puseyism revived certain Roman Catholic doctrines and rituals within the Church of England.

out. God's Holy Spirit and man's sin cannot live together peaceably. They may both be in the same heart, but they cannot both reign there.

Neither can they both be quiet there, for *"the flesh lusteth against the Spirit, and the Spirit against the flesh"* (Galatians 5:17). They cannot rest, but there will be a perpetual warring in the soul, so that the Christian will have to cry, *"O wretched man that I am! who shall deliver me from the body of this death?"* (Romans 7:24). However, in due time, the Spirit will drive out all sin and will present us blameless before the throne of His Majesty with exceedingly great joy.

Now, my friend, answer this question for yourself and not for any other. Have you received the Holy Spirit? Answer me, even if it is with a scoff. Answer me, even if you sneer and say, "I know nothing of your enthusiastic rhetoric." If that is so, friend, then say, "No." It may be that you do not care to reply at all. I beseech you, do not put away my entreaty. Answer, yes or no. Have you received the Spirit?

"Sir, no man can find fault with my character. I believe I will enter heaven through my own virtues." That is not the question, beloved. Have you received the Spirit? You may have done everything that you have said. However, if you have left the other undone and have not received the Spirit, it will go ill with you in the end.

Have you had a supernatural operation upon your own heart? Have you been made a *"new creature"* (2 Corinthians 5:17) in Christ Jesus? If not, depend on this, because God's Word is true: You are out of Christ. Dying as you are, you will be shut out of heaven, no matter who you are or what you have accomplished in this life.

The Caution

Thus I have tried to help you to answer the first question: Have you received the Holy Spirit? This brings me to the caution. He who has not received the Spirit is said to be *"sensual."* Oh, what a gulf there is between the least Christian and the greatest moralist! What a wide distinction there is between the greatest professor of faith who is destitute of grace, and the least of God's believers who has grace in his heart. As great a difference as there is between light and darkness, between death and life, between heaven and hell, is there between a saint and a sinner. Note what the text says, in no very polite phrase, that if we do not have the Spirit, we are sensual.

"Sensual!" exclaims one. "Well, I am not a converted man—I don't pretend to be—but I am not sensual!" Well, friend, it is very likely that you are not—not in the common understanding of the term *sensual*. However, understand that this word, in the Greek, really means what the comparable English word would mean if we had a word such as *soulish*. We do not have such a word, but we need one.

There is a great distinction between mere animals and men, because men have a soul, and animals do not. There is another distinction between mere men and converted men. Converted men have the Spirit, but unconverted men do not. They are soulish men—not spiritual men. They have progressed no further than mere nature and have no inheritance in the spiritual kingdom of grace. It is strange that soulish and sensual should, after all, mean the same!

Friend, if you do not have the Spirit, then you are nothing better—no matter who you are or what you may be—than the fall of Adam left you. That is to say, you are a fallen creature, having only the capacity to live here in sin and to live forever in torment. But you do not have the capacity to live in heaven at all, for you have no spirit; therefore, you are unable to know or enjoy spiritual things. And mark you, a man may be in this state and be a sensual man, yet he may have all the virtues that could grace a Christian. However, even with all these, if he does not have the Spirit, he has gone not an inch farther than where Adam's fall left him—that is, condemned and under the curse. He may attend to religion with all his might—he may take the sacrament, be baptized, and be the most devout professor—but if he does not have the Spirit, then he has not moved a solitary inch from where he was. He is still a lost soul bound by iniquity.

In addition, he may pick up religious phrases until he can talk very glibly about religion. He may read biographies until he seems to be a well-instructed child of God. He may be able to write an article about the deep experience of a believer, but if this experience is not his own, if he has not received it by the Spirit of the living God, he is still nothing more than a carnal man. Heaven is to him a place to which there is no entrance.

Further, he might go so far as to become a minister of the Gospel, and a successful minister, too. God may bless the words that he preaches to the salvation of sinners, but unless he has received the Spirit, even if he is as eloquent as Apollos and as earnest as Paul, he is nothing more than a mere soulish man, without the capacity for spiritual things. To crown all, he might even have the power of working miracles, as Judas had. He might even be received into the church as a believer, as was Simon the Sorcerer. (See Acts 8:9–24.)

After all that, though he had cast out devils, though he had healed the sick, though he had worked miracles, he might have the gates of heaven shut in his face if he had not received the Spirit. For this is the essential thing, without which all others are in vain: the reception of the Spirit of the living God.

It is a searching truth, is it not, my friends? Do not run away from it. If I am preaching to you falsehood, reject it; but if this is a truth that I can substantiate by Scripture, I beseech you, do not rest until you have answered this question: Do you have the Holy Spirit living, dwelling, and working in your heart?

The Suspicion

This brings me, in the third place, to the suspicion. How remarkable that "separation" should be the opposite of having the Spirit. I hear a gentleman saying, "Oh, I like to hear you preach smartly and sharply. I am persuaded, sir, that there are a great many people in the church who ought not to be there. Therefore, because there is such a corrupt mixture in the church, I have determined not to join anywhere at all. I do not think that the church of Christ nowadays is at all pure enough to cause me to join with it.

"At least, sir, I did join a church once, but I made such a great deal of noise in it that they were very glad when I went away. And now I am just like David's men. I am one who is in debt and discontented. I go around to hear all new preachers who arise. I have heard you now these three months. I intend to go and hear someone else in a very little time if you do not say something to flatter me. But I am quite sure that I am one of God's special elect. I don't join any church because a church is not good enough for me. I don't become a member of any denomination because they are all wrong, every one of them."

Listen, brother. I have something to tell you that will not please you. *"These be they who separate themselves, sensual, having not the Spirit."* I hope you enjoy the text because it certainly applies to you, above every man in the world. *"These be they who separate themselves, sensual, having not the Spirit."*

When I read this verse over, I thought to myself, there are some who would say, "Well, you are a dissenter. How do you reconcile this fact with the text, *'These be they who separate themselves'*? You are separated from the Church of England."

Ah, my friends, a man may be separated from the Church of England and be all the better for it, but the separation intended here is a separation from the one universal church of Christ. The Church of England was not known in Jude's day, so the apostle could not have been referring to it.

"These be they who separate themselves"—that is, from the church of Christ, from the great universal body of the elect. Moreover, let us just say one thing. We did not separate ourselves: We were turned out. Dissenters did not separate themselves from the Church of England, from the Episcopal Church. When the Act of Uniformity was passed, they were turned out of their pulpits. Our forefathers were as sound churchmen as any in the world, but they could not take in all the errors of the Prayer Book, and they were, therefore, hounded to their graves by the intolerance of the conforming professors. So they did not separate themselves.

Moreover, we do not separate ourselves. There is not a Christian beneath the scope of God's heaven from whom I am separated. At the Lord's Table, I always invite all churches to come and sit down and commune with us. If anyone were to tell me that I am separated from the Episcopalians, the Presbyterians, or the Methodists, I would tell him that he does not know me, for I love them with a pure heart fervently, and I am not separated from them. I may hold different views than they do, and, in that point, truly I may be said to be separated, but I am not separated from them in my heart. I will work with them—I will work with them heartily. Even though my Church of England brother sends me a summons, as he has done, to pay a church rate* that I cannot in conscience pay, I will love him still. If he comes to claim my chairs and tables for

---

* Abolished in 1868, this local property tax was levied by the Church of England for the upkeep of Anglican parish churches. Separatists, or Nonconformists, protested having to pay this tax.

payment, it does not matter—I will love him still. And if there is a school for poor children or anything else for which I can work with him to promote the glory of God, therein will I unite with him with all my heart.

I think this bears rather hard on our friends—the Strict Communion Baptists. I would not want to say anything hard against them, for they are about the best people in the world, but they really do separate themselves from the great body of Christ's people. The Spirit of the living God will not let them do this really, but they do it professedly. They separate themselves from the great universal church. They say they will not commune with it. If anyone comes to the Lord's Table who has not been baptized, they turn him away.

They separate, certainly. I do not believe it is a willful schism that makes them act this way; but, at the same time, I think the *"old man"* (Ephesians 4:22) within has some hand in it. Oh, how my heart loves the doctrine of the one church. The nearer I get to my Master in prayer and communion, the closer I am knit to all His disciples. The more I see of my own errors and failings, the more ready I am to deal gently with those whom I believe to be erring. The pulse of Christ's body is communion, and woe to the church that seeks to cure the ills of Christ's body by stopping its pulse. I think it is a sin to refuse to commune with anyone who is a member of the church of our Lord Jesus Christ.

I desire to preach the unity of Christ's church. I have sought to use the fan to blow away the chaff. I have said that no man belongs to Christ's church unless he has the Spirit; but, if he has the Spirit, woe to the one who separates himself from him. Oh, I should think myself grossly at fault if, coming from the pulpit, I would meet a truly converted child of God who called himself a Primitive Methodist or a Wesleyan or a churchman or an Independent, and I should say, "No, sir, you do not agree with me on certain points. I believe you are a child of God, but I will have nothing to do with you." I should then think that this text would bear very hard on me. *"These be they who separate themselves, sensual, having not the Spirit."* Yet would we do so, beloved?

No, we would give them both our hands and say, "Godspeed you on your journey to heaven. As long as you have the Spirit within you, we are one family, and we will not be separated from one another."

May God grant that the day will come when every wall of separation will be beaten down! See how to this day we are separate. You will find Episcopalians who hate that ugly word *dissent*. It is enough for them that a Dissenter has done something; they will not do it, then, even if it is something good! Furthermore, there are some to be found in the Church of England who not only hate dissenters, but also hate one another in the bargain. There are men who cannot let brother ministers of their own church preach in their parishes. What an anachronism such men are! They would seem to have been sent into the world in our time purely by mistake. Their proper era would have been the time of the Dark Ages. If they had lived then, what fine Bonners* they would have made! What splendid fellows they would have been to have helped to poke the fire in Smithfield.† However, they are quite out-of-date in these times, and I look upon such curious clergymen in the same way that I do upon the dodo—as an extraordinary animal whose race is extinct. Well, you may look and look and wonder. It will not be long, I trust, before the Church of England will love itself, and all who love the

---

* Edmund Bonner [c. 1500–1569], Bishop of London, was characterized by John Foxe, his contemporary, as a monster who burned Protestants at the stake during the reign of Mary I.

† John Lambert was chained and burned at the stake in Smithfield, England, in 1537, after being suspected of having converted to Protestantism.

Lord Jesus will be ready to preach in each other's pulpits, preaching the same truth, holding the same faith, and mightily contending for it. Then the world will "see how these Christians love one another." (See John 13:35.) Then it will be known in heaven that Christ's kingdom has come, and that His will is about to be done on earth as it is in heaven.

My friend, do you belong to the church? For outside the church, there is no salvation. However, note what the church is. It is not Episcopalian, Baptist, or Presbyterian. The church is a company of people who have received the Holy Spirit. If you cannot say you have the Spirit, go your way and tremble. Go your way and think of your lost condition. May Jesus by His Spirit so bless you that you may be led to renounce with grief your works and ways, fly to Him who died on the cross, and find a shelter there from the wrath of God.

I may have said some rough things in this message, but I am not given much to cutting corners or diluting the Gospel, and I do not suppose I will begin to learn that art now. If the thing is untrue, it is for you to reject. If it is true, reject at your own peril what God stamps with His divine authority. May the blessings of the Father, the Son, and the Holy Spirit rest upon the one church of Israel's one Jehovah. Amen and Amen.

How to Have
Real Joy

Contents

Chapter 1

All Things New

And he that sat upon the throne said,
Behold, I make all things new.
—Revelation 21:5

How pleased we are with things that are new! Our children's eyes sparkle when we talk about giving them a new toy or a new book. Our human nature loves things that are recent because they are like our fleeting lives—suddenly here for a brief time and then gone. In our love of novelty, we are all children, for we eagerly demand the news of the day and are all too ready to rush after new inventions. The Athenians, who spent their time in nothing else but telling and hearing something new (Acts 17:21), were by no means unusual; novelty still fascinates the crowd.

Therefore, I would not be surprised if the words of our text sound like a pleasant song in your ears, but I am thankful that their deeper meaning is even more joyous. The newness that Jesus brings is bright, clear, heavenly, and enduring.

As Christians, we should not be carried away by a childish love of novelty, for we worship a God who is always the same and whose years will have no end (Psalm 102:27). In some matters, *"the old is better"* (Luke 5:39). There are certain old things that are so truly new that to

All Things New

exchange them for anything else would be like exchanging old gold for new dross. The old, old Gospel is the newest thing in the world. In its very essence, it is forever the Good News. In the things of God, the old is always new. If anyone presents what seems to be new doctrine and new truth, it is soon perceived that the new dogma is only worn-out heresy cleverly repaired. The so-called discovery in theology is the digging up of a carcass of error that should have been left to rot in oblivion. In the great matter of truth and godliness, we may safely say, *"There is no new thing under the sun"* (Ecclesiastes 1:9).

Yet there has been so much evil in ourselves and our old natures, so much sin in our lives and our pasts, so much wickedness in our surroundings and old temptations, that we are not distressed by the belief that old things are passing away. Hope springs up at the first sound of such words as these from the lips of our risen and reigning Lord: *"Behold, I make all things new."* It is fitting that things so worn out and defiled be laid aside and that better things take their places.

The words that Christ speaks to us are truly divine. Listen to them: *"Behold, I."* Who is the great *"I"*? Who else but the eternal Son of God? *"Behold, I make."* Who can create but God, the Maker of heaven and earth? It is His prerogative to make and to destroy. *"Behold, I make all things."* What a range of creating power! Nothing stands outside that all-encompassing power. *"Behold, I make all things new."* What a splendor of almighty goodness shines out upon our souls! Lord, let us enter into this new universe of Yours. Let us be a part of the *"all things"* that are newly created. May others see the marvels of Your renewing love in us!

Let us thank Jesus as we hear these encouraging words that He speaks from His throne. O Lord, we want to rejoice and be glad forever in what You create. The former troubles are forgotten and are hidden from our eyes because of Your ancient promise, *"Behold, I create new heavens and a new earth: and the former shall not be remembered, nor come into mind"* (Isaiah 65:17).

I am going to write a little about the great transformation spoken of in the text: *"I make all things new."* Then I will go on to describe the earnest call in the text to consider that transformation: *"He that sat upon the throne said, Behold."* In other words, He said, "Pay attention to it; consider it; look at it!" *"Behold, I make all things new."* Oh, for an outpouring of the Holy Spirit while I discuss this theme and while you read about it!

The Great Transformation

Here is one of the greatest truths that ever came from the lips of Jesus: *"Behold, I make all things new."* Let us gaze upon the great transformation.

This renewing work has been in our Lord's hands since long ago. Originally, we were under the old covenant, and when our first father and covenantal head, Adam, broke that covenant, we were ruined by his fatal violation. The substance of the old covenant that God made with Adam was this: "If you keep My command, you will live, and your posterity will live. Yet if you eat from the tree that I have forbidden you to eat from, you will die, and all your posterity in you will die."

As we know, Adam ate the forbidden fruit, and the tremendous Fall destroyed both our Paradise and ourselves. We were broken in pieces, seriously wounded, and even killed. We died in Adam, as far as spiritual life is concerned, and our state of death revealed itself in an inward tendency to evil that reigned in our members. We were like Ezekiel's deserted infant, unclothed and unwashed, left in our uncleanness to die; but the Son of God passed by and saw us in the greatness of our ruin. (See Ezekiel 16:1–14.) In His wondrous love, our Lord Jesus put us under a new covenant, a covenant in which He became the Second Adam, a covenant in which God said to His Son, "If You will live in perfect obedience and vindicate My justice, then those who are in You will not perish, but they will live because You live."

Now, our Lord Jesus, our Surety and covenantal Head, has fulfilled His portion of the covenant, and the compact stands as a bond of pure promise without condition or risk. Those who are participants in that covenant cannot invalidate it, for it never did depend on them, but only on Him who was and is their covenantal Head and Representative before God. Of Jesus the demand was made, and He met it. By Him, man's side of the covenant was undertaken and fulfilled, and now no condition remains; the covenant is made up solely of promises that are unconditional and sure to all who are in Christ. Today, believers are not under the covenant of "If you do this, you will live," but under the new covenant that says, *"Their sins and their iniquities will I remember no more"* (Hebrews 8:12). The new covenant is not "Do and live," but "Live and do." The new covenant is not of merit and reward, but of free grace producing a holy lifestyle as the result of gratitude. What law could not do, grace has accomplished.

We must never forget this basis of everything, this making *"all things new"* by the fashioning of a new covenant. By it, we have been released from the bondage of the law and the ruin of the Fall, and we have entered into the liberty of Christ, into acceptance with God, and into the boundless joy of being saved in the Lord with an everlasting salvation. We *"shall not be ashamed nor confounded world without end"* (Isaiah 45:17).

If you know the Lord, I exhort you to thoroughly study that word *covenant*. If you do not yet know the Lord, I encourage you to study that word as soon as you come to know Him. It is a key word that opens the treasures of revelation. He who properly understands the difference between the two covenants has the foundation of sound theology laid in his mind. This understanding is the clue to many perplexities, the "open sesame" of many mysteries. Jesus makes *"all things new,"* beginning with the bringing in of a better hope through a better covenant.

The foundation having been made new, the Lord Jesus Christ has set before us a new way of life, which grows out of that covenant. The old way of life was this: "If you want to enter into life, keep the commandments." The commandments are perfect, holy, just, and good (Romans 7:12). Yet, alas, dear friend, you and I have broken the commandments. We dare not say that we have kept the Ten Commandments our whole lives; on the contrary, our consciences compel us to confess that in spirit and in heart, if not in act, we have continually broken the law of God. Therefore, we are under sin and condemnation, and there is no hope for us to be saved by the works of the law.

For this reason, the Gospel sets before us another way, and says, *"It is of faith, that it might be by grace"* (Romans 4:16), and *"Believe on the Lord Jesus Christ, and thou shalt be saved"* (Acts 16:31). Therefore, we read of being *"justified by faith"* (Romans 3:28), and being made acceptable to God by faith. To be *"justified"* means to be made truly righteous. Though we were guilty in ourselves, we are regarded as just because of what the Lord Jesus Christ has done for us. Thus, we fell into condemnation through another, and we rise into justification through Another. It is written, *"By his knowledge shall my righteous servant justify many; for he shall bear their iniquities"* (Isaiah 53:11), and this verse is fulfilled in all those who believe in the Lord Jesus and receive eternal life.

Our path to eternal glory is the road of faith: *"The just shall live by faith"* (Romans 1:17). We are *"accepted in the beloved"* (Ephesians 1:6) when we believe in the One whom God has set forth to be our righteousness. *"By the deeds of the law there shall no flesh be justified in his sight"* (Romans 3:20), but we are *"justified freely by his grace through the redemption that is in Christ Jesus"* (v. 24).

What a blessing it is for you and for me that Jesus has made *"all things new"* in this respect! I am glad that I do not have to say, "My dear reader, do this and do that, and you will be saved." You would not do as you were commanded, for your fallen nature is weak and wicked. However, I can say to you,

> Lay your deadly doing down,
> Down at Jesus' feet;
> Stand in Him, in Him alone,
> Gloriously complete.

I trust that you will accept this most gracious way of salvation. It is most glorious to God and safe for you. Do not *"neglect so great [a] salvation"* (Hebrews 2:3). After you have believed and have received life, you will do all kinds of holy deeds as the result of your new life; but do not attempt them with a view to earning life. No longer prompted by the servile and selfish motive of saving yourself, but by gratitude for the fact that you are saved, you will rise to virtue and true holiness. Faith has given us an irreversible salvation; and now, because of the love that we have for our Savior, we must obey Him and become *"zealous of good works"* (Titus 2:14).

By grace, every believer is brought into a new relationship with God. Let us rejoice in this: *"Thou art no more a servant, but a son; and if a son, then an heir of God through Christ"* (Galatians 4:7). Oh, you who are now a believing child, you were an unbelieving servant a little while ago! Or perhaps you are still an unbelieving servant; if you are, I tell you to expect your wages. Alas, your service has not been true service, but rebellion; and if you get no more wages than you deserve, you will be cast away forever.

You ought to be thankful to God that He has not paid you yet, that *"he hath not dealt with* [you] *after* [y]*our sins; nor rewarded* [you] *according to* [y]*our iniquities"* (Psalm 103:10).

Don't you know, you unbelieving servant, what is likely to happen to you as a servant? What would you yourself do with a bad servant? You would say to him, "There are your wages. Go." *"The servant abideth not in the house for ever"* (John 8:35). You, too, will be driven from your hypocritical profession of faith. Your period of probation will end, and where will you go? The wilderness of destruction lies before you!

"Behold, I make all things new," says Jesus. Indeed, He makes His people into sons. When we are made sons, do we work for wages? We have no desire for any present payment, for our Father says to us, *"Son, thou art ever with me, and all that I have is thine"* (Luke 15:31). Furthermore, we have the inheritance given to us by the covenant. We cannot demand a servant's wages because we already have all that our Father possesses. He has given us Himself and His all-sufficiency for our everlasting portion; what more can we desire? He will never drive us from His house. Never has our Great Father disowned one of His sons. It cannot be. His loving heart is too closely involved with His own adopted ones. That near and dear relationship that is manifested in adoption and regeneration binds the child of God to the Great Father's heart in such a way that He will never cast him away or allow him to perish. I rejoice in the fact that we are no longer servants, but sons. *"Behold,"* says Christ, *"I make all things new."*

The Holy Spirit has put within us a new life, with all the new feelings, the new desires, and the new works that go with it. The tree has been made new, and the fruits are new as a result. The same Spirit of God, who taught us that we were ruined in our old state of sin led us gently by the hand until we came to the new covenantal promise, looked to Jesus and saw in Him the full atonement for sin. Happy discovery for us! It was the kindling of new life in us. The moment that we trusted in Jesus, a new life darted into our spirits.

I am not going to say which comes first: the new birth, faith, or repentance. When a wheel moves, no one can say which spoke moves first; it moves as a whole. The moment the divine life comes into the heart, we believe; the moment we believe, the eternal life is there. Then we no longer live according to the lusts of the world, but we live by faith in the Son of God, who loved us and gave Himself for us (Galatians 2:20).

Our spiritual life is a newborn thing, the creation of the Spirit of Life. We have, of course, the natural life that is sustained by food and that is evidenced by the fact that we are breathing; but there is another life within us that is not seen by others and is not fed by earthly provisions. We are conscious of having been spiritually awakened. We were dead once, and we know it; but now we have passed from death into life (John 5:24), and we know this just as certainly. A new and higher motive sways us now, for we do not seek self, but God. A new hand steers our ship in a new course. We feel new desires, to which we were strangers in our former state. New fears are mighty within us—holy fears that once we would have ridiculed. New hopes are in us, bright and sure, such as we did not even desire to have when we lived a mere carnal life. We are not what we were; we are new, and we have begun a new life. I admit that we are not what we will be, but, assuredly, we are not what we used to be.

As for myself, my consciousness of being a new man in Christ Jesus is often as sharp and crisp as my consciousness of being in existence. I know that I am not solely what I was by my first birth. I feel within myself another life—a second and a higher vitality—that often has to contend with my lower self, and by that very contention makes me conscious of its existence. This new life is, from day to day, gathering strength and winning the victory. It has its hand on the throat of the old sinful nature, and it will eventually trample it like dust beneath its feet. I feel this new life within me. Do you? If you feel it, I know that you can say that Jesus Christ, who sits on the throne, makes *"all things new."* Blessed be His name. We needed the Lord Himself to make people such as we are new. No one but a Savior on the throne could accomplish it; therefore, let Him have the glory for it.

Perhaps Jesus Christ has not only made you new, but has also made everything new to you. "Oh," one woman said when she was converted, "either the world is greatly changed, or else I am." Why, either you and I are turned upside down, or the world is. We used to think that the world is wise, but we think that it is very foolish now! We used to think of it as a brave, glad world that showed us real happiness, but we are no longer deceived. *"The world is crucified unto me,"* Paul said in Galatians 6:14, and perhaps you can say the same. To believers, the world is like a vile criminal who is taken out and hanged. Meanwhile, there is no love lost, for the world thinks much the same of us, and we can agree with Paul when he added, *"And I* [am crucified] *unto the world."*

Grace greatly transforms everything in our little world! In our hearts, there is a new heaven and a new earth. What a change in our joys! We blush to think about what we used to enjoy, but we enjoy heavenly things now. We are equally ashamed of our former hates and prejudices, but these have vanished once and for all. Why, now we love the very things we once despised, and our hearts run after the things that they once detested.

How different the Bible seems to us now! Oh, this blessed Book is exactly the same in its wording, but how differently we read these precious words! The mercy seat of God, what a different place it is now! Our wretched, formal prayers—if we bothered to pray at all—what a mockery they were! Yet now we draw near to God and speak to Him with delight. We have access to Him by the *"new and living way"* (Hebrews 10:20). The house of God, how different it is from what it used to be! We love to be found within its walls, and we feel delighted to join in the praises of the Lord.

After a recent church service, I shook the hand of a man who does not often hear me preach. He expressed to me his boundless delight in listening to the doctrine of the grace of God, and he added, "Surely your congregation must be made of stone." "Why?" I asked. He replied, "If they were not, they would all get up and shout 'Hallelujah' when you are preaching such a glorious Gospel. I wanted very much to shout, but since everybody else was quiet, I held my tongue." I thought he was wise for remaining silent, yet I am not surprised if men who have tasted God's grace do feel like crying out for joy.

Why shouldn't we lift up our voices in His praise? We will. He has put a new song into our mouths (Psalm 40:3), and we must sing it. *"The mountains and the hills...break forth before* [us] *into singing"* (Isaiah 55:12), and we cannot be silent. Praise is our ever new delight. In praise, we will compete with angels and archangels, for they are not so indebted to grace as we are.

> Never did angels taste above
> Redeeming grace and dying love.

Still, we have tasted these precious things, and unto God we will lift up our loudest song forever.

The process that I have roughly described as taking place in believers is going on in the physical world in other forms. All time is groaning, providence is working, grace is striving, the whole creation is giving birth, and all for one end—the bringing forth of the new and better age. It is coming. It is coming. It is ever nearer to us. And the Beloved Apostle did not write the following in vain:

> *And I saw a new heaven and a new earth: for the first heaven and the first earth were passed away; and there was no more sea. And I John saw the holy city, new Jerusalem, coming down from God out of heaven, prepared as a bride adorned for her husband. And I heard a great voice out of heaven saying, Behold, the tabernacle of God is with men, and he will dwell with them, and they shall be his people, and God himself shall be with them, and be their God. And God shall wipe away all tears from their eyes; and there shall be no more death, neither sorrow, nor crying, neither shall there be any more pain: for the former things are passed away. And he that sat upon the throne said, Behold, I make all things new. And he said unto me, Write: for these words are true and faithful.* (Revelation 21:1–5)

What a prospect all this opens up to the believer! Our future is glorious; we must not let our present be gloomy.

The Earnest Call

Next, in the text, there is an earnest call for us to consider this work of our Lord. He who sits on the throne says, *"Behold, I make all things new."* Why should He call on us to behold this? All His works deserve study. *"The works of the LORD are great, sought out of all them that have pleasure therein"* (Psalm 111:2). Whatever the Lord does is full of wisdom, and the wise will look into His works. However, when the Lord Himself sets up a light and calls us to pause and look, we cannot help but respond.

I think that the Lord Jesus Christ specifically calls us to consider the fact that He makes all things new, so that we may be comforted, regardless of our condition.

To the Unsaved

First, this verse is a comfort to the unsaved. If the Lord Jesus makes *"all things new,"* then a new birth is possible for you, dear friend, even though you have a wrong state of heart and your sins are upon you, clutching you tightly. There is enough light in your soul for you to know that you are in darkness, and you are saying to yourself, "Oh, if only I could attain better things! I hear people praise God for what Christ has done for them. Can He do the same for me?" Listen! He who sits on the throne says in infinite graciousness to you on the trash heap, "Behold, I make all things new." There is nothing so old that He cannot make it new, and nothing so ingrained and habitual that He cannot change it.

Don't you know, dear heart, that the Spirit of God has regenerated men and women just as far gone as you are? They were as deep in sin and as hardened by habit as you could ever be. They thought that they were hopeless, just as you think that you are. Yet the Spirit of God carried out the will of the Lord Christ and made them new. Why shouldn't He make you new? May every thief know that the dying thief entered heaven by faith in Jesus. (See Luke 23:39–43.) May everyone who has been a great sinner remember how Manasseh received a new heart and repented of his evil deeds. (See 2 Chronicles 33:1–16.) Let everyone who has left the paths of purity remember how the woman who was a sinner loved much because she had been forgiven much. (See Luke 7:37–50.)

I cannot doubt the possibility of your salvation, my friend, whenever I think of my own. A more determined, obstinate rebel could scarcely have existed. Because I was a child and was kept from gross outward sin by holy restraints, I had a powerful inner nature that would not tolerate control. I rebelliously strove hard. I labored to win heaven by self-righteousness, and this is as real a rebellion as open sin. Yet, oh, the grace of God, how it can tame

359

us! How it can turn us! With no bit or bridle, but with a blessed tenderness, it turns us according to its pleasure. Oh, anxious one, it can turn you! Therefore, I want to drop this truth into your mind (and may the Spirit of God drop it into your heart): You can be born again. The Lord can work a radical change in you. He who sits on the throne can do for you what you cannot do for yourself. He made you once, and, even though you became marred by sin, He can make you new again. He says, *"Behold, I make all things new."*

To Those Who Want a New Life

This verse is also a comfort to those who desire to lead a new life. To have a new life, you must be new yourself; for as the man is, so his life will be. If the fountain is contaminated, the streams cannot be pure. Renewal must begin with the heart.

Dear friend, the Lord Jesus Christ is able to make your life entirely new. I have seen many people transformed into new parents and new children. Friends have exclaimed in amazement, "What a change in John! What a difference in Ellen!" I have seen men become new husbands and women become new wives. They are the same people, yet not the same. Grace works a very deep, striking, and lasting change. Ask someone who has seen a member of his household converted whether the transformation has not been marvelous. Christ makes new employees, new supervisors, new friends, new brothers, new sisters. The Lord can so change us that we hardly know ourselves.

He can change you who now despair of yourself. Oh, dear heart, it is not necessary for you to go downward in evil until you descend to hell. There is a hand that can pull you in the opposite direction. It would be an amazing thing if Niagara Falls were to flow backward, ascending instead of descending. It would be an incredible thing if the St. Lawrence River were to run backward to Lake Ontario. Yet God could do even these things.

Likewise, God Almighty can reverse the course of your fallen nature and make you act like a new person. He can stop the tide of your raging passion. He can make someone who is like a devil become like an angel of God, for He says this from the throne of His eternal majesty: *"Behold, I make all things new."* Come and lay yourself down at His feet, and ask Him to make you new. I implore you, do this at once!

"Well, I am going to mend myself," some people say. "I have taken a pledge that I will be honest, moral, and religious." This is a commendable decision, but what will come of it? You will break your resolutions; you will not be made any better by your attempts at reform. If you go into the business of mending yourself, you will be like the man who had an old gun. He took it to the gunsmith, and the gunsmith said, "Well, this would make a very good gun if it had a new lock, a new stock, and a new barrel." Likewise, mending would make you a very good person, if you could get a new heart, a new life, and an altogether new self, so that there was not one bit of the old self left.

You can depend on it that it is a great deal easier for God to make you new than to mend you, for the fact is that *"the carnal mind is enmity against God"* (Romans 8:7). The carnal mind is not reconciled to God; indeed, it cannot be. Therefore, mending will not do; you must be made new. *"Ye must be born again"* (John 3:7). What is needed is for you to be made a new creation in Christ Jesus. You must be dead with Christ, buried with Christ, and risen again in Him (Romans 6:4; Colossians 2:12). Then all will be well, for He will have made *"all things new."* I ask God to bless these feeble words of mine and use them to help some of His chosen out of the darkness of their fears.

How to Have Real Joy

To the Weary Christian

There are children of God who need this text, *"Behold, I make all things new."* They sigh because they often grow dull and weary in the ways of God and therefore need daily renewing. A fellow believer said to me some time ago, "Dear pastor, I frequently grow very sleepy in my walk with God. I seem to lose the freshness of it. By about Saturday, I feel especially dull." Then he added, "But as for you, whenever I hear you, you seem to be alive and full of fresh energy." "My dear brother," I said, "that is because you do not know much about me." That was all I was able to say just then.

I thank God for keeping me near Himself. However, I am as weak, as stale, and as unprofitable as any other believer. I say this with much shame—shame for myself and shame for the brother who led me to make the confession. We are both wrong. Since all our fresh springs are in God (Psalm 87:7), we ought to be full of new life all the time. Every minute, our love for Christ ought to be as if it were newborn. Our zeal for God ought to be as fresh as if we had just begun to delight in Him. "Yes, but it is not," most Christians would say, and I am sorry I cannot contradict them. After a few months, a vigorous young Christian begins to cool down. Likewise, those who have walked in the ways of God for a long time find that final perseverance must be a miracle if it is ever to be accomplished, because they tire and grow faint.

Well now, dear friend, why do you and I ever get stale and flat? Why do we sing,

> Dear Lord, and shall we ever live
> At this poor dying rate?

Why do we have to cry,

> In vain we tune our formal songs,
> In vain we strive to rise;

> Hosannas languish on our tongues,
> And our devotion dies?

Why, it is because we stray away from the One who says, *"Behold, I make all things new."* The way to perpetual new-ness and freshness is to keep going to Christ, just as we did when we were first saved.

An even better way is never to leave Him, but to stand forever at the foot of the Cross, delighting in His all-suffi-cient sacrifice. Those who are full of the joy of the Lord never grow weary of life. Those who walk in the light of His countenance can say of the Lord Jesus, *"Thou hast the dew of thy youth"* (Psalm 110:3); and that dew falls on those who dwell with Him. I am sure that if we would maintain perpetual communion with Him, we would enjoy a perpetual stream of delights.

> Immortal joys come streaming down,
> Joys, like His griefs, immense, unknown.

Still, these joys come only from Him. We will remain young if we stay with the ever young Beloved, whose hair is *"black as a raven"* (Song 5:11). He says, and He fulfills the saying, *"Behold, I make all things new."*

He can make that next sermon of yours, my fellow minister, quite new and interesting. He can make that prayer meeting no longer a dreary affair, but quite a new thing to you and all the people. My dear sister, the next time you go to your Sunday school class, the Lord can cause you to feel as if you had just started teaching yes-terday. Then you will not be at all tired of your godly work; instead, you will love it better than ever. And you, my dear brother, preaching at the street corner where you are often interrupted, perhaps with foul language, you will feel pleased with your position of self-denial. Getting near to Christ, you will partake of His joy, and that joy will be your strength, your freshness, the newness of your life. May God grant to us that we may drink of the eternal fountains, so that we may forever overflow.

There may be someone reading this who knows that he is living on a very low plane of spiritual life, but who also understands that the Lord can raise him to a new level. Many Christians seem to dwell in the marshlands. If you ever travel through the valleys of Switzerland, you will find yourself getting feverish and heavy in spirit, and you will see many who are mentally or physically afflicted. However, if you climb the sides of the hills, ascending into the Alps, you will not see that kind of thing in the pure, fresh air. Unfortunately, in this present era, too many Christians are of the sickly valley breed. Oh, that they could get up to the high mountains and be strong!

If you have been in bondage all your life, I declare that you do not need to stay there any longer. Jesus has the power to *"make all things new"* and to lift you into new delights. It might seem like a resurrection from the dead to you; but it is within the power of that pierced hand to lift you right out of doubt, fear, despondency, spiritual lethargy, and weakness, and to make you now, from this day forward, *"strong in the Lord, and in the power of his might"* (Ephesians 6:10).

Now breathe a prayer, dear brother, dear sister, to the One who makes *"all things new"*: "Lord, make Your poor, spiritually sick child strong and spiritually healthy." Oh, what a blessing it would be for some Christian workers if God would make them strong! The whole church would be better because of the way in which the Lord would help them to do their work. Why should you be living on pennies and starving yourself when your heavenly Father would cause you to live like a prince of royal blood if you would only trust Him? I am persuaded that most of us are beggars when we could be millionaires in spiritual things.

And here is our strength for rising to a nobler state of mind: *"Behold, I make all things new."*

To the Afflicted Christian

There is another application of this truth. Someone may be saying, "Oh, I do not know what to make of myself. I have had a hard time lately. Everything seems to have gone wrong. My family causes me great anxiety. My business is a thorny maze. My own health is precarious. I dread this year. In fact, I dread everything." We will not go on with that lamentation, but we will hear the encouraging word, *"Behold, I make all things new."* The Lord, in answer to believing prayer, and especially in answer to your full submission to His will, is able to make all your surroundings new. I have known the Lord to turn darkness into light all of a sudden, and to take away the sackcloth and the ashes from His dear children, for *"he doth not afflict willingly nor grieve the children of men"* (Lamentations 3:33).

Sometimes all our worry is mere discontentment, and when the child of God gets himself right, these imaginary troubles vanish like the morning mist. Yet when the troubles are real, God can just as easily change your condition, dear child of God, as He can turn His hand. He can make your harsh and ungodly husband become gentle and gracious. He can bring your children to the place where they will bow at the family altar and rejoice with you in Christ. He can cause your business to prosper. Or if He does not do that, He can strengthen your back to bear the burden of your daily cross.

Oh, it is wonderful how different a thing becomes when it is taken to God! However, you want to make it all new yourself, and you fret and worry; you torture, trouble, and burden yourself. Why not stop that and, in humble prayer, take the matter to the Lord and say, "Lord, come to my aid, for You have said, *'I make all things new.'* Make my circumstances new"? He is certainly able to free you from your captivity.

To Those Anxious about Unsaved Loved Ones

There is one more application, and that is that the Lord can convert those dear unsaved loved ones about whom you have been so anxious. The Lord who makes *"all things new"* can hear your prayers. At a prayer meeting that I attended recently, a dear brother prayed that God would save his relatives. Then another prayed with great tenderness for his children. I know that his prayer came from an aching heart. Some of you have heartbreakers at home; may the Lord break their hearts—humbling and softening them so that they will come to Him. You are grieved and troubled because you hear the person you hold the dearest blaspheming the God you love. You know that your loved ones are Sabbath-breakers and utterly godless, and you tremble for their eternal fate.

Certain people attend my church who are not saved. I can say of them that I never stand behind the pulpit without looking to their pews to see whether they are there, and without praying to God for them. I forget a great many who are saved, but I always pray for these unsaved ones. And they will be brought in, I feel assured. Oh, may it be soon!

I liked what one man said at a recent service when his brother was introduced to the church. Wondering about his brother's conversion, I asked, "Were you surprised to see him converted?" He said, "I would have been very much surprised if he had not been." "But why, my dear brother?" I asked. "Because I asked the Lord to convert him, and I kept on praying that he would be converted. I would have been very surprised if he had not been." That is the right sort of faith. I would be very surprised if some of the unsaved who attend my church time after time are not converted. They will be, blessed be God. I will give Him no rest until He answers me.

However, if you are unsaved, aren't you praying for yourself? Don't you agree with the prayers of your Christian friends and relatives who are praying for you? Oh, I trust that you do. Yet, even if you do not, they will still pray for you. Even if you are opposed to their intercessions and are even angry with them, they will undoubtedly pray all the more. They intend to have you won for Jesus, by the grace of God, and you may as well come sooner rather than later. They are determined to see you in the church confessing your faith in Jesus. They will never let you go, nor will they cease from their persistent prayers, until they get an answer from the throne and see you saved. Oh, that you would yield to the One who can make a new creation out of you (2 Corinthians 5:17). May God grant that you will!

May the Lord answer my prayers now, for Jesus' sake, for I seek the salvation of every reader of this book.

Chapter 2

This Year Also

*He spake also this parable; A certain man had a
fig tree planted in his vineyard; and he came and
sought fruit thereon, and found none. Then said he
unto the dresser of his vineyard, Behold, these three
years I come seeking fruit on this fig tree, and find
none: cut it down; why cumbereth it the ground?
And he answering said unto him, Lord, let it alone
this year also, till I shall dig about it, and dung it:
and if it bear fruit, well: and if not, then after that
thou shalt cut it down.*
—Luke 13:6–9

The interceding vinedresser pleaded for the fruitless
fig tree, *"Let it alone this year also,"* securing for it
another year. During that year, it would have to bear
fruit, or else it would be cut down. Unlike people, trees
and fruit-bearing plants have a natural way of marking a
year. Evidently, the tree's year came to its close when it
was time to seek fruit on it, and another year commenced
when the vinedresser began once again his digging and
pruning. However, men are such barren things that their
fruit-bearing marks no particular periods, and it becomes
necessary to make artificial divisions of time for them.
There seems to be no set period for man's spiritual harvest
or vintage, or if there is, the sheaves and the clusters do

not come in their season. Thus, it is necessary for us to say to one another, "Let us make this the beginning of a new year."

A Look at the Past

Look back over the past year of your life and examine it, deliberately and honestly. In the parable of the fig tree, there had been prior years of grace. It was not the first time that the vinedresser was made aware of the fig tree's failure. It was not the first time the owner came seeking figs in vain. In the same way, God, who gives us *"this year also,"* has given us others before it. His sparing mercy is no novelty; His patience has already been taxed by our provocations.

First came our youthful years, when even a little fruit for God is especially sweet to Him. How did we spend them? Did we spend all our strength on sinful pleasures? If so, we should mourn that wasted vigor, that life misspent, that sin exceedingly multiplied. Nevertheless, He who saw us misuse those golden months of youth gives us *"this year also."* We should enter it with a holy jealousy, lest the strength and fervency that are left to us be allowed to flow into the same wasteful avenues as before.

Upon the heels of our youthful years came the years of young adulthood, when we started a family and put out roots. Fruit yielded during that time also would have been precious. Did we bear any? Did we present unto the Lord a basket of summer fruit? Did we offer Him the firstfruits of our strength? If we did so, we should adore the grace that saved us so early; but if not, the past chides us, and, lifting an admonishing finger, it warns us not to let *"this year also"* follow the same path as the rest of our lives. The person who has wasted both youth and early adulthood has surely been foolish enough; he has spent enough time following the desires of his flesh. It would be an overflow of wickedness to allow *"this year also"* to be trodden down in the service of sin.

Many of you are now in the prime of life; many years of your lives are already spent. Do you still need to confess that your years are being eaten up by the grasshopper and the cankerworm (Joel 1:4)? Have you reached midlife and still do not know where you are going? Are you fools at forty? Are you half a century old by the calendar and yet far away from the years of wisdom? How unfortunate that there are men over fifty years old who are still without knowledge!

Unsaved at sixty, unregenerate at seventy, unawakened at eighty, unrenewed at ninety—each and every one of these phrases is startling! Perhaps their wording will startle and awaken someone who is reading this; but, on the other hand, that person might just gloss over them. Continuance in evil breeds hardness of heart, and when the soul has been sleeping in indifference for a long time, it is hard to wake it from its deadly slumber.

The sound of the words *"this year also"* makes some of us remember years of great mercy, sparkling and flashing with delight. Were those years laid at the Lord's feet? Were they like the horses' silver bells that were engraved with the words, *"HOLINESS UNTO THE LORD"* (Zechariah 14:20)? If not, how will we explain our neglect if *"this year also"* is musical with joyful mercy and yet spent in the ways of carelessness?

"This year also." These words cause some of us to recall our years of sharp affliction, when we were indeed dug around and fertilized. What were those years like? God was doing great things for us, cultivating carefully and expensively, caring for us very much and very wisely. Did we give back to God according to the benefits we received from Him? Did we rise from the bed of affliction with more patience and gentleness, weaned from the world

and welded to Christ? Did we produce clusters of grapes to reward the Vinedresser?

Let us not refuse to answer these questions of self-examination, for this year may be another of those years of trial, another season of the furnace and the crucible. May the Lord grant that the coming tribulation take more chaff out of us than any tribulation before it, leaving the wheat cleaner and better.

A new year reminds us of opportunities for usefulness that have come and gone, and of unfulfilled resolutions of the past that have blossomed, only to fade. Will *"this year also"* be like those that have gone before it? Shouldn't we hope for more grace so that we may build upon grace already gained? And shouldn't we seek power to turn our poor sickly promises into robust action?

Looking back on the past, we lament our foolish actions. We do not want to be held captive by them *"this year also."* At the same time, we adore God's forgiving mercy, His preserving providence, His boundless generosity, and His divine love; and we hope to be partakers of them *"this year also."*

A Gift of Mercy

The text also mentions a mercy. Because of the vinedresser's great goodness, the tree that was merely taking up space was allowed to stand for another year. Prolonged life should always be regarded as a gift of mercy. We must view *"this year also"* as a grant from infinite Grace. It is wrong to speak as if we cared nothing for life, as if we looked upon our being here on earth as torture or punishment. We are here *"this year also"* as the result of love's pleadings and to pursue love's purposes.

The wicked individual should consider that the Lord's longsuffering points to his salvation, and he should permit the cords of love to draw him to it. Oh, that the Holy

Spirit would make the blasphemer, the Sabbath-breaker, and the openly immoral to feel what a wonder it is that their lives are prolonged *"this year also"*! Are they spared to curse and to riot and to defy their Maker? Should this be the only fruit of the Lord's patient mercy? Shouldn't the procrastinator who has put off the messenger of heaven with his delays and half promises be amazed that he is allowed to see *"this year also"*? How is it that the Lord has borne with him and has put up with his vacillations and hesitations? Is this year of grace to be spent in the same manner? Short-lived convictions, hasty commitments, and speedy apostasies—are these to be the tiresome story over and over again? The startled conscience, the tyrant passion, the smothered emotion—are these to be the tokens of yet another year?

May God forbid that any one of us should hesitate and delay throughout *"this year also."* Infinite Pity holds back the ax of justice. Will His mercy be insulted by the repetition of the sins that caused wrath's instrument to be raised? What can be more tormenting to the heart of goodness than indecision? May the Lord's prophet become impatient and cry, *"How long halt ye between two opinions?"* (1 Kings 18:21). May God Himself push for a decision and demand an immediate reply. Oh, undecided soul, will you swing much longer between heaven and hell and act as if it were hard to choose between the slavery of Satan and the liberty of the Great Father's home of love? *"This year also,"* will you delay in defiance of justice and pervert the generosity of mercy into a license for still further rebellion? *"This year also,"* must divine love be made an occasion for continued sin? Oh, do not act so wickedly, so contrary to every noble instinct, so injuriously to your own best interests.

The believer, on the other hand, is kept out of heaven *"this year also"* because of God's love, not His anger. There are people who need him to remain on earth: Some need him to guide them on their way to heaven, and others need his help and instruction to lead them to the Redeemer's feet. Many saints do not have their heaven prepared for them yet because their nearest companions have not yet arrived there, and their spiritual children have not yet gathered there in sufficient numbers to give them a thoroughly heavenly welcome. They must wait *"this year also"* so their rest may be even more glorious and the additional souls that they win to Christ may give them greater joy. Surely, for the sake of souls, for the delight of glorifying our Lord, and for the increase of the jewels in our heavenly crowns, we may be glad to wait below *"this year also."*

The Limitations of Mercy

I want to emphasize that the expression *"this year also"* implies a limit. The vinedresser asked for a reprieve of no longer than one year. If his digging and fertilizing should prove unsuccessful, he would plead no more, and the tree would be cut down.

Even when Jesus is the pleader, the request of mercy has its boundaries and limits. We will not be left alone and allowed to needlessly take up space forever. If we will not repent, we must perish. If we will not be benefited by the spade, we must fall by the ax.

There will be a last year for each one of us. Therefore, let each one say to himself, "Is this year my last?" If it were to be the last for me, I would prepare to deliver the Lord's message with all my soul and to tell my fellowmen to be reconciled to God. Dear friend, is this year to be your last? Are you ready to see the curtain rise upon eternity? Are you now prepared to hear the midnight cry and to enter into the Marriage Supper (Matthew 25:6; Revelation 19:7–9)? The Judgment and all that will follow it are most surely the heritage of every person. Blessed are they who by faith in Jesus are able to face the judgment seat of God without a thought of terror.

How to Have Real Joy

Even if we live to be counted among the oldest inhabitants of the earth, we must depart at last. There must come an end, and we will hear the Lord say, *"Thus saith the LORD...: this year thou shalt die"* (Jeremiah 28:16). So many have gone before us, and are going every hour, that no man should need any other reminder that we must die. Yet man is so eager to forget his own mortality, and thereby to forfeit his hopes of bliss, that we cannot bring it too often before the mind's eye. Oh, mortal man, think! *"Prepare to meet thy God"* (Amos 4:12), for you must meet Him. Seek the Savior; yes, seek Him before another sunset.

"This year also"—and this may be the last year—the Cross is once again uplifted as the lighthouse of the world, the one light to which no eye can look in vain. Oh, that millions would look that way and live. Soon the Lord Jesus will come a second time, and then the blaze of His throne will replace the mild radiance of His Cross. The Judge will be seen rather than the Redeemer. Now He saves, but then He will destroy. Let us hear His voice at this moment. Let us be eager to avail ourselves of this gracious season. Let us believe in Jesus this day since it may be our last. Hear these pleadings for your soul's sake and live.

Chapter 3

Growing in the Lord

*But grow in grace, and in the knowledge of our Lord
and Saviour Jesus Christ. To him be glory both now
and for ever. Amen.*
—2 Peter 3:18

Beloved friends, we are perpetually in danger. Where
can we go to escape from peril? Where can we go to
avoid temptation? If we venture into business, world-
liness is there. If we retire to our homes, trials await us
there. One would imagine that in the green pastures of
the Word of God, there would be perfect security for God's
sheep. Surely, no lion is there; surely, no ferocious beast
can walk there! Unfortunately, it is not so. Even while we
are reading the Bible, we are still exposed to peril. It is not
that the truth is dangerous, but that our corrupt hearts
can find poison in the very flowers of paradise.

Notice what Peter said about the writings of the apostle
Paul: *"In which are some things hard to be understood"* (2
Peter 3:16). Also, note the danger to which we are exposed:
*"Which they that are unlearned and unstable wrest, as
they do also the other scriptures, unto their own destruction"* (v. 16). We can distort even the Word of God to our
own destruction. With the Bible before our eyes, we can
still commit sin. Pondering over the holy words of inspired
Scripture, we can receive a deadly wound from *"the error
of the wicked"* (v. 17). Even at the horns of the altar (see

Exodus 27:1–2; 29:12; 1 Kings 1:50), we still need God to cover us with the shadow of His wings (Psalm 17:8).

How wonderful that our gracious Father has provided a shield to shelter us from every evil. For example, our text will help to prevent us from falling into the evil of unorthodox doctrines, for we are in danger of misinterpreting Scripture to make God say what He does not. If we depart from the teaching of the Holy Spirit, we are in danger of distorting the letter of the Word and losing its spirit, and of deriving from the letter a meaning that can ruin our souls.

How can we escape this? Peter, speaking by the Holy Spirit, pointed out our safeguard in the words of our text: *"But grow in grace, and in the knowledge of our Lord and Saviour Jesus Christ. To him be glory both now and for ever. Amen."* While you search the Scriptures and become acquainted with them, see to it that you *"grow in grace."* While you desire to learn and understand doctrine, long, above all, to *"grow...in the knowledge of our Lord and Saviour Jesus Christ."*

However, let both your study of Scripture and your growth in grace and in the knowledge of Christ still be subservient to a higher objective: that you may live to bring *"glory both now and for ever"* to Him who has loved you and has bought you with His blood. Let your heart forever say "Amen" to this doxology of praise. In this way, you will be kept from all destructive errors, and you will not *"fall from your own stedfastness"* (2 Peter 3:17). It appears, then, that our text is a heavenly remedy for certain diseases to which even students of Scripture are exposed.

We see in our text two "trumpets." One is blown from heaven to earth: *"Grow in grace, and in the knowledge of our Lord and Saviour Jesus Christ."* The other resounds from earth to heaven: *"To him be glory both now and for ever."*

Another way to look at our text is to divide it into two matters. First, there is a matter of theology: *"Grow in grace."* Second, there is a matter of doxology: *"To him be glory both now and for ever."*

A third way to look at our text, and the way that we will look at it in this chapter, is this: First, we have a divine command with a special direction; second, a grateful doxology with a significant conclusion.

A Divine Command: Grow in Grace

I will begin at the beginning. We have here a divine command with a special direction: *"Grow in grace, and in the knowledge of our Lord and Saviour Jesus Christ."*

Who Can Grow in Grace?

"Grow in grace." What does this mean? We see in the very outset of this verse that it was written to those who have been awakened by grace. This verse does not apply to the unsaved at all. Dead things cannot grow. Those who are alive unto God by the resurrection of Jesus Christ are the only ones who have any power or ability to grow. The great Life-Giver must first implant the seeds of life, and then, afterward, those seeds can germinate and grow. Therefore, this text does not apply to you who are *"dead in trespasses and sins"* (Ephesians 2:1). You cannot grow in grace because you are still under the curse of the law, and the wrath of God remains on you (John 3:36). Tremble, repent, believe; and may God have mercy on you.

However, if you are alive from the dead, if you have been awakened by the Spirit of God who is now in you, you are instructed to grow, for growth will prove that you are spiritually alive. A post planted in the earth does not grow, but a tree rooted there increases from a sapling to a forest king. Drop a pebble into the richest soil, and many years from now, it will still be a pebble of the same size. However, plant a seed, and it will sprout and develop.

Growing in Every Virtue

You who are alive unto God, see to it that you grow in all the graces. Grow in your roots—that is, in your faith. Seek to believe God's promises better than you do now. From that trembling faith that says, *"Lord, I believe; help thou mine unbelief"* (Mark 9:24), grow upward to the faith that *"stagger[s] not at the promise of God"* (Romans 4:20). Like Abraham, believe that *"what he* [has] *promised, he* [is] *able also to perform"* (v. 21). Let your faith increase in extent; believe more truth. Let it increase in constancy; do not allow it to be feeble or wavering, always tossed about with every wind of false doctrine (Ephesians 4:14). Let your faith daily increase in simplicity, resting more fully on the finished work of your Lord Jesus Christ.

In addition to faith, see to it that your love also grows. If your love has been a spark, pray that the spark may become an all-consuming flame. If you have brought to Christ only a little, pray that you may bring your all. Pray that you may offer your all in such a way that, like Mary's broken alabaster box, the King Himself may be satisfied with the perfume. (See Matthew 26:7–13.) Ask that your love may become more extended—that you may have love for all the saints. Ask that it may be more practical, that it may move your every thought, every word, and every deed. Ask that it may be more intense, that you may become like a burning and shining light whose flame is love for God and man.

In addition to love, pray that you may grow in hope. Along these lines, pray that *"the eyes of your understanding being enlightened; that ye may know what is the hope of his calling, and what* [are] *the riches of the glory of his inheritance in the saints"* (Ephesians 1:18). Pray that you will continually look *"for that blessed hope, and the glo-rious appearing of the great God and our Saviour Jesus Christ"* (Titus 2:13). Pray that the hope not yet realized may enable you to wait patiently (Romans 8:25). Pray that you may, by hope, enter into the joys of heaven while you are on earth. Pray that hope may give you immortal-ity while you are still mortal, may give you resurrection before you die, may allow you to see God clearly where otherwise you could see only a dim reflection.

Ask that you may grow in humility, until you can say, *"[I] am less than the least of all saints"* (Ephesians 3:8). Ask that you may grow in consecration, until you can cry, *"For to me to live is Christ, and to die is gain"* (Philippians 1:21). Ask that you may grow in contentment, until you can say, *"I have learned, in whatsoever state I am, there-with to be content"* (Philippians 4:11). Advance in likeness to the Lord Jesus, so that your very enemies may notice that you have been with Jesus and have learned from Him. (See Acts 4:13.)

In short, if there is any virtue, if there is anything that is praiseworthy, if there is anything that is true and pure, if there is anything that is lovely and of good report (Philippians 4:8), if there is anything that can increase your usefulness, that can add to your happiness, that can make you more useful to man and more glorious toward God, grow in it. Growth is necessary, for we have not *"already attained,"* nor are we *"already perfect"* (Philippi-ans 3:12).

As a Tree Grows

I want to remind you, faithful believer in Christ, that the Bible compares you to a tree—a tree of the Lord's planting (Isaiah 61:3). Seek to grow as a tree grows. Pray that this year you may grow downward, that you may know more of your own vileness, more of your own noth-ingness, and so be rooted in humility. Pray that your roots may penetrate below the mere topsoil of truth into the great rocks that underlie the uppermost layer, so that you may grasp the doctrines of eternal love, God's unchangeable faithfulness, complete satisfaction, union with Christ, and the eternal purpose of God. These deep things of God will yield a rich and abundant sap, and your roots will drink from the hidden fountains of *"the deep that lieth under"* (Genesis 49:25).

This growth of your roots will not add to your fame or your vanity, but it will be invaluable during the storms of life. It will be a growth the value of which no heart can conceive when the hurricane is tearing up the hypocrite and hurling into the sea of destruction the *"trees whose fruit withere*[d], *without fruit, twice dead, plucked up by the roots"* (Jude 12).

As you root downward, seek to grow upward. Send out the top shoot of your love toward heaven. The trees send out their spring shoots and their midsummer shoots. You can see, at the top of the fir tree, that new green child of spring—the fresh shoot that lifts its hand toward the sun. In the same way, you should also long for more love and greater desires for God, a closer communion with Him in prayer, a sweeter spirit of adoption as His child, a more intense and intimate fellowship with the Father and with His Son Jesus Christ. This act of mounting upward will add to your beauty and to your delight.

In addition, pray to grow on either side. Stretch out your branches. Let the shadow of your holy influence extend as far as God has given you opportunities. However, see to it also that you grow in fruitfulness, for to increase the bough without adding to the fruit is to diminish the beauty of the tree. Labor this year, by God's grace, to bring forth more fruit for Him than you have ever done. Lord, give to each reader more of the fruits of penitence for sin, faith in the great sacrifice of Jesus, love for the Savior, and zeal for the conversion of souls. We do not want to be like the gleanings of the vintage, when there is only here and there a cluster on the uppermost bough. We want to be like the valley of Eshcol in the Promised Land, whose presses burst with new wine. (See Numbers 13:23–24; Deuteronomy 1:24–25.)

This is what it means to grow in grace: to root downward, to shoot upward, to extend your influence like far-reaching branches, and to bring forth fruit for the Lord's glory.

As a Child Grows

I will borrow another comparison from Scripture. Fellow believer, we are not only compared to trees, but also to children. Let us grow as babes do, nourished by unadulterated milk (1 Peter 2:2). Like babes, let us grow steadily, slowly, but surely and certainly. In this way, we will grow a little each day, but much through the years. Oh, that we may grow in strength, as a child does, until the little wobbling limbs of our faith are firm, muscular legs—the legs of a young man who runs without weariness. May we have untiring feet—the feet of a strong man who walks without fainting. (See Isaiah 40:31.) So far, our wings are unfledged, and we can hardly leave the nest. Lord, command our growth to proceed until we can mount as with the wings of eagles (v. 31) toward You, surmounting clouds and storms, and dwelling in the serene presence of the Most High. Let us develop all our powers. Let us ask that we may no longer be little infants, but that many inches may be added to our height until we become mature in Christ Jesus.

Let us especially pray that we may grow as healthy children—uniformly. Beloved, it is a bad sign if a child's head enlarges but not the rest of his body, or if his arm or foot is swollen disproportionately. Beauty consists in every part having the correct proportion. A vigorous judgment should not be yoked with a cold heart, nor a clear eye with a withered hand. A giant's head looks odd on a dwarf's shoulders. A virtue nourished at the expense of others is like a fattened cannibal fed on the flesh and blood of its murdered relatives; it is not fitting for a Christian to harbor such a monster. Let us pray that faith and love and every grace may be developed, that not one power may be left unnurtured or ungrown. Only in this way can we truly *"grow in grace, and in the knowledge of our Lord and Saviour Jesus Christ."*

Reasons to Grow in Grace

Do you ask why we should grow in grace? Let us say, beloved, that if we do not advance in grace, it is a sorrowful sign. It is a mark of unhealthiness. It is a sickly child who does not grow, an unhealthy tree that sends forth no fresh shoots. Furthermore, it may be a sign not only of unhealthiness but also of deformity. If a man's shoulders have grown to a certain breadth but his lower limbs refuse to lift him to a proportionate height, we call him a dwarf, and we somewhat pity him because he is malformed. O Lord, let us grow, for we do not want to be ill-formed. We want to be children who are like God our Father; we want to be pleasing in appearance, every one of us like the sons of a king.

Not to grow may be, moreover, the sign of death. Our lack of growth may say to us, "To the extent that you do not grow, you do not live." If you are not increasing in faith, love, and grace; if you are not ripening for the harvest, fear and tremble. Perhaps you have only a reputation for being alive, while you are actually destitute of life. (See Revelation 3:1.) Perhaps you are a painted counterfeit—a lovely picture of a flower, drawn by an artist's skillful hand, but lacking life, lacking the power that makes the flowers germinate, blossom, and bring forth fruit. Advance in grace, because not to progress foretells many evil things and might indicate the worst of all things: lack of spiritual life.

Grow in grace because, beloved, to increase in grace is the only pathway to lasting nobility. Oh, don't you wish to stand with that noble host who have served their Master well and have entered into their eternal rest? Who does not wish to have his name written with the great missionaries—with Judson and with Carey, with Williams and with Moffat? What Christian has no ambition to find his name written among those servants of God—Whitefield, Grimshaw, Newton, Romaine, Toplady, and others—who preached the Word with power? Do you wish to go back to the vile dust from where we sprung up, unwept, unhonored, and unsung? If so, then remain as you are; stop marching forward. Littleness and lowness lie at your door; be small and ignoble, if you desire. However, if you want to be a prince in God's Israel, if you want to be a mighty warrior for the Cross of Christ, then pray this prayer: "Lord, help me grow in grace, so I may be a faithful servant and receive Your commendation in the end."

To grow is not only to be noble, but also to be happy. The man who stops growing refuses to be blessed. With most businessmen, if they do not win, they lose. With the warrior, if he does not gain in the battle, his enemy is getting an advantage. The wise man who gets no wiser grows more foolish. The Christian who does not learn more about his Lord and become more like Him knows less about his Lord and becomes less like Him. If our armor is unused, it will tarnish. If our arms are not strengthened by effort, they will be weakened by laziness. Our happiness declines as our spirituality fades.

To be happy, I say, we must go forward. Ahead is sunlight. Ahead is victory. Ahead is heaven. Ahead is Christ! To stand still is danger; no, it is death. O Lord, for the sake of our happiness, help us to advance; for the sake of our usefulness, let us ascend. Oh, if only we would grow in grace, if only we would grow stronger in faith, mightier in prayer, more fervent in heart, holier in life, who can tell how much we might accomplish? Men who walk lightly leave faint footprints, but men who have the tread of Roman soldiers stamp their footprints on the sands of time, never to be erased. Let us live in such a way that, in our own time and in the future, the world may be better and Christ's church more prosperous for our having lived. For this reason, if for no other, let us grow in grace.

Oh, I want to fire you with holy ambition today! If I could snatch from some ancient altar a live coal such as that which fell on the lips of Isaiah, I would say to you, *"Lo, this hath touched thy lips'* (Isaiah 6:7). Go forth in the Spirit and power of God, even the Most High, and live as those who did not count their lives dear unto themselves (Acts 20:24) so that they could serve their Master *'and be found in him'* (Philippians 3:9). I point you to the redeemed who have entered *'within the veil'* (Hebrews 6:19) and who rest in eternal glory, and I say that they won the victory by grace, and growth in grace was the means of their triumph. Imitate them. Press forward, just as they did, and through grace, you, also, will inherit the same rest, will share in their triumph, and will sit down with them forever."

Ways to Grow in Grace

Do you ask how you will grow in grace? The answer is simple. The One who gave you grace must give you more of it. Where you first received grace, there you must receive the increase of that grace. The One who made the cattle and created man is the same One who afterward said, *"Be fruitful, and multiply, and replenish the earth"* (Genesis 1:28). So the One who has given you grace must speak in your heart with His omnipotent decree and say to that grace, *"Be fruitful, and multiply, and replenish'* the soul until its inherent emptiness is filled, until the natural desert rejoices and blossoms like a rose." (See Isaiah 35:1.)

At the same time, you should use all the spiritual means available, and those means are much more prayer, a more diligent search of the sacred Scriptures, a more constant fellowship with the Lord Jesus Christ, greater activity in His cause, a devout reception of all revealed truth, and so forth. If you do these things, you will never be dwarfed or stunted in your growth as a child of God because the One who has given you life will thus enable you to fulfill the word that He spoke to you by His apostle: *"Grow in grace, and in the knowledge of our Lord and Saviour Jesus Christ."*

A Special Direction: Grow in the Knowledge of Christ

I have explained the divine exhortation of our text. However, notice that our text also contains a special direction: *"And in the knowledge of our Lord and Saviour Jesus Christ."*

My fellow believer in the Lord Jesus, we must see to it that we ripen in the knowledge of Him. Oh, that we may know more of Him in His divine nature and in His human relationship to us. Oh, that we may know more of Him in His finished work, in His death, in His resurrection, in His present glorious intercession, and in His future royal advent. To know more of Christ in His work is, I think, a blessed means of enabling us to work more for Christ.

We also must study in order to know more of Christ in His character—in that divine combination of perfection, faith, zeal, deference to His Father's will, courage, meekness, and love. He was the Lion of the tribe of Judah, yet the Man on whom the Dove descended in the waters of baptism. Let us thirst to know Him of whom even His enemies said, *"Never man spake like this man"* (John 7:46), and of whom even His unrighteous judge said, *"I find no fault in him"* (John 19:4).

How to Have Real Joy

Above all, let us long to know Christ in His person. Endeavor to become better acquainted with the Crucified One. Study His hands and His feet. Stay close to the Cross. Let the sponge, the vinegar, and the nails be subjects of your devout attention. Seek to penetrate into His very heart. Search those deep, far-reaching caverns of His undiscovered love, that love that can never find a rival and can never know a parallel.

If you can add to this a personal knowledge of His sufferings, you will do well. Oh, if you can grow in the knowledge of fellowship, if you drink of His cup and are baptized with His baptism, if you abide in Him and He in you, you will be blessed. This is the only growth in grace that is true growth. All growth that does not lead us to increase in the knowledge of Christ is only the puffing up of the flesh and not the building up of the Spirit.

Grow in the knowledge of Christ, then. And do you ask why? Oh, if you have ever known Him, you will not ask that question. He who does not long to know more about Christ knows nothing about Him yet. Anyone who has ever sipped this new wine will thirst for more, for although Christ satisfies, it is such a satisfaction that we want to taste more and more and more. Oh, if you know the love of Jesus, I am sure that *"as the hart panteth after the water brooks"* (Psalm 42:1), so you will pant after Him. If you say you do not desire to know Him better, then I tell you that you do not love Him, for love always cries, "Nearer, nearer, nearer." To be absent from Christ is hell, but to be present with Christ is heaven. As we get nearer to Him, our heaven becomes more heavenly, and we enjoy it more and feel more that it is of God.

Oh, may you come to the very well of Bethlehem, and not merely to receive a pitcherful from it, as David did, at the risk of the lives of three mighty men (1 Chronicles 11:15–19). May you come to the well and drink—drink from the well itself, from that bottomless wellspring of eternal love. Oh, may the secret of the Lord be with you, and may you be in the *"secret place of the most High"* (Psalm 91:1)! My Master, if You would permit me to ask You one thing as a special favor, it would be this: *"That I may know him, and the power of his resurrection,...being made conformable unto his death"* (Philippians 3:10). Nearer to You, blessed Lord, nearer to You; this is my cry! May the Lord grant that our cry may be heard, that we may grow in the knowledge of Christ!

We wish to know Christ as our Lord—Lord of every thought and every desire, of every word and every act. We want to know Him as our Savior, too, our Savior from every indwelling sin, our Savior from every past evil deed, our Savior from every future trial. All hail, Jesus! We salute You as Lord. Teach us to feel Your kingship over us, and to feel it every hour. All hail, the Crucified One! We acknowledge You as Savior. Help us to rejoice in Your salvation and to feel the plenitude of that salvation in all and every part of spirit, soul, and body, being wholly saved by You.

Beloved, may you *"grow in grace, and in the knowledge of our Lord and Saviour Jesus Christ."*

A Grateful Thanksgiving: To Him Be Glory

In the second part of the text, we have a grateful thanksgiving with a significant conclusion: *"To him be glory both now and for ever. Amen."*

The apostles, I must remark, very frequently suspended their writing in order to lift up their hearts in praise. Praise is never out of season. It is no interruption to interrupt any task in order to praise and magnify our God. *"To him be glory."*

Let every heart joyously feel this doxology. *"To him,"* the God who made the heavens and the earth, without whom *"was not any thing made"* (John 1:3). *"To him"* who in His infinite compassion became the Surety of the covenant. *"To him"* who became a baby. *"To him"* who was *"despised and rejected of men; a man of sorrows, and acquainted with grief"* (Isaiah 53:3). *"To him"* who on the bloody tree poured out His heart's life so that He could redeem His people. *"To him"* who said, *"I thirst"* (John 19:28), and, *"It is finished"* (v. 30). *"To him"* whose lifeless body slumbered in the grave. *"To him be glory."*

"To him" who burst the bonds of death. *"To him"* who *"ascended up on high,...[and] led captivity captive"* (Ephesians 4:8). *"To him"* who sits at the right hand of the Father and who will soon come to be our Judge. *"To him be glory both now and for ever."*

Yes, *"to him,"* you atheists who deny Him. *"To him,"* you kings who vaunt your splendor and will not have this Man to reign over you. (See Luke 19:14.) *"To him,"* you people who stand up against Him, and you rulers who take counsel against Him (Psalm 2:2). *"To him"*—the King whom God has set on His *"holy hill of Zion"* (v. 6)—*"to him be glory."*

"To him be glory" as the King of Kings and Lord of Lords. *"Wonderful, Counsellor, the mighty God, the everlasting Father, the Prince of Peace"* (Isaiah 9:6). Again, *"Hosanna in the highest"* (Matthew 21:9)! Hallelujah! King of Kings and Lord of Lords! *"To him be glory"* as Lord. *"To him be glory"* as Savior. He alone has redeemed us unto God by His blood. He alone has *"trodden the winepress"* (Isaiah 63:3); He has come *"from Edom, with dyed garments from Bozrah...glorious in his apparel, travelling in the greatness of his strength"* (v. 1). *"To him be glory."*

Hear it, you angels: *"To him be glory."* Clap your wings. Cry, "Hallelujah! *'To him be glory.'"* Hear it, you *"spirits of just men made perfect"* (Hebrews 12:23). Play the strings of your celestial harps and say, "Hallelujah! Glory to Him who has redeemed us unto God by His own blood." *"To him be glory."* Church of God, respond! Let every godly heart say, *"To him be glory."* Yes, *"to him be glory,"* you fiends of hell, as you tremble at His presence and see the key of your prison swinging on His belt. Let heaven and earth and hell, let things that are and were and will be, cry, *"To him be glory."*

Peter added *"now." "To him be glory...now."* Beloved, do not postpone the day of His triumph; do not put off the hour of His coronation. Now,

> Bring forth the royal diadem,
> And crown Him Lord of all.

"To him be glory...now," for now, today, God *"hath raised us up together, and made us sit together in heavenly places in Christ Jesus"* (Ephesians 2:6). *"Beloved, now are we the sons of God"* (1 John 3:2). Now our sins are forgiven; now we are clothed in His righteousness. Now our feet are on a rock, and our steps are established (Psalm 40:2). Who would defer the time of singing hosannas? *"To him be glory...now."* O seraphim above, *"to him be glory... now,"* for you continually cry, *"Holy, holy, holy, is the LORD of hosts"* (Isaiah 6:3). Adore Him yet again, for *"to him be glory...now."*

Notice the last part of the doxology: *"And for ever."* Never will we cease our praise. Time, you will grow old and die. Eternity, your unnumbered years will speed their everlasting course. But forever, forever, forever, *"to him be glory."* Is He not *"a priest for ever after the order of Melchizedek"* (Psalm 110:4)? *"To him be glory."* Is He not King forever—King of Kings and Lord of Lords, the Everlasting Father? *"To him be glory...for ever."*

Never will His praises cease. That which was bought with blood deserves to last as long as immortality endures. The glory of the Cross must never be eclipsed. The luster of the grave and of the Resurrection must never be dimmed. Oh, my beloved, my spirit begins to feel the ardor of the immortals. I anticipate the songs of heaven. My tongue, if

389

it only had celestial liberty, would begin even now to join in those "melodious sonnets sung by flaming tongues above." O Jesus, You will be praised forever. As long as immortal spirits live, as long as the Father's throne endures, forever, forever, forever, unto You be glory.

A Significant Conclusion: Amen

Now, there is a very significant conclusion to this verse: *"Amen."* Beloved, I want to work this *"Amen"* out—not as a matter of doctrine, but as a matter of blessed ecstasy. Join your heart with mine in affirming this doxology. *"To him be glory both now and for ever. Amen."*

By the way, the Puritans pointed out—and it is a very remarkable thing—that under the old law, there was no amen to the blessings; the only amen was to the curses. When the Levites pronounced the curses, all the people said amen. (See Deuteronomy 27:9–26.) Under the old law, there was never an amen to the blessings.

Now, it is an equally remarkable and more blessed thing that, under the Gospel, there is no amen to the curses; the only amen is to the blessings. For example, 2 Corinthians 13:14 says, *"The grace of the Lord Jesus Christ, and the love of God, and the communion of the Holy Ghost, be with you all. Amen."* On the other hand, 1 Corinthians 16:22 says, *"If any man love not the Lord Jesus Christ, let him be Anathema* [accursed]." No amen. There is no amen to the curse under the Gospel, but *"all the promises of God in him* [Christ] *are yea, and in him Amen"* (2 Corinthians 1:20).

Our Hearts' Desire

What does this *"Amen"* in our text mean? Amen has four meanings in Scripture. First, it is the desire of the heart. Jesus said, *"Surely I come quickly"* (Revelation 22:20). The apostle John responded, *"Amen. Even so, come,*

Lord Jesus" (v. 20). We say amen at the end of a prayer to signify, "Lord, let it be so"—it is our hearts' desire.

Now, beloved, join your heart with mine, then, for it is all a heart matter here. *"To him be glory both now and for ever. Amen."* Is that your heart's desire? If not, you cannot say amen to it. Does your heart long, pant, thirst, groan, and cry out after Christ so much that you can say, every time you bend your knee in prayer, *"Thy kingdom come. Thy will be done in earth, as it is in heaven....For thine is the kingdom, and the power, and the glory, for ever. Amen"* (Matthew 6:10, 13)? Can you say, "Amen, Lord; let Your kingdom come"? Oh, if you can say it in this sense, if it is your heart's desire that Christ's glory be extended and that His kingdom come, say amen. My heart glows with this amen. The Judge of all knows how my heart longs to see Jesus magnified.

> Amen, with joy divine, let earth's
> Unnumber'd myriads cry;
> Amen, with joy divine, let heaven's
> Unnumber'd choirs reply.

Our Hearts' Belief

However, the word *amen* signifies more than this; it means the affirmation of our faith. We say amen only to that which we really believe to be true. We add our affidavit, as it were, to God's promise, affirming that we believe Him to be faithful and true.

Do you have any doubts that Jesus Christ is glorious now and will be forever? Do you doubt His being glorified by angels, cherubim, and seraphim today? Don't you believe, my beloved, that *"they that dwell in the wilderness shall bow before him; and his enemies shall lick the dust"* (Psalm 72:9)? If you do believe this, if you have faith today amid the world's obstinacy and the sinner's pride, amid abounding superstition and dominant evil, if you still have faith to believe that Christ will be glorious forever and ever, then say amen. *"To him be glory both now and for ever. Amen."*

There are more who can desire these things than there are who believe them. Nevertheless, God remains faithful.

> This little seed from heaven
>   Shall soon become a tree;
> This ever blessed leaven
>   Diffused abroad must be:
> Till God the Son shall come again,
>   It must go on. Amen! Amen.

Our Hearts' Joy

There is yet a third meaning to this *amen*. It often expresses the joy of the heart. When in ancient times they crowned a Jewish king, the high priest took a horn of oil and poured it on the new king's head. Then came forward a herald, and the moment he sounded the trumpet, someone said in a loud voice, "God save the king! God save the king!" and all the people said amen, and one shout went up to heaven. With joyful hearts, they welcomed the king; they hoped that he would be a prosperous ruler whom God would use to bless them and make them victorious.

Now, as you see King Jesus sitting on Mount Zion with death and hell underneath His feet, as today you anticipate the glory of His advent, as today you are expecting the time when you will reign with Him forever and ever, doesn't your heart cry out, *"Amen"*?

In a season of my life when I was in great darkness of mind and weakness of body, I remember one text that encouraged me beyond all measure. There was nothing in the text about me; it was no promise to me, but it was something about Christ. It was this:

God also hath highly exalted him, and given him a name which is above every name: that at the name of Jesus every knee should bow, of things in heaven, and things in earth, and things under the earth.

(Philippians 2:9–10)

Oh, it seemed so joyous that He is exalted! What did it matter what became of me? What did it matter what became of all believers? King Jesus is worth ten thousand of us. Let our names perish, but let His name last forever. Beloved, I bring forth the King to you. I bring Him before the eyes of your faith today. I proclaim Him King again. If you desire Him to be King, and if you rejoice in His reign, say amen. Crown Him! Crown Him! *"To him be glory both now and for ever."* Joyous heart, lift up your voice and say amen.

> Yea, amen, let all adore Thee,
>> High on Thine exalted throne!
> Savior, take Thy power and glory;
>> Claim the kingdoms for Thine own:
> O come quickly!
>> Hallelujah! Come, Lord, come.

Our Hearts' Resolution

Finally, here is a very solemn truth: *Amen* is sometimes used in Scripture as an amen of determination and resolution. It means, "I, in the name of God, solemnly pledge myself that I, in His strength, will seek to make it so; *'to him be glory both now and for ever.'*"

Last week, I walked through the long galleries that vanity has dedicated to all the glories of France. I passed through room after room, where especially I saw the triumphs of Napoleon. Surely, as you walk through the pages of Scripture, you walk through a much more marvelous picture gallery, in which you see the glories of Christ. This Book contains the memorials of His honors.

How to Have Real Joy

In another place in Paris, there stands a column made with the cannons taken by the Emperor in battle. A mighty trophy, certainly. O Jesus, You have a better trophy than this—a trophy made of souls forgiven; of eyes that wept, but whose tears have been wiped away; of broken hearts that have been healed; and of saved souls that rejoice evermore. What wonderful trophies Christ has to make Him glorious, *"both now and for ever"*—trophies of living hearts that love and adore Him, trophies of immortal spirits who find their heaven in gazing upon His beauties!

What glories will be Christ's forever when you and I and all the millions upon millions He has bought with His blood are in heaven! Oh, when we have been there thousands of years, we will feel as fresh an ecstasy as when we first came there. If our spirits should be sent on any errand and we have to leave our Master's presence for a moment, oh, with what wings of a dove we will fly back to behold His face again! When we all surround that throne, what songs will come forth from these lips of mine, the chief of sinners saved by blood! What hymns you will give Him, you who have had your iniquities cleansed and are saved today! What praise all those multitudes who have been partakers of His grace will give Him!

Yet this has more to do with *"for ever."* What do you say about our glorifying Him *"now"*? Oh, beloved, do make this your prayer today: "Lord, help me to glorify You. I am poor; help me to glorify You by contentment. I am sick; help me to give You honor by patience. I have talents; help me to extol You by using them for You. I have time, Lord; help me to redeem it, so that I may serve You. I have a heart to feel, Lord; let that heart feel no love but Yours and glow with no flame but affection for You. I have a head to think, Lord; help me to think of You. You have put me in this world for something, Lord; show me what it is, and help me to work out my life's purpose, for I do desire to say amen. I cannot do much; my amen is only a weak one. Yet as the widow put in her two mites, which was all she had to live on, so, Lord, I put my time and eternity into Your treasury. It is all Yours. Take it, and thus I say amen to Peter's doxology."

And now, will you say amen to this? I pray that you will do so. You who do not love Christ cannot say amen. Remember that you are under the law. There is an amen for all the curses to you; there is none for the blessings while you are under the law. Oh, poor sinner under the law, may this be the day when your slavery under the law will come to an end! "How can this be?" you ask. By faith in Christ. *"He that believeth on him is not condemned"* (John 3:18). Oh, believe in Him, and then your joyful heart will say amen. Then you will say, "Loudest of all the saints in heaven, I will shout amen when I see the royal crown brought forth, and Jesus is acknowledged Lord of all."

I trust that, as long as I live, it may be mine to give my amen to that doxology, *"To him be glory both now and for ever. Amen."*

Chapter 4

The Joy of the Lord

The joy of the LORD is your strength.
—Nehemiah 8:10

*And the singers sang loud, with Jezrahiah
their overseer. Also that day they offered great
sacrifices, and rejoiced: for God had made them
rejoice with great joy: the wives also
and the children rejoiced: so that the joy
of Jerusalem was heard even afar off.*
—Nehemiah 12:42–43

I would like to consider with you the subject of joy. Perhaps as we think about joy and remark on the many reasons for its existence, some of those reasons may operate on our hearts, and we may lay this book down as recipients of tremendous joy. I will consider this a beneficial book if it causes the people of God to rejoice in the Lord, and especially if those who have been weighed down and burdened in their souls will receive the oil of joy in exchange for their mourning (Isaiah 61:3). It is a significant thing to comfort the Lord's mourners. It is a work especially dear to the Spirit of God, and it is, therefore, not to be taken lightly.

Holy sorrow is precious before God and is not a hindrance to godly joy. Carefully note, in connection with our first text, Nehemiah 8:10, that the fact that there is great mourning is no reason why there should not soon be great joy, for the very people who were told by Nehemiah and Ezra to rejoice were, at the time, weeping for their sins. *"For all the people wept, when they heard the words of the law"* (Nehemiah 8:9). The vast congregation that had gathered before the water gate to hear the teaching of Ezra was awakened and cut to the heart. The people felt the edge of God's law like a sword opening up their hearts—tearing, cutting, and killing. They had good reason to cry. However, as they were crying, it was time to let them feel the Gospel's balm and hear the Gospel's music; therefore, Nehemiah and Ezra changed their tune and consoled them, saying,

> *This day is holy unto the* Lord *your God; mourn not, nor weep....Go your way, eat the fat, and drink the sweet, and send portions unto them for whom nothing is prepared: for this day is holy unto our Lord: neither be ye sorry; for the joy of the* Lord *is your strength.*
>
> (vv. 9–10)

Now that they were penitent and had sincerely turned to God, they were told to rejoice. Even as certain fabrics need to be dampened before they will absorb the bright colors with which they are to be dyed, so our spirits need the rain of repentance before they can receive the radiant coloring of delight. The glad news of the Gospel can be printed only on wet paper. Have you ever seen the world around you shine more than after a rain shower? Then the sun transforms the raindrops into gems, the flowers look up with fresher smiles and glitter with the droplets of their refreshing bath, and the birds among the dripping branches sing with notes more rapturous because they have paused awhile. In the same way, when the soul has been saturated with the rain of penitence, the clear shining of forgiving love makes the flowers of gladness blossom all around.

The steps by which we ascend to the palace of delight are usually moistened with tears. In *The Pilgrim's Progress,* by John Bunyan, grief for sin is the porch of the house Beautiful, in which the guests are full of the joy of the Lord. I hope, then, that the mourners who read this book will discover and enjoy the meaning of that divine blessing in the Sermon on the Mount: *"Blessed are they that mourn: for they shall be comforted"* (Matthew 5:4).

From our texts, I will draw several themes for consideration. First, there is a joy of divine origin—*"The joy of the* LORD.*"* Second, that joy is a source of strength for all who share in it—*"The joy of the* LORD *is your strength."* Third, I will show that such strength always reveals itself practically—our second text will help us there. I will close this chapter by noticing, in the fourth place, that this joy and, consequently, this strength are within our reach today.

Our Joy Comes from the Lord

First, there is a joy of divine origin. Since the source of this joy is the Lord, it will necessarily be a high and sublime joy.

From the time that man fell in the Garden, he has too often sought enjoyment where the serpent finds his. God said to the serpent, *"Upon thy belly shalt thou go, and dust shalt thou eat all the days of thy life"* (Genesis 3:14). This was the serpent's doom; and man, with foolish ambition, has tried to find his delight in his sensual appetites. Man has tried to content his soul with earth's poor dust. Yet the joys of time cannot satisfy an undying nature. Once a soul is awakened by the eternal Spirit, it cannot fill itself with worldly pleasure. It cannot even fill itself with the common delights of this life. To try to do so would be like trying to store up wind and eat it for breakfast.

However, beloved, we do not have to search for joy. It is brought to us by the love of God our Father—joy refined and satisfying, suitable for immortal spirits. God has not left us to wander among those unsatisfactory things that mock the chase that they invite. No, He has given us appetites that carnal things cannot gratify, and He has provided suitable satisfaction for those appetites. He has stored up at His right hand *"pleasures for evermore"* (Psalm 16:11), which He reveals by His Spirit to those chosen ones whom He has taught to long for them.

In the pages that follow, let us endeavor to analyze that special pleasure that our text calls *"the joy of the LORD."*

The Source and Object of Our Joy

First, our joy springs from God and has God for its object. The believer who is in a spiritually healthy state rejoices mainly in God Himself. He is happy because there is a God, and because God, in His person and character, is what He is. All the attributes of God become continual sources of joy to the thoughtful, contemplative believer, for such a person says within his soul, "All these attributes of my God are mine. His power is my protection. His wisdom is my guidance. His faithfulness is my foundation. His grace is my salvation."

He is a God who cannot lie, who is faithful and true to His promise. He is all love and, at the same time, infinitely just and supremely holy. Why, to one who knows that *"this God is* [his] *God for ever and ever"* (Psalm 48:14), the contemplation of God is enough to make the eyes overflow with tears because of the deep, mysterious, unspeakable bliss that fills the heart.

There was nothing in the character of Jupiter, or any of the false gods of the heathen, to make a pure and holy spirit glad. Yet there is everything in the character of Jehovah both to purify the heart and to thrill it with delight. How wonderful it is to think about all the Lord has done, how He has revealed Himself since long ago, and especially how He has displayed His glory in the covenant of grace and in the person of the Lord Jesus Christ. How precious is the thought that He has revealed Himself to me personally and has caused me to see Him as my Father, my Friend, my Helper, my God.

If there is one phrase from heaven that cannot be excelled, even by the brightness of heaven itself, it is this phrase, "My God, my Father" (see Psalm 89:26; John 20:17), along with that precious promise, *"I will be to them a God, and they shall be to me a people"* (Hebrews 8:10). There is no richer comfort to be found. Even the Spirit of God can reveal nothing more delightful to the Christian's heart.

How marvelous it is when the child of God admires God's character and marvels at His acts, and at the same time thinks, "He is my God. I have taken Him to be mine, and He has taken me to be His. He has grasped me with the hand of His powerful love. Having loved me with an everlasting love, with lovingkindness He has drawn me to Himself (Jeremiah 31:3). My Beloved is mine, and I am His (Song 2:16; 6:3)." Why, then his soul would gladly dance like David before the ark of the Lord, rejoicing in the Lord with all its might (2 Samuel 6:14).

Reconciliation, Acceptance, and Adoption

The Christian who is living near to God finds a further source of joy in a deep sense of reconciliation to God, of acceptance with God, and yet, beyond that, of adoption and close relationship to God. Doesn't it make a person glad to know that his sins, which had once provoked the Lord, are all blotted out and that not one of them remains? Isn't he delighted to know that though he was once alienated from God, and far away from Him because of his wicked works, he is brought near by the blood of Christ? The Lord is no longer an angry Judge pursuing him with a drawn sword, but a loving Father with whom he can share his sorrows and find comfort for every heartfelt grief.

Oh, to know, beloved, that God actually loves us! I have often said I cannot preach on that theme, for it is a subject to muse on in silence, a matter to sit and meditate on for hours. The fact that the Infinite loves an insignificant creature, a fleeting moth, a declining shadow—isn't this amazing? That God pities me, I can understand. That God reaches down and has mercy on me, I can comprehend. However, for Him to love me, for the pure to love a sinner, for the infinitely great to love a worm, is matchless, a miracle of miracles! Such thoughts do, indeed, comfort the soul.

Then add to this the fact that divine love has brought us believers into actual relationship with God, so that we are His sons and daughters—this again is a river of sacred pleasure. *"Unto which of the angels said he at any time, Thou art my Son?"* (Hebrews 1:5). No angel, no ministering spirit, though perfect in obedience, has received the honor of adoption. To us, even to us frail creatures of the dust, is given a gift denied to Gabriel. Through Jesus Christ the Firstborn, we are members of the family of God! Oh, the depths of joy that lie in being God's child and Christ's joint-heir! Words are useless here.

The joy springing from *"the Spirit of adoption"* (Romans 8:15) is very much a portion of the believer's bliss. There cannot be an unhappy man who can cry, *"Abba, Father"* (v. 15). The Spirit of adoption is always attended by love, joy, and peace, which are fruits of the Spirit; for we *"have not received the spirit of bondage again to fear"* (v. 15), but we have received the Spirit of liberty and joy in Christ Jesus. "My God, my Father"—oh, how sweet the sound!

You may be thinking, "But all God's people do not experience this joy." Sad to say, I agree, but I also add that it is their own fault. It is the right of every believer to live in the assurance that he is reconciled to God, that God loves him, and that he is God's child. If he does not live this way, he has only himself to blame. If there is any starving at God's table, it is because the guest cheats himself, for the feast is superabundant. If, however, a believer begins to consistently live with a sense of pardon through the sprinkling of the precious blood, and with a delightful sense of perfect reconciliation with the great God, he will possess a *"joy unspeakable and full of glory"* (1 Peter 1:8). I pray that you will begin to live this way.

Fearlessness about the Future

Yet, beloved, this is not all. The joy of the Lord in our spirits springs also from an assurance that our entire future, regardless of what may happen, is guaranteed by divine goodness. We are joyful when we know that, as children of God, the love of God toward us never changes. The believer feels complete satisfaction in leaving himself in the hands of eternal and unchangeable love.

However happy I may be today, if I am in doubt about tomorrow, there is a worm at the root of my peace. Although the past may now be pleasant in retrospect, and the present satisfying and enjoyable, if the future looks gloomy and frightening, my joy is shallow. If my salvation is still a matter of chance and uncertainty, unmingled joy is not mine, and deep peace is still out of my reach. Yet my outlook changes when I know that He in whom I have rested has enough power and grace to complete what He has begun in me and for me (Philippians 1:6). I see my future differently when I see the work of Christ as no halfway redemption, but a complete and eternal salvation. Peace comes when I perceive that the promises are established on an unchangeable basis and are *"yea"* and *"Amen"* (2 Corinthians 1:20) in Christ Jesus, confirmed by oath and sealed by blood. When I realize all this, my soul has perfect contentment.

It is true that, as I look forward, I may see long avenues of tribulation, but glory is at the end of them. Battles may be foreseen, and woe to the believer who does not expect them, but the eye of faith perceives the crown of victory. Deep waters appear on the maps of our journeys, but faith can see Jehovah fording these rivers with us, and she anticipates the day when we will ascend the banks of the nearby shore and enter into Jehovah's rest.

When we have received these priceless truths into our souls, we are satisfied with God's grace and are full of the goodness of the Lord. There is a theology that denies believers this comfort. I will not enter into controversy over it, but I sorrowfully hint that those who believe the errors of that doctrinal system will be heavily punished by losing the comfort that the truth would have brought into their souls. For my part, I value the Gospel not only for what it has done for me in the past, but also for the guarantee that it gives me of eternal salvation. *"I give unto them* [My sheep] *eternal life; and they shall never perish, neither shall any man pluck them out of my hand"* (John 10:28).

Close Fellowship with God

Now, beloved, I have not yet taken you into the great depths of joy, though these streams are certainly by no means shallow. However, there is a deepness of delight for every Christian when he comes into actual fellowship with God. I spoke of the truth that God loves us, and the fact that we are related to Him by ties most near and dear. However, when these doctrines become experiences, then we are, indeed, anointed with the oil of gladness. When we enter into the love of God and it enters into us, when we walk with God consistently, then our joy is like the Jordan River at harvesttime, when it overflows all its banks.

Do you know what it means to walk with God and to experience the joy that Enoch had? Do you know what it means to sit at Jesus' feet and to experience the joy that Mary had? Do you know what it means to lean your head on Jesus' chest and to experience the joy that John had? Oh, yes, communion with the Lord is not a matter of mere words for some of us. We have known it in the midst of affliction. We have known it in the solitude of many a night of interrupted rest. We have known it when experiencing discouragements, sorrows, defamations, and all sorts of problems. We also know that one teaspoon of fellowship with Christ is enough to sweeten an ocean of tribulation. Only to know that He is near us, and to see the sparkle in His dear eyes, would transform even hell itself into heaven, if it were possible for us to enjoy His presence there.

However, you do not and cannot know this bliss, you who spend your time greedily consuming alcohol. You do not know what this bliss means—you have not dreamed of it, nor could you comprehend it even if someone were to tell you about it. As the beast in the field does not know the far-reaching thoughts of the One who reads the stars and threads the spheres in the heavens, so the carnal man cannot even imagine the joys that God has prepared for those who love Him (1 Corinthians 2:9). However, any day and every day, when our hearts seek to know them, He reveals them to us by His Spirit (v. 10).

This is the joy of the Lord—*"fellowship...with the Father, and with his Son Jesus Christ"* (1 John 1:3). Beloved, if we reach this point, we must work to maintain our standing, for our Lord says to us, *"Abide in me"* (John 15:4). The habit of communion is the life of happiness.

The Privilege of Serving Christ

Another form of the joy of the Lord will visit us in a practical way every day; it is the honor of being allowed to serve Him. It is a joy worth worlds to be allowed to do good. To teach a little child the alphabet in Christ's name will give a true heart a taste of the joy of the Lord, if it is consciously done for the Lord's sake alone. To give a meal to the hungry, to visit the sick, to comfort the mourner, to aid the poor, to instruct the ignorant—any and all such Christian works, if done in Jesus' name, will, in their measure, clothe us in Jehovah's joy.

Moreover, happy are we if, when we cannot work, we are enabled to lie still and suffer, for submission is another silver pipe through which the joy of the Lord will come to us. It is satisfying to smart beneath God's rod and to feel that, if God would have us suffer, it is happiness to do so. It is precious to fall back with the faintness of our nature but at the same time with the strength of God's grace, and say, *"Thy will be done"* (Matthew 6:10). It is joy, when we are crushed like an olive, to yield nothing but the oil of thankfulness. It is delight, when bruised beneath the flail of tribulation, to lose nothing but the chaff and to yield to God the precious grain of entire submissiveness. Why, this is a little heaven on earth. For us also to exult in tribulations is equal to more than a few steps of ascent toward the likeness of our Lord.

Perhaps the usual times of communion that we have with our Beloved, though exceedingly precious, will never equal those that we enjoy when we have to break through thorns and briers to be with Him. When we follow Him into the wilderness, then we feel that the love of our marriage to Christ is doubly sweet. (See Jeremiah 2:2.) It is a joyous thing when, in the midst of mournful circumstances, we still feel that we cannot mourn because the Bridegroom is with us. Blessed is that believer who, in the most terrible storm, is not driven away from his God, but instead rides nearer to heaven on the crest of the enormous waves. Such happiness is the Christian's lot.

I am not saying that every Christian possesses such happiness, but I am sure that every Christian ought to. There is a highway to heaven, and all on it are safe. However, in the middle of that road there is a special way, an inner path, and all who walk on it are happy as well as safe. Many professing Christians are barely on the right path; they walk in the ditch by the roadside. Because they are safe there, they are content to put up with all the inconveniences of their walk. Yet the believer who walks in the very center of the road that God has constructed will find that no lion will be there, nor will any ferocious beast go up on it. There the Lord Himself will be his companion and will manifest Himself to him.

You shallow Christians whose faith in Christ is barely alive, whose Bibles are unread, whose prayer times are few, whose communion with God is inconsistent—you do not have the joy of the Lord, nor are you strong. I implore you, do not rest as you are, but let your weakness motivate you to seek the means of strength. That means of strength is to be found in a pleasant medicine, as sweet as it is profitable—the delicious and effective medicine of the joy of the Lord.

Too many pages would be required for me to fully share my remarks on this very fruitful subject. Therefore, I will turn to my second topic, which I began to explain in the previous section: This joy is a source of great strength.

Our Joy Is a Source of Strength

Very briefly let us consider this thought. Joy is a source of strength because joy arises from meditations that always strengthen the soul. Much of the depth of our godliness will depend on our contemplativeness. Many people, after receiving a doctrine, put it on the shelf. They are orthodox, they have received the truth, and they are content to keep that truth on hand as dead weight. Reader, how can you be benefited if you store your granary with wheat but never grind the wheat for bread or sow it in the furrows of your fields? He is a joyful Christian who uses the doctrines of the Gospel for spiritual meat, as they were meant to be used.

Some people might as well have an unorthodox creed instead of an orthodox one, for all the difference that it makes to them. Having the notion that they know the truth and imagining that simply knowing it is sufficient, they do not consider, contemplate, or regard the truths that they profess to believe. Consequently, they derive no benefit from them.

Now, to contemplate the great truths of divine election, eternal love, justification by faith through the blood of Christ, and the indwelling and perpetual abiding of the Holy Spirit in His people—to think over these thoughts—is to extract joy from them; and doing so also strengthens the mind. To press the heavenly grapes by meditation and make the red wine flow forth in torrents is an exercise as strengthening as it is exhilarating. Joy comes from the same truths that support our strength, and it comes by the process of meditation.

Again, the joy of the Lord within us is always the sign and symbol of strong spiritual life. Holy joyfulness is evidence of spiritual vigor. I said earlier that he who has spiritual joy has gained it by communion with God, but communion with God is also the surest fosterer of strength. You cannot be with a strong God without getting strength yourself, for God is always a transforming God. As we regard and look upon Him, we change until we become, in our measure, like our God.

The warmth of southern France, which perhaps you have heard a little bit about, does not come from soft, balmy winds. No, it comes from the sun, for at sunset, the temperature falls. Also, in Italy, you might be on one side of the street and think it is May, and then cross the street into the shade and find it as cold as January. The sun makes all the difference.

Even so, a man who walks in the sunlight of God's countenance is warm and strong for that very reason. The sunlight of joy usually goes with the warmth of spiritual life. As the light of joy varies, so does the warmth of holy strength. He who dwells in the light of God is both happy and strong. He who goes into the shade and loses the joy of the Lord becomes weak at the same time. In this way, the joy of the Lord becomes our strength because it is an indicator of its rise or fall. When a soul is really vigorous and active, it is like a torrent that dashes down the mountainside, scorning to be bound by frost in wintertime. In just a few hours of cold weather, the stagnant pools and slowly moving streams are enchained in ice; but the snow king must bring forth all his strength before he can restrain the rushing torrent. So, when a soul dashes on with the sacred force of faith, it is hard to freeze it into misery. Its vigor secures its joy.

Strength for Suffering and Service

Furthermore, the believer who possesses the joy of the Lord finds it his strength in another respect: It fortifies him against temptation. What is there with which he can be tempted? He already has more than the world could ever give him as a reward for treachery. He is already rich; who can entice him with the wages of unrighteousness? He is already satisfied; who can seduce him with pleasing baits? He simply says, *"Should such a man as I flee?"* (Nehemiah 6:11).

The rejoicing Christian is equally fortified against persecution. Someone who wins at the rate that a joyful believer wins can well afford to be laughed at. "You may scoff," he says, "but I know within my soul what true faith is, and your scoffing will not make me relinquish the *'pearl of great price'* (Matthew 13:46)." Moreover, such a person is made strong to bear affliction, for all the sufferings put on him are only a few drops of bitterness flung into his cup of bliss, to give a deeper tone to the sweetness that absorbs them.

Such a believer also becomes strong for service. What can a person who is happy in his God not do? By his God, he leaps over a wall or breaks through a troop (2 Samuel 22:30; Psalm 18:29). He is strong, too, for any kind of self-sacrifice. To the God who gives him everything and is his perpetual portion, the joyful believer gives up all that he has, and does not think of it as a sacrifice. He is simply storing his treasure in his own special treasure-house—the God of his salvation.

Portrait of a Strong Christian

A joyous Christian, such as I am now picturing in my mind's eye, is strong in a calm, restful manner. Regardless of what happens, he is not upset or disturbed. He is not afraid of bad news; his heart is steadfast, *"trusting in the LORD"* (Psalm 112:7). The fretful person, on the other hand, is always weak. He is in a hurry and does things poorly.

In contrast, the joy-filled believer is quiet; he bides his time and is full of strength. Such a believer, though he is humble, is firm and steadfast. He is not carried away with every wind, or blown over by every breeze. (See Ephesians 4:14.) He knows what he knows, and he believes what he believes. The golden anchor of his hope enters within the veil and holds him tightly (Hebrews 6:19). His strength is not feigned—it is real.

The happiness that comes from communion with God does not cause him to be boastful. He does not talk of what he can do, but he simply does it. He does not say what he could endure, but he endures all that comes.

He himself does not always know what he can do; his weakness is more apparent to him because of the strength that the Holy Spirit puts in him. However, when the time comes, his weakness only illustrates the divine mightiness within him, while he goes calmly on, *"conquering, and to conquer"* (Revelation 6:2).

How to Have Real Joy

The inner light of the joy-filled believer makes him independent of the outward sun. His secret granaries make him independent of the outward harvest. His inner fountains keep him safe from dread, even though the brook Cherith may dry up. (See 1 Kings 17:1–9.) He is independent of men and of angels, and fearless of devils. All people may turn against him if they please, but since God Himself is his exceeding joy, he will not miss their love or mourn their hate. He stands where others fall. He sings where others weep. He wins where others flee. He glorifies his God where others bring dishonor on themselves and on the sacred name.

May God grant us the inner joy that arises from real strength, the kind of joy that is so linked with strength that it is partly its cause.

Joy and Strength Lead to Practical Results

Now I must go on to notice that this joy and this strength lead to practical results. Please read our second text again:

And the singers sang loud, with Jezrahiah their overseer. Also that day they offered great sacrifices, and rejoiced: for God had made them rejoice with great joy: the wives also and the children rejoiced: so that the joy of Jerusalem was heard even afar off.

In these verses, we observe some of the fruits of holy joy and godly strength.

Enthusiastic Praise

First, strength and joy lead to great praise. *"The singers sang loud"*; their singing was hearty and enthusiastic. Sacred song is not a minor matter. Someone once said, "Praying is the end of preaching." Couldn't we go further and say, "Praising is the end of praying"? After all, preaching and praying are not the chief end of man; it is the glorifying of God, of which praising God vocally is one form. Preaching is sowing, prayer is watering, but praise is the harvest. God aims at His own glory, and so should we. The Lord says, *"Whoso offereth praise glorifieth me"* (Psalm 50:23). Be diligent, then, to sing His praises with understanding.

It is shocking to me to be present in places of worship where not a tenth of the people ever venture to sing at all, and these do it through their clenched teeth so very softly that one needs to have a special hearing aid to enable him to hear the dying strain. Out with such mumbling and murdering of the praises of God! If people's hearts were joyous and strong, they would scorn such miserable worship.

Let us be glad when we come together and unite in singing. Let us all sing to the Lord. Let us not rely on musical instruments to do our praising for us. The human voice is the greatest musical instrument that exists, by far. There is certainly no melody or harmony like those created by living tongues. Let us not rely on a choir or paid musicians to praise for us. God wants to hear the voices of all His people united in praise.

Couldn't our churches have more praise services? In the church that I pastor, we have had a praise meeting every now and then. Shouldn't our churches hold praise meetings every week? Shouldn't prayer meetings be made more joyous than ever by praise? The singing of God's people should be—and if they were more full of divine strength it would be—more constant and universal. How sinners chant pagan praises in the streets! Some of us can hardly rest in the middle of the night without crude sounds of revelry startling us. Should the worshippers of wine sing so enthusiastically, and we be silent? We are not often guilty of disturbing the world with our music. The days in which Christian zeal interfered with the wicked seem to have gone by. We have settled down into more orderliness, and I am afraid into more lukewarmness, as well. Oh, to be free to shout our praises!

Beloved, wake up your singing again. May the Lord help us to sing to Him more, and make us all to praise Him with heart and with voice, until even our adversaries say, "The Lord has done great things for them," and we reply, "Yes, you speak the truth. *'The LORD hath done great things for us; whereof we are glad'* (Psalm 126:3)."

Perhaps there has not been great blessing on our churches because they have not given God the thanksgiving of which He is worthy. During all the times in which we are in trouble, we are anxious and prayerful. When the leader of our country is sick, news of his progress is issued every hour or so. Yet, oh, when God's mercy comes, very little news is put out to call on us to bless and praise the name of God for His mercies. Let us praise the Lord *"from the rising of the sun unto the going down of the same"* (Psalm 113:3). *"For great is the LORD, and greatly to be praised"* (1 Chronicles 16:25).

Great Sacrifices

The next result of strength and joy is great sacrifice. *"That day they offered great sacrifices, and rejoiced."* What day does the church of God now set aside to make great sacrifices? I have not seen it on the calendar lately. Unfortunately, if people make any sacrifice, they very often do so in a way that indicates that they would avoid making it if they could. Few make great sacrifices and rejoice. You can persuade a person to give a considerable amount of money; a great many arguments overcome him at last, and he gives because he would be ashamed not to. However, in his heart, he wishes you had not come that way but had gone to some other donor.

The most acceptable gift given to God is the gift that is given joyfully. It is wonderful to feel that whatever good your gift may do for the church, the poor, or the sick, it is twice as beneficial to you to give it. It is good to give because you love to give, even like the flower that scents the air with its perfume because it never dreamed of doing otherwise; or like the bird that quivers with song because it is a bird and finds pleasure in its notes; or like the sun that shines, not by constraint, but because, being a sun, it must shine; or like the waves of the sea that flash back the brilliance of the sun because it is their nature to reflect the light and not to hoard or absorb all of it.

Oh, to have such grace in our hearts that we joyfully make sacrifices to our God! May the Lord grant that we may have much of this grace, for the bringing of the tithes into the storehouse is the way to blessing, as the Scripture says,

> *Bring ye all the tithes into the storehouse, that there may be meat in mine house, and prove me now herewith, saith the LORD of hosts, if I will not open you the windows of heaven, and pour you out a blessing, that there shall not be room enough to receive it.*
> (Malachi 3:10)

Happiness in Everyday Life

They *"rejoiced: for God had made them rejoice with great joy."* Singing and giving are not the only signs of the joy of God's people. In addition to these, other expressions of joy are sure to follow. When the wheels of a machine are well oiled, the whole machine runs easily; and when a man has the oil of joy, then in his business, and in his family, he glides along smoothly and harmoniously because he is a happy man.

On the other hand, there are some professing Christians who imagine that the sorrow of the Lord is their strength. They glory in the spirit of bondage and in an unbelieving experience, having great acquaintance—too much so—with the corruption of their hearts. They try to say that believers' deformities are their beauty, and their faults are their virtues. Such men denounce all who rejoice in the Lord; they tolerate only the unbelieving. Their strength lies in being able to take you through all the catacombs of nature's darkness, and to show you the rottenness of their evil hearts.

Well, let those who want to have such strength have it, but I am persuaded that our text is closer to wisdom: *"The joy of the LORD is your strength."* While we know a little about our corruption and mourn over it, while we know a little about the world's troubles and sometimes lament as we bear them, there is a joy in the perfect work of Christ, and a joy in our union with Him, that lift us far above all other considerations. God becomes to us such a strength that we cannot help showing our joy in our ordinary lives.

Joy Shared with Family and Friends

The text also tells us that holy joy leads to family happiness. *"The wives also and the children rejoiced."* It is so in my own church. I have lately noticed several households that God has blessed, and I have rejoiced to see that father and mother know the Lord, and that even the youngest of the family has been brought to Jesus. Oh, households are happy, indeed, when the joy is not confined to one person, but all partake of it. I greatly dislike that Christianity that makes a person feel, "My only concern is that *I* make it to heaven." Why, a person concerned only about himself is like a furnace that heats itself but does not heat the house.

Too many need all the religion they can acquire to encourage their own hearts, while their poor families and neighbors sit shivering in the cold of ungodliness. Do not be like that. Be like those well-built furnaces that send out all the heat into the house. Send out the heat of godliness into your house, and let all the neighbors participate in the blessing, for our text finishes with, *"The joy of Jerusalem was heard even afar off."* The joy of the Lord should be observed throughout our neighborhoods; then many who might otherwise have been indifferent to true religion will ask, "What makes these people glad and creates such happy households?" In this way, your joy will be God's missionary.

You Can Have Joy and Strength

This joy and this strength are both within our reach! *"For God had made them rejoice with great joy."* God alone can give us this great joy. It is within the reach of anyone, for God can give it to one as well as to another. If it depended on our good works or our natural abilities, we could never reach it. However, if God is the source and giver of it, He may give it to me as well as to you, and to you as well as to someone else.

According to our texts, what were the conditions under which God gave this joy? First, He gave it to these people because they were attentive hearers (Nehemiah 8:3). They were not passive hearers, but they listened intently as the Word was read. As it was read to them, they absorbed it, receiving it into their souls. An attentive hearer is on his way to being a joyous receiver.

Having heard the Word, they felt the power of it, and they wept (v. 9). Does that seem like the way to joy? No, but it was. They received the threats of the Law, with all their terrors, into their souls. They allowed the hammer of the Word to break them in pieces. They submitted themselves to the words of reproof. Oh, that God would incline you to do the same thing, for this, again, is the way in which God gives joy. The Word is heard; the Word is felt.

After they had felt the power of the Word, we see that they worshipped God devoutly. (See verse 6.) *"They bowed their heads"* (v. 6). Their postures indicated what they felt within. Worshippers who truly adore God with penitent hearts will never complain of boring Sundays. Adoration helps to bring us into joy. He who can bow low enough before the throne will be lifted as high before that throne as his heart can desire.

We read also that these hearers and worshippers understood clearly what they heard (v. 8). Never be content with hearing a sermon unless you can understand it. If there is a truth that is above you, strain after it; strive to know it. Bible reader, do not be content with going through the words of a chapter of Scripture. Ask the Holy Spirit to tell you the meaning, and use the proper means for finding out that meaning. Ask those who know, and use your own enlightened judgment to discover the meaning.

When will we be done with formalism in worship and come into living adoration? Sometimes, for all the true singing that there is, the songs might as well be in Latin or in Greek. Oh, to know what we are singing, to know what we are saying in prayer, to know what we are reading, to get at it, to come right into it, to understand it—this is the way to holy joy.

I need to make one other point. These people, when they had understood what they had devoutly heard, were eager to obey. (See Nehemiah 8:14–17.) They obeyed not only the common points of the Law that had been observed and demonstrated by former generations of Israelites, but they also discovered an old institution that had long been buried and forgotten. It did not matter to them that it had not been observed for a lengthy period of time. God had commanded it, and they celebrated it; in so doing, a special joy came to them.

Oh, for the time when all believers will search the Word of God, when they will not be content with saying, "I have joined myself with a certain body of believers. They do such and such; therefore, I do the same." May no one say to himself any longer, "This is the rule of my church," but may each of us say, "I am God's servant, not the servant of man, not the servant of man-made rules and regulations, not the servant of the prayer book or the catechism. To my own Master I stand (Romans 14:4), and the only law book I acknowledge is the book of His Word, inspired by His Spirit." Oh, it will be a blessed day when every person will say, "I want to know what I am wrong about. I desire to know what I am supposed to do. I am eager to follow the Lord fully." If your joy in God leads you to practical obedience, you may rest assured that it has made you strong in the very best manner.

May we be a strong people, and, consequently, a joyous people, in the strength and joy of the Lord. May sinners in great numbers look unto Jesus and be saved.

Chapter 5

The Same Yesterday, Today, and Forever

*Jesus Christ the same yesterday,
and to day, and for ever.*
—Hebrews 13:8

I have written on this text before, but I do not need to be at all afraid of writing on the same text twice. God's Word is inexhaustible. It may be trodden in the winepress many times and still generously yield wine. We should not hesitate to write a second time from the same passage, any more than anyone going to a well would be ashamed to put down the same bucket twice, or any more than anyone would feel at all distressed about sailing down the same river twice. There is always a freshness about Gospel truth. Although the subject matter may be the same, there are ways of putting it in a fresh light in order to bring new joy to those who meditate on it.

Is it unnecessary for me to repeat my teachings concerning Christ? Is it useless for you to read over and over again the same things about the King? No, we can afford to give and receive the same teachings again. Repetitions concerning Jesus are better than varieties on any other subject. As the French monarch declared that he would sooner hear the repetitions of Louis Bourdaloue,

418

the famous French Jesuit, than the novelties of another, we may declare the same concerning our Lord Jesus. We would sooner hear again and again the precious truths that glorify Him than listen to the most eloquent orations on any other theme in all the world.

There are a few works of art and wonders of creation that you could gaze upon every day of your life and yet not tire of them. Everyone who has ever looked at the ocean or at Niagara Falls knows that, look as often as you may, though you see precisely the same object, there are new tints, new motions of the waves, and new flashes of light that forbid the least bit of monotony and that give to the waters an ever enduring charm. This is the way it is with that sea of all delights that is found in the dear Lover of our souls.

Thus, we come to the old subject of this old text; may the blessed Spirit give us new anointing while we meditate on it. We will see that our text provides us with three main themes. First, note our Lord's personal name: *"Jesus Christ."* Second, notice His memorable attribute: He is *"the same yesterday, and to day, and for ever."* Third, examine His claims, which are derived from the possession of such a character.

The Personal Names of Our Lord

Jesus

"Jesus" is the first name for our Lord that is mentioned in the text. This is our Lord's Hebrew name: "Joshua," or *"Jesus."* The word signifies a Savior: *"Thou shalt call his name Jesus: for he shall save his people from their sins"* (Matthew 1:21). The name was given to Him while He was still in His cradle.

> Cold on His cradle the dewdrops are shining;
> Low lies His head with the beasts of the stall;

419

> Angels adore Him, in slumber reclining,
> Maker, and Monarch, and Savior of all.

While He was still an infant feeding at His mother's breast, He was recognized as Savior, for the fact of God's becoming incarnate was the pledge, guarantee, and commencement of human salvation. At the very thought of His birth, the Virgin sang, *"My spirit hath rejoiced in God my Saviour"* (Luke 1:47). There was hope that man would be lifted up to God when God came down to man. Jesus in the manger deserved to be called the Savior, for when it can be said that *"the tabernacle of God is with men, and he...dwell*[s] *with them"* (Revelation 21:3), there is hope that all good things will be given to the fallen race.

He was called *Jesus* in His childhood—the holy child Jesus. It was as Jesus that He went up with His parents to the temple and sat down with the teachers, hearing them and asking them questions. Yes, Jesus, as He taught the very first principles of His doctrine, was a Savior, liberating the minds of men from superstition and setting them loose from the traditions of their ancestors. Even as a child, He scattered the seeds of truth, the elements of a glorious liberty that would emancipate the human mind from the iron bondage of false philosophy and ritualism.

It was so evident in His active life that Jesus was the Savior that He was commonly called by that name by both His friends and foes. It was as Jesus the Savior that He healed the sick, raised the dead, delivered Peter from sinking, and rescued from shipwreck the ship tossed on the Sea of Galilee. In all the teachings of His midlife, in those laborious three years of diligent service, both in His public ministry and in His private prayer, He was still Jesus the Savior; for by His active, as well as by His passive, obedience, we are saved. All during His earthly life, He made it clear that the Son of Man had come *"to seek and to save that which was lost"* (Luke 19:10). If His blood redeems us from the guilt of sin, His life shows us how to overcome its power. If by His death on the cross He crushed Satan for us, by His life of holiness He teaches us how to break the dragon's head within us.

He was the Savior as a babe, the Savior as a child, the Savior as the toiling, laboring, tempted Man. Yet He was most clearly Jesus the Savior when dying on the cross. Even Pilate called Him *"JESUS,"* or Savior, when he wrote His title on the cross, which read, *"JESUS OF NAZARETH THE KING OF THE JEWS"* (John 19:19). When Pilate was asked to change this title, he said, *"What I have written I have written"* (v. 22).

Preeminently on the cross, He was the Savior, being made a curse for us so that *"we might be made the righteousness of God in him"* (2 Corinthians 5:21). In fact, it was after beholding the dying agonies of his Master that the Beloved Apostle wrote, *"We have seen and do testify that the Father sent the Son to be the Saviour of the world"* (1 John 4:14). At Calvary, it was remarked that the Son of Man *"saved others"* (Matthew 27:42) but, through blessed incapacity prompted by love, *"himself he* [could not] *save"* (v. 42). When He was made to feel the wrath of God on account of sin, and pains unknown were suffered by Him as our Substitute; when He was made to pass through the thick darkness and burning heat of divine wrath, then He was, according to Scripture, *"the Saviour of all men, specially of those that believe"* (1 Timothy 4:10).

Yes, it was on the cross that Christ was especially a Savior. If He were nothing better than our example, how unfortunate we would be! We might be grateful for the example if we could imitate it, but without the pardon that spares us, without the grace that gives us power for holiness, the brightest example would only increase our grief. To be shown a picture of what we ought to be, without being given a method to attain that standard, would only mock our misery. However, Jesus first pulls us out of the horrible pit into which we are fallen, taking us out of the mud and mire by the power of His atoning sacrifice. Then, having set our feet on a rock by virtue of His merits, He Himself leads the way onward to perfection. Therefore, He is a Savior both in life and in death.

> That Jesus saves from sin and hell,
> Is truth divinely sure;
> And on this rock our faith may rest
> Immovably secure.

Still bearing the name of *Jesus*, our Lord rose from the dead. Evangelists delight in calling Him *Jesus* when they speak of His appearance to Mary Magdalene in the garden or His appearance to the disciples when they were gathered together behind locked doors. When He is spoken of as the Risen One, He is always spoken of as Jesus the Savior. Beloved, since we are justified by His resurrection, it is fitting that we regard Him as Savior when speaking of His resurrection. Salvation is strongly linked with a risen Christ because we see Him, by His resurrection, destroying death, breaking down the prison of the tomb, carrying away, like another Samson, the gates of the grave. He is our Savior because He has already vanquished the enemy that will be the last to be completely destroyed—Death (1 Corinthians 15:26). He rose so that we, having been saved from sin by His death, can be saved from death through His resurrection.

Jesus is the title by which He is called in glory, since *"him hath God exalted with his right hand to be a Prince and a Saviour, for to give repentance to Israel, and forgiveness of sins"* (Acts 5:31). He is today *"the saviour of the body"* (Ephesians 5:23). We adore Him as *"the only wise God our Saviour"* (Jude 25). *"He is able also to save them to the uttermost that come unto God by him, seeing he ever liveth to make intercession for them"* (Hebrews 7:25). As Jesus, He will come again, and we are *"looking for that blessed hope, and the glorious appearing of the great God and our Saviour Jesus Christ"* (Titus 2:13). Our daily cry is, *"Even so, come, Lord Jesus"* (Revelation 22:20).

Yes, *Jesus* is the name by which He is known in heaven at this hour. By the name of Jesus, the angel spoke of Him before He was conceived by the Virgin (Luke 1:30–31). By the name of Jesus, the angels serve Him and do His bidding, for He said to John on Patmos, *"I Jesus have sent mine angel to testify unto you these things"* (Revelation 22:16). The angels prophesied His second coming using that sacred name. They came to Jesus' followers, who stood looking up into heaven after His ascension, and they said, *"Ye men of Galilee, why stand ye gazing up into heaven? this same Jesus, which is taken up from you into heaven, shall so come in like manner as ye have seen him go into heaven"* (Acts 1:11). Under this name, the devils fear Him, for didn't an evil spirit say, *"Jesus I know, and Paul I know; but who are ye"* (Acts 19:15)?

The name of Jesus is the spell that binds the hearts of cherubim in chains of love, and it is the name that makes the hosts of hell tremble and cower. This name is both the joy of the church on earth and the joy of the church above. It is a family name for our dear Redeemer among the family of God below, and up there, they still sing it.

> Jesus, the Lord, their harps employs:
> Jesus, my Love, they sing!
> Jesus, the life of both our joys,
> Sounds sweet from every string.

The Meaning of "Jesus"

Henry Craik of Bristol, a man of God, wrote a little book on the study of the Hebrew language. In it, he used the word *Jesus* as an example of how much may be gathered from a single Hebrew word, for the name of Jesus is particularly rich and meaningful to the mind of the

Hebrew scholar. Its root word means "amplitude, spaciousness." It later came to mean "setting at large, setting free, delivering." Then it came to mean what it commonly means today, namely, "Savior."

There are actually two words in the name *Jesus.* The one is a contraction of the word *Jehovah;* the other is the word that I have just now explained to you as ultimately coming to mean "salvation." Broken down to its simplest terms, the word *Jesus* means "Jehovah–Salvation." The first part of His name declares the glorious essence and nature of Christ as Jehovah, *"I AM THAT I AM"* (Exodus 3:14). The second part of His name reveals His great work for us in setting us free and delivering us from all distress.

Think, beloved believer, of the amplitude, the spaciousness, the breadth, the depth, the abundance, the boundless all-sufficiency laid up in the person of the Lord Jesus Christ. *"It pleased the Father that in him should all fulness dwell"* (Colossians 1:19). You do not have a limited Christ; you do not have a narrow Savior. Oh, the infinity of His love, the abundance of His grace, the exceeding greatness of the riches of His love toward us! There are no words in any language that can sufficiently describe the unlimited, infinite extent of the riches of the glory of Christ Jesus our Lord.

The word that lies at the root of this name *Jesus,* or *Joshua,* sometimes has the meaning of riches, and who can tell what a wealth of grace and glory is laid up in our Emmanuel?

According to Henry Craik, another form of the same word signifies "a cry." The psalmist said, *"Hearken unto the voice of my cry, my King, and my God"* (Psalm 5:2). Thus, salvation, riches, and a cry are all derived from the same root, and all are found in our "Joshua," or Christ. When His people cry out from their prisons, then He comes and sets them free. He comes with all the fullness and wealth of His eternal grace, with all the plenitude of His overflowing power. Delivering His people from every form of bondage, He enables them to enjoy the riches of the glory treasured up in Himself.

If this interpretation makes the name of Jesus a little bit more dear to you, I greatly rejoice. Just think, if there is so much wealth stored up in His name, what must be stored up in His very self! And, if we can honestly say that it would be difficult to give the full meaning of this one Hebrew name that belongs to Christ, how much more difficult would it be to give the full meaning of all His character? If His name alone is such a mine of excellence, what must His person be? If His name, which is only a part of Him, smells so sweetly of myrrh, aloes, and cassia (see Psalm 45:8), oh, what must His blessed person be but *"a bundle of myrrh"* (Song 1:13) that we will forever wear around our necks to be the perfume of our lives and the delight of our souls?

> Precious is the name of Jesus,
>   Who can half its worth unfold?
> Far beyond angelic praises,
>   Sweetly sung to harps of gold.
>
> Precious when to Calvary groaning,
>   He sustain'd the cursed tree;
> Precious when His death atoning,
>   Made an end of sin for me.
>
> Precious when the bloody scourges
>   Caused the sacred drops to roll;
> Precious when of wrath the surges
>   Overwhelm'd His holy soul.
>
> Precious in His death victorious,
>   He the host of hell o'erthrows;
> In His resurrection glorious,
>   Victor crowned o'er all His foes.

Precious, Lord! beyond expressing,
Are Thy beauties all divine;
Glory, honor, power, and blessing,
Be henceforth forever Thine.

Christ

I have written about the Hebrew name of God's Son. Now let us reverently consider the second title given to Him in our text—*"Christ."* That is a Greek name, a Gentile name, meaning "anointed." In our text, we have the Hebrew name *Joshua,* or *Jesus,* then the Greek name *Christos,* or *Christ,* so that we may see that there is no longer Jew or Gentile, but that all are one in Jesus Christ (Galatians 3:28). The word *Christ,* as I have mentioned, means "anointed," and as such, our Lord is sometimes called *"the Christ"* (see, for example, Matthew 16:16) or *"the very Christ"* (John 7:26). At other times, He is called *"the Lord's Christ"* (Luke 2:26) or *"the Christ of God"* (Luke 9:20). He is the Lord's Anointed, our King, and our Shield.

This word *Christ* teaches us three great truths. First, it indicates His offices. He exercises offices in which anointing is necessary; there are three of them: the office of king, the office of priest, and the office of prophet.

Christ is King in Zion, *"anointed...with the oil of gladness above* [His] *fellows"* (Psalm 45:7), even as it was said long ago,

> *I have found David my servant; with my holy oil have I anointed him: with whom my hand shall be established: mine arm also shall strengthen him....I will set his hand also in the sea, and his right hand in the rivers....Also I will make him my firstborn, higher than the kings of the earth.* (Psalm 89:20–21, 25, 27)

Saul, the first king of Israel, was anointed with only a vial of oil, but David was anointed with a horn of oil, as if to signify his greater power and his greater kingdom. Yet as for our Lord Jesus Christ, He has received the Spirit of anointing without measure (John 3:34). He is the Lord's Anointed, for whom an unquenchable lamp is ordained. The Scripture says, *"There will I make the horn of David to bud: I have ordained a lamp for mine anointed"* (Psalm 132:17).

Beloved, as we think about the name *Christ,* let us reverently yield up our souls to the One whom God has anointed to be King. Let us stand up for His rights over His church, for He is King of Zion, and no one has a right to rule there except under and in subjection to the great Head over all, who in all things will have the preeminence (Colossians 1:18). Let us stand up for His rights within our own hearts, seeking to thrust out anything that competes with Him for our affections, desiring to keep our souls chaste for Christ. Let us compel every member of our bodies, although previously they might have surrendered themselves to sin, to be subservient to the anointed King, who has an absolute right to rule over them.

Next, the Lord Christ is Priest. Priests had to be anointed. Israelites were not supposed to take this office upon themselves, nor could they become priests without going through the ceremony that set them apart. Jesus Christ our Lord has had grace given to Him that no priest ever had. The outward anointing of the priest was only symbolical, while His anointing was true and real. He has received what their oil portrayed only in type and shadow; He has the real anointing from the Most High.

Beloved, let us always look at Christ as the anointed Priest. My friend, you can never come to God except through the ever living and truly anointed High Priest of your faith's profession. Oh, never for a moment seek to come to God without Him, or through any pretender who may call himself a priest. High Priest of the house of God, we see You thus ordained, and we give our cause into Your hands. Offer our sacrifices for us; present our prayers. Take our praises, put them into the golden censer (see Revelation 8:3), and offer them Yourself before Your Father's throne. Rejoice, beloved, every time you hear the name *Christ,* knowing that He who wears it is anointed to be Priest.

Regarding the prophetic office, the Scriptures reveal that Elisha was anointed to prophesy, and likewise Jesus Christ is the Prophet anointed among His people. Peter told Cornelius of *"how God anointed Jesus of Nazareth with the Holy Ghost and with power: who went about doing good, and healing all that were oppressed of the devil; for God was with him"* (Acts 10:38). He was anointed to preach the Good News and to sit as Master in Israel. We should consider no man's teaching to be authoritative except the testimony of the Christ. The teaching of Christ is our creed, and nothing else.

I thank God that in my church we do not have to divide our allegiance between some venerable set of articles and the teaching of our Lord. We have one Master, and we do not acknowledge the right of any man to bind another's conscience. Even if a man is great in piety and deep in learning, like Augustine and Calvin, whose names we honor, for God honored them, still he has no dominance over the private judgment of God's people. Jesus Christ is the Prophet of Christendom. His words must always be the first and the last appeal.

This, then, is the meaning of the word *Christos:* He is anointed as King, Priest, and Prophet. Yet it means more than that. The name *Christ* declares His right to those offices. He is not King because He sets Himself up as such. God has set Him up as King upon His holy hill of Zion and has anointed Him to rule. He is also Priest, but He has not taken the priesthood upon Himself, for He is the atoning Sacrifice that God has set forth for human sin. The Lord God has appointed Christ to be the Mediator; He has chosen Christ to be the only mediator between God and man. And as for His prophesying, Christ does not speak on His own; on the contrary, He has revealed to us the things that He has learned from the Father. He does not come as a prophet who assumes office; God has anointed Him to preach the Good News to the poor and to come among His people with the welcome news of eternal love.

Moreover, this anointing signifies a third thing. Even as He has the office, and as it is His by right, so He has the qualifications for the work. He is anointed to be King. God has given Him royal power, wisdom, and government; He has made Him fit to rule in the church and to reign over the world. There is no better king than Christ—none as majestic as He who wore the crown of thorns—for He will one day wear the crown of universal monarchy.

He has the qualifications of a priest, too—qualifications that even Melchizedek did not have (see Hebrews 7:1–3, 15–17), qualifications that cannot be found in the long lineage of the house of Aaron. Blessed Son of God, You are perfect in Yourself, and You do not need a sacrifice for Your own sake. Yet You have presented unto God an offering that has perfected forever those whom You have set apart (Hebrews 10:14). Now You do not need to make a further offering. You have forever put away sin.

It is the same way with our Lord's prophesying; He has the power to teach. *"Grace is poured into thy lips: therefore God hath blessed thee for ever"* (Psalm 45:2). All the words of Christ are wisdom and truth. The substance of true philosophy and sure knowledge is to be found in the One who is the wisdom and the power of God (1 Corinthians 1:24).

Oh, that word *Christ!* It seems to grow on us as we think it over. It shows us the offices of Christ, His right to those offices, and His qualifications for them.

> Christ, to Thee our spirits bow!
> Prophet, Priest, and King art Thou!

> Christ, anointed of the Lord,
> Evermore be Thou adored.

Now, put the two titles together and ring out the harmony of the two melodious notes: Jesus Christ—Anointed Savior! Oh, how blessed! Don't you see that our Beloved is a Savior appropriately appointed, a Savior abundantly qualified? My friends, if God has appointed Christ to be the Savior of sinners, why do you question His decision? God presented Christ as a sinner's Savior. Come, then, sinners; take Him, accept Him, and rest in Him. Oh, how foolish we are when we begin raising questions, objections, and difficulties! God declares that Christ is a Savior to all who trust in Him. My poor heart trusts Him; it has peace. Yet why do some of you imagine that He cannot save you? Why do you ask, "How can it be that this Man would save me?" God has appointed Him. Take Him; rest in Him.

Moreover, God has qualified Him and given Him the anointing of a Savior. What? Do you think that God has not given Him enough power or furnished Him with enough merit with which to save such as you are? Will you limit what God has done? Will you think that God's anointing is imperfect and cannot qualify Jesus to remedy your condition? Oh, do not slander the grace of heaven! Do not insult the wisdom of the Lord! Honor the Savior of God's anointing by coming now, just as you are, and putting your trust in Him.

His Memorable Attribute

Jesus Christ is said to be *"the same."* Now, as far as His circumstances are concerned, He has not been the same at all times, for He was once adored by angels but afterward spit on by men. He exchanged the heavenly splendors of His Father's court for the poverty of the earth, the degradation of death, and the humiliation of the grave.

The Same Yesterday, Today, and Forever

Jesus Christ is not, and will not be, always the same in regard to His occupation. Once He came *"to seek and to save that which was lost"* (Luke 19:10), but we truly sing, "The Lord will come, but not the same as once in lowliness He came." He will come again with a very different purpose. He will come to scatter His enemies and to *"break them [as] with a rod of iron"* (Psalm 2:9).

Therefore, we are not to interpret the expression *"the same"* in the strictest sense imaginable. Looking at the original Greek, I notice that our text might be read this way: "Jesus Christ Himself, yesterday and today and forever." The anointed Savior is always Himself. He is always Jesus Christ. The word *"same"* seems to me to have the most intimate relationship with the two titles of the text. Jesus Christ is always Jesus Christ, yesterday and today and forever. Jesus Christ is always Himself. At any rate, if that is not the correct translation, it is a very correct and blessed statement. It is sweetly true that Jesus Christ is always Himself.

The Same Yesterday

An unchangeable nature is ascribed to Christ, and He was always to His people what He is now, for He was *"the same yesterday."*

Some men who are extremely wise (at least in their own opinion) have drawn distinctions between the people of God who lived before the coming of Christ and those who have lived afterward. I have even heard it said that those who lived before the coming of Christ do not belong to the church of God. We never know what we will hear next, and perhaps it is a mercy that these absurdities are revealed one at a time, so that we may be able to endure their stupidity without dying of amazement.

Why, every child of God in every place stands on the same footing. The Lord does not have some children whom He loves the best, some who are second-rate, and others whom He hardly cares about. Those who saw Christ's day before it came differ greatly from us as far as what they knew; and perhaps, to that extent, they differ as far as what they enjoyed in meditating on Christ while they were on earth. However, they were all washed in the same blood, all redeemed with the same ransom price, and all made members of the same body. In the covenant of grace, the Israel of God is not natural Israel, but all believers from all ages.

Before the First Advent, all the types and shadows pointed one way—to Christ. To Him all believers looked with hope. Those who lived before Christ were not saved with a different salvation than the eternal salvation that will come to us. They exercised faith just as we must. Their faith struggled as ours struggles, and their faith obtained its eternal reward just as ours will. Comparing the spiritual life of the believer now with the spiritual life of David is like comparing a man's face with a reflection of that face.

Sometime, when you are reading the book of Psalms, forget for an instant that you are reading about the life of someone who lived a long time ago. You might suppose that David wrote only yesterday. Even in what he wrote about Christ, it seems as though he lived after Christ, instead of before. Furthermore, both in what he saw of himself and of his Savior, he sounds more like a New Testament believer who has found his Messiah than an Old Testament Israelite still awaiting the Christ. What I am saying is that, living before Christ, he had the same hopes and the same fears, the same joys and the same sorrows. He had the same impression of his blessed Redeemer that you and I have in these times. Jesus was the same yesterday as He is today, as far as being an anointed Savior to His people. Old Testament believers received from Him similar precious gifts. If the good prophets could be here today, they would all testify that, in every office, He was the same in their time as He is today.

The Same Today

Jesus Christ is the same now as He was in the past, for the text says, *"The same yesterday, and to day."* He is the same today as He has been from eternity. Before all the worlds existed, He planned our salvation, and He entered into covenant with His Father to undertake it. His *"delights were with the sons of men"* (Proverbs 8:31) who would one day inhabit the earth, and now today He is as faithful to that covenant as ever. He will not lose those who were then given to Him (John 18:9), nor will He fail or be discouraged (Isaiah 42:4), for every stipulation of that covenant will be fulfilled. The same infinite love that was in the heart of Christ before the stars began to shine is there today.

Jesus is the same today as He was when He was here on earth. There is much comfort in this thought. When He lived among men, He was most willing to save. *"Come unto me, all ye that labour and are heavy laden"* (Matthew 11:28) was His cry. He is still calling to the weary and the burdened to come to Him. When He was on earth, He would not curse the woman caught in adultery, nor would He reject the tax collectors and sinners who gathered to hear Him. He is still merciful to sinners, and He still says to them, *"Neither do I condemn thee: go, and sin no more"* (John 8:11). That delightful sentence that so graciously came from His lips—"[Your] *sins, which are many, are forgiven"* (Luke 7:47)—is still His favorite utterance to human hearts.

Oh, do not think that Christ in heaven has become distant and reserved, so that you may not approach Him. He is the same now as He was when He lived here—a Lamb, gentle and meek, a Man to whom men drew near without a moment's hesitation. Come boldly to Him, you lowliest and guiltiest ones. Come near to Him with broken hearts and weeping eyes. Though He is King and Priest, surrounded with inconceivable splendor, yet He has the same loving heart and the same generous sympathy for the sons of men.

He is still the same in His ability as in His willingness to save. He is still Jesus Christ, the anointed Savior. In His earthly days, He touched the leper and said, *"I will; be thou clean"* (Matthew 8:3). He called Lazarus from the tomb, and Lazarus came. Sinner, Jesus is still just as able to heal or enliven you as He was able to do for others then. *"He is able also to save them to the uttermost that come unto God by him, seeing he ever liveth to make intercession for them"* (Hebrews 7:25). Now that His blood has been shed indeed, and the sacrifice has been fully offered, there is no limit to the ability of Christ to save. Oh, come and rely on Him, and find salvation in Him now.

Believer, it will encourage you also to remember that when our Lord was here on earth, He showed great perseverance in His art of saving. He could say, *"Of them which thou gavest me have I lost none"* (John 18:9). Rejoice that He is the same today. He will not cast one of you away or allow His little ones to perish (Matthew 18:14). He kept all safe in the days of His earthly sojourn; He takes care to keep all safe now in the days of His heavenly glory. He is the same today as He was while on earth.

Blessed be His name; Jesus Christ is the same today as in apostolic days. Then He gave the fullness of the Spirit; then, *"when he ascended up on high, he...gave gifts unto men"* (Ephesians 4:8)—apostles, preachers, teachers of the Word (v. 11). Do not think that we will never see days as good as the Day of Pentecost. He is the same Christ. He could just as readily convert three thousand after one sermon today as in Peter's time. His Holy Spirit is not exhausted, for *"God giveth not the Spirit by measure unto him* [Christ]*"* (John 3:34).

We ought to pray that God would raise up among us prominent men to proclaim the Gospel. We do not pray enough for the ministry. The ministry is the particular gift of the Ascension. When Jesus Christ ascended on high, He received gifts for men, and He gave what? Why, apostles, teachers, preachers. When we ask for salvation, we plead the blood of Jesus; why don't we ask for ministers and plead the Ascension? If we would do this more, we would see raised up among us more Whitefields and Wesleys, more Luthers and Calvins, more men of the apostolic kind. Then the church would be revived. Jesus Christ, being the same, is able to enrich His people with all spiritual gifts this year just as in the year when He ascended to His throne. He is *"the same yesterday, and to day."*

He is the same today as He was to our forefathers in the faith. They have gone to their rest, but they testified before they went of what Christ had been to them, how He had helped them in their times of peril, how He had delivered them in their hours of sorrow. He will do for us just what He did for them. Some who lived before us were burned at the stake for their faith, but Christ was very precious to them as they went to heaven in chariots of fire. We read the stories of Christian martyrs with wonder. How sustaining the presence of Christ was to those who lay in prison, to those who were thrown to the lions, to those who *"wandered about in sheepskins and goatskins"* (Hebrews 11:37)! England, Scotland—all the countries where Christ has been preached—have been dyed with the blood and ennobled with the testimonies of the faithful. Whatever Jesus was to these worthy believers who have now departed, He is to His people still. We have only to ask God, and we will receive the very same benefits.

"Jesus Christ the same...to day," says the text. Therefore, He is the same today as He has been to us in the past. We have greatly enjoyed God's presence. We remember the love of our first days of salvation, and if we do not have the same joys today, it is no fault of His. The same water is still in the well; if we have not drawn it, it is our own fault. We

have walked away from the fire, and therefore we are cold. We have walked contrary to Him, and therefore He walks contrary to us (Leviticus 26:23–24). Let us return to Him, and He will be as glad to receive us now as in our first moment of repentance. Let us return to Him. His heart is just as full of love, and He is just as ready to tearfully embrace us as when we first came and sought pardon from His hands.

There are many precious truths in the text, but I cannot linger any longer on this part of the subject. It is enough for us to remember that Jesus Christ is the same today as He always has been.

The Same Forever

Last, Christ will be tomorrow what He was yesterday and is today. Our Lord Jesus Christ will be changed in no respect throughout the duration of our lives. It may be a long time before we descend to our graves. Let these hairs of mine all turn gray, these legs of mine begin to wobble, and these eyes of mine grow dim, for Jesus Christ will have the dew of His youth upon Him (Psalm 110:3), and the fullness of His love will still flow to me. And after death, or, if we do not die, at the coming of Christ and in His glorious reign, Jesus will be the same to His people as He is now.

It seems that an idea is being circulated that, after His coming, Christ will deal differently with His people than now. I have been informed by a contemporary school of inventors of religion, who invent newfangled ideas, that some of us will be shut out of the kingdom when Christ comes. Saved by precious blood and brought near to God, adopted into the family, our names written on the breastplate of Christ, will we be shut out from the kingdom? Nonsense! I see nothing about this in the Word of God, although there might be a great deal of it in the imaginations of people.

The Same Yesterday, Today, and Forever

The people of God, equally bought with blood and equally dear to Jesus' heart, will be treated on the same scale and footing. They will never be put under the law; they will never come to Christ in a future state and find Him ruling them as a legal Judge, beating them with many lashes, or shutting them out of His estate of millennial majesty. He will not reward some by giving them rule and authority and at the same time exclude others of His redeemed family. His entire family will find that He always treats them as unchanging love and immutable grace dictate.

The rewards of the millennial state will always be those of grace; they will not be such that they will exclude even the very least of God's family. In fact, all believers will receive rewards from the dear Savior's hand.

I know He will not love me today, giving me glimpses of His face and allowing me to delight in His name, and yet, when He comes again, tell me I cannot enter His kingdom but must stand out in the cold. I do not have a tinge of faith in this "purgatory" of banishment, which certain despisers of the ministry have chosen to set up. I marvel that in any Protestant denomination there should arise a dogma as villainous as the dogma of purgatory. These teachers say that everyone else is wrong but that they have been taught deep things and can discover what the best theologians have never seen.

I know this: Jesus will love His people in times to come as strongly as He does now. The destruction or denial of this doctrine would cast sorrow into the whole family of God. Throughout eternity, in heaven, there will still be the same Jesus Christ, with the same love for His people. They will have the same intimate communion with Him—not only this, but they will see Him face-to-face. They will rejoice forever in Him as their unchangeably anointed Savior.

Our Lord's Claims upon Us

Since our Lord is *"the same yesterday, and to day, and for ever,"* then, according to the verse preceding our text, He is to be followed to the end. Observe the seventh verse: *"Remember them which have the rule over you, who have spoken unto you the word of God: whose faith follow, considering the end of their conversation"* (Hebrews 13:7). The meaning of the verse is this: These holy men ended their lives with Christ; their exit out of this life meant going to Jesus and reigning with Him. Beloved, if the Lord is still the same, follow Him until you reach Him. Your exit out of this life will bring you where He is, and you will find Him to be then what He always was. You will *"see him as he is"* (1 John 3:2). If He were a delusive hope, forever changing, it would be dangerous to follow Him. However, since He is always equally worthy of your admiration and imitation, follow Him forever.

Henry VI of France gave an eloquent speech on the eve of a certain battle. He said to his soldiers, "Gentlemen, you are Frenchmen. I am your king. There is the enemy!" Similarly, Jesus Christ says, "You are My people. I am your Leader. There is the foe!" How dare we do anything unworthy of such a Lord as He is, or of such a citizenship as that which He has given us? If we are indeed His, and He is indeed immutable, let us by His Holy Spirit's power persevere to the end, so that we may obtain the crown.

The next claim of Christ upon us is that we should be steadfast in the faith. Notice the verse after our text: *"Be not carried about with divers* [various] *and strange doctrines"* (Hebrews 13:9). There is nothing new in theology except that which is false. All that is true is old, though I am not saying that all that is old is true. Some speak of new developments as though we had not discovered the whole Christian religion yet; but the religion of Paul is the religion of every person who is taught by the Holy Spirit.

The Same Yesterday, Today, and Forever

We must not, therefore, indulge for a moment the idea that something has been discovered that might correct the teaching of Christ, that some new philosophy or scientific discovery has arisen to correct the declared testimony of our Redeemer. Let us hold tightly to what we have received; let us never depart from *"the faith which was once delivered unto the saints"* (Jude 3) by Christ Himself.

Moreover, since Jesus Christ is immutable, He has an obvious claim to our most solemn worship. Immutability can be the attribute of no one but God. Whoever is *"the same yesterday, and to day, and for ever"* must be divine. Forever, then, believer, bring your adoration to Jesus. At the feet of Him who was crucified, cast your crown. Give royal and divine honors to the One who stooped to the ignominy of crucifixion. Let no one prevent you from glorying in Christ, for you boast in the Son of God made man for you. Worship Him as God over all, blessed forever.

Next, He has a claim to our trust. If He is always the same, here is a Rock that cannot be moved. Build on it! Here is a haven. Cast your anchor of hope into it, and hold on in times of storm. If Christ were changeable, He would not be worthy of your confidence. However, since He is forever unchanged, rest on Him without fear.

Last, if He is always the same, rejoice in Him, and rejoice always. If you have ever had cause to rejoice in Christ, you always have cause, for He never changes. If yesterday you could sing of Him, today you may sing of Him. If He were subject to change, your joy might change. Yet if the stream of your gladness springs solely out of this great deep of the immutability of Jesus, then it never needs to stop flowing. Beloved, let us *"rejoice in the Lord alway: and again I say, Rejoice"* (Philippians 4:4). *"Until the day break, and the shadows flee away"* (Song 2:17; 4:6), until the blessed hour arrives when we will see Him face-to-face and be made like Him, let this be our joy, that He is *"the same yesterday, and to day, and for ever."*

Chapter 6

Suffering and Reigning with Jesus

*If we suffer, we shall also reign with him: if we
deny him, he also will deny us.*
—2 Timothy 2:12

Our text is the second part of one of Paul's "faithful sayings." If I remember correctly, Paul had
four of these. The first occurs in 1 Timothy 1:15,
that famous, that foremost, of all faithful sayings: *"This
is a faithful saying, and worthy of all acceptation, that
Christ Jesus came into the world to save sinners; of whom
I am chief."* Paul himself had most marvelously proved
the value of this golden saying. What should I say about
this verse except that, like the light of a lighthouse, it has
darted its ray of comfort through miles of darkness and
has guided millions of tempest-tossed spirits to the port
of peace?

The next faithful saying is in the same epistle:

*Godliness is profitable unto all things, having promise
of the life that now is, and of that which is to come.
This is a faithful saying and worthy of all acceptation.*
(1 Timothy 4:8–9)

This, too, the apostle knew to be true, since he had *"learned, in whatsoever state* [he was], *therewith to be content"* (Philippians 4:11).

Our chosen text, *"If we suffer, we shall also reign with him,"* is a portion of the third faithful saying. The last of the four you will find in Titus 3:8:

> *This is a faithful saying, and these things I will that thou affirm constantly, that they which have believed in God might be careful to maintain good works. These things are good and profitable unto men.*

There is a connection between these faithful sayings. The first one, which speaks of Jesus Christ coming into the world to save sinners, lays the foundation of our eternal salvation, which is the free grace of God. This grace was shown to us in the mission of the great Redeemer. The next faithful saying affirms the double blessedness that we obtain through this salvation—the blessings of both the lower and upper springs—of both time and eternity. The third faithful saying shows one of the duties to which the chosen people are called: We are ordained to suffer for Christ with the promise that *"if we suffer, we shall also reign with him."* The last faithful saying describes the active form of Christian service, instructing us to diligently maintain good works.

Thus you have, first, the root of salvation in free grace; next, the privileges of that salvation in the present life and in the life to come; and, last, the two great branches of suffering with Christ and service to Christ, loaded with the fruits of the Spirit of all grace.

Treasure up, dear friend, these faithful sayings. *"Lay up these my words in your heart and in your soul, and bind them for a sign upon your hand, that they may be as frontlets between your eyes"* (Deuteronomy 11:18). Let these choice sayings be printed in letters of gold and posted on the doorposts of our houses and on our gates (Deuteronomy 11:20). Let them be the guides of our lives, as well as our comfort and our instruction. The Apostle to the Gentiles proved them to be faithful. They are faithful still. Not one word of them will fall to the ground. They are worthy of full acceptance. Let us accept them now and prove their faithfulness.

This chapter will focus on a part of the faithful saying that deals with suffering. Let us look at the verse preceding our text: *"It is a faithful saying: for if we be dead with him, we shall also live with him"* (2 Timothy 2:11). All the elect were virtually dead with Christ when He died on the cross; they were on the cross, crucified with Him (Galatians 2:20). In Him, who is their Representative, they rose from the tomb, and they live *"in newness of life"* (Romans 6:4). Because He lives, they will live, also (John 14:19).

In due time, the chosen are drawn to God by the Spirit of God. When they are saved, they are made dead with Christ unto sin, unto self-righteousness, unto the world, unto the flesh, and unto the powers of darkness. Then it is that they live with Jesus; His life becomes their life. As He was, so are they also in this world (1 John 4:17). The Spirit of God breathes the quickening grace into those who were once dead in sin, and thus they live in union with Christ Jesus. A believer may be sawed in half or burned at the stake, yet, since he sleeps in Jesus, he is preserved from the destruction of death by Him; he is made a partaker of Christ's immortality. May the Lord root us and ground us in the mysterious but most comforting doctrine of union with Christ Jesus.

Let us now focus on our text: *"If we suffer, we shall also reign with him: if we deny him, he also will deny us."* The words naturally divide themselves into two parts: first, suffering with Jesus and its reward; second, denying Jesus and its penalty.

Suffering with Jesus and Its Reward

To suffer is the common lot of all people. It is not possible for us to escape from pain. We come into this world through the gate of suffering, and we leave it through the same gate. We suffer if we live, regardless of what kind of lives we lead. The wicked individual may cast off all respect for virtue; he may live riotously in excessive vice. Yet he must not expect to avoid the well-directed shafts of sorrow. No, rather, let him expect a tenfold share of bodily pain and remorse of soul. *"Many sorrows shall be to the wicked"* (Psalm 32:10). Even if a person could so completely degrade himself as to lose his intellectual powers and become like an animal, even then he could not escape from suffering, for we know that the animal is the victim of pain as much as more lordly man. In fact, the animals have the additional misery that they have no mind endowed with reason or encouraged by hope to fortify them in their pain.

Oh, man, don't you see that however you may degrade yourself, you are still under the yoke of suffering? The loftiest men bow beneath it, and the lowest men cannot avoid it. Every acre of humanity must be furrowed with this plow. There may be a sea without a wave, but never a man without a sorrow. He who was God as well as man had His full measure of pain; in fact, His share was pressed down and running over. Let us be assured that, if the Sinless One was not spared the rod, the sinful will not go free. *"Man that is born of a woman is of few days, and full of trouble"* (Job 14:1). *"Man is born unto trouble, as the sparks fly upward"* (Job 5:7).

Suffering That Does Not Ensure a Reward

If, then, a man has sorrow, it does not necessarily mean that he will be rewarded for it, since it is the common lot brought upon all by sin. You may ache under the lashes of sorrow in this life, but your sadness will not deliver you from the wrath to come. Remember, you may live in poverty and lead a wearisome life of unrewarded toil. You may be placed on a sickbed and be made to experience agony in every part of your body. Your mind, too, may be depressed with fears or plunged into the depths of despair. Yet, by all this, you may gain nothing of any value to your immortal spirit. *"Except a man be born again, he cannot see the kingdom of God"* (John 3:3), and no amount of affliction on earth can alter that unchanging rule to admit an unsaved person into heaven.

To suffer is not unique to the Christian. Neither does suffering necessarily bring with it any reward. The text clearly implies that we must suffer *with* Christ in order to reign with Him. The structure of our text plainly requires such a reading. The words *"with him"* may be as accurately placed at the end of the one clause as the other: *"If we suffer* [with Him], *we shall also reign with him."* The suffering that brings the reigning with Jesus must be a suffering with Jesus.

There is a misconception among many poor people who are ignorant of true Christianity that all poor and afflicted people will be rewarded for their suffering in the next state. I have heard workingmen refer to the parable of the rich man and Lazarus (Luke 16:19–31) with a cruel sort of satisfaction at the pains of the rich man. They have imagined that, in the same manner, all rich people will be cast into the flames of hell without a drop of water to cool their tongues, while all poor people like Lazarus will be triumphantly carried into Abraham's bosom.

A more fearful mistake could not be made. It was not the suffering of Lazarus that entitled him to a place in Abraham's bosom. He might have been licked by all the dogs on earth and then dragged off by the dogs of hell. Many a man goes to hell a pauper. A drunkard's hovel is very wretched; is he to be rewarded for bringing himself to rags? Very much of the poverty we see around us is the result of vice, extravagance, or folly. Are these things so meritorious as to be passports to glory? Let no man deceive himself so horribly.

On the other hand, the rich man was not cast into hell because he was rich and lived luxuriously. Had he been rich in faith, holy in life, and renewed in heart, his purple and fine linen would have done him no harm. Lazarus was carried above by the angels because his heart was in heaven, and the rich man lifted up his eyes from hell because he had never lifted them up toward God and heavenly things.

It is a work of grace in the heart and character that will decide the future, not poverty or wealth. Suffering here does not imply happiness hereafter. Let sensible people combat this false idea whenever they encounter it. It is only a certain type of suffering to which a reward is promised—the suffering that comes to us from fellowship with the Lord Jesus and conformity to His image.

The Necessity of Being in Christ

Let me add a few words here to help you in making the distinction between these two types of suffering. We must not imagine that we are suffering for Christ, and with Christ, if we are not in Christ. If a person is not a branch of the Living Vine, you may prune and cut until the branch bleeds and the sap flows, but he will never bring forth heavenly fruit. Prune the bramble as long as you like—use the knife until the edge is worn away—but the brier will be as sharp and fruitless as ever. No process of pruning will transform the brier into one of the vines of Eshcol (Numbers 13:23; Deuteronomy 1:24–25).

In the same way, if a person remains in a fallen state, he is a member of the earthly Adam. He will not, therefore, escape suffering, but ensure it. He must not, however, dream that because he suffers, he is suffering with Christ. He is plagued with the old Adam. He is receiving, with all the other heirs of wrath, the sure heritage of sin. Let him consider these sufferings of his to be only the first drops of the awful shower that will fall upon him forever, the first tingling cuts of that terrible whip that will lacerate his soul forever.

However, if a person is in Christ, he may then claim fellowship with the *"second man* [who] *is the Lord from heaven"* (1 Corinthians 15:47). He may expect to bear the image of the heavenly in the glory to be revealed. Oh, my reader, are you in Christ by a living faith? Are you trusting in Jesus alone? If not, regardless of what you may have to mourn over on earth, you have no hope of reigning with Jesus in heaven.

Suffering Caused by Our Own Mistakes

Even when a man is in Christ, it does not mean that all his sufferings are sufferings with Christ, for it is essential that he be called by God to suffer. If a good man were, out of mistaken views of dying to self and self-denial, to mutilate his body or to flog his flesh, as many a sincere enthusiast has done, I might admire the man's fortitude, but I would not believe for an instant that he was suffering with Christ. Who called men to such severities? Certainly not the God of love. If, therefore, they torture themselves at the command of their own inclinations, inclination must reward them, for God will not.

If I am rash and imprudent and run into situations for which neither providence nor grace has prepared me, I ought to question whether I am not sinning rather than communing with Christ. Peter drew his sword and cut off the ear of Malchus. (See John 18:3–5, 10–11.) If somebody had cut off Peter's ear in return, what would you say? You would say that Peter used the sword, and therefore he felt the sword. He was never commanded to cut off the ear of Malchus, and it was his Master's gentleness that saved him from the soldiers' rage. If we let passion take the place of judgment, if we let self-will reign instead of scriptural authority, we will fight the Lord's battles with the devil's weapons, and we must not be surprised if we cut off our own fingers.

On several occasions, excited Protestants have rushed into Catholic cathedrals, knocked down the priest, dashed the wafer to the ground, trod on it, and in other ways exhibited their hatred of idolatry. Now, when the law has intervened to punish such outrages, the offenders are hardly to be considered as suffering with Christ.

I give this as an example of a kind of action to which overheated brains sometimes lead people, under the supposition that they will join the noble army of martyrs. The martyrs were and are all chosen to their honorable estate. I may say of martyrdom, as of priesthood, *"No man taketh this honour unto himself, but he that is called of God, as was Aaron"* (Hebrews 5:4). Let us be careful that we make proper distinctions, that we do not pull a house down on our heads and then ask the Lord to console us under the trial.

Again, in troubles that come upon us as the result of sin, we must not think that we are suffering with Christ. When Miriam spoke evil of Moses, and leprosy polluted her, she was not suffering for God. (See Numbers 12:1–15.) When Uzziah went into the temple to burn incense and became a leper all his days, he could not say that he was afflicted for righteousness' sake. (See 2 Chronicles 26:3–5, 16–21.) If you speculate and lose your property, do not say that you are losing all for Christ's sake. When you invest in shaky companies and are duped, do not whine about suffering for Christ—call it the fruit of your own folly. If you put your hand into the fire, do not complain if you get burned; why, it is the nature of fire to burn you or anybody else. Do not be so silly as to boast as though you were a martyr. If you do wrong and suffer for it, what thanks do you have (1 Peter 2:20)? Hide your face and weep for your sin, but do not come forth in public to claim a reward.

Many a hypocrite, when he has had his just desserts and has been called by his proper name, has cried out, "I am persecuted." However, it is not, as some believe, an infallible sign of excellence to have a bad reputation. Who feels any esteem for a cold-blooded murderer? Doesn't every man condemn the offender? Is he, therefore, a Christian because he is spoken against and rejected? Assuredly not; he is a heartless villain and nothing more.

Beloved, honesty should stop us from making false claims. We must not talk as if we are suffering nobly for Jesus when we are troubled only as the result of sin. Oh, to be kept from transgression! Then it does not matter how rough the road of obedience may be; our journey will be pleasant because Jesus walks with us.

The Right Motives and Attitudes

Observe, moreover, that the suffering that God accepts and rewards, for Christ's sake, must have God's glory as its goal. If I suffer so that I may earn a name or win applause from others, if I undergo a trial merely so that I may be respected for it, I will get my reward, but it will be the reward of the Pharisee and not the crown of the sincere servant of the Lord Jesus.

I must be careful, too, that love for Christ and love for His elect are always the mainspring of all my patience in suffering. Remember the apostle's words: *"Though I give my body to be burned, and have not charity, it profiteth me nothing"* (1 Corinthians 13:3). If I suffer in bravado, filled with proud defiance of my fellowmen; if I love the dignity of singularity, and out of dogged obstinacy hold to an opinion—not because it is right and I love God too much to deny His truth, but because I choose to think as

I like—then I do not suffer with Jesus. If there is no love for God in my soul, if I do not endure all things for the elect's sake, I may bear many a slap and beating, but I miss the fellowship of the Spirit and have no reward.

Also, I must not forget that I must manifest the attitude of Christ or else I do not suffer with Him. I once heard about a certain minister who, having had a disagreement with several members in his church, preached from this text: *"And Aaron held his peace"* (Leviticus 10:3). He preached the sermon with the intention of portraying himself as an astonishing example of meekness, but since his previous words and actions had been quite violent, a witty hearer observed that the only likeness he could see between Aaron and the preacher was this: *"'Aaron held his peace,'* and the preacher did not." It is easy enough to discover some parallel between our situations and those of departed believers, but not so easy to carry out the parallel by holy patience and Christlike forgiveness.

If I have brought upon myself shame and rebuke, if I am quick to defend myself and to punish the slanderer, if I am irritated, unforgiving, and proud, I have lost a noble opportunity of fellowship with Jesus. If I do not have Christ's attitudes in me, I do not suffer acceptably. If, like a sheep before her shearers, I can be silent (see Isaiah 53:7), if I can bear insult and love the man who inflicts it, if I can pray with Christ, *"Father, forgive them; for they know not what they do"* (Luke 23:34), if I can submit my whole situation to Him who judges righteously, if I can consider it my joy to suffer reproach for the cause of Christ, then, and only then, have I truly suffered with Christ.

These remarks may seem very cutting. They may take away much false but highly prized comfort from you. It is not my intention to take away any true comfort from the humblest believer who really suffers with my Lord. Yet may God grant that we may have enough honesty not to pluck flowers out of other men's gardens or wear other men's honors. Only truth will be desired by true men.

The Sufferers Who Will Receive a Reward

I will now very briefly discuss the ways in which we may suffer for Jesus in our day. It is not our lot now to rot in prisons, to wander around in sheepskins and goatskins, to be stoned, or to be sawed in half, though we ought to be ready to bear all this if God wills it. The days of Nebuchadnezzar's furnace are past, but the fire is still on earth.

Some, for instance, suffer in their finances. I admit that many Christians gain financially rather than lose financially when they become believers in Christ. However, I encounter many cases—cases that I know to be genuine—in which Christians have had to suffer severely for conscience' sake. I know people who were once in very comfortable circumstances, but they lived in a neighborhood where most of the business was done on Sundays. When they became Christians and closed their shops on Sundays, their customers left them. I know that some of them are working very hard for their bread, though once they earned abundance without any great toil. They do it cheerfully for Christ's sake, but the struggle is a hard one.

I know other people who were once employed in lucrative jobs, but their jobs involved sin. When they became Christians, they were obliged to resign. Now they do not have anything like the apparent prosperity they used to have. Their incomes have been significantly reduced.

I could point to several cases of people who have truly suffered greatly in financial matters for the Cross of Christ. If this is your situation, you may possess your soul by patience (Luke 21:19) and expect as a reward of grace that you will reign with Jesus, your Beloved.

Those featherbed soldiers who are brokenhearted if fools laugh at them should blush when they think of those who endure real hardship as good soldiers of Jesus Christ. Who can waste his pity over the small griefs of faint hearts when cold, hunger, and poverty are cheerfully endured by the true and the brave? Cases of persecution are by no means rare. We who live in a more enlightened society little know the terrorism exercised in some places over poor men and women who endeavor conscientiously to carry out their convictions and walk with Christ. To all saints who are oppressed, this sweet sentence is directed: *"If we suffer, we shall also reign with him."*

More often, however, the Christian's suffering takes the form of enduring personal contempt. It is not pleasant to be pointed at in the streets and have disgraceful names shouted after you by vulgar tongues. Neither is it a small trial to be greeted in the workplace by reproachful names, or to be looked upon as an idiot or a madman. Yet this is the lot of many people of God every day of the week. Many of those who are of the humbler classes have to endure constant and open reproach, and those who are richer have to put up with the cold shoulder, neglect, and sneers as soon as they become true disciples of Jesus Christ. There is more sting in this treatment than some imagine. I have known strong men who could have borne the whip but were brought down by jeers and sarcasm. Indeed, a lion may be more troubled by the irritations of a wasp than by the attack of the noblest beast of prey.

Believers also have to suffer slander and falsehood. Undoubtedly, it is not profitable for me to boast, but I know a man who scarcely ever speaks a word that is not misrepresented or performs an action that is not misconstrued. At certain seasons, the press, like a pack of hounds, will get on his trail, harassing him with the vilest and most undeserved abuse. Publicly and privately, he is accustomed to being sneered at. The world whispers, "Oh, he pretends to be zealous for God, but he makes a fine show of it!" Mind you, when the people of the world do learn what he makes of it, maybe they will have to eat their words.

However, I will not focus on myself, for such is the portion of every servant of God who publicly testifies to the truth. Every motive but the right one will be imputed to him. His good will be spoken of as evil; his zeal will be called imprudence; his courage, impertinence; his modesty, cowardice; his earnestness, rashness. It is impossible for the true believer in Christ who is called to any prominent service to do anything right in the eyes of the world. He had better learn right now to say with Luther, "The world hates me, and there is no love lost between us, for as much as it hates me, so heartily do I hate it." He did not mean that he hated the people in the world, for never was there a more loving heart than Luther's. He meant that he hated the fame, the opinion, the honor of the world. If, in your measure, you bear undeserved rebuke for Christ's sake, comfort yourself with these words: *"If we suffer, we shall also reign with him: if we deny him, he also will deny us."*

If, in your service for Christ, you are enabled to sacrifice yourself in such a way that you bring upon yourself inconvenience and pain, labor and loss, then I think you are suffering with Christ. The missionary penetrating into unknown regions among savages, the teacher going wearily to class, the village preacher walking many toilsome miles, the minister starving on a miserable pittance, the evangelist content to deteriorate in health—all these, and those like them, suffer with Christ.

We are all too occupied with taking care of ourselves. We shun the difficulties of excessive labor. Frequently, because we are too concerned about caring for our health, we do not do half as much as we ought. A minister of God must spurn the suggestion to take it easy; it is his calling to labor. If he destroys his health, I, for one, only thank God that He permits us the high privilege of making ourselves living sacrifices. If earnest ministers bring themselves to the grave, not by imprudence, for that I would not advocate, but by the honest labor that their ministries and their consciences require of them, they will be better in their graves than out of them. What? Are we never to suffer? Are we to be summer soldiers? Are God's people to be pampered—perfumed with fragrances and indulged with quiet softnesses? Certainly not, unless they want to lose the reward of true saints!

In addition, let us not forget that war with our own lusts, denials of proud self, resistance of sin, and agony against Satan are all forms of suffering with Christ. We may, in the holy war within us, earn as bright a crown as in the wider battlefield beyond us. Oh, for grace to be always dressed in full armor, fighting with principalities and powers, as well as spiritual wickedness of every sort.

I will mention one more type of suffering, and that is, friends forsaking us or becoming our foes. Father and mother sometimes forsake their children. The husband sometimes persecutes the wife. I have even known the children to turn against the parents. *"A man's foes* [are] *they of his own household"* (Matthew 10:36). This is one of Satan's best instruments for making believers suffer, and those who have to drain this cup for the Lord's sake will reign with Him.

Beloved, if you are called to suffer for Christ in this way, will you quarrel with me if I say, in adding up all your sufferings, what very little they are compared with reigning with Jesus? *"For our light affliction, which is but for a moment, worketh for us a far more exceeding and eternal weight of glory"* (2 Corinthians 4:17). When I contrast our sufferings of today with the sufferings of Christians in pagan Rome, why, ours are scarcely a thimbleful!

Yet what is our reward? We will reign with Christ. There is no comparison between the service and the reward. Therefore, it is all of grace. We do only a little and suffer only a little, and it is grace that gives us that little bit. Yet the Lord grants us *"a far more exceeding and eternal weight of glory."*

We will not merely sit with Christ; we will also reign with Christ. All the royal splendor of His kingship, all the treasure of His wide dominions, all the majesty of His everlasting power—all this is to belong to you. It will be given to you by His rich, free grace as the sweet reward of having suffered for a little while with Him.

Who would draw back, then? Who would flinch? Young man, have you thought about running from the Cross? Young woman, has Satan whispered to you to shun the thorny pathway? Will you give up the crown? Will you miss the throne? Beloved, it is so blessed to be in the furnace with Christ, it is such an honor to be publicly humiliated with Him, that if there were no reward, we could consider ourselves happy. However, when the reward is so rich, so superabundant, so eternal, so infinitely more than we had any right to expect, will we not take up the Cross with songs and go our way rejoicing in the Lord our God?

Denying Christ and Its Penalty

"If we deny him, he also will deny us." That is a dreadful *"if,"* yet an *"if"* that is applicable to every individual. The apostles, in response to Christ's statement that one of them would betray Him, asked, *"Lord, is it I?"* (Matthew 26:22). In the same way, surely, we may ask, "Lord, will I ever deny You?" You who say most loudly, *"Though all men shall be offended because of thee, yet will I never be offended"* (v. 33)—you are the most likely to deny Christ.

Ways That People Deny Christ

In what ways can we deny Christ? Scoffers overtly deny Him: *"They set their mouth against the heavens, and their tongue walketh through the earth"* (Psalm 73:9). Others deny Him willfully and wickedly in a doctrinal way. Take, for example, those who deny His deity. Also, those who deny His atonement and those who speak against the inspiration of His Word come under the condemnation of those who deny Christ.

In addition, there is a way of denying Christ without even saying a word, and this is more common. When blasphemy and rebuke are encountered, many hide their heads. They are in company where they ought to speak up for Christ, but they put their hands over their mouths. They do not come forward to profess their faith in Jesus. They have a kind of faith, but it is one that yields no obedience. Jesus instructs each believer to be baptized, but they neglect His ordinance. Neglecting that, they also despise *"the weightier matters of the law"* (Matthew 23:23).

They go to the house of God because it is fashionable to go there, but if it were a matter of persecution, they would forsake *"the assembling of* [themselves] *together"* (Hebrews 10:25). In the day of battle, they are never on the Lord's side. If there is a parade and the banners are flying and the trumpets are sounding, if there are decorations and medals to be given away, they are there. However, if shots are flying, if trenches have to be dug, if fortresses have to be stormed, where are they? They have gone back to their dens, and there they will hide themselves until fair weather returns.

Pay attention, for I am giving a description, I am afraid, of many people. Pay attention, I say, you silent one, lest you stand speechless at the judgment seat of Christ.

Some who have been practically denying Christ for a long time by their silence go even further. They apostatize altogether from the faith they once had. No one who has a genuine faith in Christ will lose it, for the faith that God gives will live forever. However, hypocrites and formalists have a reputation for being alive while they are yet dead (Revelation 3:1), and after a while they return like the dog to its vomit (2 Peter 2:22) and like *"the sow that was washed to her wallowing in the mire"* (v. 22).

Some do not go this far, yet, in practice, they deny Christ by their lives, though they make a profession of faith in Him. Some are baptized and receive communion, but what is their character? Follow them home. I strongly wish that they had never made a profession because, in their own houses, they deny what in the house of God they have avowed. If I see a man drunk; if I know that a man indulges in immorality; if I know a man to be harsh, overbearing, and tyrannical to his employees; if I know another who cheats his customers; and if I know that such men profess allegiance to Jesus, which am I to believe, their words or their deeds? I will believe what speaks the loudest. Since actions always speak louder than words, I will believe their actions. I believe that they are deceivers whom Jesus will deny in the end.

Many people belong in one of these categories of those who deny Jesus. Perhaps you are one of them. If so, do not be angry with me, but stand still and hear the Word of the Lord. Understand that you will not perish, even if you have denied Christ, if you now run to Him for refuge. Peter denied, yet Peter is in heaven. A transient forsaking of Jesus under temptation will not result in everlasting ruin if faith steps in and the grace of God intervenes. However, if you continue in a denial of the Savior and persevere in it, this terrible text will come upon you: *"He also will deny [you]."*

Ways That Jesus Will Deny People

In musing over the very dreadful clause that closes our text, *"He also will deny us,"* I was led to think of various ways in which Jesus will deny us. He does this some-times on earth. Perhaps you have read about the death of Francis Spira. If you have ever read about it, you can never forget it to your dying day. Francis Spira knew the truth—he was a religious reformer of no low stand-ing. However, when threatened with death, out of fear he recanted. In a short time, he fell into despair and suffered hell on earth. His shrieks and exclamations were so hor-rible that their record is almost too terrible for print. His doom was a warning to the age in which he lived.

Another instance is told of one who was very earnest for Puritanism. However, when times of persecution arose, he forsook his profession of faith. The scenes at his death-bed were shocking and terrible. He declared that though he sought God, heaven was shut against him; gates of brass seemed to be in his way. He was given up to over-whelming despair. At intervals he cursed, at other inter-vals he prayed, and so he perished without hope.

If we deny Christ, we may be delivered to such a fate. If we have stood highest in God's church yet have not been brought to Christ, or if we become apostates, our high soar will end in a deep fall. High pretensions bring down sure destruction when they come to nothing. Christ will deny such people even on earth.

There are remarkable instances of people who sought to save their lives and lost them. Richard Denton was a very zealous follower of the English reformer John Wycliffe and had been the means of the conversion of a prominent believer. However, when he came to the stake, he was so afraid of the fire that he renounced everything he held and joined the Church of Rome. A short time afterward, his own house caught on fire. Going into it to save some of his money, he perished miserably, being utterly consumed by the fire that he had denied Christ in order to escape.

If I must be lost, let it be in any other way than as an apostate. If there is any distinction among the damned, it is given to those who are *"trees...twice dead, plucked up by the roots"* (Jude 12), who are *"wandering stars, to whom is reserved the blackness of darkness for ever"* (v. 13). *"Reserved"*! As if nobody else were qualified to occupy that place but themselves. They are to inhabit the darkest, hottest place because they forsook the Lord. Let us, my dear friend, prefer to lose everything else than to lose Christ. Let us sooner suffer anything than lose our ease of conscience and our peace of mind.

Marcus Arethusus was commanded by Julian the Apostate to give a large contribution toward the rebuilding of a heathen temple that his people had torn down after being converted to Christianity. Arethusus refused to obey. Though he was an elderly man, he was stripped naked and then pierced all over with lancets and knives. The old man stood firm. He was told that if he would give one halfpenny toward the building of the temple, he could be free. If he would cast one grain of incense into the censer devoted to the false gods, he could escape. However, he would not approve of idolatry in any degree. As a result, he was smeared with honey, and while his innumerable wounds were still bleeding, the bees and wasps attacked him and stung him to death. He could die, but he could not deny his Lord. Arethusus entered into the joy of his Lord, for he nobly suffered with Him.

A long time ago, when the Gospel was preached in Persia, a courtier of the king named Hamedatha embraced the faith. He was then stripped of his position, driven from the palace, and compelled to feed camels. This he did with great contentment. The king, passing by one day, saw his former favorite at his humble work, cleaning out the camels' stables. Taking pity on him, he took him into his palace, clothed him with luxurious apparel, restored him to all his former honors, and made him sit at the royal table. In the midst of the delicious feast, he asked Hamedatha to renounce his faith. The courtier, rising from the table, tore off his garments with haste, left all the delicacies behind him, and said, "Did you think that for such silly things as these I would deny my Lord and Master?" Away he went to the stable to his lowly work.

How honorable was his reaction! Yet how I detest the lowness of the apostate. Because of his detestable cowardice, he forsakes the bleeding Savior of Calvary to return to the miserable principles of the world that he once despised. In his fear, he bows his neck once again to *"the yoke of bondage"* (Galatians 1:5). Oh, follower of the Crucified One, will you do this? You will not. You cannot. I know you cannot if the spirit of the martyrs dwells in you, and it must dwell in you if you are a child of God.

What will be the doom of those who deny Christ when they reach another world? Perhaps they will come with a sort of hope in their minds and appear before the Judge and say, "Lord, Lord, open to me."

"Who are you?" He will ask.

"Lord, I once took the Lord's Supper. Lord, I was a member of the church, but there came very hard times. Mother told me to give up religion. Father was angry. Business went poorly. I was so ridiculed that I could not stand it. Lord, I had evil acquaintances, and they tempted me. I could not resist. I was Your servant—I did love You—I always had love for You in my heart. But I could not help it. I denied You and went back to the world."

What will Jesus say? "I do not know you."

"But, Lord, I want You to be my Advocate."

"I do not know you!"

"But, Lord, I cannot get into heaven unless You open the gate. Open it for me."

"I do not know you. I do not know you."

"But, Lord, my name was in the church's membership book."

"I do not know you. I deny you."

"But won't You hear my cries?"

"You did not hear Mine. You denied Me, and I deny you."

"Lord, I will take the lowest place in heaven, if I may only enter and escape from the wrath to come."

"No, you would not take the lowest place on earth, and you will not enjoy the lowest place here. You had your choice, and you chose evil. Stick with your choice. You were filthy; be filthy still. You were unholy; be unholy still."

Oh, friend, if you do not want to see the angry face of Jesus; oh, friend, if you do not want to behold the lightning flash from His eye and hear the thunder boom from His mouth when He judges the fearful, the unbelieving, and the hypocrite; if you do not want to have your *"part in the lake which burneth with fire and brimstone"* (Revelation 21:8), mightily cry to God today. Say, "Lord, hold me fast. Keep me; keep me. Help me to suffer with You, so that I may reign with You. Yet do not, please do not, let me deny You, lest You also deny me."

Chapter 7

Our Own Dear Shepherd

I am the good shepherd; and I know mine own,
and mine own know me, even as the Father
knoweth me, and I know the Father; and
I lay down my life for the sheep.
—John 10:14–15 RV

T he Bible version used for the above verses is the
Revised Version. As the passage stands in the King
James Version, it reads like a number of short sentences with hardly any apparent connection: *"I am the*
good shepherd, and know my sheep, and am known of
mine. As the Father knoweth me, even so know I the Father:
and I lay down my life for the sheep" (John 10:14–15).

In that form, it is still precious, for our Lord's pearls
are priceless even when they are not threaded together.
However, when I point out that the translators left out one
of the *and*s in the verse, you will see that they were not too
accurate in this case. Admittedly, it was John's style to use
many *and*s, but there is usually a true and natural connection between his sentences. With him, the *and* is usually a golden link, not a mere sound. We need a translation
that treats it this way.

461

It is also helpful to know that the word *"sheep,"* which appears in verse fourteen in the King James Version, is not in the original; it was added by the translators. However, there is no need for this alteration if the passage is more closely rendered.

Again, the Revised Version gives the text in its natural form: *"I am the good shepherd; and I know mine own, and mine own know me, even as the Father knoweth me, and I know the Father; and I lay down my life for the sheep."*

I admit that I do not care much for the Revised Version of the New Testament in general, and consider it to be by no means an improvement on the King James Version. It is a useful thing to have for private reference, but I trust it will never be regarded as the standard English translation of the New Testament. However, the Revised Version of the Old Testament is so excellent that I am half afraid it might carry the Revised New Testament upon its shoulders into general use. I sincerely hope that this will not happen, for the result would be a decided loss.

However, that is not my point. Returning to our subject, I believe that, on this occasion, the Revised Version is true to the original. We will, therefore, use it in this instance, and we will find that it makes good sense. *"I am the good shepherd; and I know mine own, and mine own know me, even as the Father knoweth me, and I know the Father; and I lay down my life for the sheep."*

He who speaks to us in these words is the Lord Jesus Christ. To my mind, every word of Holy Scripture is precious. When God speaks to us by priest or prophet, or in any way, we are glad to hear. When, in the Old Testament, I come across a passage that begins with "Thus saith the Lord," I feel especially blessed to have the message directly from God's own mouth. Yet I make no distinction between one Scripture and another. I accept it all as inspired, and I do not join the dispute about different degrees and varying modes of inspiration, and all that. The matter would be plain enough if learned unbelievers did not mystify it: *"All scripture is given by inspiration of God, and is profitable for doctrine, for reproof, for correction, for instruction in righteousness"* (2 Timothy 3:16).

Still, there is to my mind a special sweetness about words that were actually spoken by the Lord Jesus Christ Himself. These are like honey to me. The words of our text were not spoken by a prophet, a priest, or a king, but by one who is Prophet, Priest, and King in one, even our Lord Jesus Christ. He opens His mouth and speaks to us. You will open your ears and listen to Him, if you are indeed His own.

In addition, notice that not only do we have Christ for the speaker, but we also have Christ for the subject. He speaks, and He speaks about Himself. It would not be proper for you or for me to extol ourselves, but there is nothing more pleasing in the world than for Christ to commend Himself. He is different than we are. He is infinitely above us, and He is not under rules that apply to us fallible mortals. When He speaks about His own glory, we know that His words are not prideful. Rather, when He praises Himself, we thank Him for doing so, and we admire the humble graciousness that permits Him to desire and accept honor from such poor hearts as ours.

It would be prideful for us to seek honor from men, but it is humility for Christ to do so. He is so great that the esteem of inferior beings like us cannot be desired by Him for His own sake, but for ours. Of all our Lord's words, the sweetest are those that He speaks about Himself. Even He cannot find another theme that can excel that of Himself.

Beloved, who can speak fully of Jesus but Jesus? He masters all our eloquence. His perfection exceeds our understanding. The light of His excellence is too bright for us; it blinds our eyes. Our Beloved must be His own mirror. No one but Jesus can reveal Jesus. Only He can see Himself, know Himself, and understand Himself;

therefore, no one but He can reveal Himself. We are very glad that, in His tenderness to us, He describes Himself with many helpful metaphors and instructive symbols. By these, He wants us to know a little of that love that surpasses knowledge. With His own hand, He fills a golden cup out of the river of His own infinity and hands it to us so that we can drink and be refreshed.

Take these words, then, as being doubly refreshing, because they come directly from the Well Beloved's own mouth, and they contain rich revelations of His own all-glorious self. I feel that I must quote them again: *"I am the good shepherd; and I know mine own, and mine own know me, even as the Father knoweth me, and I know the Father; and I lay down my life for the sheep."*

In this text, there are three matters that I want to explain. First, I see here complete character: *"I am the good shepherd."* Christ is not a half shepherd, but a shepherd in the fullest possible sense. Second, I see complete knowledge: *"And I know mine own, and mine own know me, even as the Father knoweth me, and I know the Father."* Third, I see complete sacrifice. How preciously that last part concludes the two verses: *"And I lay down my life for the sheep"*! He goes the full length to which sacrifice can go. Let me say that He lays down His *soul* in the place of His sheep; this is the correct translation. He goes the full length of self-sacrifice for His own.

Complete Character

First, then, our text reveals the complete character of our Lord. Whenever the Savior describes Himself by any symbol, that symbol is exalted and expanded, yet it is not able to convey all His meaning. The Lord Jesus fills every type, every figure, and every character; and when the vessel is full, there is an overflow. There is more in Jesus, the Good Shepherd, than you could ever discover from studying a human shepherd. He is the Good, the Great, the Chief Shepherd; but He is much more.

Symbols to describe Him may be multiplied as the drops of dew in the morning, but this multitude will fail to reflect all His brightness. Creation is too small a frame in which to hang His likeness. Human thought is too small, human speech too insufficient, to adequately describe Him. When all the symbols in earth and heaven will have described Him to their utmost, there will remain aspects not yet described. You can force a square to become a circle before you can fully describe Christ in the language of mortal men. He is inconceivably above our ideas, unspeakably above our words.

The Owner of the Flock

Let us think about what Jesus was actually referring to when He described Himself as a shepherd. The shepherd He was talking about is not the type of shepherd that comes to our minds: someone to look after the sheep for a few months until they are large enough to be slaughtered. No, the shepherd in an Oriental society (biblical examples are Abraham, Jacob, and David) is quite another person. The Eastern shepherd is generally the owner of the flock, or at least the son of their owner and therefore their prospective proprietor. The sheep are his own.

On the other hand, Western shepherds seldom, or never, own the sheep they tend. They are employed to take care of them, and they have no other interest in them. In spite of this, the English shepherds I have known are a very excellent set of men as a rule; they have been admirable examples of intelligent workingmen.

Yet they are not at all like the Eastern shepherd, and cannot be, for he is usually the owner of the flock. The Eastern shepherd remembers how he came into possession of the flock, when and where each of his sheep were born, where he has led them, and what trials he has gone through with them. He remembers all this with the added emphasis that the sheep are his own inheritance. The sheep are his wealth. He very seldom has much of a house, and he does not usually own much land. He takes his sheep over a good stretch of country, which is open to everyone in his tribe. However, his flocks are his possession. If you were to ask him, "How much are you worth?" he would answer, "I own this many sheep." In Latin, the word for money is related to the word *sheep* because wool was the wealth of many of the first Romans; their fortunes lay in their flocks.

The Lord Jesus is our Shepherd; we are His wealth. If you ask Him what His heritage is, He will tell you about *"the riches of the glory of his inheritance in the saints"* (Ephesians 1:18). Ask Him what His jewels are, and He will reply, "[The believers] *shall be mine...in that day when I make up my jewels"* (Malachi 3:17). If you ask Him where His treasures are, He will tell you, *"The LORD's portion is his people; Jacob is the lot of his inheritance"* (Deuteronomy 32:9). The Lord Jesus Christ has nothing that He values as much as He does His own people. For their sakes, He gave up all that He had and died naked on the cross. Not only can He say, *"I gave...Ethiopia and Seba for thee"* (Isaiah 43:3), but He *"loved the church, and gave himself for it"* (Ephesians 5:25). He regards His church as being His own body, *"the fulness of him that filleth all in all"* (Ephesians 1:23).

The Caregiver of the Flock

The Eastern shepherd, the owner of the flock, is generally also the caregiver. He takes care of the sheep continuously. There is a fireman in my congregation who lives at the fire station; he is always on duty. I asked him whether he was off duty during certain hours of the day, but he said, "No, I am never off duty." He is on duty when he goes to bed, while he is eating his breakfast, and if he walks down the street. At any time, the alarm may sound, and he must do his job and rush to the fire.

In the same way, our Lord Jesus Christ is never off duty. He takes care of His people day and night. He has declared, *"For Zion's sake will I not hold my peace, and for Jerusalem's sake I will not rest"* (Isaiah 62:1). He can truly say what Jacob did: *"In the day the drought consumed me, and the frost by night"* (Genesis 31:40). He says about His flock what He says about His garden: *"I the LORD do keep it; I will water it* [or watch over it] *every moment: lest any hurt it, I will keep it night and day"* (Isaiah 27:3).

I cannot tell you all the cares a shepherd has concerning his flock because he has many different anxieties. Sheep have about as many complaints as people do. Perhaps you do not know much about them, and I am not going to go into detail because I do not know much about them myself! However, the shepherd knows, and the shepherd will tell you that he leads an anxious life. All the flock is seldom well at one time. One sheep or another is sure to be hurt or sick, and the shepherd spies it out and has eyes and hands and heart ready to help and to give relief. There are many varieties of complaints and needs, and all these are laid on the shepherd's heart. He is both possessor and caregiver of the flock.

The Provider for the Flock

Then, he has to be the provider, too, for there is not a woolly head among the flock that knows anything about selecting good pastures. The season may be very dry, and where there once was grass, there may be nothing but dust. It may be that grass is to be found only beside the rippling brooks, here a little and there a little. However, the sheep do not know anything about that; the shepherd must know everything for them. The shepherd is the sheep's provider.

How to Have Real Joy

Both for time and for eternity, for body and for spirit, our Lord Jesus supplies all our needs out of His riches in glory (Philippians 4:19). He is the great storehouse from which we derive everything. He has provided, He does provide, and He will provide. Every believer may therefore sing, *"The LORD is my shepherd; I shall not want"* (Psalm 23:1).

Dear friend, we often dream that we are the shepherds, or that we, at any rate, have to find some of the pasture. I could not help saying at a recent prayer meeting, "There is a passage in Psalms that says the Lord will do for us what one would have thought we could do for ourselves: *'He maketh me to lie down in green pastures'* (Psalm 23:2)." Surely, if a sheep can do nothing else, it can lie down. Yet to lie down is the very hardest thing for God's sheep to do. The full power of the rest-giving Christ has to come in to make our fretful, worrying, doubtful natures lie down and rest. Our Lord is able to give us perfect peace, and He will do so if we will simply trust in His abounding care. It is the shepherd's business to be the provider; let us remember this and be very happy.

The Leader of the Flock

Moreover, the shepherd has to be the leader. He leads the sheep wherever they have to go. I was often astonished at where the shepherds in southern France, which is very much like Palestine, take their sheep. Once every week, I saw a shepherd come down to Menton and conduct his whole flock to the beach. Honestly, I could see nothing for them but big stones. Folks jokingly said that perhaps this is what made his mutton so hard. However, I have no doubt that the poor creatures got a little taste of salt or something that did them good.

At any rate, sheep follow the shepherd, and away he goes up the steep hillsides, taking long strides, until he reaches points where the grass is growing on the sides of the hills. He knows the way, and the sheep have nothing to do but to follow him wherever he goes. Theirs is not to make the way; theirs is not to choose the path; but theirs is to keep close to his heels.

Don't you see our blessed Shepherd leading your own pilgrimage? Can't you see Him guiding your way? Don't you say, "Yes, He leads me, and it is my joy to follow"? Lead on, O blessed Lord; lead on, and we will follow Your footprints!

The Defender of the Flock

The shepherd in the East also has to be the defender of the flock, for wolves still prowl in those regions. All sorts of wild beasts attack the flock, and the shepherd must run to their aid. So it is with our Shepherd. No wolf can attack us without finding our Lord in arms against it. No lion can roar at the flock without waking One greater than David. *"He that keepeth Israel shall neither slumber nor sleep"* (Psalm 121:4).

The Good Shepherd

Jesus is our Shepherd, then, and He completely possesses a shepherd's character—much more completely than I can describe.

Notice that the text adds an adjective to the word *"shepherd,"* adorning our Shepherd with a chain of gold. The Lord Jesus Christ Himself says, *"I am the good shepherd."* He is *"the good shepherd."* He is not a thief; moreover, He is not a shepherd who deals with the sheep only when he takes them from the fold to the slaughter. He is not a hireling; He does not do only what He is paid or commanded to do. Jesus does everything with tender love, with a willing heart. He throws His soul into it. There is a goodness, a tenderness, a willingness, a powerfulness, a force, an energy in all that Jesus does. He is the best possible shepherd.

Again, He is no hireling, nor is He a loafer. Even shepherds that own their own flocks have neglected them, just as there are farmers who do not cultivate their own farms. However, it is never so with Christ. He is the Good Shepherd, good up to the highest point of goodness, good in all that is tender, good in all that is kind, good in all the roles in which a shepherd can be needed. He is good at fighting, good at ruling, good at watching, and good at leading. He is surpassingly good in every way.

Notice how Christ puts it: *"I am the good shepherd."* This is the truth that I want to bring out: We can say about other shepherds, "He is a shepherd," but Jesus is *the* Shepherd. All other shepherds in the world are mere shadows of the true Shepherd; Jesus is the substance. After all, what we see in the world with our physical eyes is not the substance, but the type, the shadow. What we do not see with our physical eyes, what only our faith perceives, is the real thing. I have seen shepherds, but they are only pictures to me. The Shepherd—the truest, the best, the surest example of a shepherd—is Christ Himself.

Moreover, you and I are the sheep. The sheep that we may see grazing on the mountainside are just types or symbols of us, but we are the true sheep, and Jesus is the true Shepherd. If an angel were to fly over the earth to find the real sheep and the real Shepherd, he would say, "The sheep of God's pasture are men, and Jehovah is their Shepherd. He is the true and real Shepherd of the true and real sheep." All the possibilities that lie in a shepherd are found in Christ. Every good thing that you can imagine to be, or that should be, in a shepherd, can be found in the Lord Jesus Christ.

Now, I want you to notice that, according to the text, the Lord Jesus Christ greatly rejoices in being our Shepherd. He says, *"I am the good shepherd."* He does not confess the fact as if He were ashamed of it, but He repeats it in the tenth chapter of John so many times that it almost reads like the refrain of a song: *"I am the good shepherd."* He evidently rejoices in the fact. He rolls it over His tongue as a sweet morsel. Clearly, this fact brings great contentment to His heart. He does not say in this passage, "I am the Son of God," or "I am the Son of Man," or "I am the Redeemer," but this He says, and He congratulates Himself on it, *"I am the good shepherd."*

This should encourage you and me to firmly grasp the word *shepherd*. If Jesus is so pleased to be my Shepherd, let me be equally pleased to be His sheep. Let me avail myself of all the privileges that are wrapped up in His being my Shepherd, and in my being His sheep. I see that He is not worried about my being His sheep. I see that my needs will not cause Him any perplexity. I see that He will not be inconvenienced by attending to my weakness and troubles. He delights to dwell on the fact, *"I am the good shepherd."* He invites me to come and bring my needs and problems to Him, and then to look up to Him and be fed by Him. Therefore, I will do so.

Doesn't it make you feel truly happy to hear your own Lord Himself say, and say it to you out of His precious Book, *"I am the good shepherd"*? Don't you reply, "Indeed, You are a good shepherd. You are a good shepherd to me. My heart puts emphasis on the word *good* and says about You, 'There is no one who is good but One, and You are that Good One.' You are the Good Shepherd of the sheep"?

We have now looked at the complete character of the Good Shepherd.

Complete Knowledge

May the Holy Spirit bless our text even more while I explain the next idea as best as I can.

The knowledge of Christ toward His sheep, and of the sheep toward Him, is wonderfully complete. I must repeat the text again: *"I know mine own, and mine own know me, even as the Father knoweth me, and I know the Father."*

Christ's Knowledge of Us

First, then, consider Christ's knowledge of His own, and the comparison by which He explains it: *"As the Father knoweth me."* I cannot imagine a stronger comparison. Do you know how much the Father knows the Son, who is His glory, His beloved, His other self—yes, one God with Him? Do you know how intimate the knowledge of the Father must be of His Son, who is His own wisdom, yes, who is His own self? The Father and the Son are one spirit. We cannot describe how intimate that knowledge is, yet that is how intimately, how perfectly, the Great Shepherd knows His sheep.

He knows their number. He will never lose one. He will count them all in that day when the sheep will *"pass again under the hands of him that telleth* [or counts] *them"* (Jeremiah 33:13), and then He will total them up. *"Of them which thou gavest me,"* He said, *"have I lost none"* (John 18:9). He knows the number of those for whom He paid the ransom price.

He knows everything about them. He knows the age and character of every one of His own. He assures us that the very hairs on our heads are all numbered (Luke 12:7). Christ does not have a sheep of which He is unaware. It is impossible for Him to overlook or forget one of them. He has such an intimate knowledge of all who are redeemed with His most precious blood that He never mistakes one of them for another or misjudges one of them. He knows their constitutions—those who are weak and feeble, those who are nervous and frightened, those who are strong, those who are presumptuous, those who are sleepy, those who are brave, those who are sick, sorry, worried, or wounded. He knows those who are hunted by the devil, those who are caught between the jaws of the lion and are

472

shaken until the very life is almost driven out of them. He knows their feelings, fears, and terrors. He knows the secret ins and outs of every one of us better than any one of us knows himself.

He knows your trials—the particular trial that now weighs heavily on you. He knows your difficulties—that special difficulty that seems to block your way. All the ingredients of our lives are known to Him. *"I know mine own...as the Father knoweth me."* It is impossible to have a completer knowledge than that which the Father has of His only begotten Son. It is equally impossible to have a completer knowledge than that which Jesus Christ has of every one of His chosen.

He knows our sins. I often feel glad to think that He always did know our evil natures and what would come of them. When He chose us, He knew what we were and what we should be. He did not buy His sheep in the dark. He did not choose us without knowing all the devious ways of our past and future lives.

> He saw us ruined in the Fall,
> Yet loved us notwithstanding all.

Oh, the splendor of His grace! *"Whom he did foreknow, he also did predestinate"* (Romans 8:29). His election of us implies foreknowledge of all our evil ways. People say that human love is blind. Yet Christ's love has many eyes, and all its eyes are open, and yet He loves us still.

It ought to be very comforting to you that you are known by your Lord in this way, especially since He knows you not merely with the cold, clear knowledge of the intellect, but with the intimate knowledge of love and affection. He knows you in His heart. You are especially dear to Him. You are approved by Him. You are accepted by Him. He knows you by acquaintance, not by hearsay. He knows you by communion with you. He has been with you in sweet fellowship. He has read you as a man reads a book, and He remembers what He has read. He knows you by sympathy with you, for He is a man like yourself.

> He knows what sore temptations mean,
> For He has felt the same.

He knows your weaknesses. He knows the places where you suffer most, for

> In every pang that rends the heart
> The Man of Sorrows had a part.

He gained this knowledge in the school of sympathetic suffering. *"Though he were a Son, yet learned he obedience by the things which he suffered"* (Hebrews 5:8). In all points, He was made like us, and by being made like us, He has come to know us. He knows us in a very practical and tender way.

Suppose that you have a watch, and it will not work, or it works very poorly. Now, suppose that you give your watch to someone who knows nothing about watches, and he says, "I will clean it for you." He will do more harm than good. However, then you meet the very person who made the watch. He says, "I put every wheel into its place. I made the whole thing, from beginning to end." You think to yourself, "I have great confidence in this man. I can trust him with my watch. Surely, he can repair it, for he made it."

It often encourages my heart to think that, since the Lord made me, He can repair me and keep me repaired to the end. My Maker is my Redeemer. He who first made me has made me again, and will make me perfect, for His own praise and glory. That is the first part of this complete knowledge: Christ's knowledge of us.

Our Knowledge of Christ

The second part is our knowledge of Christ. *"And mine own know me, even as...I know the Father."* You may be thinking, "I do not see much meaning in that. I can see a great deal more meaning in Christ's knowing us." Beloved, I see a great deal in our knowing Christ. That He should know me is great condescension, but it must be easy for Him to know me. Being divine, having such a piercing eye as His, it is not difficult for Him to know me. It is amazingly kind and gracious, but not difficult. The marvel is that I could ever know Him. That such a blind, deaf, dead soul as mine could ever know Him, and could know Him as He knows the Father, is ten thousand miracles in one.

Oh, this is a wonder so great that I do not think you and I have fully realized it yet, or else we would sit down in glad surprise and say, "This proves Him to be the Good Shepherd, indeed—not only that He knows His flock, but also that He has taught them so well that they know Him!" With such a flock as Christ has, that He should be able to train His sheep so that they are able to know Him, and to know Him as He knows the Father, is miraculous!

Oh, beloved, if this is true of us, that we know our Shepherd, we can clap our hands for joy! I think it is true even now. At any rate, I know enough about my Lord Jesus that nothing gives me as much joy as to hear more about Him. I am not boasting by saying this. It is only the truth. You can say the same, can't you? If someone were to preach to you the finest sermon that was ever delivered, would it please you if there were no Christ in it? No. Yet you open this book and read about Jesus Christ in words as simple as I could find, and you are satisfied.

> Thou dear Redeemer, dying Lamb,
> We love to hear of Thee:
> No music's like Thy charming name,
> Nor half so sweet can be.

How to Have Real Joy

Take note that this is the way in which Jesus knows the Father. Jesus delights in His Father, and you delight in Jesus. I know you do, and in this the comparison holds true.

Moreover, doesn't the dear name of Jesus stir your very soul? What is it that makes you desire to be involved in holy service for the Lord? What makes your very heart awake and feel ready to leap out of your body? What but hearing of the glories of Jesus? Play on whatever string you please, and my ear is deaf to it. However, once you begin to tell of Calvary and sing the song of free grace and dying love, oh, then my soul opens all her ears and drinks in the music. Then my blood begins to stir, and I am ready to shout for joy! Right now I want to sing,

> Oh, for this love let rocks and hills
> Their lasting silence break,
> And all harmonious human tongues
> The Savior's praises speak.
>
> Yes, we will praise Thee, dearest Lord,
> Our souls are all on flame,
> Hosanna round the spacious earth
> To Thine adored name.

Yes, we know Jesus. We feel the power of our union with Him. We know Him, beloved, so that we will not be deceived by false shepherds. There is a way nowadays of preaching Christ against Christ. It is a new device of the devil to set up Jesus against Jesus, His kingdom against His atonement, His precepts against His doctrines. The half Christ is preached to frighten people away from the whole Christ, who saves the souls of men from guilt as well as from sin, from hell as well as from folly.

However, these false shepherds cannot deceive us in that way. No, beloved, we can distinguish our Shepherd from all others. We can tell Him apart from a statue dressed in His clothes. We know the living Christ, for we have come into living contact with Him, and we could not be deceived any more than Jesus Christ Himself could be deceived about the Father. *"Mine own know me, even as...I know the Father."*

We know Him by our union with Him and by our communion with Him. *"We have seen the Lord"* (John 20:25). *"Truly our fellowship is with the Father, and with his Son Jesus Christ"* (1 John 1:3).

We know Christ by our love for Him. Our souls cling tightly to Him, even as the heart of Christ cleaves to the Father. We know Him by trusting Him. He is *"all my salvation, and all my desire"* (2 Samuel 23:5).

I remember a certain time when I had many questions and doubts as to whether I was a child of God or not. I went to a little chapel, and there I heard a good man preach. I made my handkerchief wet with tears as I heard this simple workingman talk about Christ and His precious blood. Even while I had been preaching the same message to others, I had been wondering whether this truth was mine. However, there in that chapel, hearing it for myself, I knew it was mine, for my very soul lived on it. I went to that good man and thanked him for the sermon. He asked me who I was. When I told him, he turned all kinds of colors. "Why, sir," he said, "that was your own sermon." I said, "Yes, I know it was, and it was good of the Lord to feed me with food that I had prepared for others." I perceived that I had a true taste for what I myself knew to be the Gospel of Jesus Christ. Oh yes, we do love our Good Shepherd! We cannot help it!

And we also know Him by our shared desires, for what Christ wants to do, we also long to do. He loves to save souls, and we love to see them saved. Wouldn't we win all the people on a whole street if we could? Yes, in a whole city and in the whole world! Nothing makes us as glad as the fact that Jesus Christ is a Savior. "Have you read the news in the paper?" people ask. That news is often of small importance to our hearts when compared with news of a spiritual nature.

I happened to hear that a poor servant girl had heard me preach the truth and had found Christ, and I confess that I felt more interest in that fact than in all the rise and fall of our political parties. What does it matter who is in the government, as long as souls are saved? That is the main thing. If the kingdom of Christ grows, all the other kingdoms are of small consequence. That is the one kingdom for which we live, and for which we would gladly die. Even as there is a boundless similarity of desires between the Father and the Son, so there is between Jesus and us.

We know Christ as He knows the Father because we are one with Him. The union between Christ and His people is as real and mysterious as the union between the Son and the Father.

We have a beautiful picture before us. Can you imagine it for a minute? Picture the Lord Jesus with you. He is the Shepherd. Then, around Him are His own people, and wherever He goes, they go. He leads them to green pastures and beside still waters. And there is this specialness about His people: He knows them as He looks on every one of them, and every one of them knows Him. There is a deeply intimate and mutual knowledge between them. As surely as He knows them, they know Him.

The world does not know the Shepherd or the sheep, but they know each other. As surely, as truly, and as deeply as God the Father knows the Son, so does this Shepherd know His sheep. And as God the Son knows His Father, so do these sheep know their Shepherd. Thus, in one company, united by mutual communion, they travel through the world to heaven. *"I know mine own, and mine own know me, even as the Father knoweth me, and I know the Father."* Isn't that a blessed picture? May God help us to be a part of it!

Complete Sacrifice

Last, our text reveals the complete sacrifice of our Lord. His complete sacrifice is described in this way: *"I lay down my life for the sheep."*

These words are given four times in John 10 in different forms. The Savior kept on saying, *"I lay down my life for the sheep."* Read the eleventh verse: *"The good shepherd giveth his life for the sheep."* The fifteenth verse: *"I lay down my life for the sheep."* The seventeenth verse: *"I lay down my life, that I might take it again."* The eighteenth verse: *"I have power to lay it down, and I have power to take it again."* It looks as if this is another refrain of our Lord's personal hymn. I call this passage His pastoral song. The Good Shepherd sings to Himself and to His flock, and this comes in at the end of each stanza: *"I lay down my life for the sheep."*

Did He not mean, first of all, that He was continually doing so? All His life He was, as it were, laying it down for them; He was divesting Himself of the garments of life until He came to be fully disrobed on the cross. All the life He had, all the power He had, He was always giving for His sheep. This is the first meaning of our text.

It also means that the sacrifice was actively performed. It was always occurring as long as He lived, but He did it actively. He did not just die for the sheep, but He laid down His life, which is another thing. Many a man has died for Christ; it was all that they could do. However, we cannot lay down our lives because they are due already as a debt of nature to God. We are not permitted to die at our own will. That would be suicide and would be wrong. Yet the Lord Christ's situation was totally different. He was, as it were, actively passive. *"I lay down my life for the sheep....I have power to lay it down, and I have power to take it again. This commandment have I received of my Father"* (John 10:15, 18).

How to Have Real Joy

I like to think of our Good Shepherd not merely as dying for us, but as willingly dying—laying down His life. While He had that life, He used it for us; and when the time came, He gave up that life on our behalf. He actually did this for us. When Jesus spoke the words of our text, He had not yet given His life. However, now the deed has been done. *"I lay down my life for the sheep"* may now be read, "I have laid down My life for the sheep." For you, beloved, He has given His hands to the nails and His feet to the cruel iron. For you, He has borne the fever and the bloody sweat. For you, He has cried, *"Eloi, Eloi, lama sabachthani?"* meaning, *"My God, my God, why hast thou forsaken me?"* (Mark 15:34). For you, He has breathed His last.

And the beauty of it is that He is not ashamed to declare the object of His sacrifice. *"I lay down my life for the sheep."* Whatever Christ did for the world—and I am not one who would limit the implications of the death of Christ for the world—His particular glory is, *"I lay down my life for the sheep."*

Great Shepherd, do You mean to say that You have died for such as these? What? For these sheep? You have died for them? What? The Shepherd dying for sheep? Surely, You have other objects for which to live and die besides sheep. Don't You have other loves, other joys? We know that it would grieve You to see the sheep killed, torn by the wolf, or scattered, but do You really love these poor creatures so much that You would lay down Your life? "Ah, yes," He says, "I would, and I have!"

Carry your wondering thoughts to Christ Jesus. What? Son of God, infinitely great and inconceivably glorious Jehovah, would You lay Your life down for men and women? They are no more in comparison with You than so many ants and wasps—pitiful and pathetic creatures. You could make millions of them with a word or crush them out of existence by one blow of Your hand. They are weak things. They have hard hearts and wandering wills, and the best of them are no better than they are obligated to be. Savior, did You die for such? He looks around and says, "Yes, I did. I laid down My life for the sheep. I am not ashamed of them, and I am not ashamed to say that I died for them."

No, beloved, He is not ashamed of His dying love. He has told it to His brothers and sisters up in heaven and has made it known to all the servants in His Father's house. This has become the song of that house: *"Worthy is the Lamb that was slain"* (Revelation 5:12)! Let us join in and sing, *"For thou wast slain, and hast redeemed us to God by thy blood"* (v. 9).

Whatever people may say about particular redemption, Christ is not ashamed of it. He glories that He laid down His life for the sheep. Note well, it was for the sheep. He did not say "for the world." The death of Christ has an influence on the world. However, in this verse, He boasts and glories in the particular object of His sacrifice: *"I lay down my life for the sheep."*

The verse could even be read, "I lay down my life *instead* of the sheep." He glories in His substitution for His people. When He speaks of His chosen, He makes it His boast that He suffered in their stead—that He bore, so that they would never have to bear, the wrath of God on account of sin. What He glories in, we also glory in. *"God forbid that I should glory, save in the cross of our Lord Jesus Christ, by whom the world is crucified unto me, and I unto the world"* (Galatians 6:14).

Oh, beloved, what a blessed Christ we have who knows us so, who loves us so—whom we also know and love! May others be taught to know Him and to love Him. Yes, may they come and put their trust in Him, as the sheep put their trust in the shepherd! I ask it for Jesus' sake.

The Power
in Praising God

Contents

Chapter 1

Holy Songs from Happy Saints

Now will I sing to my wellbeloved a song.
—Isaiah 5:1

A prophet inspired by God wrote these words. He did not consider singing a song of praise to be beneath his position. It was no waste of his important time to occupy himself with song. There is no activity under heaven that is more exalting than praising God. However great may be the work for which we are responsible, we will always do well if we pause to spend time in sacred praise.

I do not wish to show a preference for one spiritual exercise over another; otherwise, I think I would endorse the words of an old clergyman who said that a line of praise was even better than a page of prayer—that praise was the highest, noblest, best, most satisfying, and most healthful occupation in which a Christian could be found. If these sentiments may be regarded as the words of the church, the church of old did well to turn all her thoughts in the direction of praising God.

Though the winning of souls is a great thing, though the edifying of believers is an important matter, though the reclamation of backsliders calls for earnest attention, yet never, never, never may we cease from praising and magnifying the name of the Well Beloved. This is to be our occupation in heaven. Let us begin the music now and make a heaven of the church, even here below.

The Strains of the Soul's Song

Days without a Song

The words of the text, *"Now will I sing,"* give us a starting place. *"Now will I sing."* Does that not imply that there were times when the writer of these words could not sing? *"Now,"* said he, *"will I sing to my wellbeloved."* There were times, then, when his voice, his heart, and his circumstances were not in such a state that he could praise God.

My friends, a little while ago, we could not sing to our Well Beloved, for we did not love Him, we did not know Him, we were dead in trespasses and sins. Perhaps we joined in sacred song, but we mocked the Lord in doing so. We stood up with His people, making the same sounds as they did, but our hearts were far from Him. Let us be ashamed of those counterfeit psalms. Let us shed tears of repentance that we could so insincerely have come before the Lord Most High.

Then, after being convicted of our sinful state, our guilt lay heavily on us. We still could not sing to our Well Beloved. Our music was pitched low and in a mournful minor key. We could produce only sighs and groans.

I well remember when my nights were spent in grief and my days in bitterness. A perpetual prayer, a confession of sin, and a bemoaning of myself occupied all my time. I could not sing then, and if any of you are in that condition, I know you cannot sing just now. What a mercy it is that you can pray. Bring forth the fruit that is in season; and in your case, the most seasonable fruit will be a humble acknowledgment of your sin and an earnest seeking for mercy through Christ Jesus. Take care of that, and soon, you, too, will sing a song to your Well Beloved.

Friends in Christ, it has now been a number of years since some of us first believed in Him, but since then, there have been times when we could not sing. Sad for us, there was a time when we did not watch our steps but went astray, when the Flatterer led us from the straight road that leads to heaven and brought us into sin. Then the chastisement of God came on us. Our hearts were broken until we cried out in anguish, as David did in Psalm 51. If we did sing, we could bring out only penitential odes, but no songs. We laid aside all parts of the Psalms that had to do with praising the Lord, and we could only groan forth the notes of repentance. There were no songs for us until, at last, Immanuel smiled upon us once more. We were reconciled again, brought back from our wanderings, and restored to a sense of divine favor.

Besides that, we have occasionally had to sorrow through the loss of the light of God's countenance. It is not always summer weather with the best of us. For the most part,

> We can read our title clear,
> To mansions in the skies.

However, we have our times of fasting when the Bridegroom is not with us. (See Matthew 9:15.) He does not intend that this world should be so much like heaven that we should be willing to stop in it; therefore, He sometimes passes a cloud before the sun so that, in our darkness, we may cry out, *"Oh that I knew where I might find him! that I might come even to his seat!"* (Job 23:3).

Even the means of grace at such times will bring us no comfort. We may go to the throne of mercy in private prayer, but even there, we will perceive little light. If the Lord withdraws Himself, there is no merrymaking in the soul, but sadness, darkness, and gloom covering all. Then we hang our harps on the willows. If anyone requires a song from us, we tell them we are in a strange land, and the King has gone; how can we sing? (See Psalm 137:2–4.) Our hearts are heavy, and our sorrows are multiplied.

Also, we cannot sing the praises of our Well Beloved very well when the church of God is under a cloud. I trust we are such true patriots, such real citizens of the New Jerusalem that, when Christ's kingdom does not advance, our hearts are full of anguish. Beloved, if you happen to be a member of a divided church where the ministry appears to be without power, where there are no additions, no conversions, no spiritual life, then, indeed, you will feel that whatever the state of your own heart, you must sigh and cry for the desolations of the church of God. *"If I forget thee, O Jerusalem, let my right hand forget her cunning"* (Psalm 137:5).

This is the view of every true citizen of Zion. Our hearts may flourish, and our souls may be like well-watered gardens, yet if we see the place of worship neglected, the Lord's house dishonored, the church diminished and brought low, the Gospel held in contempt, infidelity rampant, superstition stalking through the land, the old doctrines denied, and the Cross of Christ made to be of no effect, then we feel we cannot sing. Our hearts are not in tune, our fingers forget the accustomed strings, and we cannot sing a song to our Well Beloved.

With these exceptions, however, I turn to a very different strain and say that the whole life of the Christian ought to be describable by the text, *"Now will I sing to my wellbeloved a song."* From the first moment that our sin is pardoned to the last moment that we are here on earth, it should forever be our delight to sing to our Well Beloved. How can we do this? We can do it in the following ways.

The Power in Praising God

Thanks-feeling

There is such a thing as "thanks-feeling"—feeling thankful. This ought to be the general, universal spirit of the Christian. Suppose you are not rich. Be thankful that you have food to eat, something to drink, and clothes to wear. Suppose that you did not have any hope of heaven. I might say to a sinner, "Be thankful that you are not in hell." However, to a Christian, I would add, "Be thankful that you will never be there, and that, if just now your present joys do not overflow, yet *'There remaineth...a rest to the people of God'* (Hebrews 4:9)." Let that console you.

Is there ever a day in the year, or ever a moment in the day, in which the Christian should not be grateful? Quickly, I can respond: There is never such a day; there is never such a moment. Since we are always receiving precious blessings too numerous to count, let us continuously be exalting the hand that gives them. Before the foundation of the world, our names were engraved on the Savior's hands (Isaiah 49:16). In Christ, we have always been redeemed by His precious blood, always been preserved by the power of God, always been secure of the heritage given to us in covenant by the blood of Christ. Therefore, let us always be grateful. If we are not always singing with our lips, let us always be singing with our hearts.

Thanks-living

Then, we should always be "thanks-living." I think that is a better thing than thanksgiving—thanks-living. How is this to be done? By a general cheerfulness of manner, by an obedience to the command of Him by whose mercy we live, by a perpetual, constant delighting of ourselves in the Lord, and by a submission of our desires to His will. Oh, I wish that our whole life might be a psalm; that every day might be a stanza of a mighty poem; that from the day of our spiritual birth until we enter heaven, we might be pouring forth sacred music in every thought, word, and action. Let us give Him thankfulness and thanks-living.

Thanks-speaking

But then let us add "thanks-speaking." I have written often about the matter of prayer, but perhaps I should be just as earnest in addressing the matter of praise. We do not sing enough, my friends. Do we sing as much as the birds? Yet what do birds have to sing about compared to us? Do you think we sing as much as the angels? Yet they were never redeemed by the blood of Christ. Birds of the air, will you excel me? Angels of heaven, will you exceed me? You have done so, but I intend to imitate you from now on. Day by day, night by night, I will pour forth my soul in sacred song.

Silent Thanks

We may sometimes thank God not only by feeling thankful, living thankfully, and speaking our thanks, but also by silently blessing Him. This consists of suffering patiently and accepting the bad as well as the good from Jehovah's hand. It is often better thanksgiving than the noblest psalm that the tongue could express. When you bow down before Him and say, *"Not my will, but thine, be done"* (Luke 22:42), you show Him honor equal to the hallelujahs of the angels. To feel not only submitted, but also willing, to be anything or nothing as the Lord wills it—this is, in truth, to sing a song to our Well Beloved.

Occasions When We Must Praise Him with Song

When We Are Saved

The first song of praise should come when our souls realize the infinite love of Jesus for us, when we receive the pardon of sin, when we enter into the marriage relationship with Christ as our Bridegroom and Lord. The song becomes the wedding feast. Should it be a marriage without joyfulness? Do you remember, even years ago, that day when you first looked to Him and were filled with joy, when your soul clasped His hands, and you and He were one? Other days I have forgotten, but that day I can never forget. Other days have mingled together unrecognizably, like coins that have been in circulation so long that their engravings are rubbed off. However, that day when I first saw the Savior is as fresh and distinct in all its outlines as though it were yesterday, like a newly minted coin. How can I forget it—that first moment when Jesus told me I was His, and my Beloved was mine (Song 6:3)?

Were any of you saved recently? Then consecrate the occasion. Pour out your soul before the Most High. Now, if never before, let your Well Beloved receive your choicest music.

> *My heart is fixed, O God, my heart is fixed: I will sing and give praise. Awake up, my glory; awake, psaltery and harp: I myself will awake early.*
>
> (Psalm 57:7–8)

> *And in that day thou shalt say, O LORD, I will praise thee: though thou wast angry with me, thine anger is turned away, and thou comfortedst me.*
>
> (Isaiah 12:1)

When We Come to the Lord's Table

Our first joyful days with Christ are sometimes followed by other occasions that are not always as joyful. Sometimes, however, we have our high days and holidays when the King entertains us at a feast. It is often like that when I come to the Communion Supper every Lord's Day. I do not find that it grows stale and flat. On the contrary,

I think that every time I come, I love to commemorate my Lord's sufferings in the breaking of bread better than I did before. Usually, when we do come to the Table, we, who know what it means, feel, *"Now let me sing to my Wellbeloved a song."* It was fitting that the early disciples sang a hymn after that first Lord's Supper. We need some such expression for the sacred joy that rises in our souls at this feast.

Not only when the elements are before you, but also when you hear a sermon that feeds your soul, when you read a chapter of the Bible and the promises are very precious, when you are in private prayer and are able to get very near to Jesus, I know your hearts then say, *"'Now will I sing to my wellbeloved a song.'* He has visited me, and I will praise Him. Where will my strength and rapture be spent but at His dear feet, adoring and magnifying His ever blessed name?" Oh, I wish we would often break through order and decorum to give our Lord a song. He well deserves it. May we not let cold ingratitude freeze the praises on our lips.

Now, recognizing that there are some times when we cannot sing, but that, as a rule, our lives should be a praise, let us return to the text. Sometimes, on choice occasions appointed by providence and grace, our souls will be compelled to say, "Now, if never before; now, beyond all other occasions, I will sing a song to my Well Beloved." I hope that all Christians will feel that way on many occasions. Especially when you come to the table of the Lord's Supper, upon which are the emblems of your Savior's Passion, I trust you will be saying, "I feel I must sing a song to my Well Beloved, for if ever I loved Him, I love Him now."

At a Time of Deliverance

We ought to particularly praise our Lord Jesus Christ, singing a song to our Well Beloved, when we have had a remarkable deliverance. *"You shalt compass me about with songs of deliverance"* (Psalm 32:7), David said. Were you raised from a sickbed? Have you come through great financial difficulty? Through God's help, has your character been cleared from slander? Have you been helped in some endeavor and prospered in the world? Have you seen a child restored from sickness or a beloved wife returned to you from the gates of the grave? Have you just experienced the light of Christ's countenance in your own soul? Have you been freed from a perplexing situation? Has a temptation been removed? Are you in a joyous frame of mind? *"Is any merry? let him sing psalms"* (James 5:13). Oh, give your Well Beloved a song now when the sun is shining and the flowers are blooming. When the year turns to spring and fair weather comes, the birds seem to feel it, and they renew their music. Do the same, believer. *"For, lo, the winter is past, the rain is over and gone"* (Song 2:11). Fill the earth with your songs of gratitude.

In Times of Trial

Yet remember, believer, you should sing songs to your Well Beloved even when troubles overtake you, when sorrows come. He *"giveth songs in the night"* (Job 35:10). Perhaps there is no music as sweet as that which comes from the lips and heart of a tried believer. It is real then. When Job prospered, the devil said, *"Doth Job fear God for nought?"* (Job 1:9). However, when Job lost everything and yet said, *"The LORD gave, and the LORD hath taken away; blessed be the name of the LORD"* (v. 21), then the good man shone like a star on a cloudless night. When Job blessed God, even the devil himself could not insinuate that Job was a hypocrite. Let us be sure to praise God when things go wrong. Make certain that you sing then.

Walking one night with a companion, a holy man listened to the nightingale. He said, "Brother, that bird in the darkness is praising her Maker. Sing, I pray you, and let your Lord have a song in the night." However, the other replied, "My voice is hoarse and not used to singing." "Then," said the other, "I will sing." And he sang, and the bird seemed to hear him and to sing louder still. The man sang on, and as other birds joined, the night seemed sweet with song. After a while, the good man said, "My voice fails me, but this bird's throat holds out longer than mine. I wish that I could fly away where I could sing on forever and forever."

Oh, it is blessed when we can praise God when the sun has gone down, when darkness lowers and trials multiply. Then let us say, "Let me *'sing to my wellbeloved a song.'*" I will tell you exactly what I mean by that. You may have just passed through a very terrible trouble, and you may be almost brokenhearted. If so, you are probably inclined to say, "I will ask the prayers of the church so that I may be sustained." It is quite right, my dear one, to do that, but suppose you could be a little stronger and say, "Now I will sing to my Well Beloved a song!" Oh, it will be grand work. It will glorify God. It will strengthen you. You can say, "Yes, the dear child is dead. I cannot bring him back again, but the Lord has done it, and He always does things right. I will give Him a song, even now." "Yes, the property is gone, and I will go from wealth to poverty. But now, instead of fretfulness, I will give to my Well Beloved extra music from my heart. I will praise Him now." As Job testified, *"Though he slay me, yet will I trust in him"* (Job 13:15). This is the part of a Christian. May God help us ever to act it.

At the Time of Death

Dear friends, we may well sing to our Beloved when it is near the time of our departure. It draws near, and as it approaches, we must not dread it, but rather thank God for it. The swan is said to sing her dying song—a myth, perhaps; but the Christian, God's swan, sings sweetest at the last. Like Simeon of old, he becomes a poet at the last, pouring out his soul before God. (See Luke 2:25–35.) I hope we each desire, if we are spared to old age, to let our last days be perfumed with thanksgiving and to bless and magnify the Lord while yet we linger where mortal ears may hear the song. Break, you chains. Divide, you clouds. Be rolled up, you veil that hides the place of mystery from the world. Let our spirits pass into eternity singing. What a song to our Well Beloved will we pour out from among *"ten thousand times ten thousand"* (Revelation 5:11) singers. (See also verse 12.) We will take our part; every note will be for Him who loved us, who washed us from our sins in His own blood. Each note will be undefiled by sin; each note undistracted and undivided by worldly thoughts; each note full of perfection and acceptable to Him to whom it will be presented. Oh, long-expected day, begin! Our hearts are ready to cry out, "Open, you double doors. Let my spirit pass through the gates so that I may sing a song to my Well Beloved."

Let Everyone Bless His Holy Name

Now I will linger here a minute to address every Christian. Brother, will you sing a song for the Well Beloved? Sister, do you have a song for the Well Beloved? Aged friend, will you give Him a note? Young brother, full of vigor, will you offer a verse full of praise for Him? Oh, if we might all come to the Communion table in the spirit of praise! Perhaps some can dance before the ark like David. Others, perhaps, are on their crutches like John Bunyan's character Ready-to-halt. We read in *The Pilgrim's Progress*, though, that even he laid down his crutches when he heard the sweet music of praise. Let us bless the name of the Lord. The day has passed and been full of mercy. Evening has come. As the sun goes down, let us magnify Him whose mercy lasts through the night, will come again in the morning, and will be with us until nights and days will no more change the scene. Lift up your hearts, brothers and sisters; let every one of you lift up your hands to the name of the Most High. Magnify Him who lives forever. *"Oh that men would praise the Lord for his goodness, and for his wonderful works to the children of men!"* (Psalm 107:8).

The Quality of the Song

It Is a New Song

I suppose that every Christian has found that he has one of the Lord's songs to sing about. *"Now will I sing to my wellbeloved a song."* The Lord's music has one thing about it: It is always new. How very frequently we find in the New Testament that saints and angels sing *"a new song"* (Revelation 5:9). This new song is very different from the songs we used to sing, very different from the songs the world still delights in. Ours is heart-music, soul-music. Ours is real joy—no fiction. Solid joys and lasting pleasures make up the new song of the Christian. New mercies make the song always new. There is a freshness in it of which we never grow weary.

Some of you have heard the Gospel now for fifty years; has it become flat to you? The name of Jesus Christ was known to you as the most precious of all sounds fifty or sixty years ago; has it become stale now? Those of us who have known and loved Him twenty years can say only, "The more we know Him, the sweeter He is; the more we enjoy His Gospel, the more resolved we are to keep to the old-fashioned Gospel as long as we live." We could, indeed, sing a new song, though we have sung the same praises for many years.

It Is a Harmonious Song

The saints' praises have this about them: They are all harmonious. This does not necessarily mean that their voices are. Occasionally, some brother sings very earnestly through his nose, often disturbing those around him; but it does not matter how the voice sounds to the ears of man. What is important is how the heart sounds to the ears of God. If you were in a forest, and there were fifty species of birds all singing at once, you would not notice any discord. The little songsters seem to pitch their songs in keys very different from each other, yet, somehow, all are in harmony.

Likewise, it is very strange that when the saints pray, they all pray in harmony. So it is when they praise God. I have attended prayer meetings where there were people from various Christian denominations. I believe the angel Gabriel would have had difficulty identifying their individual denominations when these saints were on their knees. This is the way it is with praise. I could say,

> The saints in praise appear as one
> In word and deed and mind,
> While with the Father and the Son,
> Sweet fellowship they find.

Though our words are broken and our notes fall short of the melody, if our hearts are right, our words are acceptable, and our music is harmonious to the ears of the Most High.

The Inadequacy of the Song

Beloved, notice that the saints' music always seems very insufficient to them. They feel that they must exceed the limits of earthly praise. There are some of David's psalms in which the Hebrew words are very disconnected and broken, as though the poet had strained himself beyond the power of language. How often do you find the psalmist calling on others to help him praise God? He summons not only other saints, but, as if he feels their numbers are insufficient, he also calls on all creatures that have breath to praise God (Psalm 150:6). How frequently do you find biblical writers invoking the dwellers above the skies, earth, air, and sea to help them lift high the praises of God? And, as if they were not content with all animated beings, you will hear them inviting the trees of the woods to break out and clap their hands while they ask the sea to roar and all creation to magnify the Most High (1 Chronicles 16:28–33).

Devout minds feel as though the whole creation is like a great organ with ten thousand times ten thousand pipes, and we little men, who have God within us, come and put our little hands on the keys and make the whole universe echo with thunders of praise to the Most High. For man is the world's priest, and the man who is blood-washed makes the whole earth his tabernacle and his temple, and everyone in that temple speaks of God's glory. He lights up the stars like lamps to burn before the throne of the Most High and bids all creatures here below to become servants in the temple of the Infinite Majesty. Oh, beloved, may God cause us to be in this state of mind, and though we might think our praises are inadequate and lowly compared to the majesty of Jehovah and His boundless love, yet we will have praised Him acceptably.

It Is a Beneficial Song

I earnestly desire to encourage you to sing a song to your Well Beloved because I am quite sure the exercise will be most fitting and beneficial. Speaking for myself, I will say this: If I did not praise and bless Christ my Lord, I would deserve to have my tongue torn out of my mouth. In addition, if I did not bless and magnify His name, I would deserve to have every stone I walk on in the streets rise up and curse my ingratitude, for I am utterly in debt to

The Power in Praising God

the mercy of God—head over heels in debt to infinite love and boundless compassion. Are you not the same? Then I charge you by the love of Christ to awaken; awaken your hearts now to magnify His glorious name. It will do you much good, my dear ones.

There is, perhaps, no exercise that, on the whole, strengthens us as much as praising God. Sometimes, even when prayer fails, praise will encourage our hearts. It seems to prepare us for action; it pours a holy anointing oil on the head and the spirit; it gives us a joy of the Lord, which is always our strength (Nehemiah 8:10). Sometimes, if you begin to sing in a halfhearted mood, you can sing yourself up the ladder. Singing will often make the heart rise. The song, though at first it may appear to drag, will soon be fitted with wings that lift the spirit. Sing more, my friends, and you will sing more still, for the more you sing, the more you will be able to sing the praises of God. Singing will glorify God; it will comfort you; it will also prove attractive to those who are hesitating to become involved in the life of the church.

The melancholy of some Christians tends to repel seekers, but the holy joy of others tends to attract them. More flies will always be caught with honey than with vinegar, and more souls will be brought to Christ by your cheerfulness than by your gloominess, more by your consecrated joy than by your misery. May God help us to sing praises to Him with heart and life until we sing them in heaven. I do not doubt that we would become more useful if we praised God more; and others would join us, for they would see that God has blessed us. If God makes you feel that you must praise Him more, my purpose will have been accomplished.

I wish I could invite you all to say, "I will sing a song to my Beloved!" However, there are some of you who do not love Him and cannot, therefore, sing to Him. Some years ago, I led my congregation in this hymn:

> Jesus, lover of my soul,
> Let me to Thy bosom fly.

One person present was a total stranger to the Gospel, but that touching expression, "Jesus, lover of my soul," reached his heart. He asked, "Is Jesus the lover of my soul? Then I will love Him, too." He gave his heart to Jesus and became a disciple of Christ. I pray that some who are reading this book will say the same. Then you, also, will sing a song to your Beloved, but first you must pray with repentance and faith. May God help you to seek and find the Savior, Jesus Christ the Lord.

Chapter 2

The Saints Blessing the Lord

Bless the LORD, O my soul: and all that is within me,
bless his holy name.
—Psalm 103:1

L isten to David talking to himself. Earnestly, he is talking to his own soul. Every Christian should learn to soliloquize. The first audience to whom a good man ought to think of preaching is himself. Before we talk to others, we should lecture within the doors of our own hearts. Indeed, if any man desires to excite the hearts of others in any given direction, he must first stir up himself. He who would make others grateful must begin by saying, *"Bless the LORD, O my soul."* David never would have risen to the height of saying, *"Bless the LORD, ye his angels"* (Psalm 103:20), or *"Bless the LORD, all his works"* (v. 22), if he had not first tuned his own voice to the joyful music.

Praise Begins with You

No man is fit to be a conductor of the choirs of heavenly music until he has first learned to sing the song of praise himself. *"Bless the LORD, O my soul"* is the preacher's preparation in the study, without which he will fail in the pulpit. Self-evident as this truth is, many people need to be reminded of it. They are ready to admonish others, but forget that true gratitude to God must, like charity, begin at home.

An old proverb says, "The shoemaker's wife goes barefoot." I am afraid this is too often the case in morals and religion. Preachers especially need to be watchful of themselves so that while they are motivating others to magnify the Lord, they are not shamefully silent themselves. My heart is personally warmed by the glow of thankfulness as I urge you to bless the holy name of Jehovah, our God.

However, what is true of preachers is true of all other Christian workers. When they grow more earnest, the tendency among humans is to turn their passion outward, frequently in the way of faultfinding. It is wonderfully easy to become indignant at the laziness, divisions, coldness, or errors of the Christian church. We can pronounce our judgments against her, declaring her to be weighed in our balances and found lacking, as if it mattered one bit to the church what the verdict of our imperfect scales might be. Instead of writing a tract on the faults of the church, it would be easy to write a lengthy book. However, when it was completed, it would be wise to put it in the fire. Friend, pay attention to those planks in your own eye, and leave the Lord Jesus to clear the specks from the eye of His church. (See Matthew 7:3–4.)

Begin at home. There is indoor work to be done. Instead of vainly pointing to the faults of others, earnestly praise God yourself, saying to your own heart, *"Bless the Lord, O my soul: and all that is within me, bless his holy name."*

How Can We Bless God?

Observe that the psalmist, with his audience of one, had a very choice subject: He was exhorting himself to bless God. In a certain sense, it is not possible for us to bless God. He has all things—what can we give to Him? He blesses us, and in this sense, we cannot bless Him. When we have given our best, we are compelled to confess, *"Of thine own have we given thee"* (1 Chronicles 29:14).

Begin with Gratitude

However, we can bless God by being thankful for the gifts He has given to us, by loving Him in response to His blessings to us, and by allowing these expressions of gratitude to influence our lives so that we speak well of His name and act in ways that glorify Him.

In these ways, we can bless God. We know that He accepts such attempts, poor and feeble though they are. God is pleased with our love and thankfulness. He is blessed by His children's desires and praises.

Bless God for Who He Is

Note that the psalmist blessed God's name, by which is meant His character. Indeed, we may take the names of God literally, for they each represent a reason to be thankful. We will praise *Jehovah*, the self-existent One. We will praise *El*, the mighty God whose power is on our side. We will praise Him who gives Himself the covenant name of *Elohim*, revealing in that name the triune nature of His sacred unity. We will praise *El Shaddai*, the all-sufficient, almighty God, and magnify Him because *"of his fulness have all we received"* (John 1:16).

Whatever other names there are in Scripture, or combination of names, will be exceedingly delightful to our hearts, and we will bless the sacred name. We will bless the Father from whose everlasting love we received our election to eternal life, the Father who has *"begotten us again unto a lively hope by the resurrection of Jesus Christ from the dead"* (1 Peter 1:3). We will bless the

Father of our spirits, who has given us an inheritance among all who are set apart. And we will bless the Son of God, Jesus our Savior, Christ, who has been anointed to redeem. Our hearts dance for joy at every remembrance of Him.

There is not a name of Jesus Christ's person, offices, or relationships that we should forget to bless. Whether He is Immanuel, Jesus, or the Word; whether He is Prophet, Priest, or King; whether He is Brother, Husband, or Friend—whatever name fits His beloved person is dear to us, and we will bless Him with it.

Bless God for the Holy Spirit

And the Holy Spirit, too—our Comforter, the Intercessor, the heavenly Dove, who dwells within our hearts in infinite graciousness—we will surely praise Him, too. Heaven cannot contain the Holy Spirit, yet He finds a home within the hearts of His servants. We are His temple. Each one of His influences will evoke from us grateful praise. If He is like the wind, we will be like wind chimes; if He is like dew, we will bloom with flowers; if He is a flame, we will glow with ardor. In whatever way He moves within us, we will be responsive to His voice. And while He blesses us, we will bless His holy name.

Bless God for His Character

Yet if the name of God is so blessed to us, certainly, the character that lies beneath the name is inexpressibly delightful. Select any attribute of God, and you find a reason for loving Him. Is He unchangeable? Blessed is His name. He loves everlastingly. Is He infinite? Then glory to Him. It is endless affection that He has bestowed on us. Is He omnipotent? Then He will put forth all His power for His own beloved. Is He wise? Then He will not misjudge us or fail to bring us safely to our promised rest. Is He gracious? Then, in that grace, we find our comfort and defense. Whatever there is in God, known or unknown, we will bless.

My God, I cannot comprehend You with my intellect, but I embrace You with my affections. I cannot know You fully with my mind, but I love You completely with my heart. My intellect is too narrow to contain You, but my heart expands to the infinity of Your majesty. I love You, whatever You are. You are unknown in great measure, but You are not unloved by my poor heart. Therefore, the psalmist calls on us to bless the Lord.

I would like to dwell on this emphatic phrase in the psalmist's exhortation: *"his holy name."* Only a holy man can delight in holy things. Holiness is the terror of unholy men. They love sin and consider it liberty, but holiness is slavery to them. If we are saints, we will bless God for His holiness and be glad that, in Him, there is neither spot nor flaw. He is without iniquity. Just and righteous is He. Even to save His people, He would not violate His law. Even to deliver His own beloved from going down into the pit, He would not turn away from the paths of justice. *"Holy, holy, holy, Lord God Almighty"* (Revelation 4:8) is the loftiest cry of cherubim and seraphim in their perfect bliss. It is a joyous song both to the saints on earth and those in heaven. The pure in heart gaze on divine holiness with awestruck joy.

Having briefly examined the words of our text, we will now consider the main points of the exhortation. First, it is comprehensive in its scope and calls us to bless God in the unity and diversity of our nature. Second, it shows us there are numerous attributes of praise that we must carefully consider.

Bless God in Unity and with Diversity

Our first observation, then, will be that this exhortation is remarkably comprehensive. *"Bless the Lord, O my soul"*—there is the unity of our nature; *"and all that is within me"*—there are the diverse powers and faculties that make up the variety of our nature. The unity and the diversity are both summoned to the delightful employment of magnifying God. The psalmist stirs us up to bless God with our whole being, and I pray that the Holy Spirit will help us to do this.

Bless God in the Unity of Your Nature

Bless the Lord with Your True Self

First, the unity of our nature is invited to yield its whole self to the praise of God: *"Bless the LORD, O my soul."* David praised God not only with his lips, not only with his hands on the harp strings, not just with his eyes lifted toward heaven, but also with his soul, his very self, his truest self. Never let me present to God the outward and superficial alone, but let me give to Him the inner and the sincere. Never let me bring before Him merely the outward senses that my soul uses, but the soul that uses these inner faculties. No whitewashed tombs will please the Lord. (See Matthew 23:27.)

"Bless the LORD, O my soul." Let my true self praise Him, the essential "I," the vital personality, the soul of my soul, the life of my life. Let me be true to the core to my God. Let that which is most truly my own vitality expend itself in blessing the Lord.

The soul is our best self. We must not merely bless the Lord with our bodies, which will become dust, but also with our inner, spiritual natures, which make us like angels. Our spiritual natures are that which cause it to be said that in the image of God we were created. My spiritual nature, my loftiest powers, must magnify God—not with a voice that sings a self-righteous song of praise, but with a sincere heart; not with lips that cry "Hosanna" thoughtlessly, but with a mind that considers and intelligently worships. Not within the narrow confines of my body would I sing this song, but I would fill with Jehovah's praise the limitless regions through which my spirit soars on wings of boundless thought. My real self, my best self, will bless the Lord.

Bless the Lord with Your Immortal Self

The soul is also our everlasting self, that which will outlast time. Being redeemed by His precious blood, it will pass through judgment and enter into the worlds unknown, forever to dwell at the right hand of God, triumphant in His eternal love. My immortal soul, why are you spending your energies on mortal things? Will you hunt for fleeting shadows while you are most real and enduring? Will you collect bubbles, knowing that you will endure forever in a life coexistent with God Himself, for He has given you eternal life in His Son Jesus? Bless the Lord, then. So noble a thing as you are should not be occupied with less worthy matters. Raise yourself and, like the angels, adore your God.

Bless God Wholeheartedly

The words suggest yet another meaning. The soul is our active self, our vigor, our intensity. When we speak of a man throwing his soul into a thing, we mean that he does it with all his might. When we say, "There is no soul in him," we do not mean that the man does not live, but that he has no vigor or force of character, no love, no zeal. My most intense nature will bless the Lord. I will not lisp His praises with whispered voice and restricted energy, but I will proclaim them vehemently and ardently in volumes of impassioned song.

Never serve God with a hand hesitant to work, which would willingly withdraw itself from labor if it could. If you do your own business in a lazy fashion, do not do God's business that way. If you go to sleep over anything, let it be over your own efforts to make money or your buying and selling. Always be awake in your service of the Lord. *"Bless the LORD, O my soul"*!

If you have ever been thoroughly awakened, awake now! If you ever were all life, all emotion, all energy, all enthusiasm, enter into the same condition again. Let every part of you be full of ardor, sensitive with emotion, nerved with impulse, borne upward by resolution, impelled by onward force. As Samson, when he smote the Philistines, used every muscle, sinew, and bone of his body in crushing his adversaries, so you should serve God with all and every force you have. *"Bless the LORD, O my soul."* O God, my hands, my tongue, my mind, my heart will all adore You:

Every string will have its attribute to sing.

My united, concentrated, entire being will bless You, You infinitely glorious Jehovah!

Beloved, do not pretend to praise God. Praise Him with all your might. If you are a Christian, be an out-and-out Christian or let Christianity alone. Nothing hinders the glorious kingdom of Christ as much as halfhearted people, who blow hot and cold with the same breath. My friends, be thorough. Plunge into this stream of life as swimmers who dive to the very bottom and swim in the broad stream with intense delight. Do this, or else make no profession of faith.

Bless God with All Your Faculties

Use Your Heart

Then David spoke of the diverse abilities within our nature when he wrote, *"All that is within me, bless his holy name."* I think the psalm itself might indicate that, in succession, all our mental powers and passions should praise God. For instance, when he said, *"Bless the LORD, O my soul,"* he meant, first of all, let the heart bless Him, for that is often synonymous with the soul. The affections are to lead the way in the concert of praise.

Use Your Mind

Yet the psalmist intended, next, to awaken the memory, for he continued by saying, *"Forget not all his benefits"* (Psalm 103:2). May I ask you, beloved friends, to recall what God has done for you? String the jewels of His grace on the thread of memory, and hang them around the neck of praise.

Can you count the leaves of the forest in autumn or number the grains of sand on the ocean floor? Only then could you give the sum of His lovingkindnesses. For mercies beyond count, praise Him without restraint.

Use Your Conscience

Then, let your conscience praise Him, for the psalm goes on to say, *"Who forgiveth all thine iniquities"* (Psalm 103:3). Your conscience once weighed your sins and condemned you. Now let it weigh the Lord's pardon and magnify His grace to you. Count the crimson drops of Calvary and say, "My sins were washed away." Let your conscience praise the Sin-Bearer, who has caused it to flow with peace like a river and to abound in righteousness like the waves of the sea (Isaiah 48:18).

Use Your Emotions

Let your emotions join the sacred choir. If you are like the psalmist, you have many feelings of delight. Bless Him *"who crowneth thee with lovingkindness and tender mercies; who satisfieth thy mouth with good things; so that thy youth is renewed like the eagle's"* (Psalm 103:4–5). Is all within you peaceful today? Sing some sweet verse, like the Twenty-third Psalm. Let the calm of your spirit sound forth the praises of the Lord. Do your days flow smoothly? Then consecrate your music to the Lord. Are you joyful this day? Do you feel the exhilaration of delight? Then praise the Lord with dance.

On the other hand, is there discord within? Does conflict disturb your mind? Then praise Him with the sound of the trumpet, for He will go forth with you to battle. When you return from the battle and divide the spoil, then *"praise him upon the loud cymbals: praise him upon the high sounding cymbals"* (Psalm 150:5). Whatever emotional state your soul is in, let it lead you to bless your Maker's holy name.

Use Your Understanding

Perhaps, however, right now your thoughts exceed your emotions. You may be considering the providence of God as you think about the histories of nations and their rise and fall. You have watched the hand of God in people's lives. So also did David, and he sang, *"The Lord executeth righteousness and judgment for all that are oppressed"* (Psalm 103:6). Let your judgment praise the Judge of all the earth. Let every day's newspaper give you fresh reasons for praise. Every Christian should read the paper with this intent or not at all. God's praise is the true end of history. His providence is the core of all the stories of the empires of the past. To the man of understanding, the centuries are stanzas of a divine epic where the great subject is the Lord of Hosts in His excellency.

Use Your Knowledge

Do not forget to bring your knowledge to help you in your song. You have the Scriptures, and you have the Spirit to teach you their deep insights. Therefore, you can soar above David when he sang, *"He made known his ways unto Moses, his acts unto the children of Israel"*

The Power in Praising God

(Psalm 103:7). God has made known His Son to you and in you; therefore, glorify Him.

The harvests of the fields of knowledge should be stored in the granaries of adoration. Even our human learning should be laid at the Lord's feet. We want to make each stream of knowledge increase our gratitude. Believer, do not know anything that you cannot consecrate to God, or else despise knowing it. Whatever fruits, new or old, are stored in your memory, let them all be laid up for the Beloved and none else. The censer of worship should always smoke with fragrant perfume. Knowledge should supply the spices for the incense, and love should ignite the flame.

Use Your Wonder

Be sure, too, that your faculty of wonder is used in holy things; let your astonishment bless God. If you tried to measure the distance from the east to the west, you would be lost in the immensity before you; bless God with your wonder as you realize that your sins have been removed from you that far (Psalm 103:12). You cannot tell how high the heavens are above the earth, but let your astonishment at the greatness of creation lead you to adoration, for *"so great is his mercy toward them that fear him"* (v. 11).

Use Your Fears

Let even your fears bow low before the Lord. Do you fear because you are frail? *"He remembereth that we are dust"* (Psalm 103:14). Do you tremble at the thought of death? Then praise Him who spares you, though you are before Him like a wildflower withered by the wind as it passes over you (vv. 15–16). From a sense of your own insignificance, magnify the splendor of that gracious love that pities you, even *"as a father pitieth his children"* (v. 13).

The Saints Blessing the Lord

Use Your Hopes

The voices of your hopes are sweet. Do not let them remain silent. As they peer into the future, let them sing, *"The mercy of the LORD is from everlasting to everlasting upon them that fear him"* (Psalm 103:17). What more could hope desire to make her raise her choicest praise? Someday, we will be where even the last verses of Psalm 103 will not be above our experience, for we will see the Lord on the throne that He has prepared in the heavens. Then we will invite angels that *"excel in strength"* (v. 20) and all the heavenly ministry to bless the Lord. How happy we are as we anticipate that day. Filled with expectation, we cry aloud, *"Bless the LORD, O my soul."*

Use Every Faculty

I think you see by now that we could look at every single mental faculty and show that David has given it room to bless God. He showed in a practical way how each individual power of the soul can praise God.

Beloved, we can no longer linger on this point. You know, each of you, what faculty you possess in the greatest strength. I pray you will use it for God. You know what attitude your soul is in just now. Bless God while you are in that mood, whatever it may be. *"All that is within me,"* says the text—then let it be all. Some of us have a sense of humor, and though at times we try to restrain it, it sneaks out. What then? Let us allow even this faculty to be under the Lord's control. It is not necessarily common or coarse. Let it be used for the Lord.

On the other hand, some of you have a touch of melancholy in your nature. Take care to bring it under subjection in praising the Lord. You are the ones to sing those serious melodies, which in some respects are the pearls of song. A little thoughtfulness is good flavoring. Music is at its best when it is pleasingly melancholic.

The Power in Praising God

Use Your Uniqueness

Praise God, my beloved, as you are. Larks do not refrain from singing because they are not nightingales. The sparrow does not refuse to chirp because it cannot imitate the finch. Let every tree of the Lord's planting praise the Lord. Clap your hands, you trees of the woods, while *"fruitful trees, and all cedars"* join in His praise (Psalm 148:9, 13). Both young men and women, the aged and children, praise the name of the Lord. Each one adds his distinct note, and all are important in making perfect harmony.

The Lord would not want you to borrow your brother's tones, but to use *"all that is within* [you],*"* all that is individual to your character, for His glory. Spend all your strength, yes, every atom of it. Keep back nothing, but give *"all that is within* [you]*"* to Him. If everything within you is the Lord's, all that is on the outside of you that is yours will also be His. All your bodily faculties will praise Him, and your inner and outer life will be all for God.

Use Your Possessions

Let your house praise Him. Beneath its roof may there ever be an altar to the God of all. Let your table praise Him. Learn to eat and drink to His glory. Let your bed praise Him. Let the very clothes that you wear, seeing they are gifts of His love, remind you to praise the Lord. Each breath you breathe should inspire a new song to the Preserver of all. Make your life a psalm, and be yourself an incarnate hymn: *"All that is within me, bless his holy name."*

The Qualities of Praise

Now let us consider what the text reveals about the characteristics of praise and the manner in which we are to praise God.

Praise Is Reasonable

First, the suggestion of the text is sensible. God has created all that is within us except the sin that mars us. All our faculties, receptivity, powers, and passions are of the Lord's fashioning. We would not be able to feel, to think, to hope, to judge, to fear, to trust, to know, or to imagine if He had not granted us the power. Who should own the house but the builder? Who should have the harvest but the farmer? Who should receive the obedience of the child but the father? To whom, then, O my soul, should you give respect but to Him who made you all that you are?

Moreover, the Lord has redeemed our entire being. When mankind had gone astray, and all our faculties, like lost sheep, had taken their own roads of sin, Christ came into the world and redeemed our entire nature—spirit, soul, and body—not a part of us, but our complete humanity. Jesus Christ did not die for our souls only, but for our bodies, too. Though at present *"the body is dead because of sin,"* and therefore we suffer pain and disease, yet *"the Spirit is life because of righteousness"*; and *"if Christ be in* [us]," we have a sure guarantee that He will also give life to our mortal bodies (Romans 8:11). We will, at the coming of the Lord, be wholly restored in body and soul by the Lord's divine power. Therefore, let body and soul praise Him who has redeemed both by His most precious blood.

Your body is not yours to pamper; you are to serve the Lord, for His blood has paid your ransom and secured your resurrection. Your soul, your spirit, whatever faculty you have, Christ's blood covers all; therefore, you are not your own. It would be sad, indeed, even to think of having an unredeemed will or an unredeemed judgment. However, it is not so. Every faculty is freed by His ransom. If the blood on the lintel and doorposts has saved the house (Exodus 12:23), then it has saved every room, and every

515

part of our lives should be consecrated to the Redeemer's praise.

Beloved, the Lord has given innumerable blessings to every part of our nature. I wrote of these faculties in the previous section, one by one. It would be very easy to show that all our faculties are the recipients of blessing. Therefore, they should all bless God in return. Every pipe of the organ should yield its quota of sound. As an eagle's every bone, muscle, and feather is made with a view to flight, so is every part of a regenerate man created for praise. As all the rivers run into the sea, so all our powers should flow toward the Lord's praise.

To prove that this is reasonable, let me ask one question: If we do not devote all that is within us to the glory of God, which part is it that we should leave unconsecrated? And the part that is less consecrated to God, what should we do with it? It would be impossible to give a proper answer to this question. An unconsecrated part in a believer's human nature would become a nest of hornets or a den of devils, out of which devils would come to prowl over our entire being. An unsanctified faculty would be a leprous spot, a valley of misery, a Dead Sea, a den of pestilence. To be sanctified, spirit, soul, and body (1 Thessalonians 5:23), is essential to us, and we must have it; it is but our *"reasonable service"* (Romans 12:1). *"All that is within [us]"* must bless God's holy name. To withhold part of the price is robbery; to reserve part of our territory from our King is treason.

Praise Is Necessary

I insist not only that praise is reasonable, but also that it is required. It is necessary that the whole nature bless God, for at its best, when all parts are engaged in the service of praise, it still fails to complete the work, falling short of the praise Jehovah is due. All humans, with all their might, always occupied in all ways in blessing God, would still be no more than a whisper in comparison with the thunder of praise that the Lord deserves. One of our poets expressed it aptly when he wrote,

> But, ah! eternity's too short
> To utter all Thy praise.

Praise Him Fully

It is true. All God's creatures would be incapable of reflecting the whole of divine glory. The mercy and grace God shows to us in the gift of His dear Son is so great that the church militant on earth and the church triumphant in heaven together are not capable of offering sufficient praise. Let us not, therefore, insult the Lord with half when the whole is not enough. Let us not bring Him the tithe, when, if we had ten times as much, we could not magnify Him as we should.

We must, moreover, give the Lord all because divided powers in every case lead to failure. Those who have succeeded in anything have almost always concentrated on one thing. He who is a jack-of-all-trades is a master of none. He who can do a little of this and a little of that never does much of any one thing. The fact is that there is enough water in the stream of our being to turn only one waterwheel, and if we divide it into many trickling brooks, we will accomplish nothing. The right thing to do is to dam up all our forces and allow them to expend themselves in one direction. Then we can pour them all forth on the constantly revolving wheel of praise to God. How can we afford to let life evaporate in trifles when one aim only is worthy of our immortal being?

We who have been baptized by profession of faith were taught in that solemn ceremony to bless the Lord with our entire being. We were not sprinkled randomly, but, by the outward sign, we were *"buried with him by baptism into death"* (Romans 6:4); we were immersed into the name of the triune God. If our baptism meant anything, it declared that, from that point on, we were dead to the world. We owned no life but that which came to us by way of the resurrection of Jesus. As the water flowed over our heads, we surrendered our minds, with all their powers of thought, to Jesus. Over the heart, the veins, the hands, the feet, the eyes, the ears, the mouth, the significant element poured itself, symbol of that universal consecration that floods all the inward nature of every sanctified believer. I charge you who have been baptized, do not corrupt your profession of faith.

All or Nothing at All

Remember, beloved, this one striking point: Jesus Christ will have all of us or nothing. He will have us sincere, earnest, and intense, or He will not have us at all. I see the Master at the table. His servants place before Him various meats so that He may eat and be satisfied. He tastes the cold meats, and He eats the bread hot from the oven. As for tepid drinks and half-baked cakes, He pushes them away with disgust. To those who are cold and are mourning their coldness, He will give heat. He will look on those who are hot, who serve Him with the best they have. However, to the man in the middle, the lukewarm, He says, *"I will spue thee out of my mouth"* (Revelation 3:16). Jesus cannot bear lukewarm religion; He is sick of it.

Much of the religion of this present time is nauseating to the Savior rather than acceptable. *"If the LORD be God, follow him: but if Baal, then follow him"* (1 Kings 18:21). Let there be no mockery, but be true to the core. Be thorough; throw your soul into your religion. I charge you to stand back awhile and count the cost. If you wish to give Christ a little and Baal a little, you will be cast away and utterly rejected—the Lord of heaven will have nothing to do with you. *"Bless the LORD,"* then, *"all that is within me,"* for only such sincere and undivided honor can be accepted by the Lord.

Wholehearted Praise Is Beneficial

I now ask you to give your attention to the next observation: Sincere praise is good for us. To be wholehearted in the praise of God elevates our faculties. There can be no doubt that many a person's powers have been debased by the object being pursued. Poets who might have been great poets have missed the highest seats of honor because they have selected trivial topics or impure themes. Therefore, the best features of their poetry have never been fully developed. *"Bless the LORD,"* and you will be a person who reaches your fullest capacity. This is the way to reach the loftiest peak of human attainment.

Praise Promotes Spiritual Growth

Consecration cultivates our spiritual development. To praise is to learn. To bless God is also useful to us in terms of preventing self-centeredness. We cannot bless God and, at the same time, idolize ourselves. Praise preserves us from being envious of others, for by blessing God for all we have, we learn to bless God for what other people have. I consider it to be a great part of praise to be thankful to God for making better men than I.

If we are always blessing the Lord, we will be saved from complaining; the spirit of discontent will be ejected by the spirit of thankfulness. This will also deliver us from laziness, for if all our powers magnify the Most High, we will scorn the soft couch of ease and seek the place of service in order to bring more honor to our Master.

Praise Is Becoming

Nothing beautifies a person like praising God. To plunge our whole nature in adoration adorns the spirit. I was told by one who experienced the revivals in Northern Ireland years ago that he never saw the human face look so lovely as when it was lit up with the joy of the Holy Spirit during those times of refreshing.

You know how pleasing landscapes appear when the sun shines on them. The scenery has not half its charms until the sun of this great world enriches the view with its wealth of color, making all things glow with glory. Praise is the sunlight of life. Beneath a cloud of indifference, some of you conceal all the beauty of your character. You are like the lovely mountains in the Lake District of Cumbria. When they are enshrouded in mist, little or nothing of them is visible.

Like a heavenly wind, may grace drive away the fog of despondency and discontent and shed the sunlight of true praise all over our souls. Then the beauty of our new creation will be observed. May we have many lovely praising Christians abounding in our world.

Praise Is Good for Others

While wholehearted praise is beneficial to us, it is also useful to others. I am persuaded that many souls are converted by the cheerful demeanor of Christians. Many who are already converted are greatly strengthened by the holy joy of their brothers and sisters in the Lord. You cannot do more effective good than by living a happy, consecrated life spent in blessing God. Do not think that contemplation is the fairest flower of piety. Some prominent Christians appear to resemble Christ in the sorrow that marred His face rather than in the joy that sustained His spirit.

Jesus sorrowed so that we might rejoice. It is truly Christlike to *"rejoice in the Lord alway"* (Philippians 4:4). We should seek to have Christ's joy fulfilled in ourselves. If anything is cheerful, joyous, glistening, bright, full of heaven, it is the life of a man who blesses God all his days. This is the way to win souls. We will not catch flies with vinegar. We must use honey. We will not bring men into the church by displaying black crepe and shrouds in the windows of our churches while standing silently at the door like funeral directors. No, we must tell the truth and show sinners the best robe, the wedding ring, and the silver sandals of joy and gladness. We must sing,

> The men of grace have found,
>   Glory began below;
> Celestial truths on earthly ground
>   From faith and hope do grow.

In Thomas Cooper's *Plain Talk*, I read a story of a Sunday school teacher who was in a sad state of mind. He announced a somber hymn for the class to sing:

> Ah, whither should I go
> Burden'd, and sick, and faint.

No one seemed too inclined to sing, so the leader asked a certain fellow named Martin to start a song. "No, no," said Martin. "I'm neither burdened, nor sick, nor faint. I'll start no tune, not I!"

"Well, then, Brother Martin," said the leader, "pick out a song you like." So, with all the power of his lungs, Martin sang,

> Oh, for a thousand tongues to sing
> My great Redeemer's praise.

That is the hymn, my friend. Keep to that. If you do not have a thousand tongues, at least let the one you have continue to bless the Lord while you have any breath.

The Power in Praising God

Praise Prepares Us for Heaven

Finally, all this praise is preparatory. If we can strive for constant praise now, it will get us ready for all that lies ahead. We do not know what will happen to us between now and heaven, but we can easily predict the final result. We are harps that will be tuned for the concerts of the blessed. The Tuner is putting us in order. He sweeps His hands along the strings. There is a discord from every note, so He begins first with one string, and then moves to another. He stays at each string until He hears the exact pitch.

The last time you were ill, one of your strings was tuned. The last time you had a bad debt or trembled at declining business, another string was tuned. And so, between now and heaven, you will have every string set in order. You will not enter heaven until all are in tune.

Have you ever gone to a place where they make pianos and expected to hear sweet music? The tuning room is enough to drive a person mad. In the factory, you hear the screeching of saws and the noise of hammers, and you say, "I thought this was a place where they make pianos." Yes, so it is, but it is not the place where they play them.

Earth is the place where God makes musical instruments and tunes them. Between now and heaven, He will put all that is within them into proper condition for blessing and praising His name eternally. In heaven, every part of our being will bless God without any difficulty. There will be no need for a preacher to exhort you. There will be no need for you to talk to yourself and say, *"Bless the Lord, O my soul."* You will do it as naturally as you now breathe. You never give any consideration as to how often you breathe, nor do you have any plan laid down as to when your blood will circulate. These matters come naturally to you. In heaven, it will be your nature to praise God. You will breathe praise. You will live in an atmosphere of adoration. Like those angels who for many ages, day without night, have circled the throne of Jehovah rejoicing, so will you. However, I will not write much on that, or you will be wanting to fly away to our own dear country—

> Where we will see His face,
> And never, never sin;
> But from the rivers of His grace
> Drink endless pleasures in.

You must stay a little longer in the tents of Kedar and mingle with the men of soul-distressing Meshech. (See Psalm 120:5.) When daybreak comes and the shadows flee away, say to your soul, *"Bless the LORD, O my soul: and all that is within me, bless his holy name."*

For Those Who Cannot Praise

I wish all my readers could, but some of you cannot bless God at all. It would be useless for me to tell you to do so. You are dead in your sin. I read a story the other day of a woman convinced of her sinful state by a single dream. She dreamed that she saw her minister standing in the middle of a number of flowerpots that he was watering. She thought that she was one of the flowerpots, but the minister passed her by and said, "It is no use watering that plant, for it is dead. I must pass by the dead plants."

Oh, sinner, can you bear this? I cannot invite you to sing the believer's song of praise. Can you bear to be left out? Though I pass you by, I pray that the Lord will look at you and say, "Live!"

Before I close, I must tell you something else, which is meant for dead sinners as well as for living saints. It is this: *"Believe on the Lord Jesus Christ, and thou shalt be saved"* (Acts 16:31). May God grant to you that saving faith, for Christ's sake.

Chapter 3

Prayer Perfumed with Praise

In every thing by prayer and supplication with thanksgiving let your requests be made known unto God.
—Philippians 4:6

A ccording to the text, we are to make our requests known to God both by prayer and supplication. If any distinction is intended here, I suppose that by prayer is meant the general act of devotion and the mention of our usual needs. By supplication, I think would be intended our distinct entreaties and special petitions. We are to offer the general prayer common to all the saints, and we are to add to it the special and definite petitions that are unique to us. We are to worship in prayer, for God is to be adored by all His saints. Then we are to request His attention for our own needs, according to the words of the text, letting God know our requests.

Do not forget this second form of worship. There is a good deal of generalizing in prayer. God forbid that we should say a word against it, insofar as it is sincere worship, but we need to have more definite pleading with God, asking Him for specific things with a clear knowledge of what we ask. You will hear prayers at prayer meetings in which everything is asked in general but nothing in particular. Yet the reality and heartiness of prayer will often be best displayed by requests for distinct blessings.

See how Abraham, when he went to worship the Lord, did not merely adore Him, and in general pray for His glory, but on a special occasion, he pleaded concerning the promised heir. (See Genesis 15:2–6.) Another time, he cried, *"O that Ishmael might live before thee!"* (Genesis 17:18). On one special occasion, he interceded for Sodom. (See Genesis 18:20–33.)

Elijah, when on top of Mount Carmel, did not pray for all the blessings of God in general, but for rain, for rain then and there. He knew what he was driving at, kept to his point, and prevailed. (See 1 Kings 18:41–45.)

My beloved friends, we have many needs that are so burdensome. As they weigh on us heavily, they become very distinct and definite. We ought to have just as many clearly defined petitions that we humbly ask God to answer. We should watch with eager expectancy for His divine response so that, when we receive His answer, we may magnify our Lord.

Combining Prayer and Praise

This is the point I want to make: Whether we are praying a general prayer or asking for a specific need to be met, we are to offer both requests *"with thanksgiving."* We are to pray about everything, and every prayer should be blended with praise. Since we are to *"pray without ceasing"* (1 Thessalonians 5:17), it follows that we should always be in a thankful condition of heart. Since we are not to pray without thanksgiving, it is clear that we should always be ready to give thanks to the Lord. We must say with the psalmist, *"Thus will I bless thee while I live: I will lift up my hands in thy name"* (Psalm 63:4). The constant tenor and spirit of our lives should be adoring gratitude, love, reverence, and thanksgiving to the Most High.

This blending of thanks with devotion is always to be maintained. We must offer *"prayer and supplication with thanksgiving."* Even if the prayer struggles out of the depths, its wings should be silvered with thanksgiving. Even if a prayer is offered by someone who is on the verge of death, in the last few words his trembling lips can utter, there should be notes of gratitude mixed with the words of petition.

The law instructed that *"with all thine offerings thou shalt offer salt"* (Leviticus 2:13). The Gospel states that all your prayers should be offered with praise (Philippians 4:6). "One thing at a time" is considered to be a wise proverb, but, in this case, I must risk contradicting it. Two things at a time are better when the two are prayer and thanksgiving. These two holy streams flow from one common source: the Spirit of life who dwells within us. They are expressions of the same holy fellowship with God; therefore, it is right that they should mingle as they flow and find expression in the same holy exercise.

Supplication and thanksgiving so naturally run into each other that it would be difficult to keep them separate. Like kindred colors, their shades run into each other. Our very language seems to indicate this closeness, for there is little difference between the phrases "to pray" and "to praise." A psalm may be either a prayer or praise or both. There is another form of utterance, which is certainly prayer, but is used as praise and is really both. I refer to that joyous Hebrew word that has been imported into numerous languages: *Hosanna.* Is it a prayer? Yes, it means "Save, Lord." Is it praise? Yes, for it is tantamount to "God save the king" and is used to extol the Son of David.

While we are here on earth, we should never attempt to make a distinction between prayer and praise. We should neither praise without prayer nor pray without praise. With every prayer and supplication, we should mingle thanksgiving as we make our requests known to God.

This commingling of precious things is admirable. It reminds me of that verse in which the king is described as coming from the wilderness in his chariot *"like pillars of smoke, perfumed with myrrh and frankincense, with all powders of the merchant"* (Song 3:6). There is the myrrh of prayer and the frankincense of praise. In ancient Israel, the holy incense of the temple sanctuary yielded the smoke of prayer, which filled the Holy Place. With it, there was the sweet perfume of choice spices, which may be compared to praise. Prayer and praise are like the two cherubim on the ark of the covenant. They must never be separated.

In the model of prayer our Savior has given us, the opening part is praise rather than prayer: *"Our Father which art in heaven, hallowed be thy name"* (Matthew 6:9). The closing part of it is praise: *"For thine is the kingdom, and the power, and the glory, for ever. Amen"* (v. 13).

The Example of David

David, who is the great tutor and example of the church as to her worship, being at once her poet and preacher, took care in almost every psalm, though the petition was agonizing, to mingle exquisite praise. For instance, in the psalm written after his great sin with Bathsheba, one would think that he might have almost forgotten or have feared to offer thanksgiving while he was trembling with sighs and groans and tears under a great sense of wrath. Yet before the psalm that begins *"Have mercy upon me, O God"* can come to a conclusion, the psalmist has said, *"O Lord, open thou my lips; and my mouth shall show forth thy praise"* (Psalm 51:15). He could not pen the last word without beseeching the Lord to build the walls of Jerusalem, adding the promise, *"Then shalt thou be pleased with the sacrifices of righteousness, with burnt offering and whole burnt offering: then shall they offer bullocks upon thine altar"* (v. 19).

I do not need to quote other instances, but it was almost always the case that David warmed himself into praise by the fire of prayer. He began with many broken notes of complaining, but he mounted and glowed and, like the lark, sang as he ascended. When at first his harp was muffled, he sang a few mournful notes. Then he became excited until he could not restrain his hand from that well-known and accustomed string reserved for the music of praise alone.

There is a passage in which he seemed to have caught the very idea that I want you to focus on: *"I will call upon the LORD, who is worthy to be praised: so shall I be saved from mine enemies"* (Psalm 18:3). He was in such a condition that he said, *"The sorrows of death compassed me, and the floods of ungodly men made me afraid. The sorrows of hell compassed me about: the snares of death prevented me"* (vv. 4–5).

Driven by distress, he declared that he would call upon the Lord; that is, he would pray. Yet he did not regard God only as the hearer of his prayer, but as One who is deserving of his praise: *"I will call upon the LORD, who is worthy to be praised."* Then, as if inspired to inform us that the blending of thanksgiving with prayer makes prayer infallibly effective, he added, *"So shall I be saved from mine enemies."*

The Example of Paul

If this habit of combining thanksgiving with prayer is found in the Old Testament saints, we have a right to expect it even more in the New Testament believers, who in clearer light perceive fresh reasons for thanksgiving. I will use Paul as an example. He told us that those things that we have seen in him, we are to do (Philippians 4:9), for his life was in harmony with his teachings.

Notice how frequently he began his letters with a mixture of supplication and thanksgiving. Look at Romans 1, and you will see this fusion of precious metals:

> *First, I thank my God through Jesus Christ for you all, that your faith is spoken of throughout the whole world. For God is my witness, whom I serve with my spirit in the gospel of his Son, that without ceasing I make mention of you always in my prayers.* (vv. 8–9)

Here we find both *"I thank my God"* and *"I make mention of you always in my prayers."* This was not purposefully written to correspond to the intention of our text; it was natural for Paul to thank God when he prayed.

Look at Colossians 1:3: *"We give thanks to God and the Father of our Lord Jesus Christ, praying always for you."* To the same effect, we read in 1 Thessalonians 1:2: *"We give thanks to God always for you all, making mention of you in our prayers."* Look also at 2 Timothy 1:3: *"I thank God, whom I serve from my forefathers with pure conscience, that without ceasing I have remembrance of thee in my prayers night and day."* And since it is so in other epistles, we are not at all surprised to find a mixture of prayer and praise in Philippians 1:3–4: *"I thank my God upon every remembrance of you, always in every prayer of mine for you all making request with joy."*

It is noteworthy in itself (and those to whom Paul wrote must have remembered the incident) that in Philippi, Paul and Silas prayed and sang praises to God at midnight so that the prisoners heard them. It is clear that Paul habitually practiced what he here preached in our text. His own prayers were not offered without thanksgiving.

With this as an introduction, I invite you to consider, carefully and prayerfully, the grounds of thanksgiving in prayer, the evil of its absence, and the result of its presence.

The Basis for Thanksgiving in Prayer

There are reasons for mingling thanksgiving with prayer. We have abundant cause, my friends, for being thankful at all times. We do not come to God in prayer as if He had left us absolutely penniless, crying to Him like starving prisoners begging through prison bars. We do not ask as if we had never received a single cent from God before and doubt that we will receive anything now. On the contrary, having already been the recipients of immense favors, we come to a God who abounds in lovingkindness, who is willing to shower good gifts on us and waits to be gracious to us. We do not come to the Lord as slaves to an unfeeling tyrant, craving a blessing. Instead, we come as children who approach their loving Father expecting to receive abundantly from His liberal hands. Thanksgiving is the right spirit in which to come before the God *"who daily loadeth us with benefits"* (Psalm 68:19). Think for a while what reasons you have to be thankful in prayer.

Prayer Is Possible

First of all, be thankful that such a thing as prayer is possible. That a finite creature can speak with the infinite Creator, that a sinful being can have an audience with the infinitely holy Jehovah is astounding. It is worthy of thanksgiving that God commanded prayer and encouraged us to draw near to Him. Moreover, it is amazing that He should have supplied all the things necessary to practice the sacred exercise. He has set up a blood-sprinkled mercy seat. He has prepared a High Priest, who *"ever liveth to make intercession for* [us]*"* (Hebrews 7:25). To these, He has added the Holy Spirit, who *"helpeth our infirmities: for we know not what we should pray for as we ought: but the Spirit itself maketh intercession for us"*

(Romans 8:26). Everything is ready, and God waits for us to come to Him with our requests.

He has not only set before us an open door and invited us to enter, but He has also given us the right spirit with which to approach. The grace of supplication is poured out upon us and worked in us by the Holy Spirit. What a blessing it is that we do not attempt prayer by chance, as if we were trying a questionable experiment. Neither do we come before God hopeless, desperately afraid that He will not listen to our cry. Rather, He has ordained prayer to be the regular business of heaven and earth and sanctioned it in the most solemn manner. Prayer may climb to heaven, for God has Himself prepared the ladder and set it down before us. At the top of that ladder is the Lord Himself in His covenant capacity, receiving our petitions and sending His attendant angels with answers to our requests. Will we not bless God for this?

Prayer Is Permissible

Let us praise His name, dear friends, especially since you and I are still spared to pray and permitted to pray. What if we are greatly afflicted? We should be glad that, because of the Lord's mercy, we are not consumed (Lamentations 3:22). If we had received our due, we would not have been on praying ground and pleading terms with Him. It is for our comfort and to God's praise that we can still stand with bowed head and cry, *"God be merciful to me a sinner"* (Luke 18:13). We are free to cry out, like sinking Peter, *"Lord, save me"* (Matthew 14:30). Like David when he was fleeing from Saul, we may be unable to go to the temple, but we can still go to God in prayer. The Prodigal has lost his wealth, but he has not lost his power to ask for restoration. Although he has been feeding pigs, he is still a man who has not lost his senses. Temporarily, he may have forgotten his father, but his father has not forgotten him. He may get up and return to his father. He may pour out his soul to his father's heart. Therefore, let us thank God that He has never said to us, *"Seek ye me in vain"* (Isaiah 45:19).

If we find a desire to pray trembling within our souls, if we feel some hope in the promise of our gracious God even though that hope is almost extinct, if our hearts still groan after holiness and after God even though they have lost their power to pray with joyful confidence as they once did, yet let us be thankful that we can pray, even if it is but a little. In the will and power to pray lies the capacity for infinite blessedness: The one who has the key of prayer can open heaven. Yes, he has access to the heart of God. Therefore, bless God for prayer.

Prayer Is Reasonable

Beyond the fact of prayer and our power to exercise it, there is a further ground for thanksgiving in that we have already received great mercy at God's hands. We are not coming to God to ask favors and receive them for the first time in our lives. Why, blessed be His name, if He never granted me another request, I have enough for which to thank Him as long as I have any being. Remember this: Whatever great things we are about to ask, we cannot possibly be seeking for blessings one-half as great as those we have already received if we are indeed His children. If you are a Christian, you have life in Christ. Are you about to ask for food and clothes? Life is more than these. You have already obtained Christ Jesus. He who did not spare Him will not deny you anything. Is there anything to compare to the infinite riches that are already ours in Christ Jesus?

Let us perpetually thank our Benefactor for what we have while we are requesting something more. Should it not be so? The memory of His great goodnesses runs over into our requests until our petitions are baptized in gratitude. While we come before God empty-handed to receive of His goodness, we should never appear before Him empty, but come with the fat of our sacrifices, offering praise and glorifying God.

Prayer with Acceptance Is Triumphant

Furthermore, when we come before God in the hour of trouble, remembering His great goodness to us in the past and therefore thanking Him, we ought to have enough faith to believe that the present trouble, about which we are praying, is sent in love. You will win with God in prayer if you can look at your trials in this light: "Lord, I have this *'thorn in the flesh'* (2 Corinthians 12:7). I beg You to deliver me from it, but, meanwhile, I bless You for it. Although I do not understand the why or the wherefore of it, I am persuaded there is love within it. Therefore, while I ask You to remove it because it seems painful to me, if it may to Your better knowledge work to my good, I bless You for it. I am content to endure it as long as You see fit."

Is that not a sweet way of praying? "Lord, I am in need. Please answer my request. Meanwhile, if You do not, I believe it is better for me to be in need, and so I praise You for my necessity while I ask You to supply it. I glory in my infirmity (2 Corinthians 12:9) even while I ask You to overcome it. I triumph before You in my affliction, blessing You for it even while I ask You to help me through it and rescue me out of it." This is a royal way of praying. Such a combination of prayer and thanksgiving is more precious than gold.

Prayer Works

Furthermore, beloved, when we are on our knees in prayer, we should bless God that our prayers have been answered so many times before. We should say, "Here Your poor petitioner bends before You to ask again, but before he asks, he thanks You for having heard him so many times before. I know that You hear me always (see John

The Power in Praising God

11:42); therefore, I continue to cry to You. My praises urge me to make fresh petitions, encouraging me in the full confidence that You will not send me away empty-handed." Why, many of the mercies that you possess and rejoice in today are answers to prayer. They are dear to you because, like Samuel, whom his mother so named because he was "asked of God," they came to you as answers to your earnest requests.

When mercies come in answer to prayer, they have a double delight about them, not only because they are good in themselves, but because they are certificates of our favor with the Lord. Well, then, since God has heard us so often, and we have the proof of His hearing, should we ever grumble and complain while we pray? Should we not rather feel an intense delight when we approach the throne of grace, a rapture awakened by sunny memories of the past?

Prayer Develops Our Faith

We should pray with complete thanksgiving because God has given us the mercy we seek. I wish we could learn this high virtue of faith. In talking with my dear friend George Müller, I have frequently been astonished at the way in which he mentions that he has for so many months and years asked for a specific request and praised the Lord for its answer. He praises the Lord for it as though he has actually obtained it. Even in praying for the conversion of a person, as soon as he has begun to intercede, he also begins to praise God for the conversion of that person. Though I think he told me that he has been praying thirty years for a certain request, and the answer has not yet been received, still all the while he continues to thank God because he knows the prayer will be answered. He believes that he has his petition and begins to magnify the Giver of it.

Is this unreasonable? How often do we thank people for actions that they have not yet accomplished? For example, if you were to promise some poor person that you would pay his rent when it came due, he would thank you directly, though not a cent had left your pocket. We have enough faith in our fellowmen to thank them beforehand, so surely we can do the same with our Lord. Should we not be willing to trust God for a few months or even for years if His wisdom asks us to wait? This is the way to win with Him. The Scripture says, *"What things soever ye desire, when ye pray, believe that ye receive them, and ye shall have them"* (Mark 11:24).

As a man's promissory note stands for his pledge to repay the money, so let God's promise be accounted as the performance. Will heaven's banknotes not pass as cash? Yes, truly, they will have unquestioned acceptance as currency among believers. We will bless the Lord for giving us what we have sought in accordance with His will since our having it is a matter of absolute certainty. We will never thank God by faith and then find that we were fooled. He has said, *"Whatsoever ye shall ask in prayer, believing, ye shall receive"* (Matthew 21:22). Therefore, we can rest assured that the thanksgiving of faith will never bring shame to the face of the man who offers it.

Surely, friends, if the Lord does not answer the prayer we are offering in the way that we desire, He is still so good, so supremely good. Therefore, we will bless Him whether or not He answers in the way we have requested. We should praise Him when He does not answer us and bless Him for refusing our desires. How devoutly might some of us thank Him that He did not answer our prayers when we sought for harmful things in the ignorance of our childish minds. If we asked for meat, He might have sent us quails in His anger. (See Numbers 11:4–6, 18–23, 31–34.) While the meat was yet in our mouths, His wrath might have come upon us. However, in love, He would not hear us. Blessed be His name for closing His ear in pity! Let us adore Him when He keeps us waiting at His doors, thank Him for denials, and bless Him for refusals, believing always that Ralph Erskine spoke the truth when he said,

> I'm heard when answered soon or late,
> Yea, heard when I no answer get:
> Yea, kindly answered when refused,
> And treated well when harshly used.

Faith glorifies the love of God, for it knows that the Lord's roughest usage is only love in disguise. We are not so low-down as to make our songs or praise depend upon the weather or the quantity of our blessings. Blessed be His name. He must be right even when He seems at cross purposes with His people. We are not going to quarrel with Him like silly children with their babysitters because He does not happen to grant us every desire of our foolish hearts. Though He slay us, we will trust in Him even if He declines our requests. (See Job 13:15.)

We ask Him for our daily bread, and if He withholds it, we will praise Him. Our praises are not dependent upon His answers to our prayers. As the prophet wrote:

> *Although the fig tree shall not blossom, neither shall fruit be in the vines; the labour of the olive shall fail, and the fields shall yield no meat; the flock shall be cut off from the fold, and there shall be no herd in the stalls: yet I will rejoice in the Lord, I will joy in the God of my salvation.* (Habakkuk 3:17–18)

This is the sum of what I have said: Under every condition, and in every need, draw near to God in prayer, but always bring thanksgiving with you. As Joseph said to his brothers, *"Ye shall not see my face, except your brother be with you"* (Genesis 43:3), may the Lord say to you, "You will not receive My smile unless you bring thankfulness with you."

Let your prayers be like those ancient manuscripts that one sometimes sees, in which the initial letters of the prayers are gilded and adorned with multiple colors, the work of masterful artists. Let even the general confession of sin and the litany of mournful petitions have at least one illuminated letter. Light up your prayers with rays of thanksgiving all the way through. When you come together to pray, do not forget to speak *"to yourselves in psalms and hymns and spiritual songs, singing and making melody in your heart to the Lord"* (Ephesians 5:19).

The Perils of Praying without Praise

Second, I will try to show the evil of the absence of thanksgiving in our prayers.

Ingratitude

First and foremost, if we pray without praising, we should be charged with ingratitude. Are we always to be receiving and never returning thanks? Aristotle rightly observed: "A return is required to preserve friendship between two persons." As we have nothing else to give to God except gratitude, let us give it abundantly. If we have no fruit of the field, let us at least give to God the fruit of our lips. Have we no thanks to bring? How, then, can we expect further blessings? Does not generosity itself close its hand when ingratitude stands in the way? What, never a word of gratitude to Him from whom all blessings flow!

Selfishness

Next, it would indicate great selfishness if we did not combine praise with prayer. Can it be right to think only of

ourselves, to pray for benefits and never honor our Benefactor? Are we going to bring the hateful sin of greed
into spiritual things and care only for our own soul's
good? What, no thought for God's glory? No idea of magnifying His great and blessed name? May God prevent
us from having such mean, greedy spirits. Healthy praise
and thanksgiving must be cultivated because they prevent
prayer from becoming overgrown with the mildew of selfishness.

Lack of Faith

Thanksgiving also prevents prayer from becoming an
exhibition of a lack of faith. Some prayer shows the
absence of faith rather than the exercise of confidence in
God. When I am in trouble, if I still bless the Lord for
all I suffer, my faith is seen. Before I obtain mercy, if I
thank God for the grace that I have yet to taste, my faith
is shown.

Is our faith such that it sings only in the sunshine?
Have we no nightingale music for our God? Is our trust
like the swallow, which leaves us in winter? Is our faith a
fragile flower that needs a greenhouse to keep it alive? Can
it blossom like the gentian at the foot of a frozen glacier,
where the damp and chill of adversity surround it? I trust
it can. It should. We ought to be able to praise and bless
God when outward circumstances would cause us to sigh
rather than to sing.

Willfulness

Not to thank God in our prayers would demonstrate
willfulness and lack of submission to His will. Must everything happen according to our plans? To refuse to praise
unless we have our own way is great presumption. It
shows that, like a naughty child, we will sulk if we cannot
be master. It is like the little boy who was very diligent

in saying his prayers, but was at the same time disobedient, ill-tempered, and pesky. His mother told him that she thought it was hypocritical for him to pretend to pray. He replied, "No, Mother, indeed, it is not. I am praying that God will lead you and Daddy to like my ways better than you do."

Numbers of people want the Lord to "like their ways better," but they do not intend to follow the ways of the Lord. Their minds are contrary to God and will not submit to His will. Therefore, there is no thanksgiving in them. Praise in a prayer is indicative of a humble, submissive, obedient spirit. When it is absent, we may suspect willfulness and self-seeking. Much of the prayer of rebellious hearts is the mere growling of an angry stubbornness, the whine of an ungratified ego. God must do this and He must do that or else we will not love Him. What baby talk! What spoiled children! A little correction will do them good.

I knew a good man whose child was on the verge of death. When I went to see her, he instructed me not to mention death to her. He said, "I do not believe God could do such an unkind thing as to take my only child away." When I assured him that it was likely that she would die in a few days and that he must not quarrel with the will of the Lord, he stood firm in his rebellion. He prayed, but he could not bless God. It was no surprise that his heart sank within him, and he refused to be comforted when at last his child did die. Afterward, he became resigned, but his reluctant submission cost him much pain.

This will not do. This quarreling with God is not good. Acceptance comes to the heart like an angel in disguise, and when we entertain it, our souls are comforted. We may ask for the child's life to be spared, but we must also thank the Lord that the dear life has been prolonged as long as it has. We must put the child and everything else into our Father's hands and say, "Lord, even if You take all away, I will still bless Your name, O Most High." This is an acceptable prayer because it is not soured by the leaven of self-will, but salted with thankfulness.

Discord

We must mingle thanksgiving with our prayers because, otherwise, we may find that our minds are not in harmony with the divine will. Dear friends, the purpose of prayer is not to try to change the mind of God. Prayer is the shadow of the laws of the Eternal. God has ordained His plans, and He molds His saints to will what He wills and to express their desires in prayer. Prayer is the rustling of the wings of the angels who are bringing the blessing to us.

It is written, *"Delight thyself also in the Lord; and he shall give thee the desires of thine heart"* (Psalm 37:4). It is not promised that He will give everyone the desires of his heart. First, you must delight in the Lord. When your mind finds all its joy in God, then it is clear that God and you, as much as can be, are standing on the same plane and moving in the same direction. Then you will have the desire of your heart because the desire of your heart is the desire of God's heart.

Powerlessness

Character, as much as faith, lies at the basis of persistence in prayer. I do not mean in the case of the prayer of the sinner when he is seeking mercy, but I mean in the habitual prayers of the godly. Some men cannot pray with strength enough to triumph because sin has made them weak. God walks contrary to them because they walk contrary to Him. He who has lost the light of God's countenance has also lost much of the power of his prayers. You do not suppose that every Israelite could have gone to the top of Mount Carmel and opened the windows of heaven as Elijah did. No, he must first be Elijah, for it is the *"effectual fervent prayer of a righteous man"* that *"availeth much"* (James 5:16). When the Lord has put your heart into agreement with His, then you will pray and prevail. Our Lord said, *"If ye abide in me, and my words abide in you, ye shall ask what ye will, and it shall be done unto you"* (John 15:7).

Without a doubt, many lose power in prayer because their lives are deplorable in the sight of the Lord, and He cannot smile upon them. Will any father listen to the requests of a child who has set himself up in opposition to parental authority? The obedient, tender, loving child, who would not wish for anything that you did not think was right to give, is he whose requests you are pleased to consider and fulfill. You even anticipate the wishes of such a child before he asks. May we be this type of children of the great God.

The Rewards of Thankful Prayer

Praise Produces Peace

In the third place, let us consider the result of the presence of thanksgiving in connection with prayer. According to our text, thanksgiving blended with prayer produces peace:

> *In every thing by prayer and supplication with thanksgiving let your requests be made known unto God. And the peace of God, which passeth all understanding, shall keep your hearts and minds through Christ Jesus.* (Philippians 4:6–7)

That peace, that conscious calm, that divine serenity, which is described as *"the peace of God,"* is not produced by prayer alone, but by prayer with thanksgiving. Some men pray, and that is commendable. However, because their prayers lack praise, praying disturbs them. They come away more anxious than when they started. If their requests were mingled with praise, like chemists who expertly mix compounds in just the right proportions, the blessing of God would flow from their prayers, resulting in rest for the heart.

If we bless our gracious Lord for the specific troubles we are praying about, if we bless Him for the mercy that we need as if it had already come, if we resolve to praise Him whether we receive the answer or not, learning to be content in spite of our circumstances (Philippians 4:11), then *"the peace of God, which passeth all understanding, shall keep [our] hearts and minds through Christ Jesus"* (v. 7). Beloved, if you value this divine rest of spirit, if you prize constant serenity of soul, I beg you to mingle praises with your prayers.

Praise Releases Prayer

In addition to bringing peace, thanksgiving often warms the soul, enabling it to pray. I believe it is the experience of many who cherish their devotional time to encounter periods when they cannot pray. Their hearts seem hard, cold, silent, and almost dead. Do not work at creating unwilling and formal prayer, my friends. Instead, take down the hymnal and sing. While you praise the Lord for what you have, you will find your stony hearts beginning to soften. You will be encouraged to enter into the presence of the Lord because you will remember what you have already received from His hand.

If you had to raise an empty wagon to the mouth of a coal pit, it might be a very difficult task for you. Yet the work is managed easily by the common sense of the miners. As the full wagons run down, they pull the empty wagons up the incline. Likewise, when your heart is loaded with praise for mercy received, let it run down the incline and draw up the empty wagon of your desires. Then you will find it easier to pray. If our hearts can be warmed and renewed by so simple a method as asking the Lord to accept our thanksgiving, let us by all means take care to use it.

Praise Precedes Victory

Finally, I believe that when a man begins to pray with thanksgiving, he is on the edge of receiving the blessing. God's time to bless you has come when you begin to praise Him as well as pray to Him. God has His set time to answer us, and He will not grant our desires until the proper season has arrived. However, the time has come for you to bless the Lord.

Look at this example from 2 Chronicles 20:20–22. Jehoshaphat went out to fight a massive army, and notice how he achieved the victory:

And they rose early in the morning, and went forth into the wilderness of Tekoa: and as they went forth, Jehoshaphat stood and said, Hear me, O Judah, and ye inhabitants of Jerusalem; believe in the Lord your God, so shall ye be established; believe his prophets, so shall ye prosper. And when he had consulted with the people, he appointed—

What? Warriors? Captains? No, that was already done, but he appointed—

singers unto the Lord, and that should praise the beauty of holiness, as they went out before the army, and to say, Praise the Lord; for his mercy endureth for ever. And when they began to sing and to praise, the Lord set ambushments against the children of Ammom, Moab, and mount Seir, which were come against Judah; and they were smitten.

The Power in Praising God

Victory came when they began to sing and praise. Your answer to prayer will come when you multiply your thanksgiving in all your prayers. Be assured of that.

Our thanksgiving will show that the reason for our waiting is now over. The waiting has answered its purpose and may now come to a joyful end. Sometimes we are not in a proper state to receive a blessing, but when we reach the condition of thankfulness, then is the time when it is safe for God to bless us.

A professing Christian once went to his minister and said, "Sir, you say we should always pray." "Yes, my friend, undoubtedly." "But I have been praying for twelve months to enjoy the comforts of religion, and I am no happier than before. I have made that my one perpetual prayer, and I do not feel joy or even peace of mind. In fact, I have more doubts and fears than I ever had before." "Yes," said his minister, "and that is the natural result of such a selfish prayer. Why, dear friend, come and kneel down with me, and let us pray in another manner: 'Father, glorify Your name. Your kingdom come.' Now, go and offer those petitions and get to work to try to make them true. See if you do not soon enjoy the comforts of religion."

There is a great truth here: If you will desire that God be glorified and aim at glorifying Him yourself, then the joys of true godliness will come to you in answer to prayer.

The time for the blessing is when you begin to praise God for it. For, dear ones, you may be sure that when you offer thanksgiving on the grounds that God has answered your prayer, you really have prevailed with God.

Suppose you had promised some poor woman that you would give her a meal tomorrow. You might forget it, you know. Yet suppose when the morning came, she sent her little girl with a basket for it. She would be likely to get it, I think. Suppose that, in addition, she sent a little note thanking you in advance for your great kindness. Would you have the heart to say, "My dear girl, I cannot pay attention to you today. Come another time"? Oh, no. If your cupboards were bare, you would go out to get something. You would find a way to meet her need because the good soul believed in you so much that she had sent you thanks for the food before she even received your gift.

Well, now, trust the Lord in the same manner. He cannot go back on His Word. Believing prayer holds Him, but believing thanksgiving binds Him. Even evil people will fulfill a pledge when they know that a thankful person is counting on them. How much more will our good God answer the prayers of a thankful heart? You can depend on God. The time for receiving is at hand because thanksgiving for the gift not yet received fills your heart. It is up to you. If you are able to pray with gratitude, great good will come to you, to the church of God, and to the world at large.

Someone reading these words may feel, "I cannot pray like that. I do not know how to pray. Oh, I wish I knew how to pray! I am a poor, guilty sinner. I cannot mix any thanksgiving with my requests."

Dear soul, do not think about that just now. These words I have written are more for the people of God. Your prayer should be a simple one: *"God be merciful to me a sinner"* (Luke 18:13). And yet, I would venture to say that there is praise even in that prayer. You are implicitly praising the justice of God and praising His mercy by appealing to Him. When the Prodigal returned, he began his plea by saying, *"Father, I have sinned against heaven, and in thy sight, and am no more worthy to be called thy son"* (Luke 15:21). In that confession was a real praise of the father's goodness, which the son felt unworthy to receive.

First, you have to find Jesus and eternal life in Him. Go and plead the merit of Jesus. Cast yourself upon the love and mercy of God; He will not cast you away. Then, after you have found Him and know Him, take care that you never stop thanking Him for the gift of your salvation. No matter what circumstances life brings you—hunger, poverty, and need or health and wealth—continue to bless your saving Lord, saying, *"This poor man cried, and the LORD heard him"* (Psalm 34:6), and *"I will sing unto the LORD as long as I live: I will sing praise to my God while I have my being"* (Psalm 104:33). God bless you, for Jesus' sake.

Chapter 4

Praise God

For of him, and through him, and to him,
are all things: to whom be glory for ever. Amen.
—Romans 11:36

My text consists almost entirely of simple words, but it contains the loftiest of thoughts. Such tremendous meaning is concentrated here that an archangel's eloquence would fail to convey its glorious teaching. Not even angels could grasp its full impact. I can truly say that no man living can preach a sermon worthy of this text. Among all the sacred orators and eloquent preachers, none ever lived nor will any live who would be capable of reaching the height of the great argument contained in this verse.

I utterly despair of successfully describing the greatness of God; therefore, I will not even attempt to explain the infinite glory contained in this verse. Only our great God can explain this Scripture, for He alone knows Himself, and He alone can worthily proclaim His own perfection. Yet I am comforted by the thought that, in answer to our prayers, God will speak from this text to our hearts, if not through the words of the writer, then through His own still small voice to which the believer's ear is so well tuned. If He will bend down to bless us, our hearts will be lifted.

Two things are presented to us in the text: doctrine and devotion. The first one is worthy of our observation,

the second of our imitation. The doctrine is high doctrine—
"Of him, and through him, and to him, are all things."
The devotion is lofty devotion—*"To whom be glory for ever.
Amen."*

The Doctrine

Let us consider the doctrine. The apostle Paul explained
the general principle that all things come from God: They
are of Him as their source; they are through Him as their
means; they are to Him as their end. They are of Him in
the plan, through Him in the working, and to Him in the
glory that they produce. Taking this general principle, you
will find that it applies to all things, and it is our job to see
those examples where it is most obvious. May the Lord, by
His Holy Spirit, open His treasures to us at this moment
so that we may be enriched in spiritual knowledge and
understanding.

God Alone

Meditate, dear friends, on the whole range of God's
works in creation and providence. There was a time when
God dwelt alone, and creatures did not exist. In that time
before all time, when there was no day but the Ancient of
Days, when matter and created mind were alike unborn,
and even space was not, God, the great I Am, was as perfect, glorious, and blessed as He is now. There was no
sun, yet Jehovah dwelt in indescribable light. There was
no earth, yet His throne stood fast and firm. There were
no heavens, yet His glory was unbounded. God inhabited
eternity in the infinite majesty and happiness of His self-
contained greatness.

The Divine Counselor

If the Lord, abiding in this majestic solitude, chose to
create anything, the first thought and idea had to come

from Him, for there were no others to think or suggest. All things had to be of Him in design. From whom could He receive counsel? Who could instruct Him? No others existed to give Him counsel, even if such an assistance could be imaginable. In the beginning of His way, before His works of old, eternal wisdom brought forth from its own mind the perfect plan of future creations. The creative design was clearly the Lord's alone.

The Master Designer

He ordained the pathway of every planet and the place of every fixed star. He created the Pleiades, and bound Orion with his belt. (See Job 38:31.) He appointed the boundary of the sea and settled the course of the winds. As to the earth, the Lord alone planned its foundations and shaped its design. In His own mind, He formed the mold of all His creatures and found for them a home and a purpose. He appointed the degree of strength with which He would endow each creature, settled its months of life, its hour of death, its comings and goings. Divine wisdom mapped this earth, its flowing rivers and foaming seas, its towering mountains and laughing valleys. The Divine Architect fixed the gates of the morning and the doors of the shadow of death. Nothing could have been suggested by any other, for there was no other to suggest. It was in His power to create a universe very different from this one if He had so pleased; He must have made it what it is because, in His wisdom and prudence, He saw fit to do so.

The All-Knowing Sovereign

He could have created a world from which sin could have been forever excluded. That He permitted sin to enter into His creation must again be attributed to His own infinite sovereignty. If He had not known with certainty that He would be Master over sin and that out of evil would evolve the noblest display of His own glory, He would not have permitted it to enter the world. However, in sketching the whole history of the universe that He was about to create, He permitted even that black spot to defile His work. He knew in advance what songs of everlasting triumph would rise to Him when, in streams of His own blood, incarnate Deity would wash out the stain of sin. It cannot be doubted that, whatever may be the whole drama of history in creation and providence, there is a high and mysterious sense in which it is all of God. The sin is not God's, but the temporary permission of its existence formed part of the foreknown scheme. Neither the interference of evil in the moral nature of man nor the purity of God's divine character diminishes the force of our belief that the whole scope of history is of God in the fullest sense.

The Supreme Creator

When the plan was all laid down, and the Almighty had ordered His purpose, this was not enough: Mere arrangement would not create *"through him"* as well as *"of him."* He had to create the universe out of nothing. He did not call for help—He does not need it, and besides, there is none to help Him. There was no raw material that He could fashion between His palms and launch forth as stars. He did not need a mine of unquarried matter to melt and purify in the furnace of His power before skillfully hammering it out upon the anvil. No, there was nothing to begin with in that day of Jehovah's work. From the womb of Omnipotence, all things must be born.

He speaks, and the heavens leap into existence. He speaks again, and worlds are created with all the varied forms of life so filled with divine wisdom and matchless skill. *"Let there be light: and there was light"* (Genesis 1:3) was not the only time God spoke into existence things that were not. He also spoke forth the rolling earth and blue heavens, which blossomed out of nothingness. *"Through him"* were all things, from the high archangel who sings His praises in celestial notes to the cricket chirping on the hearth. The same finger paints the rainbow and the wings of the butterfly. He who dyes the garments of evening in all the colors of heaven has covered the king's cup with gold and lit the glowworm's lamp. From distant, massive mountains that pierce the clouds down to that minute grain of ocean sand—all things are made *"through him."* If God were to withdraw the radiance of His divine power, everything would melt away as the foam upon the sea melts into the wave that bore it. Nothing could stand an instant if the divine foundation were removed. If He should shake the pillars of the world, the whole temple of creation would fall to ruin, and its very dust would be blown away. A dreary waste, a silent emptiness, a voiceless wilderness is all that would remain if God were to withdraw His power; no, nothing would remain if His power were removed.

The Omnipresent God

Nature exists through the energy of the omnipresent God. If the sun rises every morning and the moon walks in her brightness at night, it is *"through him."* Away with those men who think that God has wound up the world as though it were a clock and has gone away, leaving it to work for itself apart from His present hand.

God is present everywhere—not just when we tremble because His thunder shakes the solid earth or He sets the heavens in a blaze with lightning. He is present in the calm summer's eve when the air so gently fans the flowers and gnats dance up and down in the last gleams of sunlight.

Men try to forget the divine presence by calling His energy by strange names. They speak of the power of gravitation, but what is that? We know what it does, but what is it? Gravitation is God's own power. They tell us of the laws of electricity and other scientific data. We know the laws, and let them wear the names they have, but laws cannot operate without power. What is the force of nature? It is a constant issuing from the great Fountain of power, a constant flowing out of God Himself, the perpetual radiance of light from Him who is the great *"Father of lights, with whom is no variableness, neither shadow of turning"* (James 1:17).

Tread softly. Be reverent, for God is here as truly as He is in heaven. Wherever you are, and whatever you see, you are in God's workshop, where every wheel is turned by His hand. Everything is not God, but God is in everything. Nothing works, or even exists, except by His present power and might. *"Of him, and through him,...are all things."*

Creation Praises the Creator

Beloved, the greatest glory of all is that, in the work of creation, everything is *"to him."* Everything will praise the Lord: He so designed it. God must have the highest motive, and there can be no higher motive conceivable than His own glory. When there was no creature but Himself, and no being but Himself, God could not have taken His motive from a creature that did not exist. His motive must be His own. His own glory is His highest aim. Carefully, He considers the good of His creatures, but even the good of His creatures is but a means to the main end, the promotion of His glory. All things, then, are for His pleasure; and for His glory, they daily work.

Tell me that the world is marred by sin, and I lament it; tell me that the slime of the serpent is upon everything beautiful here, and I sorrow over it; but yet, even yet, will everything speak of the glory of God. *"To him, are all things,"* and the day will come when we will see, with spiritually illuminated eyes, that even the introduction of the Fall and the Curse did not mar the splendor and majesty of the Most High. *"To him"* will all things be. His enemies will bow their heads unwillingly but abjectly, while His people, redeemed from death and hell, will cheerfully praise Him. The new heavens and the new earth will ring with His praise, and we who will sit down to read the record of His creating wonders will say of them all, "Glory!" (See Psalm 29:9.)

The Victorious One

Courage, then, beloved, when you think that matters go against the cause of God. Rest on His sovereignty like you would relax on a soft couch. When the enemy hisses in your ears, "God is overcome. His plans are spoiled. His Gospel is thrust back. The honor of His Son is stained," tell the enemy, "No, it is not so; *'to him, are all things.'*" God's defeats are victories *"because the foolishness of God is wiser than men; and the weakness of God is stronger than men"* (1 Corinthians 1:25). In the end, we will see most clearly that this is so. Hallelujah!

We will see, dear friends, one day in the clear light of heaven, that every page in human history, however stained by human sin, has nevertheless something of God's glory in it. The calamities of nations; the falling of dynasties; the devastation of epidemics, plagues, famines, wars, and earthquakes, have all worked out the eternal purpose and glorified the Most High. From the first human prayer to the last mortal sigh, from the first note of finite praise to the everlasting hallelujah, *"all things work together for good to them that love God, to them who are the called according to his purpose"* (Romans 8:28). All things are *"of him, and through him, and to him."*

His Matchless Grace

This great principle is seen most clearly in the grand work of divine grace. Here everything is of God and through God and to God. The great plan of salvation was not drawn by human hands. It is no concoction of priests nor elaborate scheme of clergymen. Grace first moved the heart of God and joined with divine sovereignty to ordain a plan of salvation. This plan was the offspring of a wisdom no less than divine. No one but God could have imagined a way of salvation such as that which the Gospel presents—a way so just to God, so safe to man. The thought of divine substitution and the sacrifice of God on man's behalf could never have suggested itself to the most educated of all God's creatures. God Himself suggested it, and the plan is *of him.*

His Perfect Plan

Since the great plan is of Him, so are the details. God ordained the time when the first promise would be proclaimed, who would receive that promise, and who would deliver it. He ordained the hour when the great Promise-keeper would come, when Jesus Christ would appear, of whom He would be born, by whom He would be betrayed, what death He would die, when He would rise, and in what manner He would ascend.

Need I say more? He knew who would accept the Mediator, to whom the Gospel would be preached, and who would be the favored individuals who would respond to the gift of salvation. He settled in His own mind the name of every one of His chosen and the time when each elect vessel would be put on the wheel to be fashioned according to His will. He determined what pangs of conviction would be felt when the time of faith came and how much of holy light and enjoyment would be bestowed. All this was purposed ahead of time. He settled how long the chosen vessel would be glazing in the fire and when it would be taken up, made perfect by heavenly workmanship, to adorn the palace of God Most High. From the Lord's wisdom, every stitch in the noble tapestry of salvation most surely comes.

The Incomparable Redeemer

Neither must we stop here. *"Through him,"* all these things come. Through His Spirit, the promise came at last, for He inspired the prophets and holy men of old. Through Him, the Son of God was born of the Virgin Mary by the power of the Holy Spirit. Through Him, sustained by that Spirit, the Son of God lived His thirty-three years of perfection. In the great redemption, God alone is exalted. Jesus sweat in Gethsemane and bled on Calvary. No one stood with our Savior there. He trod that winepress alone (Isaiah 63:3). His own arm brought salvation, and His own arm upheld Him (v. 5). Redemption was through God alone.

Not one soul was ever redeemed by human suffering. No spirit was freed by self-reproach, but all through Him. And as through Him the Atonement came, so through Him the application of the Atonement comes. By the power of the Spirit, the Gospel is preached daily. Upheld by the Holy Spirit, pastors, teachers, and elders still remain with the church. The energy of the Spirit continues to go forth with the Word to the hearts of the chosen; still is *"Christ crucified...the power of God, and the wisdom of God"* (1 Corinthians 1:23–24), because God is in the Word, and through Him, men are called, converted, and saved.

God Alone Should Be Praised

My beloved, beyond a doubt, we must confess that this great plan of salvation is all *"to him."* We do not have a note of praise to spare for another. Those who would retain a single word of praise for man or angel in the work of grace will be silenced forever with everlasting confusion. You fools! Who can be praised but God, for who but God determined to give His Son Jesus? You scoundrels! Will you rob Christ of His glory? Will you steal the jewels out of His crown when He so dearly bought them with drops of His precious blood?

The Power in Praising God

You who love darkness rather than light, will you glorify man's will above the energy of the Holy Spirit? Will you worship your own freedom and dignity? God forgive you. As for His saints, they will always sing, "To God, to God alone, be all the glory. From the first to the last, let Him who is the Alpha and the Omega have all the praise. Let His name be extolled, world without end."

When the great plan of grace is fully developed, and you and I stand on the hilltops of glory, what a wondrous scene will open up before us! We will see more clearly then than now how all things sprang from the fountainhead of God's love, how they all flowed through the channel of the Savior's mediation, and how they all worked together to the glory of the same God from whom they came. The great plan of grace, then, bears out this principle of our text.

Salvation Is of God

The word holds good, dear friends, in the case of every individual believer. Let this be a matter for personal inquiry. Why am I saved? Is it because of any goodness in me or any superiority in my constitution? Of whom comes my salvation? My spirit cannot hesitate a single moment. How could a new heart come out of the old one? Who can bring a clean thing out of what is unclean? Not one. How can the spirit come out of the flesh? *That which is born of the flesh is flesh; and that which is born of the Spirit is spirit"* (John 3:6).

My soul, you must be quite clear about this: If there is any faith, hope, or spiritual life in you, it must have come from God. Can any Christian who possesses vital godliness argue with this statement? I am persuaded he cannot. If any man should claim any honor to his own physical makeup, I must, with all charity, doubt whether he knows anything at all about the matter.

Faith Comes from God

My soul, since your salvation must have come from God because He thought of it, planned it, and then gave it to you, did it not also come to you through God? It came through faith, but where did that faith have its origin? Was it not from the operation of the Holy Spirit? And what did you believe in? Did you believe in your own strength or in your own good resolution? No, you believed in Jesus, your Lord.

Did not the first ray of spiritual light you ever received come from God? Did you not look entirely away from yourself and to the Savior? The light that you now have, does it not always come to you in the same way: by being done once and for all with the creature, with the flesh, with human merit, and resting with childlike confidence on the finished work and righteousness of the Lord Jesus Christ? Dear reader, is not your salvation, if you are indeed saved, entirely *"through"* God as well as *"of"* God?

Who is it that enables you to pray every day? Who keeps you from temptation? By what grace are you led onward in spiritual duty? Who upholds you when your foot would trip? Are you not conscious that there is a power other than your own? For my part, dear friends, I know that I am not being taken to heaven against my will. Yet my nature is still so desperate and so prone to evil that I feel myself floating against its current. It seems as if all we can do is to kick and rebel against sovereign grace, while sovereign grace says, "I will save you. I will have you, whatever you may do. I will overcome your raging corruption. I will revive you out of your lethargy and take you to heaven in a fiery chariot of afflictions, if not by any other means. I will drag you to paradise rather than let you be lost."

Is this not your experience? Have you not found that, if the strong hand of God were taken from your soul, instead of going on to heaven, you would go back to eternal damnation? Is it not through God that you are saved? And, believer, is it not *"to him"*? Will you take one single jewel out of His crown? Oh, there is not one of you who would wish to praise himself. There is no song we sing more sweetly than the song of grace. No hymn seems more in keeping with our own experience than this:

> Grace all the work will crown,
>   Through everlasting days;
> It lays in heaven the topmost stone,
>   And well deserves the praise.

Whoever will may glorify the dignity of humanity; whoever will may boast of the power of free will. We cannot do it. We have found our nature to be very depraved, and our wills to be under bondage. We must, even if other creatures do not, honor that changeless, omnipotent grace that has made us what we are. It will continue to keep us until it brings us to the right hand of God in everlasting glory.

The Harvest Is from God

In every work that the Christian is enabled to do, he should bear in mind the principle of the text. Some of you are privileged to work in the Sunday school, and you have had many conversions in your classes. Others have had success in distributing tracts, going from house to house to try to bring souls to Christ. Some of us, too, have the honor of being sent to preach the Gospel in every place, and we have had an abundant harvest of souls.

Some of us seem to have received the promised blessing to its fullest extent. The Lord has made our spiritual children like the sand of the sea. (See Isaiah 48:19.) Therefore, it is necessary for us to remember that *"of him, and through him, and to him, are all things."*

"Of him." Who makes you unique? What do you have that you have not received? The burning heart, the tearful eye, the prayerful soul—all these qualifications for usefulness come *"of him."* The eloquent mouth, the pleading tongue, must have been educated and given by Him. The diverse gifts of the Spirit by which the church is edified all proceed from Him. Who is Paul? Who is Apollos or Cephas? Who are all these but the messengers of God (1 Corinthians 3:4–5) in whom the Spirit works, *"dividing to every man severally as he will"* (1 Corinthians 12:11)?

When the preacher has achieved his usefulness, he knows that all his success comes through God. If a man thinks himself capable of stirring up a revival, of encouraging even one saint or leading one sinner to repentance, he is a fool. We might as well attempt to move the stars, shake the world, or grasp a lightning flash in the palm of our hand as think we can save a soul or even stir saints out of their lethargy.

Spiritual work must be done by the Spirit. Every good thing comes from God (James 1:17). The preacher may be strong like Samson when God is with him; he will be like Samson in his degradation and shame when God is not with him. Beloved, no man was ever brought to God except through God, or ever will be. Our nation will never again be stirred up into the celestial heat of piety except by the presence of the Holy Spirit anew. I strongly desire that we would have more of the abiding sense of the Spirit's work among us, that we would look more to Him, rest less in machinery and men, and trust more in that divine but invisible Agent who works all good things in the hearts of men.

Beloved, it is through God that every good thing comes, and I am sure it is *"to him."* We cannot take credit for a single convert. We are thankful for growing churches, but we give the glory to Him alone. Give glory to humans, and they become boastful. Honor yourselves as a church, and God will soon dishonor you. Let us lay every gift on His altar, bring every lamb of the fold to the feet of the Good Shepherd. When we go out to fish for souls, let us realize that we fill the net only because He taught us how to throw it on the right side; when we take them, they are His, not ours.

What poor little things we are, and yet we think we do so much. The pen might say, "I wrote Milton's *Paradise Lost.*" Ah, poor pen! You could not have dotted an "i" or crossed a "t" if Milton's hand had not moved you. The preacher could not have done anything if God had not helped him. The ax might cry, "I have felled forests. I have made the cedar bow its head and laid the stalwart oak in the dust." No, you did not, for if it had not been for the arm that wielded you, even a shrub would have been too much for you to cut down. Will the sword say, "I won the victory. I shed the blood of the mighty. I caused the shield to be cast away"? No, it was the warrior, who with his courage and might made you of service in battle, but apart from this, you are less than nothing. In all that God does through us, let us continue to give Him the praise. Then He will continue to be with us in our efforts; otherwise, He will take His smile from us, and we will be left as weak men.

Practical Application of the Doctrine

Perhaps I have tried your patience in my efforts to clearly present this simple but very useful principle. However, before I move to the topic of devotion, I would like to make a practical application of the truth of this doctrine. Beloved, if it is true that all things are *"through him, and to him,"* do you not think that those doctrines are most likely to be correct and most worthy to be held that are most in keeping with this truth?

The Doctrine of Election

There are certain Christian doctrines commonly called Calvinistic, which I think commend themselves to the minds of all thoughtful persons for this reason mainly: They ascribe to God everything. Consider the doctrine of election. Why is a man saved? Is it the result of his own will or God's will? Did he choose God, or did God choose him? The answer "man chose God" is clearly untrue because it glorifies man. God's answer is this: *"Ye have not chosen me, but I have chosen you"* (John 15:16). God *"hath chosen us in him before the foundation of the world,... having predestinated us unto the adoption of children by Jesus Christ to himself"* (Ephesians 1:4–5). His will is the hinge of the whole matter and turns the balance. Ascribing the power of choice to God, I feel that I am in keeping with the doctrine of our text.

The Doctrine of Calling

Then take effectual calling. By what power is a man called? Some say that it is by the energy of man's own will or that, while God gives man grace, it depends upon him to make use of it. Some do not make use of the grace, and they perish. Others make use of the grace and are saved, saved by their own willingness to allow grace to be effective.

I, on the other hand, say that a man is not saved against his will, but he is made willing by the operation of the Holy Spirit. A mighty grace draws the man, disarms him, makes a new creature of him, and he is saved. I believe that the calling that saves the soul is a calling that owes nothing at all to man, but comes from God. The creature does not initiate the calling, but God molds the man as a potter molds clay. Clearly, the calling, I think, must be through God, for it coincides with the principle, *"Of him, and through him, and to him, are all things."*

The Power in Praising God

The Power of the Blood

Next comes the question of particular redemption. Some insist that men are redeemed not because Christ died, but because their choice to accept salvation gives power to the blood of Christ. They say that believing is necessary in order to make the blood of Christ effective for redemption. I believe the very opposite. Namely, that the blood of Christ has in itself the power to redeem, that it does redeem, and that faith does not give efficacy to the blood. Faith is only the proof that the blood has redeemed a man. Therefore, I believe that Christ redeemed all who will ultimately attain eternal life. I do not believe that He redeemed the damned. I think that the doctrine that men by their wills give power to the blood of Christ is derogatory to the Lord Jesus; instead, I believe that He laid down His life for His sheep, and that His laying down His life for the sheep involved and secured the salvation of every one of them. I believe this because I hold that *"of him, and through him, and to him, are all things."*

Man's Utter Corruption

Consider the total depravity of the race and its original corruption, a doctrine that is hated by those who lift up poor human nature; nevertheless, this doctrine is true. We believe that man must be entirely lost and ruined because if there is some good thing in him, then it cannot be said that *"of him, and through him, and to him, are all things."* If there are some traces of virtue and some remnants of power left in the race of man, then some things are of man, and to man will some things be. However, if all things are of God, then in man there must be nothing. Man must be regarded as ruined—hopelessly ruined—bruised and mangled by the Fall, and his salvation must be described as being, from the first to the last, in every jot and tittle, a result of that almighty grace of God. The grace of God chose him, at length redeemed him, ultimately called him, constantly preserved him, and perfectly will present him before the Father's throne.

I put these doctrines before you from the teachings of that mighty servant of God, John Calvin. I honor him not as the formulator of these doctrines, but as one through whom God spoke, and one who, next to the apostle Paul, presented truth more clearly than any other man who ever breathed. He knew more of Scripture and explained it more clearly than any other. Luther may have had as much courage, but when he saw one truth, like a bull, he shut his eyes and dashed against the enemy, breaking down gates, bolts, and bars to clear a way for the Word. Yet Calvin, following in the opened pathway—with a clear eye, searching Scripture, ever acknowledging that of God and through God and to God are all things—mapped out the whole plan with a delightful clearness, which could have come only from the Spirit of God. That man of God set forth the doctrines in so excellent and admirable a manner that we cannot too much bless the Lord who sent him, or too much pray that others like him may be honest and sincere in the work of the Lord.

This much is sufficient regarding doctrine. Now let us look briefly at devotion.

Devotion

The apostle put his pen back into the ink bottle and fell on his knees. He could not help it—he had to have a doxology. *"To whom be glory for ever. Amen."* Beloved, let us imitate this devotion. I think that this sentence should be the prayer, the motto, for every one of us.

Our Solitary Goal

"To whom be glory for ever." This should be the single desire of the Christian. I take it that he should not have twenty wishes, but only one. He may desire to see his

family well brought up, but only so that God may be glorified forever. He may wish for prosperity in his business, but only so far as it may help him to promote this praise: *"To whom be glory for ever."* He may desire to attain more gifts and more graces, but his only purpose should be that God would be glorified forever. This one thing I know, Christian: You are not acting as you should when you are moved by any other motive than the one motive of your Lord's glory. As a Christian, you are "of God and through God"; I pray for you to be "to God." Let nothing ever set your heart beating but love for Him. Let this ambition fire your soul. May this be the foundation of every enterprise into which you enter and your sustaining motive whenever your zeal would grow chilly. Make God your only object. Depend upon it. Where self begins, sorrow begins. However, if God is my supreme delight and only object:

> To me 'tis equal whether love ordain
> My life or death—appoint me ease or pain.

To me there will be no choice, when my eye looks singly to God's glory, whether I will be torn in pieces by wild beasts or live in comfort, whether I will be full of despondency or full of hope. If God is glorified in my mortal body, my soul will rest content.

Our Constant Desire

When I wake up in the morning, may my soul greet God with gratitude.

> Wake, and lift up thyself, my heart,
> And with the angels bear thy part,
> Who all night long unwearied sing
> High praises to the eternal King.

While at work, let me be looking for ways in which I can glorify Him. If I am walking in the fields, let my desire be that the trees will clap their hands in His praise. May the sun in its motion shine out the Master's glory. May the stars reflect His praise. It is yours, dear ones, to use your tongues to make the silent beauties of creation praise their God. Never be silent when there are opportunities, and you will never be silent for lack of opportunities. At night, fall asleep still praising your God. As you close your eyes, let your last thought be, "How sweet to rest upon the Savior's heart!"

In afflictions, praise Him. Out of the fires, let your song rise. On your sickbed, extol Him. Dying, let Him have your sweetest notes. In combat with Death, the last great enemy (1 Corinthians 15:26), let your shouts of victory be all for Him. When you have broken the bondage of mortality and come into the freedom of immortal spirits, then, in a nobler, sweeter song, you will sing His praise. Let this be your constant thought: *"To him be glory and dominion for ever and ever. Amen"* (Revelation 1:6).

Our Earnest Thought

Do not speak of God's glory with cold words or think of it with a chilly heart; instead, feel, "I must praise Him. If I cannot praise Him where I am, I will break through these tight chains and get where I can." Sometimes you will wish that you were bodiless so that you could praise Him as the immortal spirits do. I must praise Him. Bought by His precious blood, called by His Spirit, I cannot hold my tongue. My soul, can you be silent and dead? I must praise Him. Stand back, flesh. Away, you devils. Away, you troubles. I must sing, for if I refuse to sing, surely the very stones will speak (Luke 19:40).

Our Ever Increasing Praise

I hope, dear friends, that in your earnestness, your praise will also be growing. Let there be an expanding desire to praise Him of whom and through whom are all things. You blessed Him in your youth. Do not be content with the praises you gave Him then. Has God prospered you in business? Give Him more as He has given you more. Has God given you experience? Then praise Him by better faith than you exercised at first. Does your knowledge grow? Then you can sing more sweetly. Are you happier than you once were? Have you been restored from sickness, and has your sorrow been turned into peace and joy? Then give Him more music. Put more spices in your censer, more fragrant frankincense, sweeter sugar. Oh, I long to serve Him every day, lifting up my heart from Sabbath to Sabbath until I reach the never-ending Sabbath. Reaching from sanctification to sanctification, from love to love, from strength to strength, I will appear before my God!

In closing, let me urge you to make this desire practical. If you really glorify God, take care to do it not with lip service, which dies away in the wind, but with true reverence throughout your daily lives. Praise Him by your patience in pain, by your perseverance in duty, by your generosity to His cause, by your boldness in testimony, by your consecration to His work. Praise Him, my dear friends, not only in what you give to Him by your offerings, but praise Him every day by your service, according to the manner in which He has been pleased to bless you.

I wish I could have written more effectively, but the Holy Spirit can work better through our weaknesses. If you will try to teach these truths to yourselves, my friends, you will do it vastly better than I can. If you will meditate on this text, *"Of him, and through him, and to him, are all things,"* I am sure you will be led to fall on your knees with the apostle and say, *"To whom be glory for ever."* Then you will rise up and, in your life, practically give Him honor, putting the *"Amen"* on this doxology by your own individual service to your great and gracious Lord. May He bless you now and accept your thank offering through Christ Jesus.

Chapter 5

Wonders

*And praise the name of the L*ORD *your God,*
that hath dealt wondrously with you.
—Joel 2:26

I n the case mentioned in the second chapter of Joel, the nation of Israel had seriously gone astray. Therefore, they were visited by a very remarkable punishment. An unusual plague of locusts devoured all the fruit of the field, and the people were distressed by a severe famine. *"For the day of the L*ORD *is great and very terrible; and who can abide it?"* (Joel 2:11).

The prophet Joel was commissioned to urge the people of God to repent. If they listened to his earnest pleas, their future would be bright with mercy. Because of God's gracious hand upon them, they were moved to repent. They wept and cried to God. Then the same God who with His left hand had been amazing in discipline was with His right hand equally astonishing in blessing and enriching them. He loaded their floors with wheat, caused their vats to overflow with wine and oil, and repaid them for the years in which the locust had consumed their crops so that they had plenty to eat and were satisfied. They praised the name of the Lord, who had *"dealt wondrously"* with them. (See Joel 2:24–26.) He treated them with wonders when He afflicted them and with wonders when He returned to them in mercy.

The Israelites Saw God's Wonders

It was no unusual thing for the nation of Israel to encounter wonders. They were cradled in extraordinary events. They grew up among miracles. They lived with surprises. The history of the favored tribes is a long list of miracles. Remember how the Lord brought them *"out of Egypt with a mighty hand, and with an outstretched arm"* (Deuteronomy 26:8)? What *"marvellous things did he in the sight of their fathers, in the land of Egypt, in the field of Zoan"* (Psalm 78:12). By wonders, they were led out of Egypt and brought through the sea, upon whose shore they sang triumphantly, *"Who is like unto thee, O LORD, among the gods? who is like thee, glorious in holiness, fearful in praises, doing wonders?"* (Exodus 15:11).

Their course in the great howling wilderness for forty years was a march of wonders. When the manna dropped from heaven and the water leaped from the rock, the Lord *"dealt wondrously"* with them. Not a single day of the forty years opened or closed without wonders. The day was shaded by the cloudy pillar, and the night glowed with the light of the fiery pillar (Exodus 13:21). Not even when the desert journey was over did God's wonders cease. The river was divided before them: *"What ailed thee, O thou sea, that thou fleddest? thou Jordan, that thou wast driven back?"* (Psalm 114:5).

They entered their land and began its conquest by a wonder, for the walls of Jericho fell flat to the ground. They continued its conquest by the same marvelous power, for mighty kings fled before them. The sun and moon stood still while they struck down hostile armies. When they had driven out the Canaanites and were established in the land of promise, they sinned greatly. Yet what wonders of deliverance God worked for them when they cried to Him in their trouble! Just remember the names of Gideon, Barak, Jephthah, and Samson, and you will see before you wonder after wonder. The Lord *"dealt wondrously"* with them.

God Works Miracles Today

In all these experiences, the Israelites were a type of true believers, for with all His chosen ones the Lord has *"dealt wondrously."* We frequently hear the complaint that we live in a boring age. We have no adventures now, and remarkable events are few. We are happy that it is so, for it has been well said, "Blessed are the times which have no history." If peace and prosperity are commonplace, long may the commonplace continue.

However, no thoughtful man's life is uninteresting or devoid of marvels. A sincere life cannot be empty of memorable occurrences. He who thinks so must either be unspiritual or oblivious to his own inner history. He must be like the tribes of Israel in the wilderness of whom it is written that they *"forgat his works, and his wonders that he had showed them"* (Psalm 78:11).

Foolish people run to fiction for wonders, but godly people can tell far greater wonders. The wonders of which we can speak far surpass the inventions of imagination. Truthfully, no dreamer could dream after such a fashion.

Our days and nights have far exceeded in marvel the tales found in the *Arabian Nights*. God *"doeth great things past finding out; yea, and wonders without number"* (Job 9:10). I have seen a volume entitled *The World of Wonders* and another named *Ten Thousand Wonderful Things*. The believer is himself a world of wonders, and his life reveals ten thousand wonderful things. Mysteries, riddles, paradoxes, and miracles make up Christian experience.

Of these wonders, I will try to write, according to that precept of David's, *"Talk ye of all his wondrous works"* (Psalm 105:2). I will examine them in the following manner: First, I will testify that God's dealings toward us have been full of wonder, leading us to praise Him as Jehovah our God; second, I will remark that, because of this, we ought to look for wonders in the future; and if I may speak so paradoxically, it should not be surprising to us to see wonders; third, I will close by observing that, in a future state, we will yet more clearly see that Jehovah has *"dealt wondrously"* with us.

God's Dealings toward Us Have Been Full of Wonder

The Lord's dealings with us up until now have been full of wonder, leading us to praise Him. Let us speak of what we know, what we have tasted, and what we have handled. The Lord has *"dealt wondrously"* toward us.

God's Personal Love

Begin at the beginning. It was no small wonder that He should love us before the earth ever was. Many other things could have involved Jehovah's thoughts besides thinking about man: *"What is man, that thou art mindful of him?"* (Psalm 8:4). And if He had to think of man, there were many kinds of thoughts that the Lord might have had toward man besides thoughts of love. Yet the Lord was mindful of us. Even though we are poor and needy, the Lord thinks about us. *"How precious also are thy thoughts unto me, O God! how great is the sum of them!"* (Psalm 139:17).

Why were they thoughts of love? Gratitude and admiration toward God give us the only reply. It is a wonder of wonders that they should be thoughts of love for me! Each Christian will feel this to be the question in his own heart: "Why did divine love settle itself upon me?" Well might we say of our God what David said of Jonathan, *"Thy love to me was wonderful"* (2 Samuel 1:26).

The song of the Virgin may be on our lips: *"He hath put down the mighty from their seats, and exalted them of low degree"* (Luke 1:52). He has thought of us who were insignificant, while the great ones of the earth have been passed by. Eternal love in its sovereignty is a marvel and *"cometh forth from the LORD of hosts, which is wonderful in counsel, and excellent in working"* (Isaiah 28:29).

God's Faithful Love

That divine love should have continued faithfully, notwithstanding our unworthiness of it and the irritations with which we have tried it, is another wonder. The unchangeableness of His counsel calls for adoring wonder. Has there been a day since we have been responsible for our actions in which we have not tested the faithfulness of God by our transgressions? For forty years, the children of Israel provoked God in the wilderness. Sadly, were they not the prototypes of ourselves? Yet never, never has the Lord paused or changed in His love. As it is said of our blessed Redeemer, *"He loved them unto the end"* (John 13:1), it is also true that the Father loves you, and that He rests in His love (Zephaniah 3:17).

God's Covenantal Love

If divine love is in itself a wonder, friends, it is equally a wonder that, because of this love, God should enter into covenant with us. He has promised us a thousand mercies and has engaged Himself to the performance of these promises in a remarkable way; this increases the comfort of the promise. He has given us His oath: *"I have made a covenant with my chosen, I have sworn unto David my servant"* (Psalm 89:3). God has entered into covenant with us in the person of the Son of David, a covenant *"ordered in all things, and sure"* (2 Samuel 23:5), confirmed by oath and sealed by blood, by which He has bound Himself by His own word and oath, that, in blessing, He will bless us (see Genesis 22:17–18; Hebrews 6:13–14) and glorify His Son in us.

Behold and wonder—the Infinite enters into covenant with the finite; the Holy engages Himself to sinners. We, too, may sit before the Lord as David did, engulfed in astonishment, and then say from our heart of hearts, *"Who am I, O LORD God, and what is mine house, that thou hast brought me hitherto?"* (1 Chronicles 17:16).

It is equally wonderful that a part of the covenant states: *"[I] will be a Father unto you, and ye shall be my sons and daughters, saith the Lord Almighty"* (2 Corinthians 6:18). If God had wanted sons and daughters besides the Only Begotten, He might have chosen the bright angels who outshine the sun. Why look here upon this anthill to choose an offspring out of such ants as we? Why did He come down in the person of His Son to make a match with our frail humanity? Oh, matchless grace, that God should adopt for His children those who were *"children of wrath"* (Ephesians 2:3). Jesus looked at stones and said, *"God is able of these stones to raise up children unto Abraham"* (Matthew 3:9). Beloved, *"behold, what manner of love the Father hath bestowed upon us, that we should be called the sons of God"* (1 John 3:1).

God's Secure Love

As His sons and daughters, let us admire and wonder that the Lord should stake His honor on bringing us securely to heaven. For in the covenant, He has pledged all His attributes for His people's security. He cannot be a glorious God unless His people ultimately are a glorified people. He cannot be true unless His people are kept to the end, for He has pledged His honor for their safety.

Jesus has said, *"I give unto them eternal life; and they shall never perish, neither shall any man pluck them out of my hand"* (John 10:28). Yes, the Lord Himself has declared that *"Israel shall be saved in the LORD with an everlasting salvation: ye shall not be ashamed nor confounded world without end"* (Isaiah 45:17), and that *"heaven and earth shall pass away, but my words shall not pass away"* (Matthew 24:35). The sun and moon will cease their shining, but He will not *"alter the thing that is gone out of* [His] *lips"* (Psalm 89:34). Will He not do what He has said? Will He not make good what He has spoken?

God's Incarnational Love

By shifting the kaleidoscope, we will get another view of the same matchless wonders. The Lord has acted wondrously for us. Having loved us and covenanted with us, He gave us His only begotten Son to be born in our nature and, in that nature, to suffer even unto death! I will not attempt to show to you that this is a wonder. I believe that the angels, though they have known of the Incarnation nearly two thousand years, have never ceased from astonishment for one single moment.

That God, the Word, should become flesh and live among us and that He should bleed and die exceeds everything that is wonderful. That Jesus Christ, the King of Kings, should be a Servant of servants, that He who wrapped the earth in the ocean like swaddling clothes and spread on the firmament its garments of blue should wrap Himself with a towel and wash His disciples' feet is, beyond measure, a wonder! Yet He is virtually fulfilling this sacred office every day in His perpetual intercession for His people and in all His acts of love toward them. This is, indeed, dealing wonderfully with us.

In the gift of the Lord Jesus, we have obtained pardon, justification, sanctification, and eternal life, all of which contain a mine of wonders. Perhaps, to repentant hearts, the chief of all these is the forgiveness of sin, and of such sins as ours—

> Great God of wonders! all Thy ways
> Are matchless, Godlike, and divine;

But the fair glories of Thy grace
    More Godlike and unrivaled shine:
Who is a pardoning God like Thee?
Or who has grace so rich and free?

In wonder lost, with trembling joy
    We take the pardon of our God;
Pardon for crimes of deepest dye,
    A pardon bought with Jesus' blood:
Who is a pardoning God like Thee?
Or who has grace so rich and free?

God's Abundant Love

Having given us His Son, the Lord has also, in Him, *"given unto us all things that pertain unto life and godliness"* (2 Peter 1:3). I put these things into words and sum them up, but, indeed, there is an ocean of thought in every syllable I write, for the Lord has given us this world and worlds to come. He has given us earth and heaven; He has given us time and eternity: *"All are yours; and ye are Christ's; and Christ is God's"* (1 Corinthians 3:22–23). Believer, there is nothing in divine care that is not yours, for *"all things work together for good to them that love God, to them who are the called according to his purpose"* (Romans 8:28). That which looks harmful is good to you, and the good has a goodness in it that you do not yet perceive, an inner core of excellent mercy that will be opened for you in due time through the abounding wisdom of God. Walk now like Abraham of old. Lift up your eyes to the north and to the south, to the east and to the west, for all this has God given to you in giving you His Son. He has *"dealt wondrously"* with us in this respect.

He has made the angels to be our servants, glad to wait upon us and to bear us up in their hands for fear that we might dash our feet against a stone (Psalm 91:12). Making the angels to be our servants, He has made the angels' home to be our home, only He has brightened it with a special glory for us. It is not written that many mansions are prepared especially for angels, but Jesus our Lord has gone *"to prepare a place"* for us (John 14:2), made ready especially for our delight. He has not given us merely the angels of heaven, heaven itself, and Jesus to prepare a place for us, but He has given us Himself to be our God, for *"the LORD is my portion, saith my soul"* (Lamentations 3:24). He has confirmed it: *"I will be their God, and they shall be my people"* (Ezekiel 37:27). He has *"dealt wondrously"* for us, then.

Beloved, I now ask you to consider your own experiences. You who know the Lord, remember that the Lord has worked miracles within us. Not so long ago, we were dead, and He made us live. We were loathsome lepers, and He made us whole. We were blind, and He gave us sight. We were lame, and He made us leap. We were prisoners, and He set us free. We were condemned, and He justified us by His grace.

The changes that He made in us were incredible. We were astounded as we experienced them. We marveled to feel the hardness of our hearts removed. Years ago, nothing could move us; neither fear nor love could stir us; but the Lord came and struck us, as Moses hit the rock. Immediately, the waters of penitence gushed out. Why, the rock itself became a standing pool.

What a change the grace of God makes in the matter of repentance. The very man who was as hard as a diamond one day becomes like putty the next. He who never cared for God, nor wept for sin, hates himself with the deepest and humblest remorse. Then, blessed be God, another wonderful change comes over him. The man whom you saw broken in heart for sin, unable to derive a grain of comfort from anything around him, all of a sudden believes on the name of Jesus as it is brought home with power to his soul by the Holy Spirit. Right away, he wipes his eyes as his mourning is turned to dancing. He becomes supremely happy through faith and breaks forth with such songs as this:

> I will praise Thee every day,
> Now Thine anger is turned away.
> Comfortable thoughts arise,
> From the bleeding sacrifice.

At times, has your soul been as hard and cold as marble, and yet, suddenly, has it dissolved as ice melts in the sun? Has your soul been tossed up and down like the Atlantic in a rage, and yet, suddenly, has it been made smooth as a mirror by God's wondrous hand? Your experience within you, I am sure, is a verification of the statement that Jehovah your God has *"dealt wondrously with you."*

God's Amazing Love

What tremendous conflicts our souls have known! What wonderful victories we have won through divine grace! Immortal sins, as they seemed to be, have received their deadly wound. Unconquerable lusts have been defeated. Our victories will never be forgotten, but the crown of them will be put on the head of Him who enables us to be more than conquerors. And what wonderful revelations God has granted to us. Has He not often poured a flood of light upon a truth we saw but dimly before and made our spirits leap for joy? He has opened our eyes to behold wondrous things out of His law (Psalm 119:18). Why, I bear witness that, sometimes, when my Lord Jesus Christ Himself has been revealed in my soul, I have been unable to collect my thoughts of joy, much less to put them into a language that would make them intelligible to other people. For the glory and the beauty are transcendent, and the love and the fellowship of Christ are transporting, ecstatic, ravishing. They bear the soul away.

The Power in Praising God

God's Consoling Love

These wonders of revelation bring with them wonders of consolation. Have we not seen dying Christians full of life? Have we not seen them sinking in body but soaring in soul? Sick, weak, feeble, and breathless, yet full of glory, they are ready to burst with the new wine of the kingdom, which has been poured into their frail vessels. Have we not heard some of them sing between their groans such songs as only God's sweet love could have taught them? The angels could sing no sweeter songs, and assuredly, they know no sweeter themes! Yes, beloved, our inner experience has been full of wonders. We have committed terrible sins and suffered tremendous sorrows, but we have received wonderful pardons and enjoyed wonderful raptures. We have passed through challenging fights, but we have gained amazing victories; wondrous has been our darkness, but we have seen marvelous light.

Coleridge has said that "in wonder all philosophy begins, in wonder it ends, and wonder fills the interspace." Truly, I can say the same of all vital godliness. Another has said that "the wise man wonders once in his life, but that is always." The same may be affirmed of the man made wise unto salvation. It may be true that our first wonder is born of ignorance. At any rate, much of ignorance mingles with its surprise, but certainly, afterward, our wonder becomes the parent of adoration. We wonder when we grow in grace, not because we are not familiar with it, but we wonder at what we do know of amazing love and grace. Our children look up at the stars and think they are like little pinholes in the sky. They say,

> Twinkle, twinkle, little star,
> How I wonder what you are.

Yet when the astronomer looks through his telescope and gazes at those celestial bodies, he says with greater truth,

How I wonder what you are!

Man's wonder grows with his knowledge. As he wades into the river of wisdom, he is less and less able to keep the foothold of calm reason and is more and more likely to be uplifted and carried off his feet by the current. It is so with Christian experience: The more we know of God, the more wonderful His dealings with us appear.

God's Victorious Love

Now, beloved, I must ask you once again to consider that, as the Lord has *"dealt wondrously"* toward us, wondrously for us, and wondrously in us, so He has also *"dealt wondrously"* by us. What a field of battle, what a throne of victory, the poor child of God often becomes! Why, in this narrow plot of human clay, the powers of heaven and hell have mustered all their armies many times for conflict, and God and His grace and truth have fought with Satan in our hearts. Bless God that, on that battlefield, God has won many victories over the allied armies of the world, the flesh, and the devil.

We have been garrisoned against besieging sins, delivered by the force of heavenly arms from the power of our corruption, and brought forth by sovereign grace to delight in the Lord our God. When we get to heaven, we will be *"men wondered at"* (Zechariah 3:8), established as signs and wonders forever, immortal witnesses of God's boundless grace. In the celestial streets, we will announce His deeds of infinite love:

> *To the intent that now unto the principalities and powers in heavenly places might be known by the church the manifold wisdom of God, according to the eternal purpose which he purposed in Christ Jesus our Lord.* (Ephesians 3:10–11)

The Power in Praising God

Will not the angels say to one another, "Here are men and women who were tempted in a thousand ways, who carried about with them bodies of sin and death, who were tried with all sorts of afflictions and passed through much tribulation—but see what they are now! See how God has triumphed in them. See how He has defeated the evil one and overcome the powers of evil. For these tempted ones have come through *'great tribulation, and have washed their robes, and made them white in the blood of the Lamb'* (Revelation 7:14). There is not one in whom God has been defeated. Not one in whom the eternal purpose has failed. Not one in whom electing love has been baffled. Not one in whom the power of Christ's blood has been ineffective. Not one to whom the Spirit came without winning a complete victory. Let us praise God anew and sing, *'Worthy is the Lamb'* (Revelation 5:12)."

Our God has also worked miraculously through some of us, fulfilling His promise: *"The people that do know their God shall be strong, and do exploits"* (Daniel 11:32). His *"strength is made perfect in weakness"* (2 Corinthians 12:9). There are some among us whose lips have led many in worship, and yet they confess themselves to be emptiness itself. Their word has brought life to the dead, yet, in themselves, they have no power. They have scattered the King's enemies although they are by nature weak as water. God's ministers are but *"trumpets of rams' horns"* (Joshua 6:4), yet when God has blown through them, the blast has made the walls of Jericho rock, reel, and fall to the ground. They are but lamps enclosed in earthen pitchers, and yet by them, Midian has been routed. (See Judges 7.) Glory be to the name of Jehovah our God for this!

Thus, you see God has done wondrously by us. Praise Him; praise Him! Will you pause and sing a psalm of praise now? People, praise Him! You who know His wonders, praise Him! *"Let the redeemed of the LORD say so, whom he hath redeemed from the hand of the enemy"*

(Psalm 107:2). *"Let them sacrifice the sacrifices of thanksgiving"* (v. 22), and bless the name of the Lord. *"Praise the name of the LORD your God, that hath dealt wondrously with you."*

> Let the redeemed of the Lord
> The wonders of His grace record;
> How great His works! How kind His ways!
> Let every tongue pronounce His praise.

Look for God's Wonders

Our second and practical point is this: We ought to expect wonders.

Are You Struggling under a Sense of Sinfulness?

Are you struggling under a horrible sense of your sinfulness? Do you seem to yourself to be the blackest of all unpardoned souls, the nearest to being damned already of all living beings? Do you think that it would be the greatest wonder that ever occurred since the world began if you were to be saved? I have the most precious thought to tell you (may the Holy Spirit place it in your heart): The Lord is a God of wonders. He does only wondrous things.

He delights to find room, scope, and opportunity for wonders of grace in our sin and misery. Cast yourself upon the mercy of our matchless God, and He will make you as much a wonder of grace as you have been a wonder of sin.

Are You Spiritually Cold?

Possibly, some are saying, "I do not feel my sin as I should. I wish I did. I feel numb and insensible. If I feel anything, it is only a sort of regret that I do not have any feeling."

My dear friend, you will be a wonder, too, if God revives you and makes you tender of heart. In you, too, He finds scope for grace. He wakes the dead. He kills and makes alive; He wounds and He heals (Deuteronomy 32:29). Cry to the Lord to make you sensitive through His wounding and killing work. If your heart is as cold as ice, ask Him to melt it, for it is written, *"He sendeth out his word, and melteth them"* (Psalm 147:18). Is it not promised in His own covenant, *"I will put a new spirit within you; and I will take the stony heart out of their flesh, and will give them an heart of flesh"* (Ezekiel 11:19)? The Lord of love delights to work these transformations.

Are You Sad?

Do you feel depressed in spirit? Have you felt that way a long time? Are you one of those who feel sad without the light of the sun? Would it not be a great marvel if you should become one of the happiest of God's people? It would. I believe you will be, for God delights to work wonders. He can bring His servants out of the darkest prison. He enabled Paul and Silas to sing in the inner dungeon, and then He brought them out. He can make you sing now and bring you out into clear, full liberty. He can do it today. *"The Lord looseth the prisoners: the Lord openeth the eyes of the blind: the Lord raiseth them that are bowed down"* (Psalm 146:7–8). The prisoners of the Lord will not be prisoners forever. Release from jail is coming, and they will leap for joy.

Are You Sick?

Are you lying at death's door? Do you cry, like the singer Heman, *"My soul is full of troubles: and my life draweth nigh unto the grave"* (Psalm 88:3)? Perhaps you are sick in body, distracted in mind. Do you feel you are ready to die, and therefore you think that it is all over with you? What a desperate state you seem to be in. It would be a wonderful thing if you would obtain light and comfort, would it not?

Again, let me remind you that if it would be wonderful, it is all the more probable with the Lord. He is very compassionate. He delights in being merciful. The Lord heals the brokenhearted and binds up their wounds. Wonderful are His ways of consoling the mournful. Great is His wisdom and discernment in devising ways to bring back His banished ones. Therefore, *"ascribe ye greatness unto our God"* (Deuteronomy 32:3). Look to Him for mercy. Believe in God for immeasurable, tender affection.

Do You Need a Savior?

If I presented a little christ for little sinners, some of you would be wise to read elsewhere. However, since I have a divine calling to proclaim a great Savior for great sinners, One who is able to help us through great difficulties and to overcome great sins, why, He is the very Savior for you. Bless Him, love Him, and trust Him, and He will work wonders in your spirit.

Have You Fallen Away?

Possibly, I write to someone who has desperately backslidden. It has been years since you knew the truth, and you have, by your sins, fastened chains of iron on your soul. Well, the Lord whom you have grieved is full of compassion and can take those chains off. Yes, He can break the gates of brass and cut bars of iron in half. The Lord can work wonders of deliverance for His imprisoned children.

Are Your Problems Ordinary?

"Oh," cries another, "my case is merely a commonplace one. There is nothing remarkable about me." My dear friend, would it not be a wonderful thing if God were to save such an ordinary, insignificant person as you? Well, rest in Him, trust in Him, and there will be wonderful works performed for you, also. You will be one of those amazing people in whom God's grace is fully revealed.

Do You Feel Hopeless?

If there is anything about you, beloved, that seems to make your salvation difficult or even impossible, if there is anything in your case that causes you to feel hopeless and desperate, whether it is in your secular or your spiritual life, I would recommend that you take your case to the God of wonders. See whether He does not before long make you say, *"The LORD...hath dealt wondrously with* [me]." To sinners who believe in Jesus, salvation is promised, and they will have it. To saints who trust in the Lord, deliverance is promised, and delivered they will be. God will work ten thousand wonders, but He will never allow His promises to fall to the ground.

Are You Expecting God to Do Wonders?

I would earnestly remind all God's servants that we ought to expect wonderful answers to prayer. We should pray as if we expected the God of wonders to hear us. In times of trouble, we ought to expect to see wonderful deliverances. If we are confined by our circumstances, we should expect Him to provide a way of escape. Since we need a miracle, we should look to God to make it happen. We have grounds for expecting wonderful comfort if we are about to endure great troubles. We should look for wonderful joys between here and heaven. We ought to be on our watchtower, looking for wonderful discoveries of Christ's beauty and God's love. In fact, we should always be looking for wonders and should wonder if wonders do not happen.

In the church, we are permitted to expect wonders. We are too much in the habit of merely going to worship services and sitting down and hearing sermons; if half a dozen are converted, we are astonished. Yet we ought to expect thousands to be converted. If the church ever has faith enough to expect great things, she will see great things. When the church falls on dark times and error mars her beauty, we may expect God to work wonders to purify and exalt her.

In the darkest medieval times, God found His witnesses. When the light threatened to die out, then Martin Luther came, a man raised up by God. A train of glorious men followed him. Never tremble; never despair; never be afraid. *"The Lord of hosts is with us; the God of Jacob is our refuge"* (Psalm 46:7). We worship the God of wonders who does only wonderful things.

Our Savior is also called *"Wonderful"* (Isaiah 9:6). Stephen said of Him, *"Jesus of Nazareth, a man approved of God among you by miracles and wonders and signs"* (Acts 2:22).

Likewise, the Holy Spirit works wonders. He came at first with a *"rushing mighty wind"* (Acts 2:2) and *"cloven tongues"* (v. 3) and miraculous gifts. (See Acts 2.) Even now, His wonders have not ceased. They have only become spiritual, instead of physical. Yet the Spirit of God is working mightily now.

I bear personal witness that God has worked wonders for us far beyond all human ability. We could not perform these wonders. We did not deserve these wonders. These are wonders that we could not have expected, could not have imagined, could not have comprehended. I may add, these are wonders for which, throughout eternity, we will never be able to praise God sufficiently, though we spend our whole existence in adoring our wonder-working God! *"How great are his signs! and how mighty are his wonders! his kingdom is an everlasting kingdom, and his dominion is from generation to generation"* (Daniel 4:3).

In Heaven, God's Wonders Will Be Even Clearer to Us

My last remark is this: In our future state, these wonders will be even clearer to us. If we were to read our Bibles attentively, we would be astonished to find how much there is about heaven in them. It is not true that we have mere glimpses, for, if studiously investigated, the Word of God tells us wondrous things concerning the world to come.

Beloved, in the better land, we will wonder more than we do here, for there we will understand far more than we do now. We will have clearer views and wider perspectives. Our present capacities are narrow. There is scarcely room within our minds for great things, but in that bright world, the veil will be removed. *"For now we see through a glass, darkly; but then face to face: now* [we] *know in part; but then shall* [we] *know even as also* [we are] *known"* (1 Corinthians 13:12).

In the heavenly mansions, our growing knowledge will excite in us increasing wonder. There we will sing the praise of Him who has *"dealt wondrously"* with us. I believe the poet was right when he said,

> And sing with wonder and surprise
> Thy lovingkindness in the skies.

We Will Know What We Escaped

In our homes of endless bliss, we will see what we escaped. We will look down from our place at Abraham's side and see the sinner far off in torment. (See Luke 16:19–23.) It will be a dreadful sight, but, with hearts of gratitude, we will bless redeeming love, knowing that were it not for divine grace, that desperate fate would have been ours.

We Will Realize the Awfulness of Sin

In the heaven of perfect holiness, we will know the true character of sin. When we see the brightness of God's glory and the splendor of His holiness, sin will appear in all its hideousness. We will adore the matchless mercy that pardoned us. We will bless the precious blood that cleansed us even though we had been defiled with such pollution. We think we praise God for forgiving our iniquities, and no doubt we do in some measure, but compared with the blessing that saints in heaven give to God for deliverance from sin, our praise is nothing. We do not know sin as they know it. We do not understand its blackness as they perceive it.

We Will Understand Life's Mysteries

Up in heaven, we will see our lives and God's dealings with us as a whole. A great many matters that now appear mysterious and complex, concerning which we can only walk by faith because our reason is baffled, will be so clear to us as to excite our joyous songs in heaven. "Now I see why I was laid aside when I wanted to be busy in God's work. Now I see why that dear child, whom I had hoped would be spared as a comfort to me during my old age, was taken away. Now I understand why my business was allowed to fail. Now I comprehend why that person was allowed to defame me. Now I see why I was attacked by inward fears and was permitted to struggle with them." Such will be our confessions when the day dawns and the shadows flee away. Then we will say and sing, "Our God has dealt wonderfully with us." We will feel that the best was done for us that Eternal Wisdom could devise, and we will bless the name of the Lord.

We Will Know What It Means to Be Children of God

Reflect a moment, dear friends, and see further reasons for everlasting amazement. In heaven, we will see what God has lifted us up to be. We talk of being children of God. Do we fully understand what that means? We speak of heaven being ours. Do we know what we mean by that language? Truly, *"it doth not yet appear what we shall be: but we know that, when he shall appear, we shall be like him"* (1 John 3:2). Neither have our eyes seen nor our ears heard the *"things which God hath prepared for them that love him"* (1 Corinthians 2:9).

When we stand on the sea of glass and hear the harpists, we will join their endless music. When we see Him who laid down His life for us, yes, see Him as He is, when we behold the Lamb of God who, by bowing to death, lifted us up from our deadly fall, who, by stripping Himself of His royalty, robed us with splendors, we will be amazed, astounded, and overwhelmed with wonder.

Above all, when we see God Himself, what will be our wonder! Within our minds, we will be able to behold the infinite Jehovah and hear His voice. When we come to speak with God familiarly and stand before that throne whose brightness today would blind us, when we know Him who fills all in all, we will be plunged into adoring wonder forever. I will not say we will be amazed to think He loved us. There is no need to say that. I will not say we will be filled with astonishment to think He ever saved us. Rather, how amazing it is that He should permit us to be His sons and daughters and should, at such enormous expense, bring us to dwell with Himself forever, making us partakers of His own nature, one with His own Son. We will *"praise the name of the Lord [our] God, that hath dealt wondrously with [us]."*

Let the Praise Begin

I beg you to begin the music here. I long to spend my time perpetually adoring the God of wonders. I desire that we should rise above the spirit of discontent, the spirit that finds fault, mourns, moans, and laments, making complaints by which to provoke the Lord our God. Let it not be said of us, "They soon forgot His wonders." (See Psalm 78:10–11.) Let us go on singing to Him who does only wondrous things, speaking to one another of all His wondrous works. Day by day, hour by hour, let us admire our God, world without end.

Chapter 6

Inexcusable Irreverence and Ingratitude

They are without excuse: because that,
when they knew God, they glorified him not as God,
neither were thankful.
—Romans 1:20–21

This first chapter of the epistle to the Romans is such a terrifying portion of the Word of God that I hesitate to read it through aloud, even to myself. Read it and be startled at the terrible sins of the Gentile world. Unmentionable crimes were the common pleasures of those wicked ages, but this chapter is also a striking picture of heathenism today.

After a missionary had gone to a certain part of India and had given away New Testaments, a Hindu waited for him and asked this question: "Did you write that first chapter in the epistle to the Romans after you came here?" "No," replied the missionary. "I did not write it at all; it has been there nearly two thousand years." The Hindu said, "Well, if it has not been written since you came here, all I can say is that it might have been written about us, for it is a fearfully true description of the sin of India."

It is also true of our cities—more accurate than some of us would like to admit. Even where I live, vices are committed, the very mention of which would make a modest person blush. However, I am not going to write about Hindus; they are far away. I am not going to write about ancient Romans; they lived a couple of thousand years ago. I am going to write about us and about people whom my text aptly fits. I fear that I am addressing some who are *"without excuse: because that, when they knew God, they glorified him not as God, neither were thankful."*

Lack of Reverence

The first charge against those who are mentioned in my text is lack of reverence. *"They knew God,"* but *"they glorified him not as God."* They knew that there is a God, they never denied His existence, but they had no reverence for His name. They did not give Him the respect to which He is entitled. They did not honor Him as God.

Never Thinking of God

That is still true of people today. Some never think of God. They go from year to year without any practical thought of Him. He is not only not in their words, but He is also not in their thoughts. As the psalmist wrote, *"The wicked, through the pride of his countenance, will not seek after God: God is not in all his thoughts"* (Psalm 10:4). Whether there is a God or not makes no practical difference to the wicked. They have so little esteem for Him that, perhaps, if we could prove that there were no God, their consciences would feel relieved.

There must be something very wrong with a person who would prefer that there were no God. "Well," says one, "I do not care much whether there is a God or not; I am an agnostic." A gentleman once told me that he was an agnostic. I replied, "That is a Greek word, is it not?

The Power in Praising God

And the equivalent Latin word is *ignoramus*." Somehow, he did not like it in Latin nearly as much as in Greek. Oh, dear friends, I could not bear to be an "ignoramus" or an "agnostic" about God. I must have God; I cannot do without Him. To me, He is as necessary as food to my body and air to my lungs.

The sad thing is that many who believe that there is a God do not glorify Him as God. They do not even give Him a thought. I appeal to you to consider if this description applies to your life. Do you go from the beginning of the week to the end without reflecting on God at all? Could you do as well without God as with Him? Must there not be something very terrible in the condition of your heart if, as a creature, you can do without a thought of your Creator—when He who has nourished you and brought you up is nothing to you, One of whom you never think?

Having a False Concept of God

Further, some have a misconception of God. The true concept of God is that He is all in all. If God is anything, we ought to make Him everything. You cannot put God in second place. He is almighty, all-wise, all-gracious, all-knowing, omnipresent. His power flows to every part of the universe. God is infinitely glorious, and unless we treat Him as such, we have not treated Him as He ought to be treated. If a king is assigned to open doors or do menial work, he is not honored as a king should be. Will the great God be made a servant to our desires? Will we put God aside, saying to Him: "When it is more convenient, I will send for You. When I have more money, I will make time for religion. When I can be religious and not lose anything by it, then I will seek You"? Do you treat God so? Oh, beware. This is high treason against the King of Kings! Wrong ideas of God, groveling thoughts of God, come under the censure of our text, *"When they knew God, they glorified him not as God."*

Never Worshipping God

Again, dear friends, there are some who think of God a little, but they never offer Him any humble, spiritual worship. Do not imagine that God can be worshipped by anything that is merely mechanical or external, which is not from the heart. That god who is pleased with what some men call worship must be very strange, indeed. I have been in churches and seen decorations that would have been a disgrace to a barroom, and I have said, "Is God pleased with this kind of thing?" Then I have been in fancier buildings where I have seen crucifixes and altars adorned in jewels befitting a bride. God cares not for jewels. Is your concept of God that He desires your gold, silver, brass, fine linen, and all these adornments? Do you think that He is like humans in this way?

Surely, you have a poor concept of God. When the organ peals out its melodious tones, but the organist's heart is not in the playing, do you think that God has ears like those of a man, ears that can be tickled with sweet sounds? Why have you brought Him down to your level? He is spiritual; the music that delights Him is the love of a true heart, the prayer of a seeking spirit. He has better music than all your organs and drums can ever bring to Him. If He wanted music, He would not need to ask you to produce it. Winds and waves make melodies transcendently superior to all that your most notable musicians can compose.

Does He want candles when His touch turns mountains to great altars, smoking with the incense of praise to the God of creation? Oh, beloved, I fear that it has been true of many who externally appeared to be devout that *"when they knew God, they glorified him not as God."* Weep over your sin: Now you have glorified Him as God. Fall on your face and be nothing before the Most High: Now you have glorified Him as God. Accept His righteousness; adore His bleeding Son; trust in His infinite compassion. Now you have glorified him as God, for *"God is a Spirit:*

and they that worship him must worship him in spirit and in truth" (John 4:24). How far, my dear readers, have you complied with that command?

Not Serving God

Further, the people mentioned in our text did not glorify God, for they did not obediently serve Him. My friends, have you served God? Have you looked on yourselves as servants of God? When you awoke in the morning, did you say, "What does God expect me to do today?" When you have reviewed the day, have you applied this test: "How far have I endeavored to serve God today?" Many are the servants of themselves, and no master is more tyrannical than unsanctified self. Many are toiling like slaves for wealth, for honor, for respectability, for possessions. Yet remember, if the Lord is God and He made us, we are bound to serve Him. How is it that God has kept you alive all these years, and yet you have never glorified Him as God by serving Him at all? This is a very solemn question. I would like everyone whom it concerns to examine his own conscience.

Not Trusting God

There is another charge to be brought against those who knew God but did not glorify Him: They did not trust Him. The place for man is under the shadow of God's wings. Since He made me, I ought to seek Him in the hour of trouble. In the time of my need, I should turn to His resources. If I feel unhappy, I should look to Him for comfort. Beloved, are there some of you who have never trusted God? You run to your neighbors as soon as you are in difficulty. You trust your old uncle, but you never trust your heavenly Father. What a wretched business this is if God, who is all truth and all love, does not have the confidence of His own creatures! Remember how the Lord spoke through Jeremiah:

Cursed be the man that trusteth in man, and maketh flesh his arm, and whose heart departeth from the LORD. For he shall be like the heath in the desert, and shall not see when good cometh; but shall inhabit the parched places in the wilderness, in a salt land and not inhabited. Blessed is the man that trusteth in the LORD, and whose hope the LORD is. For he shall be as a tree planted by the waters, and that spreadeth out her roots by the river, and shall not see when heat cometh, but her leaf shall be green; and shall not be careful in the year of drought, neither shall cease from yielding fruit. (Jeremiah 17:5–8)

The people mentioned in the text knew God, but they did not trust Him.

Not Talking with God

In addition to this, they did not seek to commune with Him. Are there not some of you who have never tried to speak to God? It never occurred to you, did it? And God has not spoken to you; at least, you have not known whose voice it was when He did speak. It is a very sad business when a child who has been at home with his father and mother for years has never spoken to them. He has come down in the morning and eaten his breakfast; he has come in and devoured his lunch; he has eaten his dinner with them night after night, but he has never spoken to them. Would you have a boy of that kind living with you? You would be obliged to say, "John, you must go; it hurts me to send you away, but I cannot bear to have you sitting here in silence. When I speak to you, you never answer me." Some of you cannot remember a time when you spoke to God or God spoke to you; it was so very long ago, if it ever did occur.

Speaking Irreverently

Equally tragic is the man who calls on God with a foul and blasphemous oath. When he tells a lie, he calls on God to witness it. Yes, he has broken the silence, but it would have been better not to have spoken than to have uttered those vile blasphemies against the Most High. His horrible words have *"entered into the ears of the Lord of sabaoth"* (James 5:4). As the Lord lives, that man will have to answer to the great Judge of all men. His words will have condemned him unless he seeks God's face and finds forgiveness through His Son. Our Savior said that for *"every idle word that men shall speak, they shall give account thereof in the day of judgment"* (Matthew 12:36). How much more will they be required to answer for every evil, false, slanderous, or blasphemous word they have spoken!

Many people have never uttered an oath. Even though they are scrupulously careful about speaking the truth, they have never talked with God. They are wretched creatures, indeed. Although they may be wealthy and prosperous, they have missed the highest good, the best blessing that man can know.

Not Seeking Reconciliation

Some, although they know God, do not glorify Him because, while they are aware of their enmity against God, they do not want to be reconciled to Him. Perfect reconciliation between God and men is possible. All who believe in Christ Jesus are at once forgiven; they are adopted into the family of God; they drink of the love of God; they are saved with an everlasting salvation. There are many who know these truths in their minds, but this knowledge never stirs up any desire for them in their hearts. Whether they are reconciled or unreconciled does not trouble them. In plain language, they are saying, "I defy God; I neither want His love, nor fear His hate; I lift my face before His thunderbolts and dare Him to do His worst." Oh, fatal defiance of the blessed God! May the Spirit of God work upon your conscience now to make you see the evil of this condition and turn from it!

I feel deeply troubled to have to write these words, but I am speaking of what many consciences would confess to be true. You live, some of you, knowing God, but not glorifying Him as God.

Lack of Gratitude

Now I take from our text the second accusation, which is certainly quite as sad as the first. Those who are mentioned by Paul are accused of ingratitude. It is said of them that *"when they knew God, they glorified him not as God, neither were thankful."*

I cannot say anything much worse of a person than that he is not thankful to those who have been his benefactors. When you say that someone is not thankful to God, you have said about the worst thing you can say. Do not look merely at the people who lived in Paul's day, but at those who are living now. You will soon see how many people are guilty of ingratitude. In God's High Court of Justice, they stand accused of many counts in the indictment that is brought against them.

Ignoring God's Moral Laws

First, God's law is despised. Intelligent young men and women, if they are wise, say, "We wish that we knew what we should do in order to live long and be happy. We would like to know what to avoid so that we don't hurt ourselves." Well, the Ten Commandments provide clear instruction for moral living. They tell what will damage us and what will benefit us. We ought to be very thankful to have such plain directions. God says, "You shall," and "You shall not."

Although God has taken the trouble to give us this map of the way and to direct us on the only right road, some have despised the heavenly guide. They have gone directly against that law; in fact, it looks as if the very

The Power in Praising God

existence of the law has been a provocation to them to break it. Is this not an example of dreadful ingratitude?

Whenever God says, "You shall not," it is because it would be harmful to us to do it. Likewise, when ice on ponds is not strong enough to hold a person's weight, signs that say "Dangerous" are put up. Who but a fool would go where that danger signal is? The Ten Commandments indicate what is dangerous; even more, what is fatal. They help us to know how to keep clear of all that is forbidden. They are given in love to protect us from evil.

Dishonoring the Sabbath

Next, God's day is dishonored by those who are not thankful to Him. In His great mercy, God has given us one day in seven in which to rest and to think of holy things. Of the seven days God gave to us in a week, He said to take six and use them for our business (Exodus 20:9). Yet we think that we must have the seventh, as well. It is like someone who, while traveling, comes upon a poor man in distress. Having but seven shillings, the generous person gives the poor man six, but when the wretch scrambles to his feet, he follows his benefactor to knock him down and steal the seventh shilling from him.

How many people do this! The Sabbath is their day for sports, for amusement, for anything but the service and worship of God. They rob God of His day, though it is but one in seven. This is base ungratefulness. Could you confess that you have been guilty of it? If so, let no more Sabbaths be wasted. Let those sacred hours—and all the week between—be spent in diligent searching after God. Then, when you have found Him, the Lord's Day will be the brightest gem of all the seven, and you will sing with hymnwriter Isaac Watts,

> Welcome, sweet day of rest,
> That saw the Lord arise;

Inexcusable Irreverence and Ingratitude

Welcome to this reviving breast,
And these rejoicing eyes!

Neglecting the Bible

Moreover, God's Book is neglected by these ungrateful beings. Was there ever such a Book so full of wisdom, so full of love? Look at it on bended knee and find heaven between its pages. Although God has given us this wonderful Book, many do not take the trouble to read it. What ingratitude! It is a Father's love letter to His child, but the child leaves it unread! Here is a Book unlike any other. God has exercised His omniscience to make it a perfect Book for all ranks and conditions of men in all periods of the world's history, yet such is man's ingratitude that he turns away from it.

Refusing God's Son

However, there is something much worse: God's Son is rejected by the unthankful. God has only one Son, and such a Son: one with Himself, infinite, holy, His delight! From the heart of God, He was sent to this earth. Taking our nature, the Son became a servant, dying the death of a criminal, the death of the cross, all to save us. He died for the guilty, for men who were His enemies.

Thinking about my own guilt that caused His death, I could burst into tears. This must be one of the mysteries that angels cannot comprehend: After Christ has suffered and died for us, some sinners choose not to be saved by Him. They refuse to be washed in the fountain filled with blood; they reject eternal life, even though it streamed from the five great wounds of His body. They choose hell rather than salvation by His blood. They are so in love with their dire enemy, sin, that they will not be reconciled to God even by the death of His Son.

Oh, ingratitude, you have reached your utmost limit now, for you have *"trodden under foot the Son of God, and hath counted the blood of the covenant, wherewith* [you were] *sanctified, an unholy thing, and hath done despite unto the Spirit of grace"* (Hebrews 10:29). Is this not terrible?

Forgetting His Protection

I could stop here. However, for the sake of pricking the consciences of some, I want to say, dear friends, that some people are so ungrateful that they forget God's deliverances. Some years ago, I spoke with a cavalry soldier who had miraculously survived a disastrous, bloody battle. Almost all the saddles emptied; shots and shells flew to the right and left; death mowed down the whole brigade; yet he escaped. When he told me so, I took him by the hand; I could not help it, though he was a stranger to me. With tears in my eyes, I said, "Sir, I hope that you are God's man after such a deliverance as that." Regretfully, he still had not given his heart to Christ.

I know of a man who has been in several shipwrecks, but if he does not pay attention to God, he will be shipwrecked for all eternity! Another has had yellow fever. Oh, there are worse fevers than that for those who will not respond to God.

I cannot cite all the cases of miraculous deliverance, but I do not doubt that some of you have been between the jaws of death. You have looked over the edge of that dread precipice beneath which is the fathomless abyss. You vowed that if God would spare your life, you would never be what you were before; in truth, you are not, for you are worse than ever. You are sinning now against light and in shameful ingratitude. May God have mercy on you!

Ignoring God's Blessings

How often, dear friends, is there ingratitude on the part of unconverted men in acknowledging God's divine care? Why, look at some of you! You have never missed a meal in your lives. When you went to the table, there was always something on it. You never had to lose a night's rest for lack of a bed. From your childhood, you have had all that your hearts could wish. If God has treated you so, while many are crushed with poverty, should He not have some gratitude from you?

You had a good mother; you had a tender father; you have gone from one relationship to another with increasing comfort. You are spared; your parents are spared; your spouse and children are spared. Indeed, God has made your path very smooth. Some of you are succeeding in business while others are failing; some of you have loving support at home while others have been widowed, or their children have died one after the other. Will you never be grateful? Hard, hard heart, will you never break? Will His compassion not persuade you? Must there be a storm of wrath to break you in pieces like a potter's vessel? Will not love and tenderness melt you? I appeal to those whose paths have been so full of mercies: Think of God and turn to Him with sincere repentance and faith.

Yet one says, "I have had good luck." What can be worse than that? Here is a prime example of ingratitude to God: calling His good gifts "good luck." Some respond, "Well, you know, I have been a very hardworking man." I know you have, but who gave you the strength to work? Others say, "I have had a good supply of brains while others have not." Did you make your own brains? Do you not feel that any man who talks about his own superior intelligence writes *FOOL* across his forehead in capital letters? We owe everything to God; will we give God nothing? Will we have no gratitude for Him from whom all blessings come? May God forgive us if it has been so and give us grace to change our ways at once!

Resisting God's Spirit

Another example of ingratitude of which many are guilty is resisting God's Spirit. The Spirit of God comes to them and gently touches them. Perhaps He has come to you, and you have said, "Do not talk quite so plainly to me. Give me a little comfort, a little breathing space; do not be quite so hard on me." He has come to you a good many times, and you have tried to drive your Best Friend from your heart. You have been so stingy with Him that, when He came to lead you to Christ, you summoned all your strength to resist Him. The devil came to help you, and, up until now, you have opposed the Spirit of God with some degree of success. May the Lord have mercy on you! How true is our text, even of many who attend church: *"When they knew God, they glorified him not as God, neither were thankful."*

Irreverence and Ingratitude in spite of Knowledge

I will conclude with my third point, which is that this lack of reverence and gratitude occurred in spite of their knowledge. *"When they knew God, they glorified him not as God, neither were thankful."*

Knowledge Is Useless without Holy Practice

Will you kindly notice that, according to the text, knowledge is of no use if it does not lead to holy practice? *"They knew God."* It was no good to them to know God, for *"they glorified him not as God."* So, my theological friends who know so much that you can split hairs over doctrines, it does not matter what you think or what you know unless it leads you to glorify God and to be thankful. In fact, your knowledge may be a millstone around your neck that will plunge you to eternal misery unless your knowledge is turned to holy practice.

Knowledge Brings Responsibility

Indeed, knowledge will increase the responsibility of those who are irreverent and ungrateful. Paul said, *"When they knew God, they glorified him not as God, neither were thankful."* Whatever excuse might be made for those who have never heard of God, there was none for these people.

My dear readers, you also are *"without excuse."* Many of you have had godly parents, you have attended a Gospel ministry, your Sunday school teachers and Christian friends have taught you the way of salvation; you are not ignorant. If you do not glorify God, if you are not thankful to Him, *"it shall be more tolerable for the land of Sodom and Gomorrha in the day of judgment"* (Matthew 10:15) than for you, for they never had the privileges that you have scorned.

Remember how the Savior reproached the cities where most of His mighty works were done because they did not repent. They did not honor Him as God even though He had shown Himself to them time and time again. Instead of hearing His words of approval, they were rebuked:

> *Woe unto thee, Chorazin! woe unto thee, Bethsaida! for if the mighty works, which were done in you, had been done in Tyre and Sidon, they would have repented long ago in sackcloth and ashes.*
> (Matthew 11:21)

It is a great wonder that the people who saw Christ's mighty works did not repent.

Let Your Knowledge Bring You to Repentance

I wish, dear friends, that you could get out of this state of not glorifying God and not being thankful. Surely, as the Spirit of God speaks to your consciences, you will want to say, "I cannot bear to be in such a dreadful condition with regard to God any longer." May God enable you to repent.

Change your mind. That is the meaning of the word *repent.* Change your mind and say, "I will glorify God. He is the meaning of life. There is a Creator. There must be an omnipotent, all-wise Being. I will worship Him. I will say in my heart that this God will be my God, and I will trust Him."

Then remember the years that are past. They involve a great debt, and you cannot pay it. If you go on serving God without a flaw until the end of your lives, there is still the old debt due; there are the years that are gone, and *"God requireth that which is past"* (Ecclesiastes 3:15). However, hear what He has done for us. He has given His dear Son to bear *"our sins in his own body on the tree"* (1 Peter 2:24). If you will trust in Christ, you can know for sure that you are forgiven. *"Look"*—that is His word— *"Look unto me, and be ye saved, all the ends of the earth"* (Isaiah 45:22).

When the brass serpent was lifted up, all that those who were bitten had to do was to look at it; everyone who looked, lived. If any man of that crowd had looked at Moses, he would not have been healed. If he had looked at the fiery serpents and tried to pull them off, he would not have been healed. Yet when he looked to the brass serpent, and his eyes caught the gleam of the metal, the deadly serpents' bites were healed, and the man lived. (See Numbers 21:5–9.) Look to Jesus. Look now. May God the Holy Spirit lead you to do so!

"I do not feel able," says one. That is looking to yourself. "I do not feel my need enough," says another. That is trusting in your sense of need. Away with everything that is in you or about you. Just trust Christ, and you will immediately be saved. Whoever will simply look to Jesus will be saved on the spot. However great your iniquities, however stony your heart, however despairing your mind, look, look, look, look. Then, when you look to Christ, your ingratitude will be forgiven, and it will die. You will love Him who has loved you, and you will be saved, and saved forever.

Let Renewal Begin

I breathe an earnest prayer that our taking to heart these great truths might be the beginning of a revival. May it come today, and may all who do not know Christ be carried away by that blessed tide of mighty grace that will sweep them off their feet and land them safely on the Rock of Ages!

Will you, dear friend, pray for revival? At the family altar or at your bedside, will you make it a special subject of prayer that men who knew God, but glorified Him not as God and were not thankful, may now turn to God?

If I could reach some of you who are living without Christ, I would like to do what the Roman ambassadors used to do. When they came to a king who was at war with the empire, they said to him, "Will you have peace with Rome or not?" If he said that he must have time to think it over, the ambassador would draw a ring around the man and say, "You must decide before you cross that line, for if you do not say 'Peace' before you step out of it, Rome will crush you with her armies." If I could, I would draw a ring around you. I would pray for the Lord to hold you fast and not let you go until you say, *"Lord, I believe; help thou mine unbelief"* (Mark 9:24). May God bless you, for Jesus' sake.

Chapter 7

The Singing Army

*And Judah gathered themselves together,
to ask help of the LORD.*
—2 Chronicles 20:4

Jerusalem was startled by sudden news. For a great
while, quiet preparations had been made in the distant
countries beyond Jordan. In the mountainous region
of Edom, the enemies of Israel had been getting ready.
Their workshops in the city of Petra had been ringing with
the sound of hammers beating their pruning hooks into
spears and swords.

They were now coming down in hordes. There were
three great nations, assisted by the odds and ends of all
the nations round about, so that a great company eager
for plunder was drawn up in battle. They had heard about
the riches of the temple at Jerusalem. They knew that
the people of Judea had been flourishing for years, and
now they were coming to kill, to destroy, to loot, and to
steal. They were as numerous as grasshoppers or locusts.
What were the people of God to do? How were these poor
Judeans to defend themselves?

Their immediate resort was to their God. They do
not appear to have gathered up their armor and swords
with any particular anxiety. The case was so altogether

hopeless as far as they were concerned that it was useless to look to anything beneath the skies. Since they were driven from all visible earthly assistance, they were compelled to lift up their eyes to God. Their godly king, Jehoshaphat, helped them to do so.

A general fast was proclaimed, and the preparation to meet the armies of Moab, Ammon, and Edom was prayer. No doubt, if the Ammonites had heard of it, they would have laughed. Edom would have scoffed, and Moab would have cursed those who prayed.

"What! Do they suppose that their prayers can defeat us?" would have been the sneer of their adversaries. Yet this was Israel's artillery; this was their eighty-one ton gun. When it was ready, it would launch one missile, and only one, and that would crush three nations at once. God's people resorted only to the arm invisible, the arm omnipotent, and they did well and wisely.

Now, if the Lord will teach us to imitate them, and by His grace enable us while doing it, we will have learned a great lesson. This writer needs to learn it as much as anybody, and he prays that each one of you may be scholars in the school of faith, becoming proficient in the divine art of prayer and praise.

How They Asked for Help

First, they asked for help by calling for a general fast and prayer, but what was the style of that prayer in which they approached the Lord?

They Prayed Confidently

The answer is that they asked for help in a way that expressed their confidence:

O LORD God of our fathers, art not thou God in heaven? and rulest not thou over all the kingdoms of the

The Power in Praising God

heathen? and in thine hand is there not power and might, so that none is able to withstand thee?

(2 Chronicles 20:6)

If we begin by doubting, our prayer will falter. Faith is the tendon of Achilles, and if that is cut, it is not possible for us to wrestle with God. As long as we have that strong sinew, that mighty tendon unhurt, we can prevail with God in prayer. It is a rule of the kingdom, though God often goes beyond it, *"According to your faith be it unto you"* (Matthew 9:29).

I have known Him to give us a hundred times as much as our faith would expect, but, friends, I have never known Him to give less. That could not possibly be. I can safely say that this is His minimum rule: *"According to your faith be it unto you."* Therefore, when you are in a time of trouble, ask God for help, believing that He is able to give it. Ask expecting that He will give it.

Do not grieve the Spirit of God by unworthy doubts and mistrusts. These things will be like fiery arrows in your soul and will drink up the very life of your strength. However hard the struggle and difficult the trial, if you seek the Lord, seek Him in the confidence He deserves.

They Remembered God's Faithfulness

Then they sought God, appealing to His past acts. This is a type of prayer that has been very common among the saints, and it has proved to be very powerful:

Art not thou our God, who didst drive out the inhabitants of this land before thy people Israel, and gavest it to the seed of Abraham thy friend for ever?

(2 Chronicles 20:7)

Remember what God has done for you, and then say, as a sweet refrain, *"Jesus Christ the same yesterday, and*

to day, and for ever" (Hebrews 13:8). When you are praying, recall what He was yesterday to you. If there are
no present manifestations of divine favor, remember the
past—the days of old—*"the years of the right hand of the
most High"* (Psalm 77:10). He has been gracious to you.
Can you tell how gracious? He has abounded toward you
in lovingkindness, tenderness, and faithfulness. He has
faithfully *"led* [you] *through the wilderness, through a land
of deserts and of pits, through a land of drought"* (Jeremiah
2:6).

If in six troubles He has delivered you, will you not
trust Him for seven (Job 5:19)? If you get to sixty troubles, can you trust Him for sixty-one? Some of you have
been carried by God all your lives, and now your hair has
turned gray. How long do you expect to live? Do you think
you have ten years left? Well, do you think that the Lord
who has blessed you for seventy years will not keep you for
the other ten?

We say that we ought always to trust a man until he
deceives us. We consider a man to be honest until we find
him otherwise. Let it be so with God, I beg you. Since we
have found Him good, faithful, true, kind, and tender, let
us not think harshly of Him now that we have come into
crisis.

Let us come to Him and say, "Are You not our God? Did
You not bring us up *'out of an horrible pit,* [and] *out of the
miry clay'* (Psalm 40:2)? Did You not bring us out of the
Egypt of our sin? Surely, You have not brought us into this
wilderness to destroy us. (See Deuteronomy 1:27.) Will You
leave us now? True, we are unworthy, but we always were,
and if You wanted a reason for leaving us, You had ten
thousand reasons long ago." Say with the prophet, *"Be not
wroth very sore, O Lord, neither remember iniquity for ever:
behold, see, we beseech thee, we all are thy people"* (Isaiah
64:9). That is the style of pleading that prevails. Imitate
these men of old who asked for help by recalling the past.

The Power in Praising God

They Relied on His Promises

Going a little further in their prayer, we see that the people of Judea pleaded the promise of God that was made at the time Solomon dedicated the temple:

> *If, when evil cometh upon us,...we stand before this house, and in thy presence, (for thy name is in this house,) and cry unto thee in our affliction, then thou wilt hear and help.* (2 Chronicles 20:9)

He who understands the promise of God and grasps God with the promise does and must prevail.

I have known a man who is unable to grasp anything. Objects slip away from him because his hand is slippery. Yet I have seen him take some sand in his hand, and then he has been able to get a grip. I like to plunge my hand into the promises, and then I find myself able to grasp the mighty faithfulness of God with a grip of determination.

An omnipotent plea with God is this: *"Do as thou hast said"* (2 Samuel 7:25). You know how a man nails you when he brings your very words before you. "There," he says, "that is what you said you would do. You pledged to do this of your own free will." You cannot get away from it. It is that way with the saints if they swear to something. Even if it means that they will be hurt by following through, they must be true to their word.

Of the saints' Master, it is always true. *"Hath he said, and shall he not do it? or hath he spoken, and shall he not make it good?"* (Numbers 23:19). Here is a mighty instrument to be used in prayer: "Lord, You have said it; now *'do as thou hast said.'* You have said, *'Many are the afflictions of the righteous: but the Lord delivereth him out of them all'* (Psalm 34:19). You have said, *'He shall deliver thee in six troubles: yea, in seven there shall no evil touch thee'* (Job 5:19). You have said, *'Surely blessing I will bless thee'* (Hebrews 6:14). You have said, *'Be strong and of a good courage; be not afraid, neither be thou dismayed: for the* LORD *thy God is with thee whithersoever thou goest'* (Joshua 1:9). You have said, *'Thy shoes shall be iron and brass; and as thy days, so shall thy strength be'* (Deuteronomy 33:25). Lord, here are Your promises for my need." With such a plea, you must prevail with a faithful God.

They Admitted Their Weakness

Next, as these people asked for help, they confessed their own unhappy condition. There is great power in that. One of the strongest pleas for generosity is the urgency of poverty, and one of the most prevailing arguments to be used in prayer with God is a truthful statement of our condition—a confession of our sad state. So they said to the Lord,

> *O our God, wilt thou not judge them? for we have no might against this great company that cometh against us; neither know we what to do: but our eyes are upon thee.* (2 Chronicles 20:12)

They had no might; they had no plan. Sometimes, even if you cannot do something, it is a little comfort to know how it might be done if you had the power. Yet these perplexed people could not do it, nor did they even know how to do it. They were bewildered. A little nation like Judah, surrounded by these powerful enemies, truly had no might. Their weakness and ignorance were great pleas. Their logic was divine: *"Neither know we what to do: but our eyes are upon thee."*

It was as if they had said, "If we could do it ourselves, you might tell us, 'Go and do it. What did I give you the strength for, but so that you could use it?' Yet because we have no strength, and we do not know what to do, we come and just present the case at Your feet and say, *'Our eyes are upon thee.'"*

The Power in Praising God

Perhaps you think that is not praying. I tell you, it is the most powerful form of prayer—just to set your case before God, just to lay bare all your sorrow and all your needs, and then say, "Lord, there it is."

In some of our cities, people are not permitted to beg in the streets. The police will not allow it, and I venture to say that is a wise regulation. Yet what does the needy person do? Have you not seen him? He is dressed like a peasant and looks half starved. His knees can be seen through an old pair of corduroys as he stoops. He does not beg. He only sits down at the corner of the road. He knows quite well that the very sight of his condition is enough.

There are some people on the streets whose faces are a fortune to them; pale, thin, and woebegone, they appeal more eloquently than words. Their manner of shivering and their remarkably ill appearance, although they are not sick, take in people who are continually being duped. All the world knows that it is the look of the thing, the very appearance and show of sorrow, that prevails with people more than any words that are used.

Therefore, when you cannot pray in words, go and lay bare your sorrow before God. Show your soul. Tell God what it is that burdens and distresses you, and you will prevail with the bounteous heart of our God. He is not moved by eloquence of words or oratory of tongue, but is swift to answer the true oratory, the true eloquence of real distress, and is as able to detect false misery as to relieve real sorrow.

Do you recall any particular times of trial? I do. At any rate, there is one common affliction that has overwhelmed us all: the great affliction of sin. When sin, with its many offenses, becomes clear to us under conviction, and we do not know how to face one single sin or to answer one of a thousand of the charges that might be brought against us; when we feel that we have no strength whatsoever; when we realize that, through sin, we have brought ourselves into such terrible circumstances, and we do not know how to get out of them, though we feel that we must; when we turn to the right and that way seems blocked, and the left seems equally closed to us; when we dare not go back, and we cannot go forward, how wonderfully God clears the way! In a miraculous manner, we find that our enemies are dead—those whom we thought were going to kill us! As for those who were going to rob us, we are enriched by them. Instead of plundering us, they fall, and their riches become our right. Rejoicing, we take their riches home with us. Oh, what wonders God can do!

He loves for us to state the difficulty we are in so that, when He gets us out of it, we may remember that we were in such a condition. It was a real disaster and a time of genuine trial, yet the Lord redeemed us from it.

They Declared Their Trust

What did they do after asking for help, after pleading the promise and confessing their condition? Why, they expressed their confidence in God. They said, *"Our eyes are upon thee"* (2 Chronicles 20:12). What did they mean by that? They meant, "Lord, if help does come, it must come from You. We are looking to You for our rescue. It cannot come from anywhere else, so we look to You. Yet we believe it will come. Men will not look for what they know will not come. We feel sure it will come. We do not know how, so we are looking to You. We do not know when, but we are looking to you. We do not know what You would have us to do, but we are looking to You, Lord. Lord, we are looking."

That is a great attitude. Do you not know that is the way you are saved—by looking to Jesus? And that is the way you must be saved—all the way between here and heaven. Whatever trouble comes, looking will save you— looking, often waiting, looking like the weary watcher from the tower when he wants to see the gray tints of the coming morning, when the night is long and he is weary, but still looking. *"Our eyes are upon thee."* They are full of tears, but still they are fixed on You. They are getting drowsy with sleep, but still they are focused on You. With the eyes that we have, we look to You.

I have sometimes thanked the Lord that He did not say, "See Jesus—see Me and be saved." What He has said is "Look." Sometimes, if you cannot see, you have still done your part if you have looked—looked into the darkness. Lord, Your Cross would give me such joy if I could see it. I cannot quite see it. It looms very indistinctly on my gaze, but I do look. It is looking, you know, that saves. For as we look, the eyes get stronger, and we are enlightened. And so in this case, they looked, and they found deliverance. May God help us, brothers and sisters, to do the same.

How They Received Help

They Received a Fresh Assurance

Their help came to them, first, by a message from God. They received a fresh assurance of God's goodness. Jahaziel, a new prophet, was raised up, and he spoke with new words: *"Be not afraid nor dismayed by reason of this great multitude; for the battle is not yours, but God's"* (2 Chronicles 20:15). Now, in our case, we will not have a new promise. That would not be possible:

> What more can He say
> > Than to you He has said,
> To you who to Jesus
> > For refuge have fled?

However, you will have that promise sweetly brought home to your soul. The Spirit of God will bear witness with that promise, strengthening and comforting you. You will receive deliverance even before deliverance comes.

It often happens that to be rescued from the fear of trouble is the main need. To be quieted, calmed, and assured is really to be saved from the sting of trial. The trial itself is nothing if it does not bring a sting to your soul. If your heart is not troubled, then there is not much trouble in anything else. All the poverty and pain in the world would be powerless if the evil of it did not enter into the soul and distress it. So in this emergency, God began to answer His people by quieting them: *"Be not afraid nor dismayed by reason of this great multitude; for the battle is not yours, but God's."*

As that gracious promise calmed their fears, they were able to face the impending attack. Then they received distinct direction as to what to do on the next day, which was to be the day of the assault. That direction was this: *"To morrow go ye down against them"* (v. 16).

How often God has given His people deliverance by quieting them before He directs them to act. Already, the steps they have taken in looking to Him have delivered them before they knew it. As we will see, the Israelites, by marching out with songs and praises to meet their foes, were doing the best possible thing to rout them. As I have already said, there is no doubt that their enemies were unable to comprehend such a defense as this. They must have supposed that there was some treachery or ambush intended, so they began to slay each other. Israel had nothing to do but to keep on singing.

They Received Actual Deliverance

Then came the real providence: They received actual deliverance. When the people of Judah came to their foes, they found there were no foes. There they lay all rigid and dead. None of the men of might could raise their hands against those whom God had favored.

The Power in Praising God

After this fashion, God will deliver you, beloved. In answer to your prayers, He will be your defense. Therefore, sing unto His name. Did He not deliver you in this way when you went out to meet the great army of your sins? You saw that Christ had put them away, and your heart danced within you as you said, *"There is therefore now no condemnation to them which are in Christ Jesus"* (Romans 8:1). He has slain our sins, and they can curse us no more.

So it has been with a great many troubles that have appeared to you to be overwhelming. When you have come to them, they have disappeared. They have been cleared out of your way as you have advanced, and you have had nothing to do but sing and praise the name of the Lord.

They Responded by Worshipping

Finally, and this is the main point, let us note how they acted after they had prayed and heard God's voice. They asked for help and received it. How did they then behave?

Well, first, as soon as they had an assurance that God would deliver them, they worshipped. That is one of the purposes of trials—to revive in us the spirit of devotion and communion with God. And when mercy comes on the back of great trouble, it leads us sweetly to prayer. I maintain that there never was such profound worship in all of Jerusalem as there was that day. After Jahaziel, that young son of the Levites, had stood and delivered the Word of the Lord, the king and all the people bowed their heads and honored the God of Israel. You could have heard the sound of the wind rustling the trees at the time, for they were so hushed and quiet. Oh, when you know that the Lord means to deliver you, bow your head and give Him the quiet, deep, solemn worship of your spirit.

I do not suppose that many people practice the Quakers' form of worship, though an occasional experience of it would do us a world of good. To sit still before the Lord and to adore, and to adore, and to adore again and again, and still again, braces the spirit and clears the soul for the understanding of eternal realities.

They worshipped, but why did they do it? They were not delivered. No. Yet they were sure they were going to be delivered. Their enemies were not dead. No. They were all alive, but they were sure they would be dead, so they had a time of worship, and their devotion rose from trustful and grateful hearts. May we get into a worshipping frame of mind and be kept in it. Then God will appear for our help.

They Proceeded to Praise

As soon as the worship time had ended, or rather just before it had quite finished, they began to praise. Up went the loud voices of the trained singers under the leadership of the chief musician, and they praised the name of the Lord. They sang, as we do,

> For His mercies will endure,
> Ever faithful, ever sure.

That is the way you should deal with God. Before deliverance comes, praise Him. Praise Him for what is coming; adore Him for what He is going to do. No song is as sweet, I think, in the ear of God as the song of a man who blesses Him for grace he has not tasted yet—for what he has not received, but what he is sure will come. The praise of gratitude for the past is sweet, but that praise is sweeter that adores God for the future in full confidence that all will be well. Therefore, take down your harps from the willows. (See Psalm 137:1–4.) Oh, you people, praise the name of the Lord.

The Power in Praising God

Although the fig tree shall not blossom, neither shall fruit be in the vines; the labour of the olive shall fail, and the fields shall yield no meat; the flock shall be cut off from the fold, and there shall be no herd in the stalls: yet I will rejoice in the LORD, I will joy in the God of my salvation. (Habakkuk 3:17–18)

Though there is not enough income to meet your needs, and you are almost at necessity's door, still bless the Lord, whose mighty providence cannot fail, and will not fail, as long as there is one of His children to be provided for. Your song while you are still in distress will be sweet music to the ears of God.

They Practiced Obedience

After they had worshipped and sung, the next thing these people did was to act. They went forth marching. If there were unbelievers in Jerusalem, I know what they said. They stood at the gates and said, "Well, this is foolishness. These Moabites and Ammonites have come to kill you. They will do it, but you might as well wait until they get to you. You are just going to deliver yourselves to them." That would be the idea of unbelief, and that is also how it sometimes seems to our little faith when we go and commit ourselves to God. "What! Are you going on your knees to confess your guilt before God and admit that you deserve to be lost? Are you going to withdraw every excuse and apology, every trust of your own, and give yourself up, as it were, to destruction?" Yes, that is exactly the thing to do, and it is the highest wisdom to do it. We are going out of the city marching away according to orders, and if we are to give ourselves up, so we will.

Perhaps, in your case, you are planning to do something about which everybody else says, "Now, that will be very foolish. You should be crafty. You should show a little cunning." "No," you reply, "I cannot do other than I am directed. I must do the right thing." That will probably turn out to be the very best thing in the world to have done. The shortest distance between any two points is by a straight line. The straight way will always be better than the crooked way. In the long run, it is always so. Go right out in the name of God. Meet your difficulties calmly and fairly. Do not have any plans or tricks, but just commit yourself to God. That is the way by which you may confidently expect to find deliverance. These people of old went out of the city.

They Started to Sing

Notice again that, as they went out, they went out singing. They sang before they left the city and as they left the city. When the adversary came in sight, they began to sing again. The trumpet sounded, the harps rang out their notes, and the musicians shouted for joy. This was the song:

> For His mercies will endure,
> Ever faithful, ever sure.

When they sang the following passage, it must have had great significance for them:

> *To him which smote great kings: for his mercy endureth for ever: and slew famous kings: for his mercy endureth for ever: Sihon king of the Amorites: for his mercy endureth for ever: and Og the king of Bashan: for his mercy endureth for ever.* (Psalm 136:17–20)

Why, every singer, as he sang those lines, which look to us like mere repetition, must have felt how applicable they were to their present condition when there was a Moabite and an Edomite and an Ammonite to be overthrown in the name of the mighty God whose mercy endures forever. So they kept on singing. You will observe that, while they were singing, God was accomplishing the great deliverance for them.

They Anticipated the Reward of Their Trust

When the singing stopped, they prepared to gather up the spoil. What a different activity from what they had expected! You can see them stripping the bodies; taking off the helmets of gold and the armor of brass, the jewels from the ears and from around the necks of the princes; robbing the dead of their Babylonian garments and their wedges of gold; heaping up the tents—the rich tents of the Eastern nations—until they said to each other, "We do not know what to do."

Yet the difficulty was different from what might have happened to them at first. Previously, they did not know what to do because of their weakness in the presence of their foes, but now the difficulty was because of the greatness of the spoil. "We cannot carry it all home," they said to each other. "There is too much. It will take us days and days to stockpile this wondrous booty."

Now, child of God, it will be the same for you. I do not know how, but if you can only trust God and praise Him and go straight ahead, you will see such wondrous things that you will be utterly astonished.

They Returned Singing

Then what will you do? Why, you will at once begin praising the Lord, for that is what the Israelites did. They went home singing. *"They came to Jerusalem with psalteries and harps and trumpets unto the house of the LORD"* (2 Chronicles 20:28). When God has done great things for you and brought you through your present difficulty, you must be sure to repay Him in the courts of His house with your loudest music and your most exultant notes, blessing again and again the name of the Lord.

They Rested in Quietness

After that, they had to rest. In the narrative it is added, *"So the realm of Jehoshaphat was quiet: for his God gave him rest round about"* (2 Chronicles 20:30). Their enemies were afraid to come and touch them any more. After a very harsh storm, it generally happens that there is a long rest. So it will be with all the Lord's people. You will get through this trouble, friend, and afterward it will be smooth sailing for a very long time.

I have known a child of God who faced a cyclonic experience; it seemed as if he would be utterly destroyed. However, after it was over, there was not a ripple on the calm of his life. People have envied him and wondered at his quietness. He had had all his storms at once, and when they were over, he came into smooth water that seemed unruffled.

Perhaps you will have the same experience. Ask the great Pilot of the Galilean lake to steer you safely through your tempest, and then, when the storm ceases at His bidding, you will be glad because you can be quiet. He will bring you to your desired haven.

I have desired to speak these comforting words to God's children, for well I know how you are tried, and I pray that the Lord, the Comforter, will apply these words to your troubled hearts.

Yet I never can finish my writing without having the very sad thought that there are always some to whom these comforting truths do not apply. They are not believers. They have never trusted in Christ. If this is so with you, my friend, you have to fight your own battles. You have to bear your own trials. You have to carry your own burdens. And when you come to the last great Day and stand before the judgment seat, you will have to answer for your own sins and bear your own punishment.

The Power in Praising God

May God have mercy on you and deliver you from such a condition as this. It is a bad condition to live in. It is a terrible condition to die in. May you receive Christ as your Substitute and your Surety and glorify His name forever and ever.

About the Author

C harles Haddon Spurgeon was born on June 19, 1834, at Kelvedon, Essex, England, the firstborn of eight surviving children. His parents were committed Christians, and his father was a preacher. Spurgeon was converted in 1850 at the age of fifteen. He began to help the poor and to hand out tracts; he was known as "The Boy Preacher."

His next six years were eventful. He preached his first sermon at the age of sixteen. At age eighteen, he became the pastor of Waterbeach Baptist Chapel, preaching in a barn. Spurgeon preached over six hundred times before he reached the age of twenty. By 1854, he was well-known and was asked to become the pastor of New Park Street Chapel in London. In 1856, Spurgeon married Susannah Thompson; they had twin sons, both of whom later entered the ministry.

Spurgeon's compelling sermons and lively preaching style drew multitudes of people, and many came to Christ. Soon, the crowds had grown so large that they blocked the narrow streets near the church. Services eventually had to be held in rented halls, and he often preached to congregations of more than ten thousand. The Metropolitan Tabernacle was built in 1861 to accommodate the large numbers of people.

Spurgeon published over thirty-five hundred sermons, which were so popular that they sold by the ton. At one point, his sermons sold twenty-five thousand copies every week. The prime minister of England, members of the royal family, and Florence Nightingale, among others, went to hear him preach. Spurgeon preached to an estimated ten million people throughout his life. Not surprisingly, he is called the "Prince of Preachers."

In addition to his powerful preaching, Spurgeon founded and supported charitable outreaches, including educational institutions. His pastors' college, which is still in existence today, taught nearly nine hundred students in Spurgeon's time. He also founded the famous Stockwell Orphanage.

Charles Spurgeon died in 1892, and his death was mourned by many.